the assessment of risk of violence in a community mental health setting. She worked in a community forensic service for ten years before taking on more management responsibilities and moving back to general adult mental health. Involvement in the area of risk has continued and developed, however, in both service-related – with involvement in the *Best Practice* guidance and its implementation within her NHS Trust – and clinical settings, in which the regular, frequent assessment and management of risk with consultation and supervision is an ongoing and fundamental aspect of practice.

Phil Garnham was Head of Nursing Development at Oxleas NHS Foundation Trust at the time of writing and is now a Forensic Nurse Consultant. He has worked in the field of mental health care for over 26 years, with 17 of those in forensic mental health. He has a masters degree in counselling and psychotherapy, has published several journal articles and contributed a chapter entitled 'Managing the Psychiatric Intensive Care Unit' to the second edition of *Psychiatric Intensive Care* by Beer and colleagues. Phil is an Honorary Lecturer at the University of Greenwich and at the Centre for Health and Social Care Research, Canterbury Christchurch University. He is also an external examiner for the Institute of Psychiatry short course programme and was Chair of the Royal College of Nursing's National Forensic Forum for four years.

Dr Helen Gilburt is post-doctoral research worker in the Department of Addiction at the Institute of Psychiatry in London. She started her career as a biological scientist but, after experiencing mental health problems at university, has forged a career in mental health services research. Joining the Institute of Psychiatry in 2005, she has worked on a number of projects including a national study of innovative care provision in acute inpatient psychiatric services, the implementation of the recovery model in community mental health services, and most recently, developing assertive outreach for people with alcohol dependence. She has a particular interest in the added value of facilitating service user involvement for care provision, service development, and research itself.

Dr Beth Greenhill is a clinical psychologist working with adults with learning disabilities in the Rebuild Clinical Business Unit at Olive Mount in Mersey Care NHS Trust. Beth has worked in the Liverpool Team at Olive Mount for eight years and has drawn heavily on her learning from, and experiences with, service users and team colleagues in her contribution to her chapter. Clinically, Beth works therapeutically within a Cognitive Analytic Therapy (CAT) framework, offering direct therapy and 'relationally informed' systemic support to service users on the complex care pathway and their staff teams. Indeed, she is about to finish her CAT practitioner training. Beth has particular experience and interest in working with women who have experienced trauma and whose responses to trauma are labelled as 'complex'. Beth also has a strong personal, political and professional interest in human rights and equality issues. She is project lead for the 'Human Ri~~~~~~~ ~~ re Project' within Mersey Care's Learning Disability S~~~~

Dr Devendra Hansjee MRCPsych, is the Associate ~~~~~~~ Assertive Community Treatment (ACT) Team in ~~~~~~~~~ team serves a group of clients who have a wide r~~~~~~ health needs. In his three years with the ACT Team ~~~~~~ ~~perience in assessing and managing risk across both inpatien~ ~~~ community settings. He is a proponent of community-based psychiatric care and is committed to helping service users to achieve their full potential during their journey towards recovery.

Kate Hunt is a Consultant Clinical and Forensic Psychologist in the NHS. She is currently the Professional Lead for Psychology and Psychological Therapies in Acute and Crisis Services in Sussex Partnership NHS Foundation Trust, and has a lead role in clinical risk assessment and management across all care groups within the Trust. She was a member of the expert reference group in the recent Department of Health *Best Practice in Managing Risk* guidance and a member of the recent National Task Force on the Health Aspects of Violence against Women and Children. She is currently a member of the National Collaborating Centre for Mental Health Guideline Development Group for Self-Harm: Longer Term Management, and a member of the National Steering Group for Multiagency Risk Assessment Conferences (MARACs). Kate Hunt is a chartered clinical and a chartered forensic psychologist.

Dr Lorna Jellicoe-Jones is currently Head of Secure Psychological Services at Guild Lodge Secure Services, Lancashire Care Foundation Trust. Lorna qualified as a clinical psychologist in 1997 after a number of years working in voluntary sector mental health projects, including MIND, with the Eating Disorders Association and with young people's mental health projects. Her specialist areas of interest are women in secure services, personality disorder, self-injury and multidisciplinary team working. On qualifying, Lorna worked for three years in the Women's Services at Ashworth Hospital, after which she moved to Guild Lodge. Lorna has led on the development of the Psychological Services team at Guild Lodge and on various clinical and service initiatives, including self-injury and Trust and service strategy, the development of gender-sensitive secure women's services, risk policy and training and the establishment of specialist forensic personality disorder teams and networks. Lorna has maintained an active interest in research and has supervised and contributed to projects on trauma and psychosis, sexual offending, the management of challenging behaviour and engaging service users within secure services. A current focus of her work is on developing service user involvement in risk assessment and management and increasing multidisciplinary involvement in psychological service provision.

Dr Maria Leitner is currently Research Director of a company carrying out both medical and veterinary research and also holds an honorary Senior Research Fellow post at the University of Liverpool. Previous posts include five years as Research Director of the School of Health Sciences at Liverpool University and two years as a Manager and Senior Reviewer at the NHS Centre for Reviews and Dissemination, University of York. Maria's research background includes a BA in Experimental Psychology and Philosophy from the University of Oxford and a PhD in quantitative genetics from the University of Sheffield. In line with this diverse background, her primary research interests lie in the quantitative analysis of large-scale population datasets. Current interests in relation to human health issues include the use of systematic reviews in promoting evidence-based health care; prevention, intervention and risk assessment in the context of violent behaviour; and the epidemiology and prevention of suicidal and self-harming behaviour.

Dr Caroline Logan is a Consultant Forensic Clinical Psychologist in Greater Manchester West Mental Health NHS Foundation Trust and an Honorary Research Fellow at the University of Manchester, positions she has held since August 2009. She contributed to the development of the *Best Practice in Managing Risk* guidance while working as a Consultant Specialist Clinical Psychologist in the Secure Psychological Services based at Ashworth Hospital, part of Mersey Care NHS Trust. She has worked in forensic mental health services for 15 years, working directly with clients who are a risk to themselves and to others and, in various consultancy roles, with the multidisciplinary teams and the health and criminal justice organizations that look after and manage them. Caroline serves on the editorial board of the *International Journal of Forensic Mental Health* and is an associate editor of *Legal and Criminological Psychology* and the *Journal of Forensic Psychiatry and Psychology*. She also has ongoing research interests in the areas of personality disorder, including psychopathy, and risk and has a special interest in gender issues in offending. Caroline is both a clinical psychologist and a forensic psychologist, and has a DPhil in experimental psychology.

Mark Love is Senior Team Leader, Occupational Therapist at Guild Lodge Medium and Low Secure Services, Lancashire Care Foundation NHS Trust. After completing a fine arts degree in 1985, Mark worked as a technical instructor at Whittingham Psychiatric Hospital. In 1996, he qualified as an Occupational Therapist and commenced his first clinical post at the Rowan High Dependency Unit, Whittingham Hospital. Since 1999, he has worked as a Senior Team Leader in the Occupational Therapy department at Guild Lodge. Mark has undertaken various training courses, including psychosocial interventions with psychoses (at Manchester University in 2000), as well as cognitive rehabilitation and motivational interviewing. One of his roles within the Occupational Therapy department has been the setting up of a comprehensive range of activities as part of the treatment programme for service users – this has included coping with psychoses, anger and anxiety management, as well as social skills training. He is involved in the Risk Working Group, offering an occupational therapy perspective on the risk pathway at Guild Lodge. Mark continues to facilitate in-house training to students and staff on risk assessment and management, as well as lecturing at Salford University on the Occupational Therapy degree course.

Sally Luxton has brought up three children, and has been the primary carer on her own for her son, her youngest child, who became ill with schizophrenia when he was 17 years old. He is now 31. For the past eight years, Sally has worked as an associate trainer in the training department of Avon and Wiltshire Partnership Mental Health Trust. Together with service users and clinicians, she has developed and delivered training to staff. Training includes Working Collaboratively with Risk, CPA and Care Pathways, Working in Partnership with Families and Carers and Mental Health Awareness. Sally also teaches on the three-year pre-registration mental health nursing degree at the University of the West of England, has worked with Rethink and been engaged in other work in the mental health field, all promoting the importance of working together with families and carers.

Prof. James McGuire is Professor of Forensic Clinical Psychology and Director of the Doctorate in Clinical Psychology Programme at the University of Liverpool. He also holds an honorary post as Consultant Clinical Psychologist in Mersey Care NHS Trust. He worked for some years in a high security hospital and has carried out psycho-legal work involving assessment of individuals for Youth Court, Crown Court and for hearings of the Mental Health Review Tribunal, Parole Board and Criminal Cases Review Commission. He has conducted research in probation services, prisons, and other settings on aspects of psychosocial rehabilitation with offenders and has written or edited 13 books and numerous other publications on this and related issues. Professor McGuire serves on the editorial boards of four journals, and has contributed to a Guideline Development Group for the National Institute of Clinical

Excellence (NICE) on Antisocial Personality Disorder. In addition, he has been involved in a range of consultative work or staff training with criminal justice agencies in the United Kingdom, Sweden, Finland, Romania, Canada, Australia, Hong Kong and Fiji.

Patrick McKee is currently the head of practice and clinical quality development for the Avon and Wiltshire Mental Health Trust. He holds a dual qualification in nursing, with 30 years' experience in mental health. He trained initially in Northern Ireland, qualifying as a Registered Mental Health Nurse in 1983. Patrick moved to England in 1984, working in a number of mental health fields including drugs and alcohol, acute care, rehabilitation and later as a ward manager in an interim psychiatric intensive care, low security facility in London. Patrick moved into senior clinical managerial roles from 1990 onwards running both inpatient and community services. In 1999, he completed a BSc (Hons) in Health and Community Studies, which led to a role as associate nurse director for quality development. This eventually led to a seven-year period as Director of governance and nursing with the Avon and Wiltshire Mental Health Partnership Trust providing professional leadership for a large nursing workforce. In 2008, Patrick embarked on a new career as head of practice and quality development, with a central role in developing new and innovative clinical services. One of the founder members of the Care Programme Approach Association (CPAA), he has been involved in the development of care planning and clinical risk processes. He is currently leading his Trust's plans for the introduction of a system for payment by results, including the introduction of care clusters and clinical outcome measures.

Jane Moore is Head of Clinical Audit and Research at Oxleas NHS Foundation Trust. She has worked in the field of health care quality for over 15 years, with a background in psychology and academic research. She has a masters degree in 'Evaluation of Clinical Practice', has published several journal articles, and has a special interest in change management theory and its application. Jane has advised on several national audits, and recently spent a year working for the local quality improvement team at the Healthcare Quality Improvement Partnership (HQIP), which is a national body established to promote and support clinical audit.

Dr Rajan Nathan is a Consultant Forensic Psychiatrist in Mersey Care NHS Trust and an Honorary Senior Research Fellow at the University of Liverpool. He qualified in medicine in 1992 and the following year commenced psychiatric training, culminating in the appointment to a consultant post in 2001. As a post-doctoral research fellow, the focus of his research was the assessment of serious violence and the developmental antecedents of violence. He was awarded a doctorate in 2007. Alongside his clinical commitments, largely in the area of forensic personality disorder, he has continued to conduct research in the forensic field. He has led service development in the area of forensic personality disorder.

Prof. Dr Norbert Nedopil is Head of the Department of Forensic Psychiatry at the University of Munich, Germany, having previously been Professor and Head of the Department of Forensic Psychiatry at the University of Würzburg. Norbert studied medicine and psychology at the University of Munich, graduating in 1974. Between 1977 and 1984, he held a residency at the psychiatric hospital of the University of Munich, specializing in psychopharmacology, schizophrenia research and sleep research. He has specialized in forensic psychiatry since 1984. Norbert's special interests are psychiatric assessment, human aggression, treating mentally disordered offenders, predicting recidivism and a range of ethical and legal issues pertaining to psychiatry. Norbert is the author or editor of seven books and more than 200 scientific papers.

Beverley Quinn is a Registered Psychiatric Nurse and holds a BSc (Hons) in neuroscience and a BSc (Hons) in psychosocial interventions in psychosis, as well as a diploma in mental health nursing. She has seven years' experience of working within both inpatient and forensic psychiatric services. She is currently working at the Scott Clinic, part of Mersey Care NHS Trust, which is a medium secure psychiatric unit. The unit emphasizes working with clientele using a psychosocial intervention framework, utilizing therapeutic and cognitive behavioural therapeutic techniques, as well as traditional interventions to aid recovery. Bev currently has a dual role in the Scott Clinic, where she is involved in research projects in collaboration with the University of Liverpool and also works on the wards within the unit as a psychiatric nurse.

Claire Riding is Case Manager for the North West Secure Commissioning Team. Claire qualified as a Mental Health Nurse in March 1997 and took up her first post at the Chesterton Unit at Winwick Hospital (later changed to Hollins Park Hospital). She completed a BSc in Personality Disorder and Mental Health at Liverpool John Moores University in 1999, before moving to Guild Lodge medium secure unit in August 2000 to take up the post of Team Leader. Shortly afterwards, Claire led a project to open the unit's first women-only ward, and in 2002 completed an MSc in Forensic Behavioural Science at the University of Liverpool. Her dissertation focused on women suffering from psychopathic disorder. Claire then enjoyed a series of promotions, from ward manager to Flow and Capacity Manager, and finally Modern Matron, managing four clinical areas within the unit. She is currently on secondment as a Case Manager with the North West Specialized Commissioning Team.

Kay Sheldon has received a range of mental health services including inpatient care under the Mental Health Act. She has been involved with a wide range of service user initiatives either as an 'involved' service user herself or by developing opportunities for others. She has been a Mental Health Act Commissioner and a member of the Mental Health Act Commission board. In the latter capacity, she helped to develop an involvement strategy for the organization, which included setting up a Service User Reference Panel of people with either current or recent experience of being detained under the Mental Health Act. She is currently a Commissioner – board member – with the Care Quality Commission, the new health and social care regulator. Kay also has a background in advocacy and user-led research. For example, she was the founding chairman of a local user-controlled advocacy project and has worked as a user/survivor researcher with the Mental Health Foundation. Other voluntary sector experience includes being a trustee with MIND, having previously been co-chair of MIND Link, MIND's user/survivor network. Kay also writes and undertakes some training and consultancy work.

Prof. Tilman Steinert is a senior doctor in acute psychiatry in Weissenau, Germany, and an extraordinary professor at Ulm University. He was born in 1957 and went to school in Stuttgart, Germany. He studied medicine at Ulm University from 1976 to 1984, interrupted by 16 months of civil service, undertaken in place of national service as a conscientious objector. In 1984, he finished his dissertation on psychiatry in Nazi Germany. He has been a psychiatrist since 1990, and a neurologist and a psychotherapist since 1991. In 1997, he achieved his habilitation with several articles and books on violence and schizophrenia (*Aggression bei psychisch Kranken* (*Aggression in Mentally Ill People*); *Aggression und Gewalt bei Schizophrenie* (*Aggression and Violence in Schizophrenia*); *Basiswissen: Umgang mit Gewalt in der Psychiatrie* (*Basic Knowledge: Management of Violence in Clinical Psychiatry*)). In the same year, he founded the German Working Group for the Prevention of Violence and Coercion in Psychiatry, of which he is still the leader today. In 2007, he was commissioned by the German Association of Psychiatry and Psychotherapy to develop guidelines for the management of aggressive and violent behaviour, which was eventually published in 2009 (*Deutsche Gesellschaft für Psychiatrie, Psychotherapie und Nervenheilkunde: Praxisleitlinien in Psychiatrie und Psychotherapie* (*German Association for Psychiatry and Psychotherapy: Guidelines in Psychiatry and Psychotherapy*)). Since 2008, he has belonged to the managerial board of the hospital group Zentrum für Psychiatrie Südwürttemberg with responsibility for general psychiatry and research. He has published four monographs and about 170 papers and book contributions in German and English, and is editor of the journal *Psychiatrische Praxis*.

Dr Geraldine Strathdee OBE, MRCPsych, is the Associate Medical Director for Mental Health for London and the Specialist Clinical Adviser on Mental Health to the Care Quality Commission. For over 15 years she has held senior roles in mental health policy and regulation at national and London regional levels in organizations that have included the Department of Health and the Healthcare Commission. She advises policy bodies internationally on mental health policy and service design. Her particular commitment is to the translation of policy and best practice guidelines into routine working practice. Clinically, she has worked in a wide range of inpatient and community services for people with complex and multiple needs, and is currently the Consultant Psychiatrist for the Bromley Assertive Community Treatment team, Oxleas NHS Foundation Trust. She is committed to providing services that enable service users to live in their own homes, develop their own self-management expertise to achieve recovery, while at the same time working with community agencies to achieve risk management, which maximizes service users' chances of recovery and provides public protection.

Dr Nicola Swinson is a Consultant Forensic Psychiatrist at Guild Lodge, Lancashire Care NHS Foundation Trust and an Honorary Clinical Research Fellow at the National Confidential Inquiry into Suicide and Homicide by People with Mental Illness at the University of Manchester. She graduated from the University of Glasgow with an MB ChB in 1999, having completed an intercalated degree in Biomedical Sciences and Psychology at University College London in 1997. She trained at the Maudsley Hospital, London until becoming a member of the Royal College of Psychiatrists in 2003. She then completed her higher specialist training in Forensic Psychiatry in the north west of England. She is currently studying for a PhD in personality disorder in perpetrators of homicide. She teaches on violence risk assessment and supervises both undergraduates and postgraduates on research projects and higher degrees. Her other research interests include violence risk assessment, suicide prevention, homicide and other aspects of forensic psychiatry.

Dr Ben Thomas is the Head of Mental Health and Learning Disabilities for the National Patient Safety Agency. He is currently on secondment to the Department of Health, England as the Director of Mental Health and Learning Disability Nursing in the Professional Leadership Team. He has held a number of senior clinical, managerial and academic positions both in the United Kingdom and Australia, where he was Chief

Nurse at St Vincent's Mental Health Service, St Georges Older Peoples' Service and Associate Professor at the University of Melbourne. He was also a non-executive director for the Norwood Rehabilitation and Housing Association. Ben has served on a number of ministerial reviews and advisory committees to governments including Malaysia, South Korea, Australia and China.

Richard Whitehead is currently Head of Clinical Psychology for Rebuild Clinical Business Unit, which is based at Olive Mount and is part of Mersey Care NHS Trust. The psychology service works with learning disability, psychiatric rehabilitation, brain injury and Asperger syndrome services. Richard has worked in the NHS for over 24 years, working with people who have psychosis, personality disorder and forensic labels. His main focus over the last 12 years has been supporting people with a learning disability and complex needs into the community from secure settings. Richard is also Course Convener and honorary lecturer on the learning disability module in the Doctorate in Clinical Psychology course at the University of Liverpool. Over the last four years, the team at Olive Mount has developed practical tools for applying human rights-based approaches in learning disability services, in collaboration with the British Institute of Human Rights and the Department of Health. These have ranged from human rights-based risk assessment and management tools, benchmarking third sector providers on a range of human rights factors, to a 'Standing up for my rights group' for people who use services, and the development of Service User Consultants based on the co-production model.

Prof. Richard Whittington is Professor of Mental Health in the Institute of Psychology, Health and Society at the University of Liverpool and an Honorary Research Fellow at Mersey Care Mental Health NHS Trust. He has a PhD from the Institute of Psychiatry, London, and is a researcher and forensic psychologist with a particular research interest in the issues of violence, self-harm and mental health. He has a background in mental health nursing in intensive care and general acute settings. He is a member of the Liverpool Violence (LiVio) Research Group and was Chair of the European Violence in Psychiatry Research Group (EViPRG) from 2004 until 2009. He has published widely on psychological and social aspects of violence in both institutional and community settings, with a particular focus on the role of interaction in the generation of aggression and the use of coercive interventions. Other current research interests include the management of mental health problems in the youth justice system and the translation of complex evidence syntheses into useable decision–support guides. Together with Dr Caroline Logan, he led the team which produced the *Best Practice in Managing Risk* guidance in 2007.

Dr Kirsten Windfuhr is the Senior Project Manager and Research Fellow for the National Confidential Inquiry into Suicide and Homicide by People with Mental Illness, which forms part of the Centre for Suicide Prevention at the University of Manchester. She completed her PhD in Psychology at the University of York in 1999, having completed her BA at Hope College (in the United States) in 1995 with a double major in Psychology and German. Pursuing her interests in health care ethics, she also completed her MA in Health Care Ethics and Law at the University of Manchester in 2006. Dr Windfuhr's research interests include the epidemiology and aetiology of suicidal behaviour and suicide prevention.

Dr Thomas Wolf is a judge. He studied law at Marburg University, and practised law thereafter. In 1980, he was appointed judge at the Land Hessen, and in 1983 appointed life-time judge. In 1984, he was promoted to doctor of law science, and between 1990 and 1993, he was scientific clerk at the German Constitutional Court. In 1998, Thomas became chair judge at Marburg Regional Court, dealing with all cases of release both from prison and forensic hospital. Thomas is the director of the Führungsaufsichtsstelle Marburg (surveillance over released prisoners and mentally-ill offenders), author of a scientific commentary on the law of execution, and has published many of his court decisions in German law journals. He is a permanent lecturer at the German Judge Academy and teaches at many other institutions and meetings. He is a member of the scientific board of German journals on matters of execution (*Der Deutsche Rechtspfleger*) and on forensic psychiatry (*Zeitschrift für Psychiatrie, Psychologie und Kriminologie,* edited by Kröber, Saß *et al.*).

Foreword

Safety is at the centre of all good health care. However, in mental health, safety can be particularly sensitive and challenging. The autonomy and rights of service users have to be considered alongside risk to the public. A good therapeutic relationship must, therefore, include both sympathetic support and objective assessment of risk.

In the last decade, there have been a number of initiatives that are intended to make mental health services safer. Assertive outreach teams, for example, now provide intensive care in the community to people who may drift away from care, putting themselves and others at risk. Also, more acceptable treatments, both modern drugs and psychological therapies, are more widely available. The Care Programme Approach has recently been revised to align it more closely to the management of risk. And, to back up these changes, the Mental Health Act has been amended in various ways.

We know from the work of the National Confidential Inquiry into Suicide and Homicide by People with Mental Illness that staff have often found it difficult to recognize risk in cases where a suicide or a homicide occurs. There are complex reasons for this, to do with our training as frontline professionals, the relationships we try to make with service users and the inherent difficulties in understanding and positively managing risk as part of a collaborative venture.

This book offers a positive message and practical guidance on what can be done to improve our understanding of risk and what we can usefully do to manage it. It is unrealistic to expect services to prevent all incidents of harm to self and others, but the clinical management of risk can always be strengthened, with benefits to service users and their families, to the public and to the public perception of mental health services.

Louis Appleby
National Clinical Director for Health and Criminal Justice
May 2010

Preface

In this book, we offer a view about risk – what it feels like to be a person at risk of harming themselves or others or the close relative of such a person, what risk is and what it is not, how to understand risk in individuals and in the organizations in which they are cared for, and ultimately, how to try to manage risk using the least restrictive methods possible. It has taken us around two years to bring this book together, to gather the views that follow and to shape them into a collective whole that communicates one key message: the basis for risk management is an understanding about the risks posed by an individual interacting with his or her environment and the other people encountered within it. Consequently, this book endeavours both to enhance understanding about self-harm and violence and to offer practical solutions to the management of individuals and the organizations tasked with managing them.

Why have we put this book together? Because it is our view that despite a very great deal of research on the subject of risk assessment, we still do not know enough about what it feels like to be on the receiving end of risk management plans, what positive risk management really looks like and how it can be achieved, what a risk formulation is and how organizations can improve the way they think collectively about risk and its management. All these topics are addressed in this book by practitioners, researchers, managers, service users and carers who are in a position to offer an expert view on their area of interest or experience.

This book follows on from the publication in 2007 by the Department of Health of the document, *Best Practice in Managing Risk: Principles and Evidence for Best Practice in the Assessment and Management of Risk to Self and Others in Mental Health Services* (Department of Health, 2007). The authors of this guidance – all of whom have contributed to chapters in this book – were moved by the experience of putting the guidance together and, subsequently, in 2008, of implementing it in mental health trusts across England. We were moved by the experiences of service users and carers who were consulted on the development of the guidance and by the frequent fears and frustrations of practitioners and managers uncertain about what to do with their risky clients. This book is intended as a way of channelling their experiences into something that might be useful for practitioners and managers, service users and their carers, all grappling with risk and its safe, effective, transparent and, ultimately, proportionate management.

Work began in earnest on this book in November 2008 when many of the authors were brought together in a writer's workshop, which took place over two days at Albert Dock, Liverpool. At this workshop, the purpose of the book was discussed and individual chapters were planned. In the 12 months that followed, chapters were written and edited, reviewed and updated, in a process notable for the patience of the authors with the tiresome obsession with detail shown by the book's two editors. Consequently, in the last few months, this volume has come together into what we hope is a coherent whole – a guide to the entire clinical risk assessment and management process that complements and enhances the original *Best Practice* guidance, and reinforces the view that something good can come out of doing something positive about risk. It is our hope that you will agree that this objective has been met.

Our most heartfelt thanks go to the contributors to this book. We are grateful to you for your time and patience and for the vital information you have distilled and communicated so well in the pages that follow. We must also thank Janet Davies of the Department of Health who had faith in us to deliver the *Best Practice* guidance and who has supported our work in the delivery of this book. Our thanks also go to Dawn Fleming, who for the period during which the *Best Practice* guidance was prepared, was assistant to Ms Davies. The contribution is also gratefully acknowledged of all the members of the *Best Practice* National Mental Health Risk Management Programme 'Risk Assessment and Management Tools and Methods' Expert Advisory Group, as well as all the other experts – by training or experience – consulted in the process of the development of the guidance, its revision and in the preparation of this book. In addition, we must thank both the University of Liverpool and Mersey Care NHS Trust for supporting the development of the *Best Practice* guidance and the preparation of this book in many different ways. The support of Greater Manchester West Mental Health NHS Foundation Trust is gratefully acknowledged by Caroline Logan, in particular, the support given by Drs Adrian West and Josanne Holloway, for allowing her the time to complete her work on this book since she joined them from Mersey Care NHS Trust in August 2009. Finally, we wish to express our gratitude to Sarah Davidson whose contribution over these last few months, getting this manuscript organized and ready for Wiley and generally not missing a thing, has been invaluable.

Richard Whittington and Caroline Logan
May 2010

1

Introduction

Richard Whittington and Caroline Logan

The idea of 'risk' has begun to prevail in many areas of life over the past two decades (Gardner, 2009). Mental health services in particular find their activities increasingly dominated by the view that risks such as violence and self-harm can be calculated, predicted and managed. Service users, in turn, increasingly find their personal experiences of distress to be framed in terms of the risk they may present to themselves and to society as a whole. Such an emphasis on risk could have benefits. For instance, by encouraging more comprehensive treatment plans that take into account undesirable as well as desirable outcomes, service users can be liberated from unnecessary restrictions at an earlier stage in their recovery. On the other hand, and more negatively, the emphasis on risk can be seen as just another phase in the long history of the stigmatization routinely faced by people with mental health problems based on an exaggerated, largely false, sense of their dangerousness; fears about risk then limit rather than energize progress. Ultimately, however, the discourse of risk is here to stay in mental health services and the challenge for practitioners is to try to use it creatively and fairly – and safely – in their therapeutic work. This book is an attempt to help with that process by examining the personal experience of service users, carers and staff, the research evidence and the practice dilemmas that arise frequently in relation to risk decision-making in mental health services. By looking at these issues from several different perspectives, we hope to move forward the debate about what exactly is meant by risk in this context and, furthermore, what are the best ways of 'doing' risk management in mental health services when working with the problems of self-harm and violence.

Managing such risks as these in mental health services is a highly charged topic and ideas about the right way forward are hotly contested. There are many and varied debates about what constitutes risk and how the right balance should be struck between risk management and treatment. There is also the question of power between service users and practitioners when a particular decision needs to be made involving users' liberty or the use of coercion in care. There are also understandable anxieties about the

Self-Harm and Violence: Towards Best Practice in Managing Risk in Mental Health Services, First Edition. Edited by Richard Whittington and Caroline Logan.
© 2011 John Wiley & Sons, Ltd. Published 2011 by John Wiley & Sons, Ltd.

reality of engaging service users in their own risk *self*-management. Working and living with risk is, almost by definition, stressful. Being responsible for decisions about risk can also be demanding and often troubling for both practitioners and service users and their carers. The potential for self-harm or violence is only one small part of the full range of a person's potential needs and problems, but they are problems that tend to dominate the picture because they can generate far more anxiety and concern than any other aspect of care. At the same time, people with mental health problems are as entitled as anybody else to high quality services with an underlying philosophy that emphasizes a collaborative approach in all decisions about care and treatment. Getting the balance right in this area is exceedingly challenging, but at the same time extremely important.

This book has grown from the work of an expert panel convened by the English Department of Health in 2006 to set out the key principles that should underpin risk management in mental health services. Self-neglect and personal vulnerability were included as relevant risks alongside the 'headline' risks of self-harm and violence. The panel represented a wide range of views, including those of service users, carers, professional organizations, academics and the police. Together, they were asked to devise a 'best practice' guideline for staff faced with the task of managing these various risks in mental health services. There had been growing attempts within government to systematize and improve approaches to risk in mental health services in this way in the early years of the new millennium and the proposed 'best practice' guidance was part of this overall initiative. Other efforts included preparation for the revised 2008 Mental Health Act, reform of the 20-year-old Care Programme Approach, and dissemination of the *Seven Steps to Patient Safety* guide (National Patient Safety Agency, 2008). The urgency of the problem was emphasized by two violent incidents in London in 2004 where people with very recent service contact acted violently with fatal consequences. In one of these incidents, a man with a diagnosis of paranoid schizophrenia discharged himself from the hospital where he had been resident for 18 months following a stabbing incident. The next day, he attacked and killed a man cycling through a London park. In the second incident, a mother killed her child shortly after being visited at home by her health visitor. These were both tragic, high-profile cases where something had clearly gone wrong. Their occurrence indicated a systems failure in that both mental health services and other agencies had failed to detect the risk of imminent violence. It seemed clear that some practitioners working in mental health services were still not properly equipped to assess and manage the risky behaviours they encountered and that the time was right for a statement of basic principles and some guidance on tools that could support effective assessment and decision-making in this area.

Inevitably, there was much debate in preparing the Best Practice document. There was, for instance, an awareness of the potential over-use of the concept of risk. There was passionate debate already around the Mental Health Act and changes to the scope for compulsory treatment. Risk was seen as part of good quality care rather than as something separate or specialized. But at some point in formulating guidance, a consensus must be reached and clear ideas put forward to those who have to make the decisions. Therefore, the process of developing the guidance required, first, a systematic review of the evidence in the various risk domains (violence, self-harm, etc.) and the generation of an expert consensus view about the principles of clinical risk assessment and management practice. Then, a systematic (and independent) examination of a range of risk assessment tools was prepared, including information about their technical performance, clinical efficacy and effectiveness, cost and utility. Eventually, a collective view was achieved and a range of recommendations were made, including a set of 16 best practice principles. These principles are set out in full elsewhere (see Chapter 8, Box 1), but they can be encapsulated in six core areas (see Leitner and Barr, Chapter 4):

- clinical decisions should be based on established research evidence;
- clinicians should proactively engage with clients as partners in care;
- risk management should be flexible, dynamic and responsive;
- careful forward planning should be integral to the clinical process;
- care should be multidisciplinary but well coordinated; and
- structural, procedural and organizational factors should be addressed in addition to individual (client-specific) factors.

In sum, the guidance – entitled *Best Practice in Managing Risk* – was designed to improve effectiveness in mental health care, especially in relation to clinical risk, and to be an instrument for quality assurance for practitioners, the services they work for and the service users and carers with whom they work. Nothing radically new was being put forward here – the basic tenets of good mental health practice were being crystallized and restated in the new context of risk management as they seemed to have been lost in some settings over time. Since production of the guideline, the basic vision of mental health services has been revisited again in the *New Horizons* strategy (Department of Health, 2009) and many of the messages remain the same around issues of, for instance, personal control in care and recovery through involvement in developing personal care plans.

Therefore, consensus is vital in establishing policies and providing formal guidance to staff on what constitutes best practice. However, improving practice for the future also relies on debate and on contesting ideas about what works and what is desirable or acceptable. This is where this book moves on from the work of the guidance. Here, especially in the first three sections of this volume, there is scope for competing voices. Each of these voices has space within the book to develop their argument for consideration by the reader. It is crucial, for instance, to get the balance right between care and risk management. Safety is, of course, central to effective care, but most clinicians from every discipline are motivated by a desire to help people achieve wellbeing and recovery, rather than to act purely as a risk management agent whose relations with the service user are framed entirely in terms of risk. Many of the views here are probably incompatible with each other, but we believe the creative tension between them contributes to new thinking on these important topics. In the final section, the book builds on the original project to develop 16 principles of best practice in managing risk. Such principles are meaningless unless they can be translated into better practice in real settings, and the final section considers the specific challenges of implementation. Overall, the book aims to take the next step after developing the idea of best practice in risk management by contextualizing the principles contained within the original guidance and testing their application to real-world settings.

Two key themes emerging from the chapters that follow are particularly worth highlighting. First, several contributors are concerned with the issue of *positive* risk management; how can practitioners retain a sense of optimism when working with service users and avoid the temptation to take as few risks as possible in the hope of avoiding personal and professional criticism? The stakes are always high when working with clients who are violent or who self-harm – very occasionally things can go seriously wrong and s can have major consequences for everyone involved, including the practitioners who took the key decisions. Imagining these painful consequences if things go wrong is an inevitable part of the process of risk decision-making and practitioners deserve maximum support when deciding to go beyond the risk-averse mindset of 'safety at all costs'. Several of the chapters that follow recognize this dilemma and the consequences it can have for the ongoing therapeutic relationship. However, they try to explore some ways in which positive approaches to working with risk can be justified, developed and sustained.

Secondly, there is much discussion here about the continuing struggle to develop a philosophy of care and risk management with a real commitment to *collaboration* at its core. For centuries, the experience of receiving mental health care has been one in which the recipients of the service feel estranged from the system and the passive target of allegedly therapeutic interventions – an abusive feeling at worst. More recently, the notions of collaboration and shared decision-making have become popular in the rhetoric of mental health but, to date, it has been little more than just rhetoric – many service users still report feeling uninvolved and unengaged, their fears and preferences ignored or patronized. Perhaps inevitably, this can lead to a passive and even reluctant compliance with risk management plans and, in the worst case scenario, a dangerous disengagement from services and potentially increased risk leading to more imposed risk management and even less talk of collaboration. Consequently, advocates of collaborative care can be accused of naivety when some service users are seen to be beyond the pale in terms of partnership and engagement in realistic decision-making. It is clear that we still have some way to go to change the mindset of many mental health staff to one in which real collaboration is the starting point for developing risk management plans rather than an add-on or token gesture. However, while it is realistic for practitioners to question the potential for collaboration in some situations, they have a duty to ask themselves if their reluctance to work with other service users in decision-making is truly because of that person's incapacity or if, in fact, it may be more to do with the practitioner's worldview. Are they, for instance, becoming cynical about the scope for change and meaningful clinical engagement, perhaps due to excessive workload or poor supervision? How much of this reluctance to work collaboratively is really to do with the service user?

Elsewhere, one of us (Logan, in press) has highlighted the major challenges faced by mental health services working with people with a personality disorder, and many of these challenges can also be seen when working with the linked problems of self-harm and violence. For instance, as mentioned above, sometimes practitioners lose their capacity for therapeutic optimism and stop believing that a particular service user can change in a positive direction. Similarly, the public and the government can expect too much from services in terms of their capacity to manage risk effectively and at all times, perhaps because these services have in the past promised to do so thus inflating expectations to an unrealistic level and dooming themselves to failure. Inadequate resources will always be an element of this problem, especially in the economic future we are currently facing. In both these areas of practice, there is the real danger of clinging to risk assessment tools based on an ill-founded belief in their seemingly scientific qualities, credibility and simplicity – that the tool will make the decision for the practitioner rather than aid what is ultimately his or her decision-making responsibility. Finally, as with the management of all complex mental health problems, where diverse agencies are responsible for various aspects of care and treatment, there is the scope for poor communication, unclear relationships and risky people disappearing in the gaps between agency boundaries. These challenges are not going to disappear any time soon. However, it was these problems of pessimism and unrealistic thinking, over-reliance on tools, inconsistent decision-making and poor communication that drove the development of what became the *Best Practice* guidance and what has since become this book.

Many of the contributors to the book participated in the debates surrounding the development of the *Best Practice* document or are now leading on the implementation into practice of the principles set out in the document. Together, they have a wide range of experience in thinking about the notion of risk in this area, conducting risk management in real-world mental health settings, living with a label of risk and making everyday practice reflect best practice in the full range of mental health professions. They combine theoretical, research and personal knowledge with a wealth of practical skills in care and management. Further, they emphasize the collaborative and recovery-focused nature of modern risk management – working with the service user, building on strengths – but trying at the same time to remain aware throughout of the realities of mental health care.

In the forthcoming pages, there is much discussion about the evolving evidence base, for violence and self-harm as well as clinical risk assessment and management, and how this can be incorporated into designing and delivering services in ways that can make a real difference to their efficacy and to the experience of service users. Some chapters explicitly deal with the relevant evidence base, most acknowledging appropriately that there are still worrying gaps in what we know. However, while the 'science' of structured risk assessment tools and specific interventions (particularly cognitive–behavioural therapy and pharmacological interventions) is quite advanced and sophisticated, it does not capture the service user experience. Much of this experience is mediated via the dynamic relationship with the practitioner and the subtle aspects of this relationship, which can be crucial in underpinning an effective therapeutic alliance, are still poorly understood and very difficult to study using approaches valued in the traditional research methods hierarchy. Consequently, most of the contributors draw on the evidence base available to them in relation to their topic, but also draw on sound clinical and real-life experience to fill the gaps.

The book is structured into four sections. The four themes of personal experience, research evidence, practice and implementation run through most of the chapters, but are prioritized in different ways in each section. We have tried to move from the direct experience of service users and carers, through some of the relevant research evidence, to explore some key aspects of clinical practice. The final section then looks at ways in which a variety of trusts have attempted to implement the principles of best practice in this area.

In the first section, 'Experience', Kay Sheldon (Chapter 2) and Sally Luxton (Chapter 3) write about their personal experiences as a service user and a carer, respectively, involved in the process of risk management. Both acknowledge that there is good work going on, but their personal experience on the receiving end indicates that we are still a very long way from achieving best practice (i.e., collaborative care) in this area. Hence, the title of this book, which emphasizes movement towards, rather than arrival at, best practice in current services.

In the second section, 'Evidence', there is an attempt to examine and, where possible, to summarize research evidence as it relates to the problems with which we are concerned. In Chapter 4, Maria Leitner and Wally Barr use a systematic review approach to tackle the voluminous literature from around the world on the management of self-harm. In Chapter 5 Richard Whittington, James McGuire, Tilman Steinert and Beverley Quinn provide an overview of key points from the even more vast literature relating to violence risk management. Then, in Chapter 6, Kirsten Windfuhr and Nicola Swinson complement these two reviews by drawing conclusions from the UK National Confidential Inquiry on Suicide and Homicide, which underpins much policy in this area in England and Wales. Finally, in this section, and building on the experiences outlined in Chapter 2, Helen Gilburt (Chapter 7) examines the emerging evidence base relating to service user involvement in risk management decision-making.

Both personal experience and research evidence should provide the raw material for improving practice and moving it towards best practice. Therefore, the third section is concerned explicitly with 'Practice' and considers various aspects from a number of angles. The first two chapters are pitched at the national policy level. In Chapter 8, Caroline Logan, Norbert Nedopil and Thomas Wolf look at the growing desire around the world to articulate the principles of best practice and the consistency that is emerging across different countries. Ben Thomas (Chapter 9) works from a national policy perspective to emphasize the role that organizations, as well as individual practitioners, play in embedding best practice into their everyday endeavours. Then, the other three chapters in this section take a detailed look at what might be called the mechanics of practice. Caroline Logan, Rajan Nathan and Andrew Brown (Chapter 10) discuss the core skill, often implicit rather than explicit, of formulation and argue for its centrality in the bridge between risk assessment and risk management. In Chapter 11, Paul Clifford examines the idea, often celebrated but very difficult to implement, of positive risk management, the capacity for both service user and clinician to be cautiously creative in working with risk. Richard Whitehead, Ged Carney and Beth Greenhill (Chapter 12) then conclude this section by discussing an example of implementing positive risk management with one particular client group, namely, people with learning difficulties.

The final section is made up of a collection of case studies in which clinicians describe their efforts to move towards best practice in managing risk in four English mental health trusts. The *Best Practice* guidance drove many of these changes, but each organization took an individual approach and brought their own particular experiences to bear on the innovations. In Case Study 1 (Chapter 13), Geraldine Strathdee, Phil Garnham, Jane Moore and Devendra Hansjee introduced changes to risk management procedures in a large general mental health trust in London and describe the four-step approach they followed. Kate Hunt (Case Study 2, Chapter 14) led innovations across another general mental health trust in the south of England and discusses, among other things, the need to narrow the gap between policy and practice in this implementation process. Louise Fountain and Patrick McKee (Case Study 3, Chapter 15) led a similar implementation project in south west England and describe their experiences, including the challenge for practitioners of balancing clinical flexibility and formal standards. Finally, in a forensic mental health context, Lorna Jellicoe-Jones, Mark Love, Roy Butterworth and Claire Riding (Case Study 4, Chapter 16) describe their initiative to improve practice in accordance with the key principles in a medium secure unit in north west England.

In conclusion, clinical risk assessment and management in mental health services is a highly complex area with a multiplicity of competing viewpoints alongside high stakes for practitioners, service users and their carers and the public in terms of making the right decisions. Ideas on how to get it right are evolving all the time and, rightfully, there is passionate debate about the best way forward. Many of the current ideas informing this debate are discussed in the chapters of this book, and our hope is that overall this book on best practice in managing risk contributes to the quality and content of that ongoing discussion.

REFERENCES

Department of Health (2009). *New Horizons: A Shared Vision for Mental Health*. London: Department of Health.

Gardner, D. (2009). *Risk: The Science and Politics of Fear*. Virgin Books.

Logan, C. (in press). Managing high risk personality disordered offenders: Lessons learned to date, in B. McSherry and P. Keyser (eds), *Managing High Risk Offenders: Policy and Practice*. Routledge.

National Patient Safety Agency (2008). *Seven Steps to Patient Safety in Mental Health*. London: National Patient Safety Agency, available to download at: http://www.nrls.npsa.nhs.uk/resources/collections/seven-steps-to-patient-safety, retrieved 23 May 2010.

Part I

Experience

2

Service Users: Experiences of Risk and Risk Management

Kay Sheldon

Introduction

This chapter describes and reflects on what it is like to experience risk first-hand and how it feels to be subject to risk management in mental health care. It is written from the perspective of people using services, or patients, including my own experiences of receiving mental health services. The apparent risks that I faced were through self-neglect and at times self-harm. However, there were also unseen, or at least less obvious, risks posed by the inherent and prevalent practices of mental health services. Many of my experiences, especially when I have been in crisis and 'at risk', have been characterized by feelings of disempowerment and hopelessness: a passive recipient of care with little meaningful voice and a sense that I had no real future ahead of me. As such, the chapter also considers a range of issues that are pertinent to our experiences of risk as service users such as stigma, powerlessness and fear, as well as the importance of information, involvement and rights in helping to counter these potentially damaging experiences.

There are views here on what works well and what doesn't. In particular, the need to involve us in our own risk management, including why and how, is discussed. Rather than simply relying on my own perspective, I have also drawn on the views and experiences of many other service users that I have come across in other roles I have undertaken in mental health including as a Mental Health Act Commissioner, an advocate and a researcher.

The chapter aims to challenge thinking and encourage all those involved with developing and implementing risk management in mental health, to consider the implications, good and bad, for people receiving services. The chapter ends with a manifesto that details the key facets of an approach to risk management that not only puts service user experiences and needs at the centre, but optimizes risk management so that it becomes less of a controlling and largely malevolent experience and more one which provides safety, respect and hope.

Self-Harm and Violence: Towards Best Practice in Managing Risk in Mental Health Services, First Edition.
Edited by Richard Whittington and Caroline Logan.
© 2011 John Wiley & Sons, Ltd. Published 2011 by John Wiley & Sons, Ltd.

Experiences and Views

The value of direct experience

The overriding theme of this chapter is the importance and value of direct experience in the provision of mental health care. That is, what we, as service users, feel about the care we receive and how we can influence it to achieve positive outcomes, or successes, in our lives. This is true both for individuals, as well as more widely at service and national policy levels.

Having the opportunity to describe what it is like to be subject to, and indeed not subject to, risk management in the context of receiving care from mental health services has many benefits. It provides us as users of the services with a chance to have a voice in this important aspect of care that can have major implications in our lives. We can say what we think about risk and its management and how it has or has not affected us, both positively and negatively. We can describe our direct experiences of risk management, how it felt, and what it did to us and for us. Stemming from experiences of the process, we can provide an insight to help mental health professionals optimize risk management in a way that is both protective when necessary but also, crucially, becomes an important therapeutic activity that supports recovery rather than hinders or prevents it.

Because of my own largely unhelpful experiences, I was motivated to try and improve this situation. I started at 'grass roots' as an activist (described further below in the section 'Involvement?'), becoming involved in setting up a local service user forum and advocacy project and subsequently being appointed as a Mental Health Act Commissioner. Rather than relying solely on my own experiences for this chapter, I surveyed the Service User Reference Panel (SURP) of the Mental Health Act Commission[1] (MHAC) to explore more experiences and perspectives, good and bad, and to find out how, or if, service users were involved in their own risk planning. I also asked the SURP for suggestions and recommendations for improving both the experience and the effectiveness of risk management with a view to changing practice.

Many of the experiences that are described here are negative, in fact quite traumatic, and shocking at times. However, it is vital that these voices are sought, heard, and acted upon for compelling reasons of respect, rights, and equality. Similarly people working in services can be encouraged to work in a more user-focused way, aspiring to be user-defined or directed, and through this to improve the life outcomes of people that they care for. In turn, it is suggested that a more rewarding role for practitioners and workers will emerge, enabling them to feel that they are helping people rather than just controlling or restricting them.

It can be difficult hearing some tough messages in service user feedback and there is always the chance of alienating people. However, what many overlook is that, as people with experience of mental health problems, we want our experiences and perspectives acknowledged and valued, but we can also respect other points of view. Many people are angry because they know that if they had been listened to, engaged, or provided with help and support that would either have prevented a crisis or facilitated a quicker recovery. If this anger – energy – can be used to help influence and change things for the better, we

---

[1] The Mental Health Act Commission was abolished and its functions and activities (including the Service User Reference Panel) transferred to the new health and social care regulator, the Care Quality Commission from April 2009.

will have moved on. The perspectives we bring as service users and valuing our direct experience can – should – have a positive impact on how the risk management process can be improved for all concerned.

Meanings

To start to understand what risk management feels like when you are the person whose 'risks' are being 'managed', it is necessary to take a step back and consider what the word 'risk' means to people in everyday life, its associations and its implications. The term has many meanings and interpretations depending on context and perspective. It can be applied in many walks of life and can, for example, relate to business, finance, and governance. The term is always associated with potential dangers, threats, or problems. Within mental health services, the term is mostly attributed to the management of people receiving services. An individual who has led a relatively ordinary life can almost overnight be catapulted into a situation where they are likely to be deemed as a 'risk' simply because they have become unwell and have required the intervention of mental health services. The way that a person is regarded and approached – assessed, interviewed, and 'managed' – can mean that he or she is then viewed in terms of problems, symptoms, interventions, and risks. This has a devastating impact on people's lives. It affects both how they see themselves and how others see them. They become forever (it seems) associated with danger, whether it is towards him- or herself and/or to others. Once this association has been made, it will always be there: for the person concerned, their family, maybe also friends and neighbours, and in the eyes of health (not just mental health) and social care services. No matter if they feel better or have 'recovered', the association persists, cropping up again and again, perpetuated by stigma, prejudice, and a pervasive lack of self-worth.

While the word 'risk' in connection with mental health care has become a permanent fixture, it is important not to lose sight of the effects the actual word can have on service users, in their own eyes, those of people working in services and wider including the general public. Stigma is the biggest risk facing people with mental health problems. It is well known that the risks that service users face are predominantly as victims of abuse, violence and self-neglect, yet the perception remains and, indeed, policy suggests and perpetuates the myth that people with mental health problems are dangerous. Even within these scenarios, a common factor of subsequent inquiries is the lack of support and engagement of mental health services, despite in many cases the service user and their family repeatedly contacting services. It raises the question about who the victim is in such situations.

On the receiving end

In the past I have posed a significant risk to myself through self-neglect and self-harm. My experiences of mental health services have been largely traumatic, and I have literally survived. I have experienced numerous compulsory admissions to hospital after breaking down again and again in the community. I was viewed as the problem in this 'revolving door' situation and deemed as 'non-compliant' when I was unable to tolerate the excruciating side-effects of antipsychotic medication. I was seen as difficult to engage, because I could not express myself or trust the staff. There was no meaningful attempt to establish a rapport, to listen to me, and to work *with* me. I was very much the passive, and sometimes resistive, recipient.

Interactions with staff took the form of trying to persuade me to agree with their point of view. I became alienated, hopeless, and actively suicidal. The worst of my experiences took place in the late 1980s and 1990s and have fuelled my determination to both provide a voice for service users and to contribute to a better and more humane experience for service users. Unfortunately, I know that I am not alone in my experiences, even up to the present time. In my roles as researcher, advocate and as a Mental Health Act Commissioner, I have heard and seen hundreds of examples that confirm this experience. It is overwhelmingly further confirmed through the survey of the MHAC's SURP that follows below.

My own risk management consisted of being placed under a Section of the Mental Health Act, followed around by a member of staff 24 hours a day for weeks at a time, reprimanded for taking an overdose, put on depot injections, and forcibly restrained and medicated when I refused the horrific depot injections or tried to go out for walk or to my flat. The dangers that I posed to myself were far from the only risks I faced. My contact with mental health services at times served to either perpetuate risks or to create new ones. Sometimes, this was an oversight; for example, I absconded to my flat and took a life-threatening overdose. I had been detained under the Mental Health Act and was supposed to have been on 15-minute checks. It took the ward staff 3 hours to discover that I was absent without leave. Another time, when I was supposedly under continuous observation, I got up one night to go to the toilet and found the nurse 'observing' me fast asleep in an armchair wrapped in blankets! It was only because it was pouring with rain and I had no shoes, that I went back to bed.

More often, my experiences were aligned with alienation: I was reprimanded for attempting to hang myself and it was suggested that I was trying to take my distress out on staff; I was told that I had not attended outpatient appointments, although no appointments had been sent; I was told that a Community Psychiatric Nurse (CPN) would visit weekly, but this didn't happen. I had a potentially lethal combination of an untreated depression and severe akathisia (an excruciating inner feeling of restlessness caused by the antipsychotic medication), yet this was unrecognized for a long time and then when it was identified it was dealt with inadequately. I really don't know how I managed to quite literally survive – the biggest risk of all.

You come to believe yourself that you cannot cope or be trusted, that you need to live where you can be 'supported' or 'supervised'. Somehow, I resisted being installed in a nursing home. It was a significant and scary 'risk' for me to take, yet I instinctively knew that the long-term risks of such a move would be a disaster, a greater risk to leading a full and independent life. Over the years, I have been given 'advice' by the mental health services that, although well meant, would have – if I had heeded the advice – restricted and impoverished my life. I have been told that I should not work, buy a house, stop depot injections, and have even been told not to have children. Anger has, in fact, been my saving grace. So outraged was I that other people should define how I should live my life, I set out to prove them wrong. While the anger was draining, it did provide me with the impetus to change things in my life. Without this motivation, I'm not sure that I would have been able to resist the direction in which I was gradually being propelled. Suffice to say, I am now self-supporting, a house owner, free of depot injections and married with two gorgeous children.

A view from the inside

In the mental health magazine, *Open Mind* (No. 146), a psychiatric nurse described her experiences of suddenly being on the receiving end of coercive care on a mental health unit. Her observations make sobering reading. Having been just detained under the Mental Health Act, she relates the following:

> I had believed in my job as a psychiatric nurse. I could have justified everything I did. But now that I was a patient I was horrified to discover just how terrifying and restricting it is to be on the receiving end of mental health services. The psychiatrist and nurses were in total control of everything I did. They not only dictated the treatment I would receive but also how I spent my day. I felt utterly powerless. I had no-one who was on my side or who would explain to me what I was doing there. (pp. 19–20)

And on witnessing the control and restraint of 'aggressive' patients:

> I agreed with this [Control and Restraint] as I felt it was the best management of patients in a highly emotional state. However, when I saw nurses carrying out this procedure on the locked ward I found it barbaric. To see someone so completely restrained was . . . horrifying and totally unnecessary. (p. 20)

More experiences

After several years of working as a Mental Health Act Commissioner, I applied for a position on the organization's management board. I felt that the Commission could do more to improve the direct experiences of people detained in hospital and that a key aspect in achieving this was to actively engage detained patients in the work of the Commission. Rather to my surprise, I was appointed and became the board lead for service user involvement to oversee the development and implantation of an involvement strategy for the Commission. The lynch pin of the strategy was the establishment of a Service User Reference Panel (SURP), which comprises of approximately 30 people, all of whom have current or recent experience of being detained under the Mental Health Act.

As mentioned above, to access more experiences and views of risk management to inform this chapter, I asked members of SURP to describe their experiences and views. SURP members have a diverse range of experiences and backgrounds. For example, about one-third describe themselves as coming from a black or other ethnic minority background. Some members have physical disabilities in addition to mental health issues, and there are service users with learning disabilities. The Panel membership also has a wide age range and there is a geographic representation from England and Wales. Members also have a wide range of mental health services experience, including low, medium and high secure care, Psychiatric Intensive Care Units, rehabilitation/recovery units, community-based care and acute inpatient care.

Six Questions

I used six questions to help members structure, although not restrict, their contributions aimed at eliciting personal experiences of risk management, both positive and negative, the level of involvement, if any, and whether members had any suggestions for improving risk management from a user perspective. The questions I posed are set out in Box 2.1.

Box 2.1: Topics covered in the SURP survey of risk management experiences

Q1 Please describe what your *experiences* of risk management in care planning have been, i.e., what happened or what didn't happen.

Q2 We would like to know what you think was *good or helpful*, if anything, about your experiences of risk management:
  (a) please describe what was good or helpful;
  (b) if possible, can you give *examples* of how risk management helped you.

Q3 We would like to know what was *bad or unhelpful*, if anything, about your experiences of risk management:
  (a) please describe what was bad or unhelpful;
  (b) if possible, can you give *examples* of how risk management has been bad or unhelpful to you.

Q4 Please describe how you were *involved or not involved* in your own risk management assessment or plan.

Q5 What *suggestions* do you have for *improving* risk management in care planning from the point of view of service users/patients?

Q6 Do you have any other comments about risk management in care planning?

The responses to these questions were collated and have been used to shape and inform the whole of this chapter and this section in particular.

Experiences: good, bad and indifferent

The answers to the first three questions provided some very traumatic responses, many of which I could identify with personally. I have made use of many direct quotes so that the real voices of individuals come through:

> I was severely disturbed and isolated in a room. I received no care or assessment. I began cutting my upper wrist with strips, cut by my teeth, from a used plastic cup . . . Cutting began about 8.15/30 and stopped about 12.30pm. I cut beneath and around the tendon. The blood was everywhere. I fell asleep. I would hear a thud at my door. I would hear death threats at my door and around nearby occult literature. In that same room I suffered repeated sexual abuse.
>
> I have had the experience of distressing bad protocol and lack of experience and efficiency from certain staff . . . physical aggression towards patients where patients have been attacked; verbal abuse and intimidation when 1-1 talk time has been asked for by patients to members of staff.
>
> I experienced not only a lack of effective risk management but a total failure of any risk intervention whatsoever. I was left at serious risk to self and possibly others for many months.

In my early years in [a high secure] hospital, my experiences of risk management were quite oppressive. Not only was I not allowed out of the hospital for any reason, I also had only restricted access to my own room and therefore only restricted privacy.

The 'observation' by staff made you feel like a prisoner and that it was your fault that you were in hospital . . . They did not communicate with you except to chastise you, for example for having a beaker of water in your room.

The experiences described by SURP members about risk and risk management, sometimes the lack of it, were overwhelmingly negative. Predominant experiences were of coercion, restriction, and feeling unsafe. Strong feelings of distress, fear, and anger were expressed. Some people were not aware if risk assessments had been completed on them. In fact, those that had not had risk assessments (or were unaware of them) felt that they should have had better management of the difficulties that they faced and people who had experienced risk management felt the process had been damaging rather than helpful. A clear impression emerged suggesting that mental health services were part of the problem either through omission or through inherent damaging practice, which at times would seem to amount to an infringement of human rights:

At the start of my stay in hospital I felt very alone, scared, frightened, and disorientated.

The very first moment of arriving . . . the door slamming and locking very loudly behind me . . . feeling totally helpless, hopeless, vulnerable, not just scared but terrified . . .

Being admitted to a mental health unit, particularly if you have never been in one before, is often a very frightening experience. When people are admitted, they are usually very ill and vulnerable. Women service users in particular reported feeling unprotected and unsafe from their own actions, other patients, and some staff. It is noteworthy that very little was done to make people feel safe, and simply to talk to people, to reassure and explain. It would seem that simple human compassion could go a long way, setting the foundations for a meaningful, therapeutic relationship and, in turn, reducing risk:

Nothing good has come out of risk management except that I have had to learn to cope and rise above the issues that became commonplace in my life when and since being in hospital and becoming unwell. So all in all determination and self preservation is where I'm at as well as aware of what corruption goes on in facilities set aside to protect and serve.

Nothing helpful has been volunteered.

I was an exceptionally high risk patient and detained. There was no risk management by staff. I was very lonely and very frightened with no-one to trust or to speak to . . . There is no good, only bad. I was severely traumatised and suffered flashbacks for three years until I spoke out. I've been told that I am suffering from post traumatic stress disorder.

I was not protected from all on-going harm.

Service users found it difficult to identify examples of when risk management had been helpful:

the only time that robust risk management surfaced, by all mental health professionals concerned [was] to protect themselves from possible recriminations and accountability. Never, during all this time, did one person stand up and ask '*What are we doing to "S"?*'

It doesn't say how you will be dealt with if you feel upset. [You could] be restrained when feeling upset, C&R, being dragged out of your room. Also, in the past [I have been] threatened with being returned to [a high secure] Hospital.

No interest in patient perception. Pathologizing of patient perceptions, i.e., 'If you think you are well, you are ill', 'If you cannot see what I'm talking about you must be ill'.

Until now filling in this form, I had never heard of risk management.

Very little meaningful engagement of service users in the risk management process was described. The experience was very much of 'being done to'. It is not uncommon to come across blanket policies in mental health services that put restrictions on individuals irrespective of whether it is required. The justification for this is usually 'security'. Often an individual approach is absent. SURP members recall:

Referred to 'Assessment Unit' to be assessed on transfer from another High Secure Hospital. No continuity of leave plan or individual treatment plan formulated on past behaviour or trust levels in previous hospital; blanket procedure apparently all patients admitted to [a high secure hospital] are assessed in the Assessment Unit.

A patient ran off whilst on day leave to hospital in London, because of this I was told I would have to handcuffed to staff when visiting the local hospital – cuffed the whole time to staff – man – or would not be able to attend hospital appointment.

No incident for 10 years not taken into account.

However, more positively, there is some indication that, particularly more recently, the risk management process is starting to be used in a more constructive way:

After nearly 6 years at [a high secure hospital], the risks were considered to have decreased enough for me to go to [a Medium Secure Unit]. A more community-orientated and positive regime there, combined with my continued progress, saw me discharged to a community care hostel.

Presumably because staff felt I may make complaints about them, I was put on 2:1 interviews . . . When I got a new named nurse, she formed a good therapeutic relationship with me and wanted the 2:1 sessions to finish. . . . I agreed to our 1-1 interviews being taped and then after a while the tape recording was not considered necessary any more.

My previous crime-free record, my hard work, good behaviour and progress and my insight into my mental illness were all taken into account in the risk assessments. My risk factors and the care team's views of them were regularly explained to me (in person and/or in writing) in a clear manner. For most of time in 2 hospitals, I felt that clinical teams were on my side and had my best interests at heart. Part of this was because it was emphasised that the more progress I was making, the less my risks. Thus the positive side of events was being emphasised.

The risk assessment is very good at [a particular hospital] and it helps me very much and when you go outside . . . it was very good to go out for most of the day. The risk assessment allows me to get out of the house.

The responses that I received from SURP members were at times shocking, but they were also incisive, articulate, and powerful. More than anything, the content, and nature of the responses underlined the importance and value of direct experience and meaningful engagement of service users to both inform and direct mental health care. These and other contributions from SURP members, together with many other service user views and experiences, have been used to illustrate salient issues in the Mental

Health Act Commission's Thirteenth (and final) Biennial Report (2007–2009), *Coercion and Consent*.

Involvement?

There should be no question that, as service users, we should be involved in our own risk assessment and management plan. While service user involvement is covered elsewhere in the book (see Chapter 7), the *experiences* of how, or indeed whether, people have been engaged in their own risk management is pertinent to this chapter. It is noteworthy that the individual on the SURP who felt most positive about his risk assessment and management was the person who had the most detailed knowledge of and involvement in the process:

> I had one-to-one psychology sessions geared towards my specific risk factors. The psychologist would then be able to evaluate how significant these factors remained. Furthermore, for every CPA . . . I completed a patient self assessment form. This was then discussed at the CPA and was part of the CPA report.

However, most SURP members described very little meaningful involvement in risk management or in their care planning:

> Decisions made without patient involvement. No professional led initiatives. My requests yielding limited information. My intelligence not respected. My viewpoint not being taken seriously enough. No proper discussions about risk. No proper discussions about the need for detention.
>
> The plans were typed up, given to me. I didn't get a say in it.
>
> I was not consulted about the decisions. They are made in meetings. I haven't always agreed with them.
>
> In the bad and unhelpful examples, I was just told what was going to happen. If I didn't like it or go along with it, there would be consequences: no handcuffs, no hospital appointment. Not moving rooms into a room where I was told to go, would be looked on as refusing to comply with 'treatment'.
>
> I was informing doctors repeatedly . . . that something was wrong, and I was unwell, felt unsafe. Psychiatrists constantly reassured me that I was fine, no reported incidents, no problems, I posed no risk, I was safe in the community. . . . Totally without warning the police arrested me, I was also sectioned under the Mental Health Act. I was absolutely terrified as I could not understand why. No one explained anything to me.
>
> I was not consulted about my treatment at all. . . . It was a regime of compliance and punishment with the threat of increased medication of injection.

Service users value being meaningfully involved in the risk management process, together with clear information about the process, our rights, and how it is possible to progress and move on. Where risk management has been used as an active tool in the recovery process, to provide better care or quality of life, for instance, service users, understandably, can see the benefits of risk management. It is not difficult to come to the conclusion that the more people are involved and the more ownership an individual has of the process, then the more likely we are to make it work and assume responsibility. This seems an obvious concept, but it is clear that a collaborative and progressive approach is far from the norm.

Getting Involved: A Personal Perspective

Like many people who have been on the receiving end of bad or unhelpful experiences of care, I decided to channel my energy into getting involved with a view to improving the experiences of mental health service users. Initially, this consisted of helping to establish local involvement projects, including a user forum, an advocacy service, and an advice and information project, to ensure service users had a voice, both collectively and individually, as well as sufficient and appropriate information to make decisions and choices. The advocacy service was a user-led initiative and a relatively new concept at the time, especially in my local area. While we were supporting other service users to speak up and to be listened to, we were also challenging the prevalent paternalistic culture and contributing to the establishment of one based more on empowerment, respect, and self-determination.

The early days of these initiatives were both exciting and challenging. It was exciting because I was aware that we were potentially part of a major shift in how people with mental health problems experienced services. The challenge was in confronting attitudes. These ranged from dismissal and even ridicule from some working in services, to a lack of confidence and self-belief in service users. It was also scary because we were challenging, even fighting back. In fact, I was subject to a two-year harassment campaign by a mental health nurse because of the impact we were having. It was exhilarating because there was a vision and commitment that things could be different and I felt fortunate that I was able to contribute to this.

Based on my local involvement experience and my own direct experiences, I applied to become a Mental Health Act Commissioner in an attempt to improve the care and rights of people detained in hospital. To my surprise, I was appointed and I was encouraged that my personal experience of detention, together with my advocacy work, were seen as valid and relevant backgrounds for the role.

As a Mental Health Act Commissioner, I have visited hundreds of mental health units and so have been exposed to risk management 'at the coal face'. It is evident to me that very few places are using risk management as a way of providing holistic care so that service users can progress and move on in their lives rather than live unnecessarily restricted lives or end up in unsafe or damaging situations. Many places now have risk screens and/or risk assessment protocols, but these are frequently little more than a form-filling process. They are rarely reviewed or updated, and have often been completed in a hurry and without checking accuracy or facts. Where risks have been highlighted, there is rarely a coherent plan in place to manage the risk. Most patients have no idea that they have been subject to a risk assessment, and those that do have only the vaguest notion of what it is, what it is for, and what it means or could mean for them.

From my experiences as a service user and a Mental Health Act Commissioner, it is clear to me that in order to improve the experience of service users, both in terms of satisfaction and successful outcomes, the way forward is in working together through meaningful involvement and direct experience. Involvement is becoming more embedded and commonplace, but there is still a long way to go, especially I would hazard, for people with severe or complex mental health problems.

Barriers to involving users: food for thought

The understanding of what is meant by 'meaningful' user involvement can vary, notably between what people receiving mental health services and those providing mental health services say.

Service users sometimes say that, yes, they were involved in that the care or risk plan was put together with them, that they had signed the plan, and they may even have a copy, but that they did not feel that their views were genuinely sought or that their opinions counted only when they accorded with what the professionals wanted. Immediately, this raises the question of what if a service user requests or suggests something that a professional does not feel can be provided either because of risk or possibly due to lack of resources or capacity. What is the point of asking someone's opinion if you cannot act on it? Is it appropriate, ethical even, to ask?

I recall an occasion when I was speaking to a group of mental health professionals about my personal experiences of mental health services and the importance of user/patient involvement in our own care planning and delivery. A rather cynical nurse working in the local medium secure unit said that involvement sounded a good idea but in reality it didn't work. He relayed that he had given a patient a copy of her care plan and asked her for comments, but she had immediately torn it up and thrown it in the bin! He argued that there was little point in trying to involve most patients in their care as they were too angry or disinterested. I suggested that anger was not a bad place to start and the nurse sighed loudly and left the room.

Sometimes professionals will say that someone is difficult to motivate or to engage. Once this observation, or judgement, has been made, this seems to signal that little or no further effort is required in terms of developing a relationship with the individual, to ask for views or to talk to the person. One of my most striking memories of being in hospital was when I started to open up about my thoughts and feelings with a particular nurse. She left saying she would have another 'chat' with me the next day. I waited and waited, but she did not come and talk to me. In fact, she did not approach me again in such a manner during the following months I was there. To protect myself, I closed off my feelings to others. The irony was that I was described as withdrawn and difficult to engage, yet I was desperate to talk to someone.

Involvement and engagement are ongoing processes. When people have their liberty removed even though they have done nothing wrong and/or are ill, it is not surprising that anger is a common emotion! You are often suddenly plucked from your life – 'interrupted' – and subject to a restrictive and sometimes coercive regime. Many people when they are new to mental health services are horrified by how they are viewed and treated not only by the people in their lives, but also those within the mental health services. You cannot impose involvement and, to be meaningful, involvement has to start with the service user. Sometimes this can take time. It requires the service user to be in control as much as possible. It requires listening, gaining an understanding of the individual, taking an interest, not judging or imposing values. Sometimes the involvement of other (former) service users or advocates can be helpful in making a ward or a service seem less threatening or confusing.

Involvement does not relate only to individual care. It is also a culture with a value base of respect, equality, and humility. It is not something that should be seen as an 'extra', to be undertaken when there's time or for a particular occasion. Sometimes the issue is raised of evidence in relation to the benefits or 'added value' of involvement, or even whether it 'works' at all. For me, involvement is a rights issue. It is not a question of whether it should happen or not, but how. Research should be geared at establishing meaningful or useful ways on how involvement can work (see also Chapter 7). To take this a step further, when looking at 'best practice' for involvement it is essential that service users lead or are active participants in developing involvement and research around involvement. The same values that are required for meaningful involvement in individual care also hold for wider involvement initiatives. Involvement is not something you can do to, or require of, people. Involvement can start to be meaningful only if service users have ownership and influence of it.

Rights as Human Beings

Some of my own experiences and those described by SURP members could be described as 'dehumanizing'. That is, feeling that you are much less worthy than are most other people in society. Experiences of mental health care, particularly in inpatient settings, and more specifically, in secure units, can serve to underline or perpetuate these feelings of worthlessness and exclusion. Your identity becomes that of a psychiatric patient. People detained under the Mental Health Act are often subjected to needless impositions and restrictions: I have experienced and witnessed petty and unnecessary 'rules' that exist predominantly to support the institutional regime: you can't have a bath after 9 p.m.; you won't get a takeaway if you don't go to occupational therapy; you can't have visitors until you 'behave'; you can go to your room only at certain times; you can use the washing machine only once a week; no coffee for supper. The fact that you're 'sectioned' can serve to justify particular restrictions or approaches irrespective of your personal circumstances.

Information as Evidence

Clearly, risk assessments and plans rely on information. As such, accurate, relevant, and up-to-date information would seem to be essential to the effectiveness of risk management. However, how this information is collected and updated is subject to huge variation. Verification of information, or rather the lack of it, rarely happens and interpretations are awash with bias and partiality. It seems that you have to go to extraordinary lengths to 'clear' your name and some people feel that they will never manage this. You have to prove that you are a safe and capable person, often competing with partial, incomplete, and false 'evidence' that is being used by the mental health services to justify certain interventions such as levels of security or restrictions:

> You don't know when you're getting out. I've been in too long. They should give me my freedom . . . how do you convince Tribunals that you are no longer a risk if they don't give you the chance or the support you need outside of the hospital to prove it?

I have read many reports and letters written about me by the mental health services and none have been an accurate reflection of the situation. Notwithstanding the numerous factual errors, there have been many inappropriate and erroneous comments made. For example, my notes stated that I had been to Glasgow University and that I was living with my parents, both of which were incorrect. Then there are judgements and comments made by professionals. I had commented that I thought going back to work would help and this had been categorized as a delusion! While it was true that none of the professionals thought I should go back to work, that is, they did not share my 'belief system', the therapeutic benefits – personal and social – of work are well documented. This is an example of how perceptions and value judgements within the context of mental health services can distort the reality of an ordinary, normal concept.

Another example of 'risk' rearing its head as a vague but obstructive force is in the issue of access to clinical case notes. I was denied access to my notes because it was claimed that the rapport that clinicians had with me (which was non-existent at the time!) would be jeopardized, and that the content of the notes would be too distressing for me (irrespective of the fact that not knowing what was written about me was causing me considerable distress). Eventually I gained access to my notes, which ultimately was a positive and empowering experience but I was horrified by some of things that were written, so inaccurate, partial, and judgemental were they.

I remember one particular occasion when I had just been admitted to hospital under the Mental Health Act and was very distressed. A nurse was trying to get me to take a pot of liquid medication of the sort that had previously caused me very unpleasant side-effects. I tried to explain, but the nurse pushed the pot up to my face. I instinctively responded by pushing it away. Some years later when I gained access to my notes the incident report stated that I had attacked the nurse, wrestled her to the ground, and had to be pulled off by a student nurse. This is a complete fabrication. What is additionally worrying is that the student nurse had counter-signed it as true!

I am still experiencing a battle in getting copies of letters written about me to my general practitioner. Presumably, this is because I sent letters to correct the errors and misunderstandings when I have on the odd occasion received a copy of a letter. However, I am simply correcting and explaining. I know from bitter experience how information can become distorted or accepted as correct without any checking:

> I have seen little or no risk management documentation in the last 13 years and the need for my detention has never been justified except VERY weakly and VERY subjectively without any clear understandable arguments. Requests for clear arguments are always ignored.

It seems that once an opinion has been formed, irrespective of whether the opinion has been shown to be wrong or circumstances have changed, the opinion and the ensuing consequences continue. Professional judgements are rarely objective. If there are gaps in information, assumptions are made using information that is available even though the accuracy or relevance of the information is not examined. One has the feeling that you are being tried for a crime you did not commit but with the prosecution using a range of 'evidence' against you, the truth or robustness of which is hardly questioned. The defence – that is, the patient's views – is put in a hopeless situation and is written off with such phrases as 'lack of insight' or 'a chronic patient'. Even at Mental Health Review Tribunals where you can have legal representation (like in a criminal court!) there can be a feeling that the solicitor is fighting a different battle to the one you are. You end up feeling even more desperate because you have exercised your 'rights' but your views have hardly entered into the consciousness of those involved.

A hypothesis can become a fact with minimal 'evidence'. Being prescribed certain drugs can lead to a diagnosis even in the absence of definitive signs and symptoms:

someone on an antipsychotic is or has been psychotic; an antidepressant means you are or have been depressed. These kinds of conclusions can be made both within and without mental health services, for example, by your general practitioner, a midwife, dentist, health visitor, and so on:

> On my first and second recalls, I was left to stew in ignorance with no response to my insistent questioning of why I was being held and for what reason I was not able to see a psychiatrist or make phone calls, as well as not being able to mix with other patients for the best part of 24 hours.

The accuracy and timeliness of information has huge implications for service users, to ensure both safety and fairness in our mental health care system. While making notes in clinical records is subject to professional standards and is even audited at times, this is usually too superficial and minimal for it to have any real effect. Standardized assessments can also be used but, again, these have to be used appropriately with regular re-assessments to ensure accuracy and consistency.

Human rights or wrongs?

I have experienced profound emotions of anger, frustration, and hopelessness because of injustice, prejudice, and powerlessness. Several of the issues that have arisen in my own experiences of mental health care could be viewed as an infringement of human rights. These include a lack of dignity, prevention of a family life including becoming a mother, a home of my own, a job and my own income, expressing my opinion, nearly losing my life. Other service users also speak of similar feelings and experiences:

> I am acutely aware that my life is dictated for me within an institutional framework charac-terised by flux, control, whim, and chance.
> The intrusion of privacy caused major problems between patients and staff which led to restraints or higher doses of medication being administered.

As well as my own experiences, I have come across many instances where there have been both obvious and potential infringements of the human rights of people with mental health problems. Some have been due to deliberate action, for example, a person being held naked in seclusion, while others are more about inherent practice, for example, an individual being detained hundreds of miles from his or her family:

> I was told at one point I should sell my home and enter residential care; had it not been for the intervention of my son, this might have happened. Older women on these wards are treated with contempt, disregarded as a nuisance.
> The very first moment of arriving (far from home on a PICU [Psychiatric Intensive Unit]) . . . so many emotions fighting for first place . . . left all alone, isolated.

It seems that issues relating to human rights are tightly woven into the fabric of mental health care and it is possibly within forensic settings that the issues are most dominant. Certainly, risk management is more prominent in these services but arguably is not working any better, albeit for different reasons. Service users in secure units often experience risk management as unnecessarily restrictive and coercive. The regime of the ward and defensive ways of working can lead to people feeling that they have been locked up with no real prospect in the foreseeable future of moving on and having some kind of life:

> I was detained from the age of sixteen – can you imagine being detained at sixteen until now – forty three years. They tell you that you're institutionalised, one place to another, these Sections go on too long. You're going to be institutionalised with being in these places so long.
>
>   I was frogmarched . . . down long bare corridors through many locked gates to . . . acute admissions. Given medication. No choice, drink this. Swallow these. Shown a room which was bare, dark and grimy with locked shutters on windows, bare floor, bed and a cupboard . . . I felt I had walked into a living nightmare.

It is not uncommon to come across locked units that are experiencing challenging behaviours, such as verbal and physical assaults from the patients there. Of course people can find themselves in secure units for understandable reasons, for example, because their mental health problems and associated actions are such that it has been deemed necessary and/or there is thought to be an ongoing risk. However, any observer can immediately see why, in some of these units, there are so many 'incidents': patients not being listened to or given sufficient opportunity to voice their views; an overly coercive regime with numerous 'rules'; little or no access to fresh air; insufficient activities, including leisure opportunities and trips out; few or even no opportunities to talk about their problems or receive psychological input; limited therapeutic opportunities; minimal choice about anything; overcrowded or cramped living conditions; no knowledge of future plans or of treatment goals; social isolation or loneliness.

Bullying, particularly between patients, and self-harm are common events. Boredom and lack of control of most, if not all, aspects of your life cause you to behave in a way that ordinarily you would not. Within the 'toxicity' of these environments, it is difficult to function normally even when you are (relatively) well. Yet, as a patient, if you react you 'risk' being judged as an ongoing risk to yourself or others, and so need further detention and treatment.

Many of these issues (which are not new, although they are often still unacknowledged and unaddressed) should be viewed in the context of the protection and promotion of human rights. This is not to suggest that people working in the services are deliberately contravening rights, but that the situation is due to the inherent nature of how mental health care, and within this risk, is regarded and provided. The focus of risk management is often symptomatic rather than taking a more holistic approach that also looks at causes including the environment (in the widest sense), as well as positive or mitigating factors such as motivation or progress made. The ultimate purpose of risk management should be to support people to lead lives like any other citizen of society.

What Needs to Change?

As well as highlighting problems, service users can provide valuable insights to help change services for the better and, crucially, suggest how such improvements can be sustained. This section of the chapter considers the key elements necessary to make this a reality. As before, I draw on my own experiences and those of other service users, particularly members of SURP whose direct quotes are incorporated once again.

Respecting experience

I recall one morning in hospital when a nurse appeared with a kidney-shaped dish saying that my doctor had written me up for 'an injection'. No further information was offered. I asked why and was told that it was a 'test' and would make me feel 'a lot better'. It didn't. In fact it made me worse. To my surprise, the next week another nurse appeared with the kidney dish. I said the 'test' hadn't worked and was simply told that I was 'written up for it every week'. Again, I asked why and was told it would mean I wouldn't have to take tablets. By the third week I was practically climbing the walls (I now know that this was due to the excruciating side-effect akathisia, an unbearable, inner restlessness) and was told that I had to have the injection. I refused and several nurses descended on me, pulled down my trousers, and forcibly injected me. I had no idea why they were doing this to me. I was frightened and confused. What was clear to me was that I had to be seen to be 'consenting' in order to be discharged so that I could stop these painful injections with their excruciating side-effects.

I have had to fight the system in order to get my voice heard and get the support that was right for me rather than having 'interventions' imposed on me. Sometimes this has been through the use of the Mental Health Act, but it has also been under the auspices of clinical or professional opinion that effectively sidelined my views on what my needs were and how I wanted to lead my life. Although this was very difficult for me and caused numerous short-term problems, ultimately, I have proved that I know what I'm talking about. There needs to be more respect for the experience and expertise that we bring to the table. Others have had similar experiences:

> I eventually. . . took my care into my own hands after being detained for 2.5 years with no psychology or any therapy. I asked for information about mental illness that I could read up on for insight into the diagnosis I had been given. After receiving and studying these, I asked for information on appropriate medication choices for me to take as alternatives to the ones I had already taken – the most effective with the least side effects. I then presented my choice after consulting a pharmacist to my psychiatrist and the team which was then agreed.
>
> The main risks that are usually considered are suicide, self-neglect, and violence. However, it could include other risks that are caused by your mental health problem or being in hospital. For example: poor physical health; losing your job; becoming homeless; using drugs and alcohol; side effects.

Engaging service users in the solutions to problems, whether in individual care or more widely, can only serve to improve a service and make it more responsive to the needs of the people that are using the service.

Involvement

While most mental health services seek to involve service users in both their own care and the service more generally, few are doing it in a way that is systematic and embedded, and in a way that many service users would describe as meaningful. I know that if I had been listened to, a lot of time, money, and distress would have been avoided.

There is a significant and increasing body of information and guidance on user (and carer) involvement, not least that contained in the NHS Evidence specialist library on patient and public involvement (www.evidence.nhs.uk), so there can be no excuses for not knowing how or where to start. Similarly, lack of resources and time are not valid as it is a question of ethos, priorities, and taking a longer-term perspective. On the issue of risk management, engagement is often absent or ad hoc but is highly valued by service users:

> I would very much like to attend my CPA meetings from start to finish . . . I am only allowed in for ten to fifteen minutes at the end of what is often a one or two hour meeting. Feel there should be an option to attend . . . After all it's your life and you should be able to be part of it.
> If they talked to you first before it was all done, explained what it is, discussed it. I would like my views taken into account.

Advocacy can play an important part in the lives of service users by facilitating communication with mental health professionals. Mental health services should encourage and support high quality independent advocacy. From a user perspective, this means a service that promotes self-advocacy and focuses on the views and needs of service users as expressed by service users, so that we can put across our perspectives even if this is difficult for the services or the advocate. This does not mean confrontation. It means putting across views, discussing them, having the views taken on board, accommodated, and responded to. It is about getting explanations and negotiating. If the relationship breaks down, which it does if there are completely opposing views, then keep trying. Doors should be kept open.

A rights-based approach

Risk management should always be provided within a rights-based framework (see also Chapter 12). At present, many mental health service users are either having their rights removed inappropriately or their rights are not being adequately promoted. All individuals should be seen as having full human rights. When rights are removed in accordance with the law, this should be undertaken in a systematic and transparent manner. That is, the following should be made explicit for and to each individual: what rights are being taken away, why, to what degree, and when and how this situation is to be reviewed. There should not be automatic generalizations simply because someone is detained or being cared for in a particular type of facility.

> Human Rights issues to be taken into account to a much greater degree in all mental health systems and processes. Human Rights specialists to be involved in key processes to ensure this.

Communication

Service users repeatedly raise communication, or rather the lack of it, as a key issue and, indeed, most professionals would see it as fundamental to good quality mental health care and a routine part of professional practice. However, the clear message from service users is that communication, particularly around risk issues, is inadequate and could be vastly improved. This discrepancy could be explained in part by the perceived conflict that might arise if service users ask for something that cannot be provided, perhaps due to ongoing risk issues or lack of resources. However, this should not mean the issue is ignored. If reasons are given, service users can understand these. It is much more difficult to understand actions or omissions that are not explained or addressed. Discomfort around talking about risk issues, especially if you have to tell someone that they are viewed as an ongoing risk, could also hinder effective communication with service users. However, it is a matter of fundamental respect that information and explanation should be provided to service users clearly, accurately, and honestly.

> Communicate – involve person in proactive objective risk assessment and management.
> Communication and trust is highly important and should never be underestimated by key staff in care planning for the patient. There is far too much emphasis on academic qualifications and professionalism rather than experienced staff in psychiatric care.
> Must not leave person unaware for any length of time.
> If I had been given information about perceptions of risk, then this would have helped me to make good decisions.

Information and explanation

Linked with good communication, is the provision of clear, unambiguous information about the risk management process, rights, and how the process can be used as a way of progressing. Advocacy services also have a role to play and service users should be involved in identifying information needs. The provision of information is often indiscriminate and piecemeal. Leaflet racks are often sparse and irregularly refilled. Information should be ongoing and accessible, tailored to the needs of individuals. Access to the Internet and the provision of advice surgeries should be established:

> Patients to get monthly document on risk assessment and need for detention. Document to be highly rational and convincing and free of institutionalised thinking. Patients to be able to challenge content with the help of advocates and solicitors and specialists in the production of fair and reasonable assessments.
> I feel strongly about the need for pictures on the risk management forms.

Accurate, consistent, and up-to-date information is vital to upholding rights and the provision of appropriate and progressive care. Service users should expect to be able to freely access their notes, have copies if desired, and to be actively involved in writing and/or verifying notes, assessments, and plans. Notes should be viewed as *belonging* to service users rather than as a potentially malevolent force that can have a major, although surreptitious, impact on your life. Professionals should be able to account for the things they write in patients' notes with clear evidence and reasoned arguments:

> Ensure clear comprehensive and accurate multi-disciplinary risk assessment is carried out, enabling robust risk management. Defining appropriate action to be taken. Transparency of process. Translate identifiable known risk assessment into management plans. . . . Clinical

decision-making and judgements must be safe, sound, and good practice. Not the exclusive domain of staff with the exclusion of the person.

There should be rules that all patients on admission, should have a conference on the ward with all the staff responsible for his/her care. His/her rights as a patient should be fully explained. He/she should be introduced to his/her named nurse. I did not know my named nurse for 3 months.

Focus on the individual

People working in mental health services need to guard against labelling and making judgements about service users based on potentially arbitrary factors such as diagnosis, ethnicity, gender, or the type of facility in which a person is being cared for. On the latter, the type or location of units a person is admitted to can depend on many factors, such as bed availability and regional variations in services which say nothing about the person.

There is a clear need for risk management to be personalized to individuals. While standardized risk assessment tools may help to provide consistency, the planning must be interlinked with individual needs and aspirations:

Risk management should be personalised to the individual patient as far as possible and their views and impact taken into account. Risk management should be therapeutic rather than controlling.

For *every* patient/service user, of course, the professionals have to err on the side of caution but pragmatism and a case-by-case approach is surely still the best way forward.

Ensuring that service users are aware of their risk factors; informing service users that these factors are not fixed, and can be reduced with treatment and therapy; devoting quality and regular time to addressing the questions of risk, preferably via 1:1 sessions between service user and professional.

A Future: Light at the End of the Tunnel

Risk management should be enabling rather than simply controlling. It should be aimed at enhancing care and supporting a way of moving forward. Just like anyone else, service users need to be able to grow and to have aspirations. This is also true, maybe more so, for people who spend lengthy periods in secure units. While there has to be realism and honesty, this should not be overshadowed by defensive care planning or institutional indifference:

On many occasions I have demanded information about next step milestones sometimes resulting in me getting the information that I want and sometimes revealing thinking about risk. But there is no collective will to assess patients accurately or generously and there is no collective will to move patients on as quickly as possible.

I think the risk management in care planning should be ongoing. Just because something has been refused once or thought to be inappropriate at one time, does not mean that it should remain so.

It seems that once you start to take an interest in your future yourself then movement starts. But a lot of patients can't do this and are held back.

A therapeutic milieu with a hopeful and open philosophy, that works in partnership with service users, focusing on aspirations and goals, has to be the most appropriate environment for supporting people with mental health problems.

Carrot and stick

Monitoring and audit of the risk management should take place, both by the provider and by an independent organization. This can support and assure good practice, a positive service user experience and ensure a rights-based approach.

> Tighter reins need to be in place on staff, patients, doctors and management especially management as they are the responsible body.

User-focused monitoring, preferably undertaken by service users, would improve quality from a service user perspective. Having regular feedback mechanisms (these can be anonymous) play a part in a responsive and inclusive culture.

Having high level guidance on risk management is the first step towards addressing some of the serious issues. There are also other factors that stem from this and that are equally as important. These include a shared value base, implementation, and a systematic, independent oversight at organizational and national levels.

Staff should be properly trained in a way that ensures good practice and a rights-based approach. The definition of 'good practice' should focus on the experiences and outcomes that are important to, and defined by, service users. Asking service users to participate in or lead staff training and supervision can further embed a more empowering, positive culture for staff as well as service users.

A user-led example

I came across a gem of a user-led initiative within forensic services in the north of England called 'My Future Plan'. The forensic services in the Trust set up an involvement strategy group that came up with and shared out various projects. 'My Future Plan' was one of the ideas and is based on the concept of an advance directive that has been developed in a user-friendly and straightforward way.

'My Future Plan' consists of a form and an advice document (these can be obtained by contacting Rosie.Ayub@BarnsleyPCT.nhs.uk or alternatively, Joanna.Wright@ BarnsleyPCT.nhs.uk) and was written by Robin A. Crowe, a patient in the services, together with the head occupational therapist there. The beauty of the initiative is that it has both common sense and simplicity, covering issues that may seem small but are highly important to individuals when they are detained in hospital, particularly for lengthy periods. Service users can identify what is important to them, what they need, how they would like to be treated, and what is helpful and unhelpful, particularly on admission to hospital and at times of significant distress. Robin realized that many incidents could have been prevented if the 'low level' needs of service users had been met. The 'low level' needs are simply things that are part of everyday life, but which due to ward routine often get overlooked as there are seemingly more important issues for staff to deal with.

Thus, 'My Future Plan' is completed by/with the service user and filed in an accessible place in patients' notes with the risk assessment.

There are five parts to the 'My Future Plan' form: Part 1 contains personal information; Part 2, 'Care and Treatment' provides service users with the opportunity to record wishes about treatment, such as what they want and don't want, what has and hasn't worked before (including in a crisis), and the name of an advocate; Part 3 is a 'Personal and Social Statement' in which service users can specify who they want informed about their situation and any arrangements that need to be made, for example, in relation to dependants, pets, and finances; Part 4 is an 'Open Statement' so service users can record any other important information or wishes; and Part 5 is a declaration for the service user to sign with two witnesses. The form and advice document were developed with legal advice and the parameters and limitations are clearly spelled out, for example, if a service user's wish cannot be adhered to. Robin commented:

> It is the only written record of patients' wishes. It makes it easier for staff to supply patients with 'low level' needs, e.g., favourite drinks or correct brand of cigarettes, leading to a more settled ward environment. Patients also have the opportunity to comment on medication.
>
> My Future Plan is far better than any of the usual forms patients are given to fill in because it addresses issues that are important to patients on a day-to-day basis. With these 'low level' needs met, patients should get better faster.

To ensure the continued use and development of 'My Future Plan', it has been included as part of the commissioning process and is being monitored through Key Performance Indicators in contracts. Additionally, an involvement for improvement (i4i) Network has been established to support and share learning. Such an example is encouraging, not least because of the realization that the best person to write such a document is a service user with direct experience.

Call for Change: A Manifesto

The suggestions made by SURP members are simple and obvious: the importance of and the need for information, communication, and personalization. Similarly, the rationale behind 'My Future Plan' is straightforward and based on common sense. It seems that somehow services lose sight of the obvious. Alternatively, they have not really considered *what it is like* to be held in hospital or under mental health legislation and the implications this can have for people's lives. So immersed are they in their roles as professionals, that they forget, or maybe never really understand, what service users are experiencing. While your primary nurse may pass on a decision made in the ward round, she or he does not explain how the decision was arrived at, what it means, what will happen.

The issues and comments on risk management by service users speak for themselves. While there is some good practice developing this is still very limited both in relation to the experience of service users as well the extent to which the good practice is progressing, that is, there is very little of it! With regard to the service user/patient experience of risk management, we are still at the stage of asking people to describe their experiences. These experiences are predominantly about coercion and restriction, on the one hand, and an absence of guidance and support where people have felt unsafe or at risk, on the other hand. The next stage is to listen to these experiences and to act on them: to work in partnership with service users to improve practice.

To bring together the many issues that this chapter has raised and as a call to arms, I have produced a manifesto that outlines ten key areas that require addressing to make risk and its management a positive and helpful experience for people receiving mental health services (see Box 2.2).

I look forward to a time when the prevalent culture in mental health services, both in and out of hospital settings, is one that views people with severe mental health problems with equality and respect: the biggest risk still facing many mental health service users and patients is in not being seen as human beings with opinions, rights, and aspirations.

Box 2.2: Call for change: A manifesto

Making risk management a positive and helpful experience for people who receive mental health services:

1 *Respect us.* Don't ever forget we are people with needs and feelings – not risks to be managed. Do not confuse needs with risks. Risk management should not be used to impose arbitrary restrictions or unjustifiable interventions on our lives. Do not put us in unreasonable, demanding, and damaging – 'toxic' – situations. We need a supportive, safe, and non-judgemental environment to progress and recover.
2 *Put our experiences at the centre of risk management.* Try to imagine how you would feel in a similar situation. Make sure that the risks that we see are taken into account even if you feel that those risks are due to mental illness. If we are scared or confused, we need reassurance and support, and to know that there is someone we can trust. If we are involved in a serious incident, talk to us about it to find out why it happened, how we feel about it, and how to stop the same thing happening again.
3 *Involve us.* We should be involved as soon as possible in our own risk assessment and management. Ensure involvement is ongoing. Do not give up on us. We should be able to influence – preferably write or co-produce – our own risk plans. Listen to what we are saying. Make sure our views and experiences are written down as part of the assessment, management, and reviews. Ask us if we would like any family members or friends involved in our risk management. Discuss the boundaries of this with us and write it down.
4 *Base your approach on promoting and protecting our rights.* We should have our rights explained, including our human rights. Risk management should not compromise our rights to dignity, privacy, and respect. The parameters of any restrictions should be made clear to us and regularly reviewed: we should understand the situation and our rights. We should know how to access good independent advice. Advocacy should be readily available.

(continued)

5 *Explain.* Explain what risk assessment is to us, explain how it works, and why it is being undertaken. The risk assessment should be clear and understandable. Show us or tell us what our risk assessment and management plan contain. Offer us a copy of it or make sure we know we can see it if we wish to. Ensure that staff and clinicians assume accountability for their assessments and actions.

6 *See us as individuals, and not defined by a particular diagnosis or situation.* Being detained under the Mental Health Act or the type of unit a person is in, should not define our risk management per se. A personalized approach should prevail, not a 'one size fits all' one. Blanket policies should be avoided or kept to a bare minimum. Work with us to find the most appropriate care and support that is best suited to our needs and preferences. See us as the drivers in our own care.

7 *We need hope and aspirations.* We should know what is required to reduce or manage risks, and how we can progress. We need a longer-term perspective to give us a sense of how things will or could progress. Risk assessments and management should be linked with care planning and the goals, outcomes, or aspirations we have in our lives.

8 *Risk assessments should be accurate, based on facts and kept up-to-date.* Don't assume that entries in our notes are true or factual. It is very unlikely that there are no errors of fact or judgement in our notes. Be prepared to keep an open mind. We should know what the 'evidence' is to support the risk assessment and management plan. We should have the opportunity to ask for information that substantiates risk assessments and the right to put forward a different version.

9 *There should be user-focused processes to support risk management.* This should include documentation, staff training, and audit. Staff should be trained in risk assessment and risk management; they should understand their responsibilities, accountabilities, and limitations. Service users should be actively involved in this training, the audit process, and in developing paperwork.

10 *There should be independent monitoring of risk management.* This should focus on service user experiences and views, with a strong emphasis on rights and outcomes associated with recovery. This can be commissioned by providers as well as being integral to the regulation of mental health services. It should be either user-led or undertaken in equal partnership with service users/service user groups.

Acknowledgements

The Care Quality Commission's Service User Reference Panel and Robin A. Crowe and the Clifton House 'My Future Plan' project group, Yorkshire and Humberside Regional Involvement Strategy Group.

References

Mental Health Act Commission (2007–2009). *Coercion and Consent – Monitoring the Mental Health Act*. Thirteenth Biennial Report.

Risk, *Open Mind* (July/August 2007), No. 146.

Yorkshire & Humberside Regional Forensic Involvement Strategy Group (2008). *Reaching Joint Solutions: (i) My Future Plan Advice Document, (ii) My Future Plan Form*, September.

3

Carers: Experiences of Risk and Risk Management

Sally Luxton

The assessment and management of risk in mental health can cause much stress to all parties involved. As the carer of my son, who has suffered from schizophrenia for 12 years, we have had varied experiences with mental health services. In this chapter, I hope to describe some of these experiences in order to show how a consistent approach by all parties involved in risk assessment and management can lead to better communication at all levels. In particular, I hope to show that collaborative working, with better communication among practitioners, service users, and their carers and families, can lead to increased confidence and trust, which can help to enhance the outcome of efforts towards risk management. Collaborative working really does enable and encourage service users to claim back their lives along their recovery road.

Therefore, in this chapter, I will look at how an understanding of the carer's viewpoint can help to make carers a valuable asset. I will also explore how making the most of the strengths of a service user can help enable better engagement with families, and how a valuable tool such as family work can enhance understanding in all parties. I shall look at two very important aspects of working in mental health. The first is confidentiality. Confidentiality is often seen as a barrier to collaborative working with families, and can lead to diminishing trust between parties and unnecessary misunderstandings. The second important aspect of working in mental health is stigma. Stigma can also be a barrier to engagement with families and individual service users, affecting their attitude to their illness and inhibiting their recovery. This is unfortunate, because it is the personal connection with the service user, their carer, and family – the effort of listening and caring about their point of view – that can make all the difference to the experience of those at the receiving end of mental health services. Stigma – around service providers and service users and their carers – needs to be taken into account and challenged.

Risk-taking is a part of all our lives in our everyday actions. Many of the risks we take are positive risks, which enable us to grow and progress in our lives. We take risks in small tasks such as catching a train, crossing the road, walking in the hills, or even

Self-Harm and Violence: Towards Best Practice in Managing Risk in Mental Health Services, First Edition.
Edited by Richard Whittington and Caroline Logan.
© 2011 John Wiley & Sons, Ltd. Published 2011 by John Wiley & Sons, Ltd.

cooking in our kitchen. These activities, as is the case with everything we do, have the potential to go wrong. The train may break down and make us late, you may fall over on a walk, you may be hit by a car as you cross the road, or the cooker catch fire in the kitchen. However, we mostly don't think about the risks we take as we go about our daily lives – because we manage them by taking precautions, such as setting off in good time for our meetings or taking a mobile phone when we go hill-walking. If we thought too much about the risks inherent in every little action, we may not do much at all.

In mental health, risk management requires a lot more thought and planning in order to balance safety with progress. This is because if things went wrong – if there were negative or harmful outcomes for the service user resulting from the action they took – this could set back their recovery as well as affect other people. Incorporating positive risk-taking into patient care is an important step towards recovery (see also Chapter 11). But the risks must be realistic and relevant to the stage the service user is at in his or her recovery pathway. They may sometimes involve the smallest thing that may feel a real accomplishment, which can enhance wellbeing and sense of achievement. After the first year or so of my son's illness, I felt quite low and felt that no real progress had been achieved. I was helped by a member of staff to look back over that time and see that, in fact, very small things had happened that were indeed helping him. Therefore, in this chapter, I would also like to give an example of positive risk taken early on in my son's illness.

Our Story

At the time of the onset of my son's illness, I was sharing the house with him. My two older daughters had left for university, travelling, and jobs. My husband had left us just as my son turned 16 years of age, which had had a very bad effect on him. He bottled his feelings up inside himself which, as his mother and main carer, made these roles all the harder for me to undertake.

My son took his GCSEs and obtained five passes. He chose not to stay on at school for his A levels, but went on to college to do an engineering course. The first indication that something was wrong came when his tutor told me that he was not handing in his homework. I talked to my son about this, but did not make too much of it as many teenagers do not hand in course work on time. But the problem continued and, towards the end of his first year, he dropped out of the college. He managed to get some part-time work locally, but he was not able to sustain that for long. It was now apparent that things were not right with him. However, until he asked for help and admitted something was wrong, it was very difficult for me to offer help to a teenager. 'Is everything OK?' and other tentative enquiries were met with 'Yes, fine, don't fuss Mum.' Finally, one morning he told me that he thought there was a problem and that he needed some help. I felt such relief and our general practitioner (GP) was the first port of call.

The GP saw my son a couple of times and depression was diagnosed. My son was put on an antidepressant, which he took for a short while. Soon, however, he told me he couldn't go on taking this medication as 'it was doing terrible things' to his head. I felt despairing as I realized the wrong diagnosis had been given and his initial treatment appeared to be exacerbating things. Therefore, we went back to the doctor.

At this time, GPs had a limited knowledge of mental illness; not a great deal of time in their training was given to mental health. Now much has improved in GP surgeries and health centres and there is more communication and working between primary and secondary services. Early intervention teams have been established to work with primary care with people showing signs of early onset of mental illness. By enabling patients to have access to the right treatment as early as possible, their outcome in their recovery will be that much better.

My GP had made a referral to secondary mental health services for my son, which took a while to come through. All the time, my son was becoming more unwell and psychotic. One day, he filled empty wine bottles with petrol in order to set our house on fire. Fortunately, my eldest daughter was staying with us at the time. In his psychotic state, he became angry if I tried to talk with him but he allowed his sister to speak to him and, between us, we managed to drive him to the hospital where he was finally admitted into the mental health system. From the point that his college tutor told me of his difficulties with course work to his admission into hospital was around 16 months.

We were fortunate in having a small local hospital with mental health beds near to us. This meant that my son was admitted into a place that was familiar to both of us; my son had grown up in the area and I had worked for a short time in the hospital, and we knew some of the staff. This greatly lessened the trauma and stress, which can be so much a part of someone's experience of admission into mental health care. However, in addition to the stress I was feeling, I was also feeling relief. I knew my son was very unwell and I was extremely anxious that he should receive help. I had guessed that cannabis may have been a part of my son's life before he became unwell and, on admission, it became clear that he had been using cannabis and speed, as well as alcohol. What I hadn't known, however, was that he had also been abusing solvents, deodorant and lighter fuel, in the weeks before his admission to hospital. Twelve years ago, when all this happened, not as much was known about solvent abuse and it came as a great shock to me to hear this about my son. I felt huge guilt that I hadn't realized this was happening and that it was my fault, but I had no idea these substances could be abused. My two daughters, as worldly young people, said even *they* wouldn't have known. I saw deodorant in his room, but actually felt pleased my teenage son was looking after himself. I thought nothing of the lighter fuel I also saw in his room, as he had always used refillable lighters since he began smoking. I look at these simple things differently now.

Therefore, as his illness became clearer and he felt better understood, I was increasingly able to let the professionals take over with my son. The ward staff were friendly and helpful, including those whom we had known from before his admission. A collaborative three-way partnership was a little known phrase at this time, but this is what we developed. In those first few weeks after my son entered hospital, we worked together: the professionals, my son, and I. My son was happy to sign the hospital's confidentiality form, and happy too for me to speak to the staff about him. I was fortunate. However, even if I hadn't been, such reservations on the part of the patient should not make a difference to the first admission, when a friendly face, smile, a cup of tea, and a listening ear go a very long way to calming the apprehension and fear of families entering secondary mental health services.

Towards the end of what became a 10-month stay in hospital, my son was allowed home for overnight stays. These went well, but I was beginning to feel I needed a break. I hadn't had any kind of a break for nearly a year and decided I would like to go away for a weekend, to be away on my own for just one night on a weekend. My son was still very keen to be allowed to come home that weekend, despite the fact he would be on his own. As we had all been working together – the staff, my son, and I – this enabled us to sit down together to discuss the pros and cons of letting him be at home alone for one night. Eventually, it was agreed that he would be allowed to do so. As this happened 12 years ago, I don't know if any formal risk assessment was done. However, to ensure my son was safe some safeguards were put in place. One of the staff would go to our house to have supper with him and make sure he took his medication. A little later on in the evening, one of my daughter's friends, who had a key to the house, was to call round to make sure all was well and he was on his way to bed. Both of these supportive measures took place.

However, when I arrived back in town at the end of my little break, as I stepped off the train I was met at the station on the platform by not one but two friends and I knew immediately that something must have happened. My son had taken an overdose. Fortunately, he had not harmed himself, but he had been transferred to a bigger hospital for tests and observation. He returned to our local hospital that night none the worse for wear really, but having triggered a lot of anxiety and shock among those who looked after him – including myself.

Because the decision to allow my son home on his own had been taken collaboratively, there were no recriminations towards anybody by anybody. Except by me; as his mother, I felt more guilt for allowing myself to go away. I did, however, have a lot of support after this event. It was very helpful to be able to talk to staff about the decision we had made with my son. We felt that if we had gone against his wish to go home and not allowed him to do so, he may have harmed himself more seriously or run away from the hospital. He was apologetic towards me and philosophical when I asked how he felt on waking up the next morning after swallowing the pills. He shrugged his shoulders and said he had thought he had better phone the ward to tell them what he had done. He had bought the headache pills in the afternoon and offered no explanation as to why he had bought them. My feeling was that what he did was planned and it was in his mind that this is what he would do when alone. I wondered if command voices made him do it. Alternatively, I wondered if his improving mental health and insight made him realize what might be ahead of him – breakdown after breakdown for the rest of his life. Or maybe he simply didn't know why he took the overdose. To my knowledge, my son has not attempted suicide since.

After 10 months in the hospital, my son moved into 24-hour supported housing. At this time, we both wanted a diagnosis to know what it was we were coping with. It was quite difficult to get to see the psychiatrist but, when I did see him, I asked him for a diagnosis of my son's condition. Because I have two cousins with schizophrenia, I realized that there may be a genetic link in the family, but I wanted confirmation. My son also wanted to know what was causing his illness. He had been tried on various medications, which had produced unpleasant side-effects, and it was difficult to find one that agreed with him. When I saw the psychiatrist, shortly before my son was discharged, he told us he believed the illness was indeed schizophrenia. But he explained he wanted to observe my son for some time in case it was drug-induced psychosis rather than schizophrenia. I wanted to know more about what he thought was the cause. The consultant felt that emotional stress and drugs were triggers for the illness, and the fact we seemed to have a genetic factor in the family for schizophrenia would have made him more susceptible to developing the condition. This was hard news to take and accept, but it was what we all needed to hear.

When my son took the overdose it was a difficult time in all our lives, but we all got through it, and we got through it by managing to work together. Twelve years ago, working together in a meaningful three-way partnership was not the norm. Because it made such a difference to us – to me – I am going to look at collaborative working in the next section.

Collaborative Working

Working in a successful three-way partnership can sometimes feel to clinical staff working at the front line like a mirage that never quite materializes rather than a real possibility. It is a different way of working from the usual one-to-one between staff and patient, and requires quite a shift in thinking for practitioners. In my case, I was able to work in partnership from my son's first admission to hospital as the staff were immediately friendly and sympathetic, making it possible for me to feel I could entrust them with my son's wellbeing. As I said earlier, at the point of a family's first contact with secondary mental health services – at hospital or in the community – it is a smile, a cup of tea, and empathy that is the first important step towards three-way partnership working. Working in this way with service users and their carers can positively change risk. Having formed a relationship wherein we know we are working together, the confidence and support are there to enable all parties to proceed with making positive risk decisions. Things don't always work out and sometimes will go wrong by the very nature of mental illness. When this happens – as in my example above – if you have already begun to work collaboratively and have a relationship with the service user and carer, and have already gained their trust, then that base will always be there as a cushion to support and nurture communication between all parties. Staff shortages and heavy workloads can conspire against the development of a three-way partnership, but ways should be found to manage working collaboratively.

When carers have trust and confidence in the people looking after their loved one, they are able to step back to enable the staff to do their work and the service user to progress. If the staff and support are deemed by the carer not to be there for the service user, then they become more involved and more hands on. It has been suggested to me a couple of times that I should step back a little, but if I do not feel happy about where my son is at that moment, it is difficult for me, like most caring families, not to become involved. I still sometimes do an occasional load of washing for my son and have stopped feeling guilty about this – I am his mum and it's what we do.

Families and carers, as well as service users, can feel vulnerable in society when mental illness affects one of their relatives or friends. Though wanting support, carers may present to clinical staff in different guises, which may cause staff to feel defensive; they may present as aggressive or timid, withdrawn or challenging, or in myriad other ways. It is important to remember that if a family has no experience of mental health services and this is the first admission into hospital then, underneath, however they are presenting, they will be feeling *frightened and scared*. They will be frightened about what may happen to their loved one. They will be wondering many things, such as what a mental hospital is like – is it all padded cells? And they will be worrying about whether they will be able to talk to someone about their loved one's likes and dislikes. This may be particularly the case when it is the partner of an older adult; they may have lived together for a very long time. The families know their loved one better than anyone else and have a wealth of information about them.

I have had the opportunity in Avon and Wiltshire Mental Health Partnership NHS Trust to channel my experiences as a carer into training staff, working as an associate trainer together with service users and Trust trainers. During one particular training day for staff, I remember talking to a clinician about working with carers and he said when families and carers approached him, he felt a wave of defensiveness rushing over him. He couldn't easily explain it to me and he was trying to understand these feelings while we spoke. After a little while, he decided that his defensiveness arose from the fear that the family or carer might be critical of him or his colleagues and that they might tell staff how to do their job. All parties, not just the service user and carer, feel anxiety and fear. Acknowledging the possibility of its existence and talking about it can help disperse this fear and reduce its potential to be a barrier to collaborative working.

A further example shows how working collaboratively can help to prevent a negative outcome. This incident occurred at the first admission of my son into hospital. He was beginning to be allowed out on day leave as he made progress. A doctor working with my son realized that one of the voices he heard was mine. Sometimes my son heard my voice speaking to him in a negative and derogatory way. The doctor decided this was something I should know, especially as I would take my son out on the days he was allowed leave. My son had no problem with the staff and me talking together about him. So, when we spoke, the doctor told me what she suspected. I was very upset to think that this was happening and that he should be hearing me say negative things to him. Later, while I was driving him home, he turned his head sharply several times to look at me, staring at me and frowning. Mindful of what the doctor had told me, I realized what was happening and made sure my lips were firmly shut and that I looked straight ahead so he could see it wasn't really me talking to him. We got home safely and a little later on that day, I talked to him about this voice. I was so upset I felt I had to say something. I said if he ever did think he heard my voice saying horrid things, he should know this wasn't really me as I would never speak like that to him. He didn't say anything, but he did listen to me, and gradually, over time, the problem appeared to lessen and there were no further incidents. If I hadn't known the facts and my son kept looking at me sharply while we were driving, I might have asked him 'Why are you looking at me like that?' or 'What's the matter?' He might then have believed that what he was hearing in his head was really coming from me and the situation could have escalated dangerously. But because the doctor had seen the risk potential in the situation and wanted to prevent a potentially unpleasant incident, she told me what she knew and I felt very relieved that she did so. It was a small but very important detail the doctor had picked up on, and even if my son had not given permission for staff to speak to me the doctor could have broken confidentiality because she deemed I might have been at risk. This collaboration from the doctor further endorsed my feelings of trust and confidence towards staff. By trying to keep an overview in mind of the service user and his or her carer, as well as the clinical staff, collaborative working can become a reality.

Finally, the sensitive and careful use of well-chosen words can go a long way to helping collaborative working. An ambiguous – a poorly explained or ill-chosen – word or phrase used to describe a particular risk can be interpreted by different people in different and potentially disastrous ways. Clinical staff doing a risk assessment may individually have a different understanding of the risk situation and describe issues in varying ways and in varying levels of detail. This can lead to confusion and creates risks over and above those already there. Therefore, it is important if not essential for clinical staff to discuss with work colleagues how they interpret different situations, how they are understood, and what needs to be done and why in order to demonstrate transparency in care-giving and clarity for those who come after. Collaborative working *among* clinicians is as important to the process of a three-way partnership as collaborative working *between* clinicians and service users and carers.

The *Ten Essential Shared Capabilities* (Department of Health, 2004) is a very useful document to which to refer for more guidance on and endorsement of collaborative working. Number nine of the ten capabilities is 'promoting safety and positive risk-taking' and it endorses 'empowering the service user' and 'working with the tension that arises between promoting safety and positive risk-taking . . .'. I mentioned this in the introduction and firmly believe that these tensions can be resolved by working collaboratively and in partnership in the ways illustrated above. In the next section, I am going to develop this theme by looking at things that may help clinicians to help carers to see things from their perspective.

Carer Perspective: What Helps?

The service user and carer may have different interpretations of words or phrases describing risk, and the possibility of this should always be taken into account by clinicians in their discussions or meetings, however informal. In addition, some of the language used in the mental health workplace – jargon – may not make much sense to carers. *Exercise care in the words you choose as a practitioner to communicate with your clients and their carers and families.*

A carer who is fairly timid and who doesn't often speak to staff may come forward to say she or he is feeling anxious about her or his family member. They may be a person who does not like making a fuss, so when they *do* say something they really mean it and should be listened to. Another carer who is always talking to staff and in regular contact who says the same thing may not give such a strong meaning to the words or phrase but should also be listened to. You may have a better relationship with a carer who does communicate a lot with you and may be able to put his or her worries into better context than with someone who is only in intermittent contact, but both should be listened to with equal importance. *Either way, be flexible in your approach to carers. Think about where they are coming from and respond sensitively to the needs they express and/or demonstrate.*

It is also worth bearing in mind that staff who have worked a long time in mental health settings may become slightly inured to the risks inherent in their client group, because they work with these risks every day and have perhaps become complacent. All the more reason for staff to listen to the service user and carer and for team discussion. Indeed, when there is a tragic murder or homicide, it is often found that the mother or a family member had been asking for help for some time prior to the incident and had not been listened to. *Therefore, avoid complacency and listen – and talk to your colleagues about your concerns.*

Carers often experience high levels of stress when living with the service user for a long period. They may not acknowledge or even know their own needs or recognize the feelings of guilt and grief they may be experiencing for what they are. Instead, they are anxious that the service user should receive the help they need and all their energies will go into this with small regard for themselves. What helps then?

Carers need to know they are not alone in what can often seem like an uphill struggle. Some research has been done into the different stages a carer may go through when a family member becomes mentally ill (Mohr, Lafuze and Mohr, 2000). Mohr and colleagues found that carers move through three stages that require different interventions at each stage.

The first stage is dealing with the catastrophic event, the realization that a member of the family is suffering from mental illness and needs to be in hospital. Shock and chaos come into their lives and they may be in denial as a way of coping. *Comfort and support will be needed at this stage – and small amounts of information.* When my son was admitted on to a mental health ward, it caused shock and chaos in the life of my family. As well as myself, his two sisters found it very hard to come to terms with what was happening to him. Siblings in the family are not always considered. Rethink now has a space on their website for siblings. I was greatly helped by being in a familiar local hospital and by the staff being friendly and acknowledging me as the mother and main carer. I felt included in the ongoing care and in the support being given to my son. On first admission, it is just basic information that's needed – practical things such as visiting times and who you can contact when you need more information. A carer's pack can be given, but may not be properly read for a while. Even though I knew a bit about mental illness, I shut my mind for some time to the fact he might have a serious, enduring mental disorder and what the future might hold for my son. In addition to information and signposts into future mental health care, *carers need to see a friendly face with a smile.* Even if the ward is short-staffed and everyone rushed off his or her feet, this is something that *can* be provided. A friendly greeting and recognition that they are someone involved with the patient who is being admitted can create a feeling of working together, which is the first small step towards working collaboratively with this service user and their family. Being inclusive of families engenders respect on both sides.

The second stage in caring described by Mohr and colleagues is *coming to terms with what is happening and dealing with feelings of guilt, anger, or resentment.* Historically, it was the mother who was at fault when mental illness appeared in the family and sometimes there is a feeling of this still. The family begins to look at what has happened to them and why. It may affect different family members in different ways. Siblings should be considered and may need special support for their needs, especially if still at school.

Two things particularly helped me at this stage. It was quite difficult to get to talk with the psychiatrist who was working with my son. They were not terribly accessible 12 years ago and I am pleased to say – on the whole – they are more integrated now and more inclined to work collaboratively. When I did get to see the psychiatrist, he recognized the stress I was feeling from seeing my son so ill and he wondered if I would like to *talk to someone.* I most definitely *did* and so was offered a clinical psychologist who saw me regularly for some years. At the time, she was a huge support and it was most timely and played a great part in helping me come to terms with what was happening in our family. This intervention was helpful in working through the stress, anxiety, and unhappiness that I felt. Don't forget, *a high number of carers will suffer from mental illness.* Carers who have a family member becoming unwell or who are already diagnosed with a serious mental illness may experience extreme anxiety, stress, or depression. Often they may not acknowledge or disclose how they are feeling because of feelings of guilt and grief. Initially, they may be most anxious for the family member to receive help so will not want to detract from that by mentioning their own distress. However, it is important that their feelings of grief are acknowledged, because it can feel like bereavement when a relative or friend is lost to serious mental illness and they can no longer have the life they planned.

The second helpful thing I did was attend a Rethink meeting. In those days, Rethink was called the National Schizophrenia Society. I felt quite emotional as I entered that first meeting, because I suddenly realized that I could talk to anyone in the room about what was happening to my son and they would understand. I have remained a member of Rethink ever since this time. They are an invaluable source of information for carers and service users and run a national network of support groups. Indeed, I now belong to a local Rethink group, which is lively and active and continues to be a support.

The third stage in caring described by Mohr and colleagues is when *more understanding and acceptance of mental illness finally comes*. When that happens, when the illness and its fluctuations become routine, some balance is restored to families. They may take stock of their situation and make plans for a different life. The carer may want to get more actively involved by, for example, helping out at meetings like Rethink or even doing some advocacy work with service users and carers, or working in some other way in the mental health system. About four or five years after my son became unwell, I was asked if I would be interested in helping to train staff in my local mental health trust. I agreed and have been doing this ever since. I have found this work very rewarding, and I seem to have something worthwhile to say because after some time working on staff training, I was asked to do some teaching to students on a three-year mental health graduate course. This is progress. When these students go out into the workplace, they will know it is important – necessary – to work with families and carers, which means that doing so will be their expectation of the services in which they work. My local mental health trust has always been innovative in using service users and carers in training, and I now also present, as well as training on Working in Partnership with Families and Carers, the two-day Risk and Care Programme Approach (CPA) training. Indeed, service users and carers, together with the organization, put the programme for both sets of training together. The feedback is very positive from clinicians – they find it so beneficial to their work to have 'real live' (as one attendee put it) service users and carers to talk to and this makes the training very worthwhile. *Therefore, because carers have immense experience from working through the illness with their relative and are able to say what help is most valuable and at what stage, use them.*

However, I feel there is another stage of caring that is just as important to consider. That is the time before the carer and the family member first present to mental health services. This time can vary in length. In the case of older adults, it might be a very long time before they admit something is wrong. In my case, it was around 16 months from when my son first showed signs that things may not be quite right, when he was at college, to when he was finally admitted to hospital and obtained the help he very much needed. *During this time, though they may not realize it, carers are acquiring coping skills and amassing experience, which may be useful in their relative's future care plans and so should not be overlooked.*

These stages are not set in stone and carers may move backwards and forwards through them depending on their situation and that of their relative. I know I have found myself doing this. Some carers reading the stages of caring described above may recognize in themselves the experiences described. In others, it may validate what they have been through and give reassurance and confidence that they – you – are not alone.

I am now going on to describe further top tips for carers. *Get involved* in clinical meetings, risk management planning, and in the CPA reviews because this is where collaborative working really happens. Carers are a valuable asset and an essential resource for the whole process of care planning. They have a wealth of information about the service user, and sharing information promotes collaborative working. It should be remembered that, often in a meeting, it may be difficult for carers to say things about their situation in front of their relative, and, similarly, the service user may not want to say some things in front of his or her family. Bearing this in mind, a debrief should always be carried out for the service user and carer to make sure they have understood what was said and what will be happening and, if needed, follow-up meetings arranged. If necessary, a separate worker could be assigned to the family. Because of the stress and mental health problems families may themselves suffer from, being included in these ways can help to improve their own wellbeing by enhancing their involvement and understanding.

I have been asked how I cope when tensions arise between the staff looking after my son and myself, or when there is something in particular I would like to see them offering my son that they are not already doing. The first thing I would say is to *keep the lines of communication open*, regardless of the disagreements between you. I remain positive and try to *pre-empt any tensions* that may arise and make sure I am always able to talk with the people looking after my son. When my son has moved onto another supported house, which has often been in a new area of our NHS trust, we usually start from the beginning with new staff. When this happens, I make a point of introducing myself rather than waiting to be included, and I ask for an appointment with the new psychiatrist and key worker. On the whole, I am pleased to say that clinical teams are now much more open to working with families. My son is always happy about my being so involved and, in fact, we always have a discussion together on *our* impressions of the new staff!

If the service user is not happy about his or her family speaking to staff, *it is still all right to see staff to introduce yourself*. It is all right for staff to listen and signpost you to support in your new area, and the service user needs to understand that you, as his or her carer, may need support and information. On rare occasions when there has been a difference of thinking, I will ask for an appointment with that person to try to sort any specific differences. I will also ask for someone to help guide me through the system. It can be like landing in a strange country and even the language can sound quite foreign to somebody new to the workings of the mental health system.

However, I am occasionally aware of a reticence on the part of the staff when they meet me for the first time. They may have heard that I work in training in our NHS trust – presenting to all staff – so they may think I am going to criticize them on their practice. I reassure them that when I am talking to them it is solely as the mum of someone who has a severe mental illness who needs their help – and I will often need their help in the form of reassurance, planning, or information.

When I think about how I feel when I think my son may be at risk and of his vulnerability in society, I can feel that horrid, anxious, tummy-sinking moment. In the past, he was most at risk when abusing drugs and alcohol, and though drugs are no longer part of his life alcohol is still present, though to a much lesser degree. Recently, I have become anxious in case he neglects himself by not bothering about his appearance or his clothes, or by not bothering to cook for himself. Self-neglect is a serious risk in those with severe mental illness. While my son has always been most risk to himself – he has never shown any aggressive characteristics or abuse towards others – the situation may be very different for other carers and their loved ones. This is all the more reason for working together with clinical staff, because it means that risks in all areas stand the best chance of being understood and managed.

Family Work

Family work for psychosis is an approach whereby family workers – practitioners working in mental health services – work with the carer and/or the family as a whole to support them and to enable them to provide more comprehensive support for their relative who is unwell (Smith, Gregory and Higgs, 2007). In order to become confident enough to accept and then provide this support, families need an understanding of psychosis and information about the illness. Such an approach to the family, rather than the individual carer, is warranted because of the way psychosis affects each individual member and how they relate – or not – to one another.

The structured approach of family work, together with information and education about mental illness, can help to improve understanding and establish confidence within the group, in them as an integrated unit and in them as carers. It can enable all members of a family to look at what has been happening to them and to speak directly to each other in ways that may have become limited over time. An approach to the family of a service user rather than an individual carer can also help stigma by encouraging family members to talk about and understand their experiences of psychosis. In family work, carers are viewed as therapeutic agents, and practitioners will look for family strengths to build communication skills between all members. It is used not as an alternative but in conjunction with medication. Overall, family work encourages three-way partnerships by providing a firmer base for positive risk management. It is a great tool and resource for staff to have available to them to implement with service users and families (NICE, 2009). Possibly, when the family and carer are in the second stage of caring (Mohr, Lafuze and Mohr, 2000), family work could be a useful intervention, though it can be used at anytime.

I have experienced family work with my son and found it extremely beneficial. He was living in supported housing after his first admission to hospital, but he was still using alcohol and drugs, much to my distress. I became very anxious about his mental and physical state, but when I attempted to talk with him he became angry with me. I was concerned about losing contact with him and worried about seeing him sinking down. His community psychiatric worker saw all this happening and asked if we would like to have some family work. At that time, I didn't know what that was. However, I had learned to say yes to any offers of help. The community psychiatric worker outlined how the process of family work would be and, amazingly, my son agreed to come and so the process was set up. It involved two community psychiatric nurses working with my son, and I. My two daughters would have come, but lived some way away and were working. Some assessments are completed to begin with, followed by a discussion and the provision of some information about my son's illness. I was able to talk to the clinicians and say how I felt about the present situation and they would feed this back to my son sitting beside me. Sometimes he would say something and sometimes not, and he sometimes left the room for a cigarette or a break. But he *did* listen – and we both felt heard.

I found that the greatest benefit from this intervention was that it defused the emotion and stress that had been building between my son and myself. We had family meetings like this for several months, but it can last for much longer if needed. What happened for us restored the precious lines of communication between my son and myself and gradually things improved. Drugs disappeared from his life and have not reappeared. Alcohol, however, still makes an appearance. But we continue to talk – and to listen to one another, and family work ensured that this was so. As Smith suggests, 'family work helps individuals work on the things that can be improved and accept things that cannot change' (Smith, 2007).

What Hinders Collaborative Working?

In this section, I address the two areas of confidentiality and stigma. Misunderstandings about confidentiality and ignorance about mental illness can significantly hinder the collaborative working on which good and effective and safe mental health care is based.

Confidentiality

Above, I mentioned confidentiality as a subject with which service users, carers, and staff frequently struggle. Beliefs about what confidentiality is can be a serious hinderance to engagement. However, there is no need for it to become a barrier.

Families and carers are often left on the outside, the value they can add to the recovery of their friend or relative remains unknown and unacknowledged. Things are changing, however. Currently, involving carers and families has become part of many, if not most, local and national policies. It features in training, as my own experience attests, and now more than ever there is recognition of the importance of partnership working. Indeed, the third principle of best practice in managing clinical risk (Department of Health, 2009) says exactly that – 'risk management should be conducted in a spirit of collaboration and based on a relationship between the service user and their carers that is as trusting as possible'.

It is recognized that there are absolutely no confidentiality issues in *listening* to carers. As part of the three-way partnership, it is important to have families on board with the care being given to their loved one. They can be a valuable asset. If the service user has not given permission for a member of the care team to talk to the family, perhaps a different more independent member of staff can work with them to see where their needs might be.

Carers have a legal right to a *Carer's Assessment* and to their own plan. It is the Care Coordinator's responsibility to make sure the Carer's Assessment is done. This is not an assessment of whether the carer is competent to look after their loved one, as occasionally carers think. Instead, it is an opportunity for them to have a one-to-one with a mental health practitioner, to tell their story, and describe how they are coping – or not coping – and to say what their needs are. Contact with the carer should be made within four weeks of their family member being admitted into care in order to commence this assessment. Carers will probably still be feeling a lot of trauma and stress from coming to terms with the admission of a loved one. Therefore, a meeting for a cup of coffee and chat would be most welcome. This may be a good time to go through a carer's pack or the range of leaflets that are available, providing information about mental illness and mental health services – there may be much that is not clear to them – it can also be a time for them to tell their story. Taking things slowly and building a relationship with the family or carer at this stage will pay dividends later towards working in a three-way partnership.

Carers have a right to information. Sometimes concerns about confidentiality can be resolved with just discussion or negotiation. The service user needs to know that their family has a right to a Carer's Assessment and that somebody will be working with their family to support them. Lack of time is often used as a reason for not sharing information or getting to know the family. This isn't acceptable. If it is not convenient to speak with the family then this should be explained and an appointment made and time assigned for this important meeting.

Different cultures should be respected and worked with accordingly. For example, in New Zealand, Maori families work as one. When a member of their family becomes unwell the whole family is involved automatically – if the doctor is to be seen, then the whole family will be present. Provided that the person who is unwell agrees, then that is fine. Diversity in mental health is important, particularly with respect to confidentiality, and clinicians should make sure they are aware of any cultural differences – as well as physical disabilities, differences arising from gender identity or preference, and so on – when working with the service user and carer.

If the service user is very unwell and says staff may not speak to his or her family, this should be reviewed regularly as often later on or by the next day, they may be happier for such contact to take place. If the service user is going home to live with his or her family, then it is necessary for the carer and wider family to have information on caring for their relative. Confidentiality cannot be used as an excuse to limit the quality of the care provided or the safety of those who provide it.

When the service user is well, an *Advance Statement* can be prepared saying what the service user would like to happen should they become unwell again. Though this is not a legal document and can, if necessary, be overridden by the Mental Health Act, it can be very useful for practical things that may cause anxiety to the service user, such as looking after pets, watering plants, and who should have a set of their house keys. Copies of the document should be in the patient's notes, with their GP, the carer, and anyone else who is relevant to that person.

In conclusion, if there is a problem with confidentiality, then there is work to be done with both parties to enable them to see the other person's perspective and to respect each other. If staff are unsure about a confidentiality issue, there will be a designated person in their mental health trust – such as the *Caldicott Guardian* – to answer such queries.

Stigma

Stigma is a huge barrier for service users and carers, and sometimes for staff too. Schizophrenia is a particularly stigmatized illness because of its mistaken association in the media with violence and crime, generating fear and apprehension (Vellerman *et al.*, 2007). And it seems this situation has not improved greatly over the years – mental illness still feels like something to be ashamed of. For carers, stigma around the mental illness of a loved one can create a feeling of isolation, guilt that somehow the illness is their fault, and perhaps that they deserve the troubles that have befallen them all. Historically, when a person developed a mental illness, the family, usually the mother, was considered to be to blame – I still think this is the case. Stigma like this – from outside or generated from within – can make the burden of care-giving even more lonely and stressful. Carers may not feel free to speak to neighbours about what is happening in their family. Friends may have only limited knowledge of mental illness, so any discussion with them may be limited and unhelpful. For service users and carers, mental illness can lead to more withdrawal from society rather than the improved engagement and support they more justifiably need.

My son found out about the stigma attached to mental illness quite early on after his diagnosis. He had just been discharged from hospital after his first admission and he met up with some friends in a pub. As you do when a friend has been in hospital, they asked how he was now and what had been the matter. Without hesitation, my son said, 'Oh, apparently I've got schizophrenia.' He learned from the silence and awkwardness that greeted this statement that schizophrenia was not something to which you admitted too readily. In the hospital, the staff and I had been open about his illness and had talked to him about his diagnosis and he was able to ask us questions and discuss his options. Outside hospital, it was a very different situation. His friends had limited knowledge about mental illness and what knowledge they did have was likely to be influenced by biased media coverage emphasizing the madness of murderers and other violent people. My son has since been careful not to put himself in situations that might be difficult for him to cope with, or distressing to him, and does not go out very much any more. He probably spends more time in his flat with his music and television than he might have done had he felt more accepted into the community.

The Service User's Perspective

In this section, I will examine what might be helpful to promote the engagement of service users like my son in their care, whether provided by professional services or by carers and family members.

When a person is newly admitted to a psychiatric hospital and is very unwell, it is essential to remember that this person had a life before their mental illness became an unwelcome part of their existence. They may have had a job and friends and interests. These facts can be an excellent way of engaging with the person now and in the future. Our lives are all a bit of a jigsaw, made up of the different aspects and parts of us that come together to make our whole selves. It is the same with service users like my son – mental illness is just one bit of the jigsaw that is their life. We are all on the continuum of mental health, which we will move around on during our lives, but some may veer further towards one end of the scale or the other than is acceptable for their mental health, so they need some help and support to find an acceptable place on this continuum.

On a person's first admission, somewhere during that process, there will be a 'window of opportunity' to engage with the person either directly or, if there is a family member or carer present, then perhaps through them. A bad initial experience with mental health services may be very detrimental to the quality of all future contact. Staff must attend to any descriptions of the service user's occupation or interests – their pre-illness selves – that can be used to engage them and their family and perhaps be used in later conversations and interactions.

An example of this came from a friend whose son was admitted under a Mental Health Act section when he was very unwell indeed. My friend was upset and very much wanted her son to receive support and help; she really wanted staff to engage with her son in order to help him. Therefore, she took into his ward some paintings that he had completed thinking they might provide that window of opportunity. Unfortunately, the staff were very busy and thin on the ground; the paintings were put to one side and forgotten. Her son ran away from the hospital and the opportunity for engagement was lost.

Another example relates to choice of language. I talked about the importance of language earlier. Friends and family members often do not understand the term 'carer' and likewise it can be misunderstood by service users. My son was recently asked to fill in another form on which it asked for his 'main carer'. He put down the lady who took him swimming and to football. His social worker and myself were with him and the social worker asked him who was it that did most things with him and was always around, his instant answer was 'Mum'. So often family members, particularly mothers, see themselves as doing what they would be doing anyway – being a mum, dad, sister, or brother. On admission, a service user will be asked who their main carer is and they may not realize what is meant.

The strengths approach (e.g., Ryan and Morgan, 2004) is a model that should be evident in all areas of working in mental health services. It is a positive base from which to work, focusing on enhancing the strengths of a person in order to minimize the negatives and the influence of other life problems. By looking at the person's abilities, interests, and capabilities and working with these, the service user feels empowered to lead in their own programme of growth and change in their recovery. While working with this approach, it is important that the service user feels that they are as involved in it as the care staff and that staff appreciate exactly where they are at that moment and that they are working with a true representation.

The CPA has changed recently and new care pathways are described; all service users will be guided to follow one of the recovery care pathways. It is important service users feel as though they are in the driving seat of their recovery care pathway and that the support is there for them to keep up the tempo at their own level and pace.

The *Wellness Recovery Action Plan* (WRAP) (Copeland, 1989) is a very useful tool to use with service users and their carers, and with clinical staff as well. Mary Ellen Copeland is an American who uses mental health services. The WRAP was initially developed for service users but, in fact, could be adapted to benefit everybody to enable them to think about what they need to do in order to keep themselves well. It encourages awareness of one's wellbeing. One of the service users I work with in training has personalized their WRAP with glitter, bright colours, pictures, and photos. It is something to develop, to check, to use as a reminder, as evidence of progress – or deterioration and, therefore, a reminder of what action needs to be taken. When working in the three-way partnership of service user, carer, and professional, all sides of the triangle are equally important for the working relationship to be successful. It is necessary for everyone to think about their wellbeing, mental and physical, and the things they can do for themselves in order to relax and notice how they might be feeling. Mental health should be as important to everyone as their physical health – they work together for a person's whole wellbeing and should not be separated.

Recovery means something different for everybody and everybody will have their own pace in moving forward. It is important to recognize even the smallest signs of recovery so the expectations of recovery do not become a burden and actually prevent someone from going forward. Recently, I planned to take my son on holiday. He has always found managing his money quite challenging, so a few months before we left I told him we needed to start saving so that we would have some spending money. I asked him if he could save £5 or £6 a week. He thought that might be difficult, so I wondered if perhaps he could manage a £1 a day? This seemed acceptable to him and he subsequently managed to do this and so had quite a good lump sum to spend on our holiday. It was a small thing but put in a way that made it seem possible to him to manage, and the spin offs from this were huge. He was really pleased with himself that he had managed to save and felt he had contributed to the holiday. I was really pleased that he had managed this and had helped my budget. It was also very satisfying to him on the holiday to have his own money and not to have to ask me for handouts.

Top Tips for Carers

I've been a carer for many years now and have picked up a lot of ideas and tips that I have used myself and passed on to others. Here is a selection of what I think are my best top tips – for carers and for professionals working in mental health services.

Top Tips

- Smile – to encourage you as well as them!
- Have an open attitude.
- Be honest.
- Respect others – and yourself.
- Aim to establish trust in your working relationships with clinical staff.
- Ask to see where your relative will be living.
- Ask anything you need to know.
- Don't feel intimidated.
- Ask for an appointment to meet the psychiatrist.
- Write down questions to ask – and any notes to help you remember what has been discussed.
- Notice even the tiniest signs of recovery in your loved one.
- Tears are okay.
- Explain how you are feeling.
- Write down your feelings.
- Keep lines of communication open.
- Above all, look after yourself.

Top tips for professionals to involve carers in risk management

- Remember that welcoming smile.
- And a friendly face and helpful, caring attitude.
- Honesty – tell carers if you are rushed off your feet and if its difficult to talk at that moment, but make an appointment to talk with them later – and keep that appointment.
- Respect your patients and their families, whatever.
- Regard carers as an asset – they know their family members better than anyone, including you, and can give you their history.
- Keep lines of communication open.
- Recognize the strengths of your patients and their carers and families.
- Recognize their stress too.
- Establish trust.
- Tears are okay.
- Listen.

- Look for all windows of opportunity to engage.
- Think of some tips of your own!
- Look after yourself too.

Conclusions

My hope is that after reading this chapter, clinicians will have more confidence in working with families and carers as part of their everyday working life. I especially hope that clinicians will see families and carers as an important part of collaborative positive risk management. Many do work in this way already, but there are still large areas where this does not happen. I hope that any new confidence gained from reading this chapter will be put towards successful collaborative working and that practice might change – improve – even just a little bit. I also hope this chapter will give carers the confidence to work with staff. If carers are not happy about something, I hope they will feel more confident about talking to the people looking after their relatives and work with them to put things right. Carers are vital to their relative's or friend's recovery.

A lot is changing in mental health today, which I hope will be for the better for everyone, especially the service user. At the time of writing, the previous government had a new 10-year plan for mental health called *New Horizons*. This was an inspirational, optimistic outlook for mental health services with an emphasis on prevention and recovery. These concepts have already been introduced into practice and there is now much more liaison between primary and secondary mental health services. However, this new coordinated, focused plan will make a huge difference to the lives of service users and families when it is implemented. I sincerely hope the present financial restraints on services will ease and the funding will be found to put the *New Horizon* vision into practice. Mental health has too long been the Cinderella of the health system.

We are all on a continuum of mental health, as I mentioned earlier, on which we will go up and down throughout our lives. I know I certainly do. If it is – or becomes – your family that needs mental health services in the future, you would surely hope to work in a collaborative way to enable your relative to obtain the best possible practice to help them to recovery. Encourage collaborative working now.

The last of the sixteen best practice principles described in the Department of Health publication *Best Practice in Managing Risk* states 'a risk management plan is only as good as the time and effort put into communicating its findings to others'.

This is true.

References

Copeland, M. E. (1989). *The Wellness Recovery Action Plan.* Available at www.mentalhealthrecovery.com.

Department of Health (2004). *The Ten Essential Shared Capabilities.* London: Department of Health, available at www.dh.gov.uk/en/Publicationsandstatistics/Publications/PublicationsPolicyAndGuidance/DH_4087169.

Department of Health (2009). *Best Practice in Managing Risk: Principles and Evidence for Best Practice in the Assessment and Management of Risk to Self and Others in Mental Health Services.* London: Department of Health, available at www.dh.gov.uk/en/Publicationsandstatistics/Publications/PublicationsPolicyAndGuidance/DH_076511.

Mohr, W., Lafuze, J., and Mohr, B. (2000). Opening caregiver minds: National Alliance for the Mentally Ill (NAMI), provider education program, *Archives of Psychiatric Nursing*, 14, 235–243.

National Institute for Health and Clinical Excellence (NICE) (2009). Schizophrenia: Core interventions in the treatment and management of schizophrenia in primary and secondary care (update), *National Clinical Practice Guideline*. No. 82. London: NICE.

Ryan, P. and Morgan, S. (2004). *Assertive Outreach: A Strengths Approach to Policy and Practice*. Edinburgh: Churchill Livingstone.

Smith, G. (2007). Consultant nurse and family work coordinator for Avon and Wiltshire Mental Health NHS Trust.

Smith, G., Gregory, K., and Higgs, A. (2007). *An Integrated Approach to Family Work*. London: Jessica Kingsley.

Vellerman, R., Davis, E., Smith, G., and Drage, M. (eds) (2007). *Changing Outcomes in Psychosis: Collaborative Cases from Practitioners, Users and Carers*. Chichester: John Wiley & Sons, Ltd.

Resources

For more information about Advance Statements, go to: www.mentalhealthshop.org/products/rethink_publications/advance_statements_f.html.

For more information about the Care Programme Approach, go to: www.rethink.org/about_mental_illness/peoples_experiences/jesss_journey/care_programme.html.

For more information about the work of the Caldicott Guardians, go to: www.dh.gov.uk/en/Managingyourorganisation/Informationpolicy/Patientconfidentialityandcaldicottguardians/DH_4100563.

For more information about Carer's Assessments, go to: www.carersuk.org/Information/Helpwithcaring/Carersassessmentguide.

For more information about *New Horizons*, go to: www.newhorizons.dh.gov.uk/index.aspx.

For more information about Wellness Recovery Action Plans, go to: www.workingtogetherforrecovery.co.uk/Documents/Wellness Recovery Action Plan.pdf.

See also:

Carers UK: www.carersuk.org.

Department of Health: www.dh.gov.uk.

MIND: www.mind.org.uk.

Rethink: www.rethink.org.

Princess Royal Trust: www.princessroyaltrust.org.uk.

Libraries, Internet.

Part II
Evidence

4

Understanding and Managing Self-Harm in Mental Health Services

Maria Leitner and Wally Barr

Synopsis

In this chapter, we critically review the current research evidence that might guide the clinician in preventing, or at least ameliorating the impact of, suicidal behaviours in their clients. This includes suicidal ideation, self-harm as well as acts of attempted suicide, and completed suicide itself. We begin with a discussion of the research evidence for the relationship between these various suicidal behaviours and a range of risk factors, including mental health, substance abuse, and employment. We next consider the evidence relating to structured risk assessment and move on to a discussion of interventions, with a specific focus on both high quality and moderate quality research as it pertains to the suicidal behaviours noted above. Finally, we suggest a way forward that will both progress knowledge and extend the evidence base, while minimizing the burdens usually associated with a costly programme of research.

Introduction

Best Practice in Managing Risk (Department of Health, 2009), the guideline document that promoted the commissioning of this book, identified 16 best practice points for effective risk management. These points can be subsumed within the following core responsibilities:

- clinical decisions should be based on established research evidence;
- clinicians should proactively engage with clients as partners in care;
- risk management should be flexible, dynamic, and responsive;
- careful forward planning should be integral to the clinical process;
- care should be multidisciplinary but well coordinated; and
- structural, procedural, and organizational factors should be addressed in addition to individual (client-specific) factors.

Self-Harm and Violence: Towards Best Practice in Managing Risk in Mental Health Services, First Edition. Edited by Richard Whittington and Caroline Logan.

We suggest that the first of these core principles, basing practice on the existing research evidence, is pre-eminent among all sixteen recommendations since evidence-based practice is most likely to improve outcomes in health care. On this assumption, this chapter will outline what evidence there is to support key decisions regarding service planning and organization, risk prediction, and intervention with people who experience suicidal ideation or engage at some level in the range of self-harming or suicidal behaviours.

However, we should first mention some common problems with terminology in this field. Research evidence has tended to focus on several specific elements of what might broadly be called 'suicidal behaviours'. Our recent systematic review (Leitner, Barr and Hobby, 2008) identified these as suicidal ideation, self-harm, attempted suicide, and completed suicide. These terms frequently recur in the literature and a broad review requires use of them. However, there is currently no agreed nomenclature underpinning this terminology and consequently behaviours referred to as, for example, 'attempted suicide' in one context may not be directly comparable with the behaviours to which the same term is applied in a different context. Nor has there been any significant attempt to explore the underlying association between these behaviours more fully. In particular, there is a need to establish the nature of any causal relationship between suicidal ideation, self-harm, attempted suicide, and completed suicide and to establish the factors and mechanisms that result in an individual moving from one form of behaviour to another. Bearing this in mind, we now move to a discussion of the evidence base for links between specific risk factors and suicidal behaviour.

Evidence-Based Risk Prediction

In recent years, the terminology of risk *prediction* has been overshadowed by the advent of tools concerned more with aiding clinical formulation and action rather than estimating the likelihood of an event. However, we feel that, in the context of the current chapter, our concern with past literature in the field allows us some leeway in using the term more freely than is now commonly the case. Indeed, until recently, the concept of risk prediction had become so deeply ingrained in the everyday parlance of practice and research that failure to refer to it would do the extensive literature available a disservice.

Risk prediction in the context of suicide at the broad population or national level, can be seen as comparatively well-served by the evidence, given the extensive epidemiological data available. Unfortunately, the risk factors identified at this level (such as relative deprivation and population age structure) are somewhat intransigent to intervention. At the local level, due to the comparative rarity of completed suicide and regional variations, even the prediction of likely rates of suicide presents something of a challenge to service planning and service delivery.

At both the national and local levels, evidence to inform effective population-level risk prediction in respect of attempted suicide, non-fatal self-harm, and suicidal ideation is very limited indeed. National-level data regarding suicidal behaviours *other* than completed suicide are restricted to infrequent self-report surveys and to the 'tip of the iceberg' estimates provided by routine accident and emergency (A&E) and hospital inpatient admission statistics. Reliance on such limited data sources inevitably distorts the true picture of risk and, hence, subverts our ability to plan services according to need. By way of example, people who self-poison are known to be more likely to seek help than those who self-injure (Hawton *et al.*, 2002; Meltzer *et al.*, 2002), so, where A&E and similar data are used to estimate local need, services are likely to underestimate the needs of people who self-injure. This will hamper outreach work and also prevent accurate forward-planning.

Where there is a real paucity of evidence, however, is in respect of individual-level risk prediction. Some have argued that individual risk prediction is impossible because it is not feasible to extrapolate from the group to the individual (Hart, Michie and Cooke, 2007). Certainly, the development of robust actuarial scales, even in respect of the comparatively common event of suicidal ideation, is in its infancy. As is the case also for other-directed violence (see Chapter 5), the most robust predictor of self-harm so far identified is previous self-harming behaviour. Interestingly, while in the context of violent behaviour, specific *modes* of behaviour appear to be relatively discrete in this respect (armed robbery predicts armed robbery, but not necessarily murder), the spectrum of self-harming and suicidal behaviours appears to be more diffuse: prior self-harm is not only the best predictor of future self-harm, but also the single best predictor of completed suicide (Neeleman, 2001).

Mental health, self-harm and suicidal behaviour

Relative to other predictors of self-harming behaviour, considerable attention has been paid to mental health. Systematic reviews identified by McLean *et al.* (2008) confirm an association between mental health and suicide at the population level, with around 88% of those dying by suicide identified as having a mental health disorder (Arsenault-Lapierre, Kim and Turecki, 2004; Fleischmann *et al.*, 2005). Overall, the disorders most commonly found to associate with risk of suicidal behaviour are affective disorders, in particular depression (cf. also Wulsin, Vaillant and Wells, 1999) and substance-related disorders. However, while there is a strong association at the population level between a mental health diagnosis and completed suicide, the nature of this association remains unclear. The small number of systematic reviews that have included studies providing insight into mental health and suicide at the individual level do not help to resolve this issue. These reviews report either *no* individual level association (e.g., Bostwick and Pankratz, 2000), or report associations with completed suicide that are compromised. That is, they either fail to control for other shared risk factors (e.g., Palmer, Pankratz and Bostwick, 2005 in the context of schizophrenia) or are limited to an association with depression or substance abuse.

Only two reviews were identified by McLean *et al.* (2008) as addressing potential links between mental health and forms of self-harming behaviour *other* than suicide, either at the population or the individual level. Outcomes from both reviews are reported using 'suicidal behaviour' as a generic term encompassing different forms of self-harm. The first review (Hawton *et al.*, 2005a) noted an *inverse* association between hallucinations and the likelihood of suicidal behaviour in people with schizophrenia. The second (Hawton *et al.*, 2005b) identified a number of characteristics of bipolar disorder as being associated with an increased likelihood of suicidal behaviour. Although the latter review reports quite a strong link at the individual level between several characteristics of at least one mental health disorder and suicidal behaviour, the number of studies addressing individual characteristics was small. It should also be borne in mind that, in the case of a number of mental health diagnoses, in particular personality disorder, an assumed association with self-harming behaviour can be somewhat circular. A tendency to self-harm, for example, is one of the diagnostic criteria leading to a diagnosis of personality disorder. Further work then is needed to tease out the nature of any associations between mental illness and self-harming behaviour, notably in the context of self-harming behaviours other than suicide.

Substance abuse, self-harm and suicidal behaviour

Within the general population as well as the mental health population, the association between substance misuse and self-harming behaviour has been a strong focus of attention. Three reviews (Cherpitel, Borges and Wilcox, 2004; Neeleman, 2001; Wilcox, Conner and Caine, 2004) concur in their conclusion that rates of completed suicide are generally higher in populations misusing alcohol. Standardized mortality ratios cited in the latter two reviews show the number of observed deaths in a population relative to the number of expected deaths. These average around 9:1 in respect of suicide rates in those with an alcohol misuse disorder (i.e., there were more than nine times the expected number of suicide deaths among drinkers). There were also high rates of suicide-related deaths in populations with opioid disorder, intravenous drug use, and mixed drug use. The link shown between alcohol misuse and suicide is reported to be stronger in women than in men (Wilcox, Conner and Caine, 2004). However, while the data are consistent, the primary studies incorporated in these three reviews show substantive heterogeneity (e.g., the proportion of people testing positive for blood alcohol following their death by suicide ranged between 10% and 70%), as well as large variations in sample size and a number of significant methodological flaws (e.g., high proportions of individuals not having been tested for the presence of alcohol). Only one of the reviews addressed self-harming behaviours other than suicide (Cherpitel, Borges and Wilcox, 2004, attempted suicide), and here outcomes were equivocal (again due to significant heterogeneity in the primary studies). Only one primary study (in the same review) evaluated the association between alcohol use and suicide at the individual level. While this study provided support for the link between alcohol use and suicide (identifying a substantially higher risk of suicide during or shortly after the use of alcohol in comparison with during alcohol-free periods), there remains a query regarding the likely direction of effect here. Taken overall, there is again stronger evidence of an association between substance use and suicide at the population level, albeit with some caveats regarding study quality, than there is at the individual level. Further studies at the individual level, better controlled studies at the population level, and additional studies addressing self-harming behaviours other than completed suicide are needed to confirm the reliability of substance use as a specific risk factor. This notwithstanding, it remains unfortunate from the clinical perspective that the intervention literature, in particular, fails to identify, evaluate, and control for the impact of alcohol and substance misuse in addressing the needs of people engaging in self-harm or suicidal behaviour.

Employment, self-harm and suicidal behaviour

One further factor that has been addressed by a substantial proportion of the risk assessment literature (over 200 primary studies) is employment. Four of the reviews identified by McLean *et al.*, (2008) (Hem, Berg and Ekeberg, 2001; Lindeman *et al.*, 1996; Neeleman, 2001; Rehkopf and Buka, 2006) focused on associations between completed suicide and various aspects of employment and unemployment. One additional review (Platt and Hawton, 2000) addressed both suicide and self-harm. All five reviews evaluated outcomes at the population level, using a comparison of rates and standardized mortality ratios. Summarizing the evidence from across these reviews, while again inconsistent results are found between primary studies, unemployment and low socioeconomic status show an association with the likelihood of suicide (with suicide rates in both cases being more than double the rates in the population as a whole). Although an association between self-harm and unemployment emerged in some primary studies, the evidence supporting this link is more equivocal than that identified for completed suicide. The nature of the association, even in the case of suicide, is in any event not straightforward. Time-based analyses suggest that the link with unemployment holds only for certain periods in recent history (e.g., during the 1970s, but not the 1980s: Platt and Hawton, 2000). Area-based analyses suggest that the link with socioeconomic status is based on relative (not absolute) poverty rather with socioeconomic status per se (Rehkopf and Buka, 2006). Furthermore, studies evaluating the links between particular professions and suicide (cf. Hem, Berg and Ekeberg, 2001; Lindeman *et al.*, 1996; Platt and Hawton, 2000) suggest that while low socioeconomic status may be a factor influencing overall rates of suicide, the rates of suicide in individual professions are highest within high-status groups (e.g., medical professionals). The 'highest risk' professions identified overall are the medical and allied professions (with rates exceeding four times those in the general population); male, but not female, farmers; and health, education, and welfare professionals, and personal service workers. Despite an assumption that high stress levels must exist in the police force, population-level data suggests that this occupational group, in fact, has the *lowest* occupational suicide rate in the United Kingdom (Hem, Berg and Ekeberg, 2001). Clearly, the picture is a complicated one.

Other risk factors, self-harm and suicidal behaviour

A broad range of other potential risk factors has been evaluated by a smaller number of primary studies within the literature. In general, outcomes are heterogeneous and dependent on the precise nature of the study, notably in respect of the definitions used for the risk factor, the population or sub-population group considered, and the nature of the suicidal behaviour in question. McLean *et al.* (2008) report some evidence of an association between higher rates of completed/attempted suicide and epilepsy (Pompili *et al.*, 2005), ADHD (James, Lai and Dahl, 2004), aspects of the menstrual cycle (Saunders and Hawton, 2006), pregnancy (Shadigan and Bauer, 2005), adolescent neuroticism (Neeleman, 2001), and deficits in social problem-solving skills (Speckens and Hawton, 2005). Although research has been limited, studies attempting to identify a link between genetic factors and either completed or attempted suicide have met with less success to date. McLean *et al.* (2008) cite two systematic reviews addressing this issue (Lalovic and Turecki, 2002; Li, Duan and He, 2006). While McLean *et al.* (2008) summarize the data as showing no overall positive outcomes from these studies, in fact, a significant association between one polymorphism at the 5-HT2A locus (A-1438G) and suicidal behaviour *was* identified by Li and colleagues (2006) from the primary studies included in their review.

Summary

In summary, it is fair to say that a very broad array of risk factors has been implicated in the aetiology of the spectrum of suicidal behaviours. The evidence base for population-level risk for completed suicide is the strongest, while the evidence for individual-level risk factors frequently remains equivocal. Nevertheless, work has continued on the assessment of risk and it is to this that we now turn.

Evidence-Based Risk Assessment

Given the complexity of the picture identified to date, subjective decisions made by the clinician on the basis of individual risk factors inevitably provide only a partial account of a client's actual risk profile. This is one factor in the rationale behind the Department of Health's recommendation (Department of Health, 2002) that risk management should be structured and consistent. The bottom line here is that achieving this level of consistency entails the use of some form of risk prediction tool – either an actuarial scale or some form of guided assessment tool that constrains and informs clinical judgement. The literature in respect of suicidal behaviour has to date been rather shy in respect of developing scale-based prediction. Recent Department of Health guidance (Department of Health, 2009) was able to identify only six structured risk assessment approaches that justified inclusion in a guide to best practice. Furthermore, even the limited number of tools identified was found to be lacking in sufficient evidence to be recommended without caution. Table 4.1 summarizes key features of these six prediction tools and clearly demonstrates how limited is the clinician's armoury for structured risk assessment. This situation has not been helped by the large-scale roll-out of training packages without any accompanying outcomes evaluation component. Currently, the best-evidenced tools available to assist in risk assessment would seem to be the very well-established Beck Hopelessness Scale (BHS) and the Scale for Suicidal Ideation (SSI), although each has its limitations.

As the Department of Health guidance (Department of Health, 2009) indicates, currently available structured tools should not be used as a 'stand-alone' device for risk assessment. Unfortunately, the efficacy of clinical decision-making has also been under-evaluated in this context. Therefore, currently we have access to only a very small number of tools to assist the clinician. Other areas that have received little attention in the research literature are the accuracy of clinical judgements of risk and risk prediction based on self-assessment by the client themselves or their families and carers. This is an important gap in the essential evidence base that could, in the short term, readily be addressed by the collection and collation of robust routine data.

Evidence-Based Intervention

An overview of the intervention evidence

The evidence cited in this section is taken from a recent systematic review conducted by Leitner, Barr and Hobby (2008). This review considered the effectiveness of interventions to prevent suicide and suicidal behaviour. It was unrestricted by date and was based on a search of 17 electronic databases. The review identified 200 primary studies, which

Table 4.1 Overview of structured risk-to-self assessment tools.

	Format	Focus	Research evidence base
ASIST (Applied Suicide Intervention Skills Training)	Two-day interactive suicide risk management training course.	Management of immediate risk.	Minimal. However ASIST has been adopted as a national programme in Scotland, so the potential exists for detailed evaluation.
BHS (Beck Hopelessness Scale)	Self-report 'actuarial' type scale comprising 20 items assessing feelings about the future.	No explicit link to risk management, but the scale has been shown to correlate well with changes in clinical symptoms and research indicates that hopelessness is a risk factor for completed suicide.	An extensive research evidence base including a meta-analysis (McMillan *et al.*, 2007) has evaluated the structure of the tool and the association between hopelessness and completed suicide. This provides moderate evidence of the tool's efficacy in risk management.
STORM (Skills-based Training on Risk Management)	Modular training package delivered over either one or two days.	Risk assessment, crisis management, crisis prevention and problem-solving.	Research evidence exists to support changes in staff knowledge, confidence and attitudes following training, but we are not aware of any research evidence evaluating the impact on client outcomes.

(*Continued*)

Table 4.1 (Continued)

	Format	Focus	Research evidence base
SSI (Scale for Suicidal Ideation)	A 21-item 'actuarial' type scale completed via either interview or self-report.	Designed to assess the intensity of a person's attitudes regarding suicide and their behaviours and plans to complete suicide during the past week.	Robust evidence from systematic review to support an association between scores on the interview version of the scale and completed suicide in outpatients. Evidence from one primary study suggest an association between change in self-harm and scores on the self-report version of the scale.
SADPERSONS	Brief tool assessing the presence or absence of 10 risk factors.	Originally developed as an easy to administer tool for novice risk assessors.	There is a lack of evidence regarding the reliability and validity of this very short scale, although it appears to be adequate if used as one part of a more extensive clinical assessment.
SIS (Suicidal Intent Scale)	A 15-item scale designed to assess the level of intent in people who have attempted suicide. Items are separated into circumstances related to the attempt and self-report items regarding intent. The scale can be administered by self-report or by interview and case note review.	Intention to die.	There is conflicting research evidence regarding this scale. Some primary studies report associations between total or sub-scale scores and suicide-related outcomes, but systematic review evidence suggests that SIS score is not a risk factor for completed suicide.

together evaluated 150 distinct interventions. Despite the evident breadth of research in this area, the review was unable to identify any single well-validated intervention for the prevention of any suicidal behaviour, including completed suicide, attempted suicide, self-harm, and suicidal ideation. This finding very clearly illustrates a fundamental feature of the available evidence for effective intervention in suicidal behaviour, namely, that research has adopted a truly 'scattergun' approach, leaving individual interventions without the support of more than a tiny number of studies.

This state of affairs is not, in fact, uncommon in clinical practice, but nevertheless makes for uncomfortable reading. A key take-home message in respect of intervention is that most, if not all, interventions should be regarded with caution in the clinical setting. Where specific interventions have been evaluated by a reasonable number of studies (which is only the case for a small number of pharmaceutical interventions), outcomes also tend to be rather equivocal. This suggests that the impact of intervention is likely to be context-dependent. So again, in order to have any confidence in their choice of intervention, clinicians need to assess whether the available evidence base supporting an intervention applies to the profile of the client they are treating. The lack of a research evidence base supporting a given intervention is not, of course, equivalent to a statement that the intervention does *not* work. However, if robust evidence from regularly collected and collated routine data is also lacking and/or fails to support the effectiveness of an intervention, the clinician would be best advised to exercise caution in pursuing the intervention without maintaining very close observation of the client's progress and any potential side-effects. Starting treatment with the least invasive approach and taking into account the client's preferences is likely to be the most appropriate way forward. This can be a daunting position for the clinician to take with a potentially suicidal client. However, the limited research evidence available suggests that, in fact, comparatively minimalist interventions, such as the maintenance of ongoing contact with the suicidal person and restricting access to means, may have the potential to prevent even the most extreme forms of suicidal behaviour. While 'doing nothing' is clearly not being advocated here, evidence-based practice does not currently dictate the need for intensive or invasive interventions. It is, of course, imperative that the evidence base for these and other promising interventions is expanded substantially.

Focus on specific suicidal behaviours

Although there was considerable overlap in stated outcomes, of the 200 studies identified by Leitner and colleagues (2008), nearly half (47%) evaluated the outcomes of interventions aimed at reducing suicidal ideation. Over one-third of studies reported outcomes for either attempted suicide (37%) or completed suicide (33%), and only around one-fifth of studies (22%) evaluated outcomes for self-harm. Why there should be less of a focus on the treatment of self-harm in the research literature is unclear, given its ubiquity in the clinical setting. Part of the explanation may lie in the strong focus of the literature on pharmaceutical trials. One-third of all primary studies focused on evaluating the outcomes of pharmaceutical intervention. For whatever reason, the evaluation of pharmaceutical products is less likely to take place in the context of self-harm. Only 15% of studies addressing self-harm evaluated pharmaceutical interventions. In contrast, between 30% and 40% of studies addressing other forms of suicidal behaviour, including suicidal ideation, did so. The figures in Figure 4.1 summarize other interesting

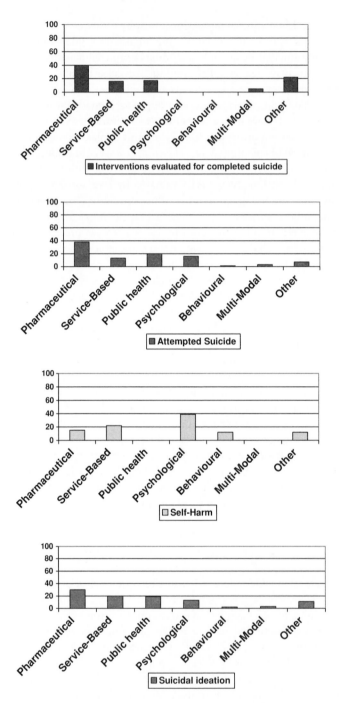

Figure 4.1 Percentage of interventions evaluated for the prevention of different suicidal behaviours.

patterns in the distribution of interventions that have been evaluated for the range of suicidal behaviours.

Aside from pharmaceutical intervention, the most commonly evaluated interventions to prevent completed suicide include service-based initiatives (altering the format for service delivery, training staff, etc.), public health initiatives (educational campaigns, programmes based in schools, prisons, etc.), and an eclectic mix of 'other' initiatives, the most prominent of which, with respect to promising outcomes to date, are the restriction of access to means and the maintenance of ongoing contact. In part due to the relative infrequency of completed suicide (which encourages studies evaluating outcomes at the population rather than the individual level), there has been no attention in the literature to the potential for psychological or cognitive and/or behavioural intervention to prevent completed suicide. This is a significant gap, which could be overcome in the short term via the national collation of regional or local routine data identifying where such interventions have been utilized and the subsequent short-term and long-term outcomes.

As with the prevention of completed suicide, service-based and public health initiatives are also among the most commonly evaluated non-pharmaceutical interventions to reduce the rate of attempted suicide. However, attempted suicide, unlike completed suicide has also attracted the attention of a relatively large proportion of studies (16%) evaluating psychological, cognitive, or social-educational interventions. Purely behavioural therapies in contrast have received virtually no attention. While the evaluation of service-based and 'other' initiatives are prominent in the literature relating to self-harm, the *most* commonly evaluated interventions are psychological or cognitive and/or behavioural intervention. The evaluation of interventions for suicidal ideation, in contrast, mimics far more closely the pattern for completed and attempted suicide, with a strong focus on service-based and public health initiatives.

While it is important to note that studies reporting positive outcomes are more likely to be published (Sackett, 1979), the fact that between 30% and 40% of studies reported a reduction in the suicidal behaviour evaluated following intervention does give some hope for the future of clinical practice. The concomitant fact that the majority did *not* report successful outcomes suggests strongly that we need to fine-tune the interventions on which both clinical practice and research are focused. Taken together, input from routine clinical data and a more targeted programme of research would help to provide a more robust, less diffuse evidence base to take clinical practice forward. As things currently stand, there are a small number of interventions that are consistently supported by a small number of studies, including one or more high quality studies. The nature of these interventions varies with the type of suicidal behaviour, as indicated in the following section.

Interventions supported by high quality research evidence

Completed suicide In respect of the prevention of completed suicide, interventions supported by high quality research evidence include the restriction of access to means, maintenance of ongoing contact with the suicidal person, and service delivery via specialist centres with highly trained personnel.

Attempted suicide With regard to attempted suicide, the evidence base is more equivocal, but promising interventions are treatment with lithium for bipolar disorder, restriction of access to means, and setting up informal social support networks to provide people with continuity of support and interaction. One caveat here is that although a number of studies report positive outcomes with lithium treatment, two studies report, respectively, subsequent increases in suicide (above baseline) following discontinuation of treatment (cf. Baldessarini, Tondo, and Hennen, 2003; Tondo *et al.*, 1998) and increases in suicide *during* the treatment of psychiatric patients with lithium (Oerlinghausen *et al.*, 1994).

Self-harm The research evidence with respect to interventions for self-harm is particularly limited and is also scattered across a particularly broad range of interventions. Many studies in this section of the literature are little better than an ad hoc evaluation of a particular aspect of clinical practice. The only clearly identified intervention finding consistent support from a number of studies is dialectical behaviour therapy (DBT) and here study outcomes are primarily restricted to the treatment of people with borderline personality disorder. This having been said, promising approaches identified by a very small number of studies include cognitive behaviour therapy (CBT) and, again, the maintenance of ongoing contact, both of which approaches merit further investigation.

Suicidal ideation Despite the comparatively large number of studies devoted to evaluating outcomes for suicidal ideation, no specific intervention is consistently supported in the literature. Promising approaches supported by a very small number of studies are the treatment of depression with either sertraline or fluvoxamine and the provision of crisis support via the use of non-directive telephone counselling.

Interventions supported by moderate research evidence

Pharmaceutical interventions

Completed suicide As noted previously, the intervention literature shows a distinct 'bias' towards the evaluation of pharmaceutical products, at least in respect of suicidal behaviours *other* than self-harm. Nevertheless, with the exception of lithium, none of the drugs evaluated to date have the benefit of having been evaluated by more than one or two studies in the context of a particular form of behaviour. Of the antidepressants listed in Table 4.2, a reduction in completed suicide was identified only by one study evaluating selective serotonin re-uptake inhibitors (SSRIs) as a composite group and two studies evaluating 'antidepressants', also as a composite group. All three studies evaluated outcomes against baseline alone. It is of particular note that when evaluated against placebo, no significant reductions in completed suicide were found for antidepressants evaluated as a composite group.

Attempted suicide Outcomes for interventions aimed at reducing attempted suicide are slightly more promising. While neither 'antidepressants' as a composite group nor fluoxetine were shown to improve outcomes, SSRIs, evaluated as a composite group, were shown by one study to reduce attempted suicide in comparison with baseline and paroxetine was shown to reduce attempted suicide in two studies, in comparison, respectively, with amitryptyline and to placebo.

Table 4.2 Antidepressants evaluated in the research literature.

	Completed suicide	Attempted suicide	Self-harm	Suicidal ideation
Duloxetine				* √
Escitalopram	*		*	
Fluoxetine	*	*		* √
Fluvoxamine				* √
Imipramine				* √
Mianserin			*	*
Moclobemide				* √
Nortriptyline				*
Paroxetine		* √		* √
Sertraline				* √
Venlafaxine			*	
Viloxazine				*
SSRIs[a] > as a composite group	* √	* √	*	
Antidepressants as a composite group	* √	*		*

[a] Selective serotonin re-uptake inhibitors.
* Target behaviours where antidepressants have been tested.
√ Evidence of favourable effects.

Self-harm The very limited number of studies (N = 4) evaluating antidepressant intervention to prevent self-harm failed to report any positive outcomes supported by formal data analysis.

Suicidal ideation A particularly broad range of antidepressants has been evaluated for the prevention of suicidal ideation, although the number of studies addressing any given type of antidepressant is again very small and a surprisingly high number of studies report narrative outcomes only, unsupported by any formal data analysis. The relative ubiquity of evaluation in this context seems to derive primarily from the tendency of researchers to include suicidal ideation scales as an additional measure when evaluating outcomes for the impact of drugs in treating depression. Nevertheless, and in contrast to other forms of suicidal behaviour, studies evaluating outcomes for suicidal ideation following treatment with antidepressants report quite promising outcomes. It should, of course, be noted here that these studies were primarily carried out in the context of treatment for clinical or sub-clinical depression and that any generalization of treatment outside this context would need further evaluation.

Of the other drug classes that have been evaluated in preventing suicidal behaviour, clozapine has been reported to reduce both *completed* and *attempted suicide* in comparison with olanzapine; *attempted suicide* in comparison with 'traditional antipsychotics' and *self-harm* in comparison with baseline. Olanzapine has been reported to reduce *suicidal ideation* in comparison with baseline when paired with either adjunctive valproate or adjunctive lithium. Lithium, for which the largest number of studies is available (N = 8 studies evaluating lithium for the prevention of *completed suicide*, five for *attempted suicide* and one for *suicidal ideation*), has been reported to reduce *completed suicide* in comparison with baseline and both *completed* and *attempted suicide* in comparison with divalproex and carbamazepine, respectively. As noted earlier, some caution should be exercised here given additional findings relating to potential increases in suicide over the longer term and on cessation of treatment with lithium. It should also be noted that lithium has not been compared against placebo in the context of any of the spectrum of suicidal behaviours. Finally, ketamine has been shown to reduce *suicidal ideation* in comparison with baseline. All other outcomes for studies relating to these drugs are either null or negative.

Non-pharmaceutical interventions The intervention literature for quantitative evaluations of non-pharmaceutical interventions is of a good methodological quality. In contrast, qualitative studies – which can provide valuable insight into the lived experience of risk and intervention – are both relatively scarce and also of generally poor quality when assessed against qualitative research benchmarks. Non-pharmaceutical interventions that have been evaluated for the prevention of suicide are shown in Table 4.3, along with those demonstrating evidence of unequivocally favourable effects.

A substantial number of studies evaluating non-pharmaceutical interventions for the prevention of completed suicide ($N = 11$, 32%) present no formal analysis of data, quantitative or otherwise. Clearly, these studies represent something of a missed opportunity. With respect to the remainder, *no* evidence of any maintained reduction in suicide attributable to the intervention was found for training GPs, integrated versus standard treatment, school-based prevention programmes, programmes for the elderly, 'other' public health programmes, neurosurgery, or electroconvulsive therapy (ECT). Some of these null findings do, however, merit closer attention. The training of health professionals, for example, is a particular goal of the NHS in the context of suicidal behaviour, as evidenced by the available national guidelines. Yet three suitably powered and well-conducted studies (Morriss *et al.*, 2005; Owens, Lloyd and Campbell, 2004; Rutz and Walinder, 1992) failed to identify any long-term reduction in suicides as a result of training GPs to recognize and treat mental health disorders, in particular depression. Direct evidence from Morriss *et al.* (2005) and *indirect* evidence from Rutz and Walinder (1992) (the latter based on overall population rates rather than direct outcomes from the study participants as such) suggest that there may be an initial 'training effect', but that, if so, this is restricted to the immediate time period around the training and that regular ongoing training would therefore be necessary to maintain any effect. Given that Owens and colleagues (2004) found no such effect in a very well-conducted trial set in the United Kingdom, and that the costs of such regular training rolled out at a national level are likely to be high, it is unclear that this represents an intervention that is likely to prove viable as a national strategy in the immediate future.

The failure to identify any reduction in suicide as a consequence of integrating the care pathway (Nordentoft *et al.*, 2002) also runs counter to prevailing principles of ideal practice. Further, more broadly-based evaluation is likely to be warranted here, however, since the study focused on one population sub-group (people with first episode schizophrenia) and the most salient outcome with respect to completed suicide was the presence of command hallucinations. (Note that this does not run counter to the findings of Hawton *et al.*, (2005a) cited earlier, since in the latter review command hallucinations were the one exception to the 'protective' effect of hallucinations overall.)

The overall failure to identify any significant impact on suicide for a diverse range of public health programmes, defined as population-level educational or other initiatives, is of greater note since such initiatives are both a recurrent theme in national health policy

Table 4.3 Non-pharmaceutical interventions evaluated in the research literature.

Intervention	Behaviour targeted for prevention			
	Completed suicide	Attempted suicide	Self-harm	Suicidal ideation
Behavioural activation training for depression			*	
Bibliotherapy		* √	*	
Brief manual-assisted cognitive therapy			*	
Case management by trained GPs			*	
Change in hospital protocol				*
Cognitive behaviour therapy		*		*
Coordinated care plus intensive outreach		*		
Developmental group psychotherapy			*	*
Dialectical behaviour therapy		*	* √	*
Differential reinforcement			*	
Doing nothing (non-intervention)				*
Drug misuse programmes		*		*
Electroconvulsive therapy (ECT)	*		*	
Electromagnetic field therapy				*
Empowerment-based parent education groups			*	*
General hospital admission versus discharge			*	*
Home-based family intervention			*	* √
Hypno-behavioural treatment			*	
Integrated treatment versus standard treatment	*	*		*
Intensive inpatient psychotherapy		*		
Intermediate care management programme in prison		* √		
Interpersonal and social rhythm therapy		*		
Interpersonal psychotherapy		*	*	
Intervention by psychiatrists and family versus GP				*
Intervention in the A&E setting				* √
Introduction of trained mental health services in rural areas		*		
Meeting patient's treatment preferences				*
Motivational visits to 'non-compliant' patients		* √		
Multi-modal therapies	* √			*
Neurosurgery	*	* √		
Nurse training			*	
Occupational therapy				*
Ongoing contact	* √	*	*	*

(Continued)

Table 4.3   (*Continued*)

Intervention	Behaviour targeted for prevention			
	Completed suicide	Attempted suicide	Self-harm	Suicidal ideation
Palliative care for cancer patients	*			
Prison-based programmes	*			
Proactively involving the patient in therapy				*
Problem-solving therapy				*
Programmes for elderly people	*			
Programmes for military personnel	*	*		*
Psychoanalytic psychotherapy				*
Psychoanalytically-oriented partial hospitalization		* ✓	*	
Psychodynamic interpersonal therapy			*	*
Public health programmes	*	*		*
Residential versus community treatment				*
Restriction of access to means	* ✓	*		* ✓
School-based prevention programmes	*	* ✓		* ✓
Short-term hospitalization in a crisis centre				*
Step-down care versus long-term residential or community care		* ✓	*	
Stress inoculation training			*	
Suicide prevention centres	* ✓	* ✓		* ✓
Telephone intervention style				*
Token economy/time out			*	
Token for re-admission		*		
Training GPs to recognize and treat mental health disorders	*			
Training health and other professionals				*
Training health professionals/non-professionals		*		
Treatment matched to cognitive distortion				*
Writing with cognitive change or exposure				*

* Target behaviours where non-pharmaceutical interventions have been tested.
✓ Evidence of unequivocally favourable effects.

and a popular focus of research. Nearly one-third of the studies identified by Leitner, Barr and Hobby (2008) as evaluating non-pharmaceutical interventions to prevent suicide evaluated public health initiatives. Unfortunately, fewer than one-half of these presented concrete empirical data. While the anecdotal evidence favours public health initiatives, where hard statistical evidence is presented (cf. Metha, Weber and Webb, 1998) this apparent effect tends to melt away. Exceptions to this general principle are public health initiatives that are targeted on a specific population or population sub-group and involve quite intense input (e.g., May *et al.*, 2005; Oyama *et al.*, 2004, 2006a, 2006b). In essence, these forms of 'public health intervention' are closer in format to intensive outreach than to the more distanced population-level educational initiative usually favoured in national campaigns.

Non-pharmaceutical evidence-based interventions identified by Leitner and colleagues (2008) that were aimed at specific suicidal behaviours include the following:

Completed suicide No specific intervention is supported by more than one or two studies. However, there is some evidence to support four approaches: restriction of access to means (primarily studied at the population level and in the context of restriction of access to firearms (e.g., Brent *et al.*, 1993; Leenaars *et al.*, 2003); treatment provision via specialist suicide prevention centres (Leenaars and Lester, 2004; Miller *et al.*, 1984); offering ongoing support and contact to the suicidal person (e.g., De, Carollo and Dello, 1995); and multi-component interventions (e.g., Knox *et al.*, 2003).

Attempted suicide A broad range of interventions has been evaluated for the prevention of attempted suicide but, again, outcomes have proven rather equivocal. The majority of public health programmes evaluated with respect to attempted suicide have taken place in schools. The specific nature of the interventions evaluated vary, but the general model followed is either 'informational' (educational initiatives directed at allowing school children to gain a better understanding of the nature of suicidal behaviour, in particular, signs of risk) or 'supportive' (crisis counselling, encouraging help-seeking, peer support and so on). Interestingly, the three studies showing concrete evidence of positive outcomes (Aseltine and DeMartino, 2004; Thompson, Eggert and Herting, 2000; Thompson *et al.*, 2001) combine elements of *both* educational and supportive components. Taken together, the three studies suggest that the combination of educational/practical 'skills building' sessions combined with social and/or crisis support by peers, teachers, or specialists may be effective in helping to reduce attempted suicide in young people.

Of the remaining approaches outlined, firm evidence of effectiveness in reducing attempted suicide is available from eight studies. These include service delivery through a specialist centre (Nordentoft *et al.*, 2005); 'step-down' care (Chiesa and Fonagy, 2003; Chiesa *et al.*, 2004); intermediate care for prison inmates (Condelli, Bradigan and Holanchock, 1997); bibliotherapy (Evans *et al.*, 1999); neurosurgery (Sachdev and Sachdev, 2005); psycho-analytically oriented partial hospitalization for people with borderline personality disorder (Bateman and Fonagy, 1999); and motivational visits by nurses to 'non-compliant' patients (van Heeringen *et al.*, 1995). Note that the latter study might perhaps raise some ethical concerns if the intervention were to be carried out in clinical practice, since it would involve contacting people who have already indicated that they do not wish to engage with the intervention being offered. This highlights the point that not all interventions that may show evidence of effectiveness in the research context are naturally suited to transfer into the clinical setting. Unfortunately, the 'implementation' phase of an intervention is an aspect of evaluation that has been consistently ignored in the research literature to date.

It is noteworthy that studies evaluating either CBT or DBT for the prevention of attempted suicide have been equivocal and so are not marked as having 'unequivocally

favourable effects' in Table 4.3. Since the range of studies addressing other psychological therapies for this behaviour also failed to show positive outcomes, it may be
that attempted suicide is more intractable to psychological intervention than self-harm
without acknowledged 'intent'. Alternatively, it may be that the tailoring of the therapy
to individual client groups' and individuals' needs is of importance. Leitner, Barr, and
Hobby (2008) noted that studies evaluating psychological and cognitive therapies in the
context of self-harm were more likely to focus on a specific patient group.

Self-harm Despite the relative ubiquity of self-harm in the general population, no studies evaluating public health initiatives for self-harm were identified in the 2008 review
by Leitner and colleagues. This contrasts quite starkly with the available literature for
completed and attempted suicide. The focus with regard to self-harm seems to be primarily on individual-level interventions, in particular, psychological/psychotherapeutic
interventions. Of those studies providing data, the majority were also unable to identify positive outcomes. The interventions evaluated that *failed* to identify any positive
change include a number of approaches that are common coinage in clinical practice,
specifically, specialist nurse training, family intervention, general hospital admission,
individual case management/counselling by trained GPs, parent education groups, interpersonal psychotherapy, and related therapies (such as behavioural activation training
for depression). Since none of these interventions was evaluated by more than one study,
it is entirely possible that subsequent evaluations may find more promising outcomes.
As things stand, however, use of these very common interventions to prevent self-harm
cannot be said to be evidenced-based.

Approaches that showed promise in the Leitner, Barr, and Hobby (2008) review include
both the maintenance of ongoing contact and CBT. However, because further evidence
of their effectiveness in this context is still needed, these approaches cannot be listed
as having unequivocally favourable effects in Table 4.3. In fact, overall, only one currently practiced non-pharmaceutical intervention for self-harm (DBT) emerges as truly
'evidence-based', and this only in the broadest sense. While outcomes are consistently
positive and a relatively large number of studies ($N = 7$) are available, the bulk of information stems from one particular patient group only (people with personality disorder
or borderline personality disorder). Generalization beyond this client group is currently
not justified in clinical practice, although the consistency of outcomes is such that the
research evidence would justify *evaluation* of this intervention for other client groups in
clinical practice. Two other therapies that have shown promise, but have each been evaluated by only one study to date and cannot be considered to be supported by unequivocally
favourable evidence, are Psychodynamic Interpersonal Therapy (Guthrie *et al.*, 2001) and
Psychoanalytically Oriented Partial Hospitalization (Bateman and Fonagy, 1999, a study
that also showed positive outcomes for the prevention of attempted suicide).

Suicidal ideation The range of interventions evaluated for the prevention of suicidal
ideation is particularly broad and diverse. However, outcomes again suggest little or no
support for the majority of interventions that have been evaluated, many of which are
also routinely implemented in clinical practice. Public health programmes (notably in
schools) have been a particular focus for interventions for suicidal ideation, but again
fail to find substantive support from available studies. Exceptions to this rule (e.g.,
Houck, Darnell and Lussman, 2002; Orbach and Bar-Joseph, 1993), map the approaches
identified as promising with respect to completed and attempted suicide in combining

'skills training' with ongoing support. Similarly, targeted public health interventions, such as culturally tailored programmes (e.g., LaFromboise and Howard, 1995) also show promise. Aside from these quite specific and fairly intensive 'public health' programmes, there is little support for this consistently popular method of intervention. This appears to be a common theme across the spectrum of suicidal behaviour where such 'broad brush' programmes have been evaluated.

A similar commonality of outcome across the behavioural spectrum is shown by the positive outcomes identified for service provision via suicide prevention centres in preventing suicidal ideation and, perhaps more surprisingly in this context, restriction of access to means. Other interventions with evidence of positive outcomes in reducing suicidal ideation include family therapy for children who self-poison (Harrington *et al.*, 1998, 2000) and interventions in the A&E setting designed to educate families about self-harming behaviour (e.g., Rotheram-Borus *et al.*, 1996).

All other studies identified by Leitner and colleagues (2008) as evaluating interventions to prevent or reduce suicidal ideation indicate either equivocal or no support for the intervention in question. Of those studies with 'equivocal' support, the most promising interventions (supported by at least one study with adequate statistical analysis) are the range of cognitive therapies, including DBT, CBT, cognitive therapy, interpersonal psychodynamic therapy or problem-solving therapy (e.g., Brent *et al.*, 1997; Brown *et al.*, 2004; Guthrie *et al.*, 2001; Joiner, Voetz and Rudd, 2001; Low *et al.*, 2001); primary care treatment guidelines for care management of the depressed elderly (Bruce *et al.*, 2004); the provision of social support networks (Eagles *et al.*, 2003); and telephone counselling (e.g., King *et al.*, 2003). These interventions would, however, require substantive further evaluation to confirm their effectiveness.

A Way Forward

A very brief summary of the evidence outlined above is that research into the risk factors underpinning suicidal behaviour and the interventions that may help to prevent such behaviours has for a long time been the Cinderella of health care research. As a consequence, the available evidence, although broad-ranging, has a scattergun profile with only a very small number of studies evaluating each possibility. This is particularly true in the context of intervention research, though risk factors have been much better explored. However, an outstanding issue here is that those factors that reliably predict risk at the population level (e.g., age, poverty) tend to be factors that are intransigent to change. In contrast, factors identified as potentially important at the individual level (e.g., substance abuse) find only equivocal support within the research evidence. Suicidal behaviour currently remains a complex and poorly understood phenomenon, and even the 'diagnosis' remains to an extent controversial. Is suicidal behaviour a pathology or a natural response to the human condition? How can one define 'intent'? Can a line be drawn between 'self-harm' and 'attempted suicide'?

Given the subjective and uncertain 'pathology' of suicidal behaviour and the weak evidence base for effective interventions, the key to 'best practice' must be for the clinician to establish common ground with the client (see also Chapter 2). Currently, both clinician and client must also accept that there are limitations to the clinical role. In recognizing the individual nature of suicidal behaviour and the equivocal evidence for risk profiles, clinicians (as per the guidelines) need to question and seek proactively to inform and update their clinical practice, both via reference to principles relating to a well-constructed philosophy of care and via reference to improvements in the evidence base as this develops. Current clinical practice frequently relies on pharmaceutical interventions, but clinicians need to maintain a level of rational scepticism about all approaches to intervention until the emerging evidence base is substantially stronger. Interventions that are currently practised, but that have little or no research evidence, should be implemented only in the context of 'evaluative research' to provide the outcome data that are currently lacking.

It can readily be seen that one clear priority is to improve the evidence base, notably with respect to possible interventions and risk assessment (and/or risk *prediction*) at the individual level. It is unclear that further funding to address this issue will be made available anytime soon. In comparison with physical health disorders, which account for a similar number of deaths and reduced quality of life, research into suicidal behaviour currently attracts only a trivial research budget. This has remained the case despite the high profile given to suicide prevention in national health initiatives over the last decade. Pragmatically then, in the absence of any substantive investment of capital, the most cost-effective way of addressing the inadequate evidence base is to utilize to a much greater extent existing and forward-going routine data and to incorporate where possible an evaluative element into ongoing practices.

This obvious and yet novel approach has a couple of implications. First, clinicians and researchers will need to work closely together on a regular and ongoing basis. Secondly, the many known problems with the collection and collation of accurate and objective routine data need to be addressed as a matter of urgency. Both issues have been tackled effectively in a small number of monitoring centres across the United Kingdom. However, to provide the evidence base we need to support effective clinical practice, this approach needs to be extended far more widely. The current focus on monitoring risk also needs to be supplemented with a gathering of evidence relating to the interventions currently employed and novel interventions that may safely be evaluated in the course of clinical practice.

Finally, it is important to recognize that there are some fundamental gaps in our evidence base, which, until resolved, make 'best practice' in the strictest sense something of a distant goal. One such fundamental gap is the fact that, currently, we have very little information on the extent of self-harm in the population. We know that there is likely to be a significant 'hidden' population of people who self-harm, but we have no evidence regarding either the likely size of this population or the epidemiology of suicidal behaviour within it. With such very fundamental gaps in our knowledge base, forward planning and structuring of services according to need is likely to remain an uphill struggle. Perhaps focusing research efforts on building the evidence to bridge these gaps is the first priority if we are aiming for 'best practice' to become 'usual practice'.

References

Arsenault-Lapierre, G., Kim, C., and Turecki, G. (2004). Psychiatric diagnoses in 3,275 suicides: A meta-analysis, *BMC Psychiatry*, 4 November, 4, 37.

Aseltine, R. H. and DeMartino, R. (2004). An outcome evaluation of the SOS Suicide Prevention Program, *American Journal of Public Health*, 94, 446–451.

Baldessarini, R. J., Tondo, L., and Hennen, J. (2003). Lithium treatment and suicide risk in major affective disorders: Update and new findings, *Journal of Clinical Psychiatry*, 64, Suppl. 5, 44–52.

Bateman, A. and Fonagy, P. (1999). Effectiveness of partial hospitalization in the treatment of borderline personality disorder: A randomized controlled trial, *American Journal of Psychiatry*, 156, 1563–1569.

Bostwick, J. M. and Pankratz, V. S. (2000). Affective disorders and suicide risk: A re-examination, *American Journal of Psychiatry*, 157(12), 1925–1932.

Brent, D. A., Perper, J. A., Moritz, G., *et al.* (1993). Firearms and adolescent suicide. A community case-control study, *American Journal of Diseases of Children*, 147, 1066–1071.

Brent, D. A., Holder, D., Kolko, D., *et al.* (1997) A clinical psychotherapy trial for adolescent depression comparing cognitive, family, and supportive therapy, *Archives of General Psychiatry*, 54, 877–885.

Brown, G. K., Newman, C. F., Charlesworth, S. E., *et al.* (2004). An open clinical trial of cognitive therapy for borderline personality disorder, *Journal of Personality Disorders*, 18, 257–271.

Bruce, M. L., Ten Have, T. R., Reynolds, C. F., III, *et al.* (2004). Reducing suicidal ideation and depressive symptoms in depressed older primary care patients: A randomized controlled trial, *Journal of the American Medical Association*, 291, 1081–1091.

Cherpitel, C. J., Borges, G. L. G., and Wilcox, H. C. (2004). Acute alcohol use and suicidal behavior: A review of the literature, *Alcoholism: Clinical and Experimental Research*, 28(5), 18S–28S.

Chiesa, M. and Fonagy, P. (2003). Psychosocial treatment for severe personality disorder. 36-month follow-up, *British Journal of Psychiatry*, 183, 356–362.

Chiesa, M., Fonagy, P., Holmes, J., *et al.* (2004). Residential versus community treatment of personality disorders: A comparative study of three treatment programs, *American Journal of Psychiatry*, 161, 1463–1470.

Condelli, W. S., Bradigan, B., and Holanchock, H. (1997). Intermediate care programs to reduce risk and better manage inmates with psychiatric disorders, *Behavioural Sciences and the Law*, 15, 459–467.

De, L. D., Carollo, G., and Dello, B. M. (1995). Lower suicide rates associated with a Tele-Help/Tele-Check service for the elderly at home, *American Journal of Psychiatry*, 152, 632–634.

Department of Health (2002). *Mental Health Policy Implementation Guide: Adult acute inpatient care provision*. Department of Health, London, available at www.dh.gov.uk/publications.

Department of Health (2009). *Best Practice in Managing Risk: Principles and Evidence for Best Practice in the Assessment and Management of Risk to Self and Others in Mental Health Services*. Department of Health, London, available at www.dh.gov.uk/publications.

Eagles, J. M., Carson, D. P., Begg, A., *et al.* (2003). Suicide prevention: A study of patients' views, *British Journal of Psychiatry*, 182, 261–265.

Evans, K., Tyrer, P., Catalan, J., *et al.* (1999). Manual-assisted cognitive-behaviour therapy (MACT): A randomized controlled trial of a brief intervention with bibliotherapy in the treatment of recurrent deliberate self-harm, *Psychological Medicine*, 29, 19–25.

Fleischmann, A., Bertolote, J. M., Belfer, M., and Beautrais, A. (2005). Completed suicide and psychiatric diagnoses in young people: A critical examination of the evidence, *American Journal of Orthopsychiatry*, 75(4), 676–683.

Guthrie, E., Kapur, N., Kway-Jones, K., *et al.* (2001). Randomised controlled trial of brief psychological intervention after deliberate self-poisoning, *British Medical Journal*, 21, 135–138.

Harrington, R., Kerfoot, M., Dyer, E., *et al.* (1998). Randomized trial of a home-based family intervention for children who have deliberately poisoned themselves, *Journal of the American Academy of Child and Adolescent Psychiatry*, 37, 512–518.

Harrington, R., Kerfoot, M., Dyer, E., *et al.* (2000). Deliberate self-poisoning in adolescence: Why does a brief family intervention work in some cases and not others? *Journal of Adolescence*, 23, 13–20.

Hart, S. D., Michie, C., and Cooke, D. J. (2007). Precision of Actuarial Risk Assessment Instruments: Evaluating the 'margins of error' of group versus individual predictions of violence, *British Journal of Psychiatry*, 190, s60–s65.

Hawton, K., Rodham, K., Evans, E., *et al.* (2002). Deliberate self-harm in adolescents: Self-report survey in schools in England, *British Medical Journal,* 325(7374), 1207–1211.

Hawton, K., Sutton, L., Haw, C., Sinclair, J., and Deeks, J. J. (2005a). Schizophrenia and suicide: Systematic review of risk factors, *British Journal of Psychiatry,* 187(1), 9–20.

Hawton, K., Sutton, L., Haw, C., Sinclair, J., and Harriss, L. (2005b). Suicide and attempted suicide in bipolar disorder: A systematic review of risk factors, *Journal of Clinical Psychiatry,* 66(6), 693–704.

Heeringen, C., van, Jannes, S., Buylaert, W., *et al.* (1995). The management of non-compliance with referral to out-patient after-care among attempted suicide patients: A controlled intervention study, *Psychological Medicine,* 25(5), 963–970.

Hem, E., Berg, A. M., and Ekeberg, A. O. (2001). Suicide in police – A critical review, *Suicide Life Threat Behaviour,* 31(2), 224–233.

Houck, G. M., Darnell, S., and Lussman, S. (2002). A support group intervention for at-risk female high school students, *Journal of School Nursing,* 18, 212–218.

James, A., Lai, F. H., and Dahl, C. (2004). Attention deficit hyperactivity disorder and suicide: A Review of possible associations, *Acta Psychiatrica Scandinavica,* 110(6), 408–415.

Joiner, T. E., Jr., Voelz, Z. R., and Rudd, M. D. (2001). For suicidal young adults with comorbid depressive and anxiety disorders, problem-solving treatment may be better than treatment as usual, *Professional, Psychology, Research and Practice,* 32, 278–282.

King, R., Nurcombe, B., Bickman, L., *et al.* (2003). Telephone counselling for adolescent suicide prevention: Changes in suicidality and mental state from beginning to end of a counselling session, *Suicide and Life Threatening Behaviour,* 33, 400–411.

Knox, K. L., Litts, D. A., Talcott, G. W., *et al.* (2003). Risk of suicide and related adverse outcomes after exposure to a suicide prevention programme in the US Air Force: Cohort study, *British Medical Journal,* 327, 1376.

LaFromboise, T. and Howard, P. B. (1995). The Zuni life skills development curriculum: Description and evaluation of a suicide prevention program. *Journal of Counselling Psychology,* 42, 479–486.

Lalovic, A., and Turecki, G. (2002) Meta-analysis of the association between tryptophan hydroxylase and suicidal behavior, *American Journal of Medical Genetics,* 8, 114(5), 533–540.

Leenaars, A. A., Moksony, F., Lester, D., *et al.* (2003). The impact of gun control (Bill C-51) on suicide in Canada, *Death Studies,* 27, 103–124.

Leenaars, A. A. and Lester, D. (2004). The impact of suicide prevention centers on the suicide rate in the Canadian provinces, *Crisis,* 25, 65–68.

Leitner, M., Barr, W., and Hobby, L. (2008). *Effectiveness of Interventions to Prevent Suicide and Suicidal Behaviour: A Systematic Review.* Edinburgh: Scottish Government Social Research, ISBN 978-0-7559-6904-3, available at www.scotland.gov.uk/Resource/Doc/208329/0055247.pdf.

Li, D., Duan, Y., and He, L. (2006). Association study of serotonin 2A receptor (5-HT2A) gene with schizophrenia and suicidal behavior using systematic meta-analysis, *Biochemical and Biophysical Research Communications,* 340(3), 1006–1015.

Lindeman, S., Laara, E., Hakko, H., and Lonnqvist, J. (1996). A systematic review on gender-specific suicide mortality in medical doctors, *British Journal of Psychiatry,* 168(3), 274–279.

Low, G., Jones, D., Duggan, C., *et al.* (2001). The treatment of deliberate self-harm in borderline personality disorder using dialectical behaviour therapy: A pilot study in a high security hospital, *Behavioural and Cognitive Psychotherapy,* January, 85–92.

May, P. A., Serna, P., Hurt, L., *et al.* (2005). Outcome evaluation of a public health approach to suicide prevention in an American Indian tribal nation, *American Journal of Public Health,* 95, 1238–1244.

McLean, J., Maxwell, M., Platt, S., *et al.* (2008). *Risk and Protective Factors for Suicide and Suicidal Behaviour: A Literature Review.* Edinburgh: Scottish Government Social Research, available at www.scotland.gov.uk/Publications/2008/11/28141444/0.

McMillan, D., Gilbody, S., Beresford, E., and Neilly, L. (2007). Can we predict suicide and non-fatal self-harm with the Beck Hopelessness Scale? A meta-analysis, *Psychological Medicine*, 37, 769–778.

Meltzer, H., Lader, D., Corbin, T., *et al.* (2002). *Non-Fatal Suicidal Behaviour Among Adults Aged 16 to 74 in Great Britain.* London: The Stationery Office.

Metha, A., Weber, B., and Webb, L. D. (1998). Youth suicide prevention: A survey and analysis of policies and efforts in the 50 states, *Suicide and Life Threatening Behaviours*, 28, 150–164.

Miller, H. L., Coombs, D. W., Leeper, J. D., *et al.* (1984). An analysis of the effects of suicide prevention facilities on suicide rates in the United States, *American Journal of Public Health*, 74, 340–343.

Morriss, R., Gask, L., Webb, R., *et al.* (2005). The effects on suicide rates of an educational intervention for front-line health professionals with suicidal patients (the STORM Project), *Psychological Medicine*, 35, 957–960.

Neeleman, J. (2001). A continuum of premature death. Meta-analysis of competing mortality in the psychosocially vulnerable, *International Journal of Epidemiology*, 30(1), 154–162.

Nordentoft, M., Jeppesen, P., Abel, M., *et al.* (2002). OPUS study: Suicidal behaviour, suicidal ideation and hopelessness among patients with first-episode psychosis. One year follow-up of a randomised controlled trial, *British Journal of Psychiatry*, Suppl., 43, s98–s106.

Nordentoft, M., Branner, J., Drejer, K., *et al.* (2005). Effect of a suicide prevention centre for young people with suicidal behaviour in Copenhagen, *European Psychiatry*, 20, 121–128.

Oerlinghausen, M. B., Wolf, T., Ahrens, B., *et al.* (1994). Mortality during initial and during later lithium treatment, *Acta Psychiatrica Scandinavica*, 90, 295–297.

Orbach, I. and Bar-Joseph, H. (1993). The impact of a suicide prevention program for adolescents on suicidal tendencies, hopelessness, ego identity, and coping, *Suicide and Life Threatening Behaviour*, 23, 120–129.

Owens, C., Lloyd, K. R., and Campbell, J. (2004). Access to health care prior to suicide: Findings from a psychological autopsy study, *British Journal of General Practice*, 54, 279–281.

Oyama, H., Koida, J., Sakashita, T., *et al.* (2004). Community-based prevention for suicide in elderly by depression screening and follow-up, *Community Mental Health Journal*, 40, 249–263.

Oyama, H., Ono, Y., Watanabe, N., *et al.* (2006a). Local community intervention through depression screening and group activity for elderly suicide prevention, *Psychiatry and Clinical Neuroscience*, 60, 110–114.

Oyama, H., Goto, M., Fujita, M., *et al.* (2006b). Preventing elderly suicide through primary care by community-based screening for depression in rural Japan, *Crisis*, 27 (2), 58–65.

Palmer, B. A., Pankratz, V. S., and Bostwick, J. M. (2005). The lifetime risk of suicide in schizophrenia: a re-examination, *Archives of General Psychiatry*, 62(3), 247–253.

Platt, S. and Hawton, K. (2000). Suicidal behaviour and the labour market, in K. Hawton and K. van Heeringen (eds), *The International Handbook of Suicide and Attempted Suicide.* Chichester: John Wiley & Sons, Ltd., pp. 309–384.

Pompili, M., Girardi, P., Ruberto, A., and Tatarelli, R. (2005). Suicide in the epilepsies: A meta-analytic investigation of 29 cohorts, *Epilepsy and Behavior*, 7(2), 305–310.

Rehkopf, D. H. and Buka, S. L. (2006). The association between suicide and the socio-economic characteristics of geographical areas: A systematic review, *Psychological Medicine*, 36(2), 145–157.

Rotheram-Borus, M. J., Piacentini, J., Van, R. R., *et al.* (1996). Enhancing treatment adherence with a specialized emergency room program for adolescent suicide attempters, *Journal of the American Academy of Child and Adolescent Psychiatry*, 35, 654–663.

Rutz, W. K. L. von and Walinder, J. (1992). Long-term effects of an educational program for general practitioners given by the Swedish Committee for the Prevention and Treatment of Depression, *Acta Psychiatrica Scandinavica*, 85, 83–88.

Sachdev, P. S. and Sachdev, J. (2005). Long-term outcome of neurosurgery for the treatment of resistant depression, *Journal of Neuropsychiatry and Clinical Neuroscience*, 17, 478–485.

Sackett, D. L (1979). Bias in analytic research, *Journal of Chronic Diseases*, 32 (1–2), 51–63.

Saunders, K. E. and Hawton, K. (2006). Suicidal behaviour and the menstrual cycle, *Psychological Medicine*, 36(7), 901–912, epub 30 Mar. Review.

Shadigan, E. M. and Bauer, S. T. (2005). Pregnancy-associated death: A qualitative systematic review of homicide and suicide, *Obstetrical and Gynecological Survey*, 60(3), 183–190.

Speckens, A. E. and Hawton, K. (2005). Social problem solving in adolescents with suicidal behavior: a systematic review, *Suicide and Life Threatening Behaviour*, 35(4), 365–387.

Thompson, E. A., Eggert, L. L., and Herting, J. R. (2000). Mediating effects of an indicated prevention program for reducing youth depression and suicide risk behaviors, *Suicide and Life Threatening Behaviour*, 30, 252–271.

Thompson, E. A., Eggert, L. L., Randell, B. P., *et al.* (2001). Evaluation of indicated suicide risk prevention approaches for potential high school dropouts, *American Journal of Public Health*, 91, 742–752.

Tondo, L., Baldessarini, R. J., Hennen, J., *et al.* (1998). Lithium treatment and risk of suicidal behavior in bipolar disorder patients, *Journal of Clinical Psychiatry*, 59, 405–414.

Wilcox, H. C., Conner, K. R., and Caine, E. D. (2004). Association of alcohol and drug use disorders and completed suicide: An empirical review of cohort studies, *Drug and Alcohol Dependence*, 76, Suppl., S11–S19.

Wulsin, L. R., Vaillant, G. E., and Wells, V. E. (1999). A systematic review of the mortality of depression, *Psychosomatic Medicine*, 61(1), 6–17.

5

Understanding and Managing Violence in Mental Health Services

Richard Whittington, James McGuire, Tilman Steinert and Beverley Quinn

Introduction

Successful risk management in mental health is based on the complex task of drawing together knowledge and expertise from many different sources and then making a decision on the best way forward. One of the key sources that should underpin effective decisions on how to work with problems of violence is the research evidence base relating to it. This chapter will examine research relating to some of the key aspects of violence, including both the causes of violence and interventions to treat or manage the problem. Awareness of the evidence base should enable practitioners to make more informed choices when working with potentially violent service users. In addition, service users themselves and their carers should be able to engage more effectively with the care planning process if they have an appreciation of the key themes emerging from this global research effort. This chapter is not a systematic review, but instead attempts selectively to pick out some key themes in the violence literature and where possible to identify some more in-depth reviews and studies which the interested reader might want to pursue. With such effort being made to address relevant issues in the violence research literature, there is much that has been produced in recent years that will be useful and of interest to the practitioner and others.

There is immediately a problem, though. Practitioners know they need to know 'the evidence', but the literature in this area is both vast and rapidly expanding. Approximately 60 to 70 new studies evaluating an intervention for violence by offenders or people with mental health problems were published each year in the 1990s and 2000s, and more than 200,000 articles that in some way relate to the interface between violence and mental health have been published in the past half-century (Leitner *et al.*, 2006). Even focusing on those studies deemed high quality in the standard hierarchies of evidence does not help much as over 400 randomized controlled trials relating to violence and mental health have been published over the same time period (Cure *et al.*, 2005). This mass of

Self-Harm and Violence: Towards Best Practice in Managing Risk in Mental Health Services, First Edition.
Edited by Richard Whittington and Caroline Logan.
© 2011 John Wiley & Sons, Ltd. Published 2011 by John Wiley & Sons, Ltd.

information contains much that could be of value to those who want to be informed, but anybody who wants to use the evidence to inform their practice or daily choices will inevitably struggle to digest and incorporate it meaningfully into their work. It must be sifted and refined to get access to the relevant ideas and to allow them to be evaluated. This chapter, therefore, aims to identify some of the key themes in the violence literature and to consider some of the relevant evidence that may be of use to practitioners. It will examine the broad concept of aggression, the factors that are significant in raising the risk of violence occurring in specific situations and the main psychological and pharmacological interventions available to mental health services and their users.

The Concept of Aggression

Before turning to the evidence, it is important to clarify the concept of violence and to map out the various dimensions along which any particular act of violence can be analysed. First, a definition of violence is needed to ensure the observed behaviour is properly classified. *Violence* here refers to the physical act of assaulting another person with a harmful intention, and *aggression* to the wider concept incorporating both physical and psychological assault (Baron and Richardson, 1994). Risk management is, of course, often concerned with pathways between low-level psychological aggression such as abuse and threats, which may act as early warning signs, on the one hand, and physical violence, on the other.

While apparently straightforward, such definitions cover a hugely diverse range of human behaviours and, consequently, aggression is a hugely complex problem to explain, predict, and prevent. Single-factor explanations either in research or clinical practice are unlikely to contribute much to understanding or solving either a theoretical problem or the problems experienced by an individual service user (Volavka and Nolan, 2008). It is more productive to recognize the different types of aggressive act or the various dimensions along which an event can be analysed. One key dimension for understanding an act of aggression is the distinction drawn between affective (or reactive, hostile, impulsive) aggression, on the one hand, and instrumental (or predatory, provocative) aggression, on the other (Cornell *et al.*, 1996). The processes underlying these two types of aggression are often divergent and call for different types of intervention in both non-clinical and mental health settings. The distinction between distal and proximal factors in any violent encounter is also crucial (Geen, 2001; Krahe, 2001). Distal factors are much removed in time and space from the actual violent situation under consideration (e.g., a history of childhood abuse), while proximal factors operate at or near the actual time of the event (e.g., being intoxicated, hearing voices giving orders). These dimensions are similar in some ways to the distinction of static and dynamic risk factors commonly used to structure approaches to risk assessment and management (Douglas and Skeem, 2005). Clearly, distal, static factors require a different, longer-term focus for intervention (e.g., violence prevention through education), which will be beyond the scope of many care teams, while proximal factors are much more amenable to change by mental health professionals working with service users.

Violent Acts: Individual or Culture?

Because acts of violence are committed by individuals, attempts at explaining them generally focus on individual factors as the origin of them. In other words, the causal process is assumed to reside *within* the perpetrator of an aggressive act, and to be a product of some feature of his or her biological or psychological make-up. Certainly, individual or personal factors are one important category of variables in contributing to violence and are the focus of much research. However, in order to gain a fuller understanding of violence in its various forms, it is important to take account of situational or contextual variables (Gadon *et al.*, 2006). They can include factors in the immediate surroundings or environment in which the violence took place and larger-scale and more diffuse influences categorized under the broad heading of 'culture'; violent neighbourhoods and disempowering inpatient ward cultures are two examples of direct relevance to violence in mental health settings. Such influences are often highly relevant and may be critical, but are the focus of far less research. For the best explanation available, a model that embraces both types of variables (personal and situational) and also provides an understanding of how they interact is likely to be superior to one that concentrates on one class of variables alone.

When we consider the nature of human violence and the different ways it is manifested, it is also important to keep in mind that the most violent acts in history were committed by people who were mentally normal, that is, they were functioning within a range that would be considered acceptable in their communities and were not suffering from mental disorder of any kind. These acts account for a far higher proportion of violent death and injury than the types of behaviour classified as 'violent crime' in most societies. Leaving aside military conflict, which is considered legitimate under specified circumstances, this applies to genocide, which accounted for over 100 million deaths during the twentieth century, but which historical and psychological evidence suggests was largely carried out by people who would be considered 'ordinary' according to most criteria (Staub, 1989, 2003; Waller, 2007). It can also apply to what has been called structural violence, such as avoidable mortality among children under five, gender-selective abortion, female genital mutilation, socially approved spousal abuse, dowry killing, and related forms of harm (Roberts, 2008).

This tension between the psychological and the sociological levels of explanation has been a feature of thinking about violence for many years and integration remains a desirable goal (Douglas and Skeem, 2005). Violence can be viewed both criminologically and clinically, and understanding the clinical problem can be enhanced by drawing upon criminological and social theories about violence, such as ideas about the role of social disorganization and dislocation (Silver, 2006). The rest of this chapter focuses on individual factors, and there are important lessons that have been learned from extensive research in this area, but this social context is always an important backdrop to this discussion.

How Does Childhood Aggression Relate to Adult Aggression?

Violent acts do not just come out of nowhere. They are connected with other aspects of an individual's history, development, and personal functioning. Research has illuminated a number of aspects of this.

First, the tendency to act aggressively in a range of circumstances has been shown to be a relatively stable aspect of individual behaviour. This emerges from follow-up studies, covering periods of up to 21 years, in which ratings of aggressiveness have been correlated at two points in time (Olweus, 1979; Zumkley, 1994). As we might expect, the size of such correlations gradually diminishes as the gap between measurements increases, but for intermediate time periods of between five and eight years there are moderate to high correlations. Thus, for a proportion of developing children, there is significant continuity between displays of aggression at an early age and the likelihood of their being maintained across a period of several years into middle childhood. Aggression in middle childhood is predictive of aggression in the teenage years; and adolescent aggression is correlated with that in early adulthood. For longer time spans, on the other hand, the degree of continuity is lower. The possibility of risk assessment and prediction is based on using this type of evidence (among others).

Secondly, the kinds of factors that play a part in the continuities and discontinuities within this tendency are reasonably well understood, at least at a broad-brush level. Newly born children display differences in temperament prior to any opportunities for learning: for example, in overall activity level, motor restlessness, distractibility, and other respects. These appear to be inherent in their psychophysiology, and they may be genetic in origin. For a small proportion of children, there is a cluster of features in evidence collectively known as hyperactivity-impulsivity-attention deficit (HIA), which research suggests may be an early forerunner of a later aggressive tendency (Farrington, 2007). Various aspects of socialization overlaid on this pattern serve to increase or decrease the likelihood of aggressive behaviour emerging, and influence whether it is maintained and even magnified, or gradually defused. They include inconsistent parenting, modelling of aggression, a high level of familial conflict, coercive processes in family dynamics, experience of emotional degradation, physical or sexual victimization, and later, exposure to peer influence. Each of these has been shown to play some part in developmental pathways towards or away from expressing aggression (Loeber *et al.*, 2008). That is, they affect the extent to which aggression is translated into physical violence, and whether its pattern escalates over time.

The above outline suggests that aggressive behaviour is learned: that is, it is an outcome of a process of behavioural and cognitive change that is primarily a function of interactions with significant others in the social environment throughout development. This is the cognitive social learning theory of aggression and it draws on the psychological models propounded by Bandura (2001). There is, however, an alternative standpoint regarding this. According to this view, children do not start out somehow 'neutral' and learn to be aggressive; on the contrary, through an evolutionary process they are born with an aggressive propensity and learn through socialization to be non-aggressive. The research of Tremblay (2000, 2003), based on his work in the Montreal Longitudinal Developmental Project, has suggested that the peak age for aggressiveness is in early childhood, but that socialization processes instil in the majority of children an ability to control and suppress aggressive urges.

What Psychological Factors Make Violence More or Less Likely to Happen?

Psychological research on the development of aggression and violence draws on several principal sources. One is the findings from a series of more than 20 longitudinal studies that have been carried out, following age cohorts of participants through various phases of the life span (early childhood, middle childhood, adolescence, adulthood). These have been done at a number of sites around the world, though almost entirely in relatively richer, industrially developed nations (the United Kingdom, the United States, Canada, Denmark, Sweden, New Zealand), with the majority in the United States (Farrington, 2006). A second set of findings comes from cross-section group comparison studies, where data are collected from children, adolescents, or adults who have manifested aggression or violence and compared with corresponding data from a matched 'control' sample with no history of that behaviour. A third type of evidence comes from intervention trials, where an effort has been made to reduce levels of aggression. Where this has been found to be effective, it arguably provides a form of support for the theoretical model that informed the design of the intervention that was used (McGuire, 2004).

Criminological and psychological research has suggested that a number of variables can be identified as 'risk factors' for violence. However, they are not always distinct from those variables that are predictive of involvement in crime in general. They include:

(a) inappropriate parental modelling and discipline;
(b) low attainment in the school/work context;
(c) social support for crime and a network of criminally oriented associates;
(d) antisocial attitudes and cognitions;
(e) poor self-control, difficulty in suppressing or re-directing impulses;
(f) lack of pro-social activities and attachment to non-offending others;
(g) persistent or heavy substance abuse;
(h) antisocial personality.

For some specific manifestations of personal violence, other factors also play a part. They include, for example, poor control over anger (Novaco, 2007), or low levels of empathy (Gannon *et al.*, 2007), though evidence concerning them is not always consistent. Nevertheless, following the type of functional analysis to be briefly described below, these can provide useful 'targets of change' in intervention programmes both at the individual and group level.

Research has demonstrated the importance of separating psychological factors into what have been called 'criminogenic' and 'non-criminogenic' needs (Andrews, 2001; McGuire, 2004). The former are the risk factors that contribute to antisocial acts and, therefore, are the ones that, if changed, may result in reduced offending or other problem behaviour. The others include a range of separate needs (such as low mood or self-esteem), which may be targets of therapy or other initiatives, but would not be expected to yield outcomes in terms of reductions in aggression.

There is some evidence, though it cannot be regarded as wholly conclusive, that there are two patterns in antisocial behaviour by young people, defined as 'adolescence time limited' versus 'life course persistent' offending (Moffitt, 1993, 2003). As the term suggests, the latter form the group who are likely to continue offending into adulthood, and who may become repeatedly involved in the criminal justice or secure mental health systems. The presence of psychological risk factors that are predictive of involvement in crime underpins the potential importance of risk assessment as a procedure for making decisions concerning the allocation and management of those who have committed serious crimes.

While risk factors are important, attention has more recently moved towards identifying protective factors as well. Loeber *et al.* (2008) have proposed a range of terms for describing factors that reduce the likelihood of involvement in delinquency in the general population (*preventive promotive factors*), that predict desistance from offending among those who have done so previously (*remedial promotive factors*), or that predict a low probability of offending among individuals exposed to risk factors (*protective factors*) (de Vogel *et al.*, 2008). Identifying the third of these has proved to be very difficult as they are not simply the reverse of risk factors (e.g., absence of criminality among parents), but are separate influences that may override, or counter, the operation of risk factors when those are present.

During the process of socialization, even in stressful childhood circumstances, the presence of at least one secure attachment can provide emotional support and nourishment and ameliorate the effects of an otherwise criminogenic environment. Higher intelligence, achievement in school, and development of friendships with non-offending peers, can all have similar effects at a later age range, and enable children to develop resilience and embark on a pathway that avoids behavioural or mental health problems. The development of skills – problem-solving, social, coping, self-management, and other competences – for addressing every-day problems and solving them without resorting to antisocial acts, can also be significant in this respect. The availability of resources and opportunities that allow alternative routes to be followed is likely to be a pivotal component if an individual developing in the midst of aggravating risk factors is not to be influenced more by them.

Some of the evidence concerning this has emerged from the longitudinal studies to which reference was made earlier. Other portions of the evidence have emerged from studies of *primary prevention*: attempts to reduce the likelihood of harmful outcomes either in general populations, across communities, or in identified high-risk groups. Work of this kind, usually targeted towards developing children and their families, has shown beneficial effects through the introduction of parent training or family support programmes, and a range of allied initiatives (Farrington and Coid, 2003).

How is it possible to create an ethos in which the protective factors that have been identified can be extensively promoted, such as an environment in which they are more likely to flourish? This is a compelling question, and one to which only tentative answers can be offered. However, to return to issues raised earlier, there is strong evidence of an association between violence and social and economic inequality. Messner (2003) has reported an analysis of economic indicators of relative prosperity and comparative inequality and their association with rates of violent crime over time. Messner's summary of the evidence showed that 'the relative economic well-being of the population is one of the most reliable predictors of national rates of criminal violence' (2003, 713). Lowering the stresses that are placed upon families, reducing poverty and adversity, and expanding opportunities to live healthy and stable lives hold the most promising prospects in this regard. This is not simply an ideological position, but one supported by the best science currently available. At a macroeconomic and political level, therefore, reducing disparities in income and wealth may be the largest-scale preventive initiative that any nation could take.

What is the Relationship between Violence and Mental Disorder?

In order to make sense of an act of violence or of a pattern of aggressive or violent behaviour over time, it is necessary to gather a range of information about individuals, their histories, and the circumstances in which the actions occurred. Research has shown that there are common factors that influence the development of aggression, certain situations that are more likely than others to elicit aggressive responses, and a number of psychological variables that, if operative, will more easily induce some individuals rather than others to act in a violent way.

However, there are also numerous variations within this. The interconnections of factors that contribute to causing violence need to be understood at an individual level if the most appropriate action is to be taken to reduce the chances of its recurrence. Functional analysis and case formulation provide valuable tools in this process and the links between violence and mental disorder can be elucidated using these methods.

In a large-scale review of the evidence concerning prediction of violence in people with mental disorders, Bonta *et al.* (1998) found that the best predictors were not clinical variables, such as psychiatric diagnoses, but the same kinds of factors that have been shown to have predictive power in studies of offenders in general. They include 'static' risk factors such as age at first offence, number of previous convictions, and other 'criminological' variables. Recent reviews of the risk assessment research literature have lent support to the finding that measures using these variables alone are superior to others that incorporate other kinds of data such as clinical variables (Farrington, Jolliffe and Johnstone, 2008). These findings apply, however, to what can be concluded at an aggregate level, across large samples of prisoners or patients.

At an individual level, it remains essential to assess the influence of 'dynamic risk factors' that fluctuate over time and may have a crucial impact on the likelihood of a violent act at a particular moment, or in a particular set of circumstances. Delusional states, preoccupations with conflict, oscillations in anger, frustration, hostility, hatred, or other strong negative emotions need to be understood and monitored if risks are to be minimized and violent incidents averted. Attitudes of callousness, contempt, a willingness to exploit others, or other features of personality pathology are also established risk factors for employing violence to achieve goals. The role of substance abuse may be additionally significant, and some evidence suggests that heightened risk of violence among some psychiatric patients may be a function of this rather than of clinical variables in themselves (Steadman *et al.*, 1998). The configuration of these problems is likely to be unique in every case. Therefore, the relationship between violence and mental disorder is virtually never the same, even for individuals diagnosed with a particular type of disorder.

Are People with Mental Health Problems More Likely to be Aggressive than the Rest of the Population?

This question has been debated and researched extensively now and has major implications for society and for the degree of stigma faced by people with mental health problems. Some research suggests that serious mental disorders are associated with an elevated risk of violent offending (e.g., Silver *et al.*, 2008), though the extent of this is less than many people seem to assume. The whole issue has recently been thoroughly reviewed (Choe, Teplin and Abram, 2008). Comparisons across studies are always hampered by differences in the reference period (violent in the past two weeks or the past year?) and by basic definitions of what constitutes violence (e.g., arrest, self-reported aggression), but some conclusions are possible. Several American studies of community samples have indicated higher rates of violence among people with severe mental illness compared with base rates among people with no diagnosable disorder in the same communities. Figures cited for the Epidemiological Catchment Area (ECA) study (Swanson, 1994), for instance, indicate a rate of 2% for violence in the past year by people with no disorder compared with 7% for those with severe mental illness. More recently, the National Comorbidity Survey (Corrigan and Watson, 2005) has indicated rates of 12% for violence in the past year by people with active bipolar disorder but only 3% for those with current psychosis. The relative importance of substance use and the relative unimportance of psychosis compared with no disorder has been demonstrated in a British sample (Coid *et al.*, 2006). While these community samples considered people as members of the general public, other studies have looked at people recently discharged from hospital, including the MacArthur programme of studies (see below). Compared with the 2% baseline annual rate of violence for people in the community from the ECA study above, Steadman *et al.* (1998) reported a prevalence rate of 6.3% at one year among the discharged sample.

The great problem with these headline figures is that they rely on a blunt instrument in that all mental disorders are lumped together, or at best various broad categories are compared, for example, major mental disorders. In this way more precise descriptions of the key factors, such as particular types of symptom, are not picked up. We need greater precision to avoid all people with mental health problems being tarred with the same stigmatizing brush. If major disorders are considered specifically (i.e., schizophrenia and major affective disorder without substance abuse) rates of violence are higher in this group than in the community (16% versus 7%), but lower than those with a substance abuse diagnosis (35%), and much lower than that for people with both major mental disorder and substance abuse (43%; Swanson *et al.*, 1993, cited in Friedman, 2006). There are also repeated demonstrations that rates of violence are associated with antisocial personality disorder (Leitner *et al.*, 2006; Scott and Resnick, 2006), although there is circularity here since, unlike schizophrenia, the diagnosis itself includes the propensity towards violence.

Yet, to drill down further, much of the violence associated with schizophrenia is probably attributable to a specific sub-group with a particular set of symptoms. The most widely cited evidence on violence in the community by people discharged from hospital after an acute phase of mental disorder is the MacArthur Violence Risk Assessment Study (Monahan *et al.*, 2001). Some very specific types of hallucinations and thinking styles were found to be important: voices commanding a violent act; a generally suspicious attitude towards other people; and persistent thoughts or daydreaming about harming other people. These very specific risk factors may end up being inaccurately generalized and stigmatizing all service users with a diagnosis of major mental disorder.

Turning the question on its head, contemporary risk management is moving towards a bidirectional approach, which recognizes that people with mental health problems are very vulnerable to violence *from* other people and that in most cases this vulnerability is more important than any risk presented by the person with mental health problems towards others. There is clear evidence that people with mental health problems face a high risk of being assaulted (Schomerus *et al.*, 2008), with up to half of respondents reporting exposure to physical assault in some studies (Choe, Teplin, and Abram, 2008). This victimization is much higher for people with mental health problems who are women and/or homeless. This risk has often been obscured by the past emphasis on dangerousness. It is worth noting that the predictors of violent victimhood are similar to those for violence perpetration in that both are associated with a high level of positive symptomatology and substance abuse. Such a close association supports an interactive view of the nature of violence where victimhood and perpetrator status are usually very difficult to disentangle. Nor are people with mental health problems immune to all the various specific abuse problems recognized in the wider population, such as domestic violence against people, especially women, with schizophrenia (Friedman and Loue, 2007).

What are the Most Effective Ways of Judging the Risk of Violence?

The most significant development in this area over the past 20 years has been the proliferation of structured scales and tools which claim, with more or less credibility, to locate the individual service user on a continuum of risk. Several hundred structured scales relating to violence have been published since the 1970s, but very few of these have been systematically tested to see how well they perform in the real world. Nevertheless, those few that have been widely and rigorously evaluated over the past decade can be meaningfully compared in a number of ways to inform any choice that needs to be made. Such comparisons can be made on the basis of how accurate the instrument is in indicating the presence of a risk and the need for an intervention (accuracy, predictive validity), but also, and of increasing importance more recently, on a whole range of other factors that are pragmatically important such as clinical utility and cost. This leads to the vexed question of which instruments are 'best' and which, if any, should be recommended for use with particular populations and in specific services.

The *Best Practice* document (Department of Health, 2009) lists six tools designed for work with violent, antisocial, and offending behaviour and which have met a basic criterion of acceptability. The review underpinning the National Institute for Health and Clinical Excellence (NICE) (2005) guidelines for the management of imminent violence in acute settings examined a wide range of instruments including general measures of psychopathology (e.g., *Brief Psychiatric Rating Scale, Positive and Negative Symptom Scale*), structured checklists for recording the occurrence of violence (e.g., *Staff Observation of Aggression Scale, Modified Overt Aggression Scale*), as well as instruments more usually recognized as risk assessment tools (e.g., *Psychopathy Checklist* [PCL], *Historical-Clinical-Risk Management-20* [HCR-20]). The reviewers noted that there is little agreement across instruments on which risk factors are important or how they should be weighted, and they also noted the relative lack of research with these instruments in United Kingdom or other European settings. There is also a mismatch between the factors examined by leading risk assessment tools and the factors clinicians use in their everyday risk assessments (Elbogen *et al.*, 2002). For NICE, none of the examined instruments was found to stand out as the obvious gold standard, but actuarial and structured clinical judgement approaches were found to be equivalent to each other and equally superior to unstructured clinical judgement alone.

A more systematic head-to-head comparison of 20 instruments has been conducted by the Scottish Risk Management Authority (RMA, 2006) for its *Risk Assessment Tools Evaluation Directory* (RATED) framework. While this comparative assessment was designed with a very specific forensic population in mind, much of the evaluation can be drawn upon to further compare the various instruments now available. The tools deemed to have the best ability to identify a person's violence, sexual violence, or offending risk *level* in this review were the *STATIC-99* (sex offenders only), the *HCR-20*, the *Level of Service Inventory–Revised* (LSI-R) and both Revised and Screening versions of the *PCL*.

Structured clinical judgement approaches attempt to identify risk *factors* as well, or instead, in order to underpin effective formulation, and when the instruments were compared on this capacity, the *Spousal Assault Risk Assessment Guide* (SARA), the *LSI-R*, and the *Risk Assessment Guide Framework* (RAGF) were considered to have the strongest support. The issue of predictive validity has recently been taken further in a systematic review of research on six tools (*General Statistical Information on Recidivism* [GSIR], *Offender Group Reconviction Scale* [OGRS], *HCR-20*, *PCL-R*, *Violence Risk Appraisal Guide* [VRAG], and *LSI-R*) by Farrington, Jolliffe and Johnstone (2008). This established that, apart from one pair, the *GSIR* and *LSI-R*, there was no significant difference between the tools in how effective they are at identifying risk accurately. However, it should be noted that structured clinical judgement tools such as the *HCR-20* have been designed to understand the potential mechanisms underlying a person's potential for violence and to provide a platform for interventions rather than for the task of predicting violence. In a further caution against comparing 'apples with oranges', the RMA (2006) supports the view that actuarial assessments should not be used in isolation from structured clinical judgement because actuarial approaches indicate nothing about a person's individual risk level. More recently another review of risk assessment tools has been reported by Yang, Wong and Coid (2010). Data on nine widely used methods were extracted from 28 studies (published or unpublished) in the period 1999 to 2008. Yang et al. (2010) found a moderate level of predictive accuracy across all the measures and concluded that "... if prediction of violence is the only criterion for the selection of a risk assessment tool, then the tools included in the present study are essentially interchangeable" (p. 759). The only exception to this was Factor 1 (items concerned with interpersonal and affective personality traits) of the Psychopathy Check List (Revised) (PCL:R) which achieved no greater than chance levels of predictive power.

While the first generation of risk assessment tools were actuarial and largely concerned with predicting the likelihood of a particular outcome, later generations have evolved into tools for supporting practitioners in understanding the range of problems and making a judgement on the best approach. Douglas and Skeem (2005), among others, have described the shift away from a purely 'predictionist' risk assessment perspective to a philosophy of violence prevention and management, and this shift has been reflected in the design of the relevant tools to aid decision-making. With this shift away from predictive validity, a much wider range of clinical and pragmatic features must now be taken into account in judging how effective a tool is in practice. Some of these features, such as the availability of a user manual, cost, accessible training and specified user qualifications, were examined in the *Best Practice* guidance (Department of Health, 2009). Other potentially important features are ease of use, appropriate administration time, specified user qualifications, competencies and skill levels, and recognition of protective factors. Farrington, Jolliffe and Johnstone (2008) compared a number of instruments on these broader features and found that the HCR-20 was the most comprehensive because it met all but one of the 22 standards they examined. All the instruments surveyed, including the HCR-20, missed out the specification of protective factors.

Assessment should form the basis for effective risk management and interventions. Given the complexity of violence causation, the variety of factors that influence it, and the intricate ways in which they interact we should not be surprised that there is no single approach to addressing the problem of violence that has been shown to work consistently across all its forms. Pharmacological and psychological interventions, either alone or in combination, are the most well-researched types of intervention and these will now be considered.

What Role does Pharmacotherapy Play in Treating Violent Behaviour?

Pharmacological intervention with violent behaviour has two different targets: rapid containment of the violent patient and long-term treatment in order to prevent future violence. 'Rapid tranquillization' (RT) refers to the use of psychotropic medication to bring about immediate behavioural control of the violent patient (Tuddenham and Logan, 2005). RT is used only in emergency situations when violence is imminent or already occurring. In this kind of situation, sedation or even sleep induction is the primary objective: it is not a side-effect. The NICE RT guidelines (2005) recommend that when the behavioural disturbance occurs in the context of psychosis an oral antipsychotic in combination with oral lorazepam, should be considered first. However, there is no clear evidence that the combination of an antipsychotic with a benzodiazepine is superior to either one alone even in psychotic individuals. Where RT through oral therapy is unworkable (e.g., it is refused, is not indicated by previous clinical response, is not a proportionate response, or is ineffective), a combination of an antipsychotic and/or a benzodiazepine (haloperidol and/or lorazepam) is recommended. Research evidence is available only on intramuscular (IM) application. However, there is no evidence that intravenous (IV) application of haloperidol, carefully administered, is less safe or less effective. Intravenous application might even be ethically preferable, since forcible undressing for IM application can be distressing and traumatizing, especially for women. For this reason, in the German guidelines (DGPPN, 2009), for instance, IV application is suggested as an alternative to be considered. However, recently (2010) the drug company producing haloperidol recommended that haloperidol should no longer be applied IV or IM without ECG monitoring. So the topical alternatives are either giving lorazepam alone or other substances with evidence of efficacy such as olanzapine or aripiprazole.

When haloperidol is used as a means of managing disturbed/violent behaviour, an antimuscarinic agent (e.g., procyclidine) should be immediately available to reduce the risk of dystonia and other extrapyramidal side-effects, or it should be given prophylactically if patients wish according to prior experiences. Zuclopenthixol acetate (acuphase) injection is not recommended for rapid tranquillization due to its long onset and duration of action. However, zuclopenthixol acetate injection may be considered as an option for rapid tranquillization in various situations, such as when it is clearly expected that the service user will be disturbed/violent over an extended period of time or a service user has a past history of good and timely response to this drug. It should never be administered to those without any previous exposure to antipsychotic medication.

For imminently violent people who are not psychotic, benzodiazepines alone are recommended. The best evidence is available in relation to lorazepam. A drawback of the NICE guideline is that no recommendation is given for violent service users who are intoxicated or are suspected to be intoxicated. Alcohol or drug intoxication, especially in combination with psychotic or affective disorders, is quite frequent in real life but is a common reason for exclusion from any kind of study. Therefore, no evidence-based recommendations are available for this group of patients, but extensive clinical experience would suggest that the use of lorazepam is not recommended. In the case of alcohol intoxication, additional benzodiazepines might exponentiate toxic effects and there is a danger of breath depression. Drug-dependent service users are frequently used to very high doses of benzodiazepines and some additional lorazepam would almost certainly yield no additional effect at all. In such situations, clinical experience suggests that haloperidol is preferable with regard to both efficacy and safety.

The other focus of pharmacotherapy is long-term treatment with the aim of preventing future violence. Here two different aims can be identified and their relative importance is based on a theoretical question about the relationship of symptoms and 'personality'. Violent behaviour in mentally ill people can be seen as having its origin either in symptoms (e.g., delusions) or as part of a wider pattern of antisocial behaviour that is not directly related to the illness or, again, in a general tendency towards impulsivity (which in most cases is a consequence of the illness, e.g., schizophrenia or substance abuse). So the aim of pharmacotherapy can be either to optimize the treatment of the underlying mental disorder or to directly influence aggressive or violent behaviour. There is some evidence available that lithium may be helpful for aggressive behaviour among children with childhood conduct disorder (Campbell *et al.*, 1995) and beta-blockers can prevent violent behaviour among people with organic brain disorder (Greendyke and Kanter, 1986). Apart from that though, there is no clear evidence that aggressive behaviour based on antisocial behaviour can be influenced pharmacologically without inducing sedation. Such sedation might be induced by all kinds of drugs including neuroleptics, benzodiazepines, or valproic acid, but it is usually unacceptable to the individual. It is a primary goal of treatment in RT, but becomes an unappealing side-effect in long-term therapy.

So, in most cases, pharmacotherapy for recurrent violent behaviour by optimizing the treatment of the underlying mental disorder is preferable to targeting specific aggressive features. Given the importance of psychosis discussed above, this makes pharmacotherapy for the underlying disorder a central approach to managing violence associated with schizophrenia and affective disorders. Antipsychotics have been the most well-researched group of drugs, and since the 1990s there has been much optimism about the various second-generation antipsychotics (SGAs), including clozapine, risperidone, olanzapine, quetiapine, amilsulpride, aripiprazole, and ziprasidone. The promise that these substances would be more effective in both acute therapy and relapse prevention and, additionally, would have a better profile of side-effects and would enable a better quality of life, has unfortunately not been fulfilled to any great extent (Jones *et al.*, 2006; Lieberman, Stroup, and McEvoy, 2005). The latest update of the NICE schizophrenia guidelines (NICE, 2009), for instance, gives no indication that SGAs are preferable to first-generation antipsychotics (FGAs).

Nevertheless, a recent large meta-analysis (Leucht *et al.*, 2009) did provide evidence that, while FGAs and SGAs do not differ as a group, individual drugs do differ in their efficacy. Clozapine, amisulpride, olanzapine, and risperidone (in that order) were more effective than haloperidol, while the other SGAs were equally or less effective. Clozapine, in particular, seems to be the most effective substance known so far in the treatment of both treatment-resistant schizophrenia and schizophrenia-related violent behaviour and is recommended as the treatment of choice in these cases (NICE, 2009). Indeed, some studies have suggested a substance-specific anti-aggressive effect of clozapine on aggression independent of its antipsychotic action (Citrome *et al.*, 2006; Krakowski *et al.*, 2006), although these effects were not confirmed under community conditions (Bitter *et al.*, 2005).

Interesting findings on the effectiveness of different neuroleptics on violent behaviour under real-life conditions in the community have been provided by the CATIE study (Lieberman, Stroup and McEvoy, 2005). Parts of the wide-ranging CATIE study were designed primarily to address the question of pharmacotherapy for violent behaviour

(Swanson *et al.*, 2008). The incidence of violent behaviour in this sample was reduced from 16% at baseline to 9%. Ziprasidone performed the best out of the five SGAs examined.

Taken together, pharmacological treatment is strongly recommended for people with aggressive behaviour due to psychotic conditions. Improvement in their mental health due to pharmacological treatment often leads to improvement of the linked aggressive behaviour, if the aggression is not based on antisocial personality traits. In all other cases, pharmacological interventions are of limited value and are usually accompanied by sedation that the individual patient may find unacceptable. The use of these substances should be carefully considered by balancing information on dangers, responsibilities, and alternatives.

How Effective are Psychological Interventions for Violent Behaviour?

In order to understand a violent offence or a recurring pattern of an individual's violence over time, it is important first to carry out a *functional analysis* of the factors likely to have influenced it. To be done thoroughly, this is likely to include collecting information on the behaviour itself; on aspects of prior learning, attitudes, social interaction and communication skills, cognitive and problem-solving abilities, emotional self-management, and other variables. This would be examined alongside information about the environment and situational factors operating before, during, and after an act of violence occurred. Where possible, this should be extended into a *case formulation,* which is an explanatory model of an individual's distress or of the behaviour that is causing problems for others (see also Chapter 10).

To date, a range of interventions has been tested and evaluated, though evidence concerning them is uneven, with regard to both the methodological quality of the research that has been conducted, and the pattern of outcomes obtained. Information has been surveyed and findings collated through a series of meta-analytic reviews, and patterns of effects within them can be used to identify the methods able to produce the largest effect sizes with the greatest consistency (McGuire, 2008).

For young offenders, the interventions that have yielded effects of this type have included interpersonal skills training, structured counselling, teaching family homes (a type of fostering), and a range of behavioural training programmes (Garrido and Morales, 2007; Lipsey and Wilson, 2007). For the most serious young offenders, a composite type of institutionally-based intervention known as a *decompression* programme has been shown to be valuable, and positive effects have been found even for those individuals with psychopathic features (Caldwell *et al.*, 2007).

For adult offenders, the most consistent effects to date have been obtained from evaluations of structured, group-based cognitive–behavioural therapy (CBT) programmes (Lipsey, Landenberger and Wilson, 2007). These draw on a similar model of change as that used in CBT in mental health settings, though with a wider emphasis on problem-solving and interaction skills rather than on addressing dysfunctional thoughts alone. These types of interventions and variations of them have been widely disseminated in the criminal justice system in England and Wales (and other jurisdictions) with beneficial effects (Hollis, 2007), though it should be emphasized that the conclusions draw more heavily on 'practical trials' than on the randomized experiments familiar in medical settings (Harper and Chitty, 2005).

There is extensive evidence, including several meta-analyses, that indicates the efficacy of anger control training and variants of it for reducing anger-related problems in the general population. When applied with violent adult offenders, however, outcomes have been more mixed, with some studies yielding dramatically positive outcomes, but others only marginal effects close to zero (McGuire, 2008). It is of vital importance in allocating offenders to intervention programmes to carry out the kind of detailed assessment and functional analysis described above; it is unwise to assume that all violent offences are an outcome of unmanaged anger, as violent offences can be of several types. Interventions that address anger-related, expressive, or emotional aggression will be unlikely to work with those who have acted aggressively for 'instrumental' or acquisitive reasons (e.g., in armed robbery)

How Important are Engagement and Collaboration in the Risk Management Process?

Interventions can be delivered effectively only as part of a broader therapeutic relationship. A major theme of this book, and an emerging area of interest for practitioners and service users, is the quality and influence of these relationships within mental health services. Service users often feel that risk assessment and risk management are things that are done to them rather than with them (see Chapter 2), and they may even be unaware when they are undergoing a formal process of risk assessment. This perception does not fit well with at least the rhetoric of modern mental health services. Disengagement from services and subsequent loss of contact is also a significant risk factor for breakdown and increased risk in itself (Shaw *et al.*, 2006), and the therapeutic alliance is a key factor in protecting against heightened risk states (Douglas and Skeem, 2005). At the heart of an effective relationship between the service user and their carer is a sense of trust and a sense, on the part of the user, that the formal services being provided are worthwhile and beneficial. While it is important not to be naive about the scope for collaboration and alliance with all service users regardless of the severity of their problems and differing perceptions on what constitutes risk, practical approaches are beginning to be explored which may enhance this aspect of risk management. Elbogen *et al.* (2007), for instance, argue that clinical interventions such as motivational interviewing, which address a service user's perceptions of the need for treatment and its likely effectiveness, appear to hold promise as risk management strategies for clinicians providing services for people with serious and enduring mental illness.

Conclusion

We have selected some interesting and important themes in the violence research literature here and attempted to summarize their implications for improving risk management in this difficult area. The vastness of the literature brings both problems and benefits. It remains difficult, if not impossible, to stay on top of this huge output, despite the development of systematic review techniques. The practitioner in search of an evidence-based approach to risk management remains at the mercy of the high-profile, attention-grabbing or personally recommended article, which may or may not provide the 'right' answer. However, the scale of intellectual and financial investment in research illustrates the significance given to this problem and the importance of getting it right in delivering care for people who are at risk. There is a much greater understanding now, compared with even just 20 years ago, of both the context and causes of violent behaviour. There is also a stronger sense of meaningful interventions for, and with, the service user who may be prone to act violently.

References

Andrews, D. A. (2001). Principles of effective correctional programs, in L. L. Motiuk and R. C. Serin (eds), *Compendium 2000 on Effective Correctional Programming*. Ottawa: Correctional Service Canada, pp. 9–17.

Bandura, A. (2001). Social cognitive theory: An agentic perspective, *Annual Review of Psychology*, 52, 1–26.

Baron, R. and D. Richardson (1994). *Human Aggression*. New York: Plenum Press.

Bitter, I., Czobor, P., Dossenbach, M., and Volavka, J. (2005). Effectiveness of clozapine, olanzapine, quetiapine, risperidone, and haloperidol monotherapy in reducing hostile and aggressive behavior in outpatients treated for schizophrenia: A prospective naturalistic study (IC-SOHO), *European Psychiatry*, 20(5–6), 403–408.

Bonta, J., Law, M., *et al.* (1998). The prediction of criminal and violent recidivism among mentally disordered offenders. A meta-analysis, *Psychological Bulletin*, 123, 123–142.

Caldwell, M. F., McCormick, D. J., Umstead, D., and van Rybroek, G. J. (2007). Evidence of treatment progress and therapeutic outcomes among adolescents with psychopathic features, *Criminal Justice and Behavior*, 34, 573–587.

Campbell, M., Adams, P. B., Small, A. M., Kafantaris, V., Silva, R. R., Shell, J., Perry, R., and Overall, J. E. (1995). Lithium in hospitalized aggressive children with conduct disorder: A double-blind and placebo-controlled study, *Journal of the American Academy of Child and Adolescent Psychiatry*, 34(4), 445–453.

Choe, J. Y., Teplin, L. A., and Abram, K. M. (2008). Perpetration of violence, violent victimization, and severe mental illness: Balancing public health concerns, *Psychiatriatric Services*, 59(2), 153–164.

Citrome, L., Volavka, J., Czobor, P., Sheitman, B., Lindenmayer, J., McEvoy, J.,Cooper, T., Chakos, M., and Lieberman, J. (2006). Effects of clozapine, olanzapine, risperidone, and haloperidol on hostility among patients with schizophrenia, *Archives of General Psychiatry*, 63, 622–629.

Coid, J., Yang, M., *et al.* (2006). Violence and psychiatric morbidity in the national household population of Britain: Public health implications, *British Journal of Psychiatry*, 189(1), 12–19.

Cornell, D. G., Warren, J., *et al.* (1996). Psychopathy in instrumental and reactive violent offenders, *Journal of Consulting and Clinical Psychology*, 64(4), 783–790.

Corrigan, P. W. and Watson, A. C. (2005). Findings from the National Comorbidity Survey on the frequency of violent behavior in individuals with psychiatric disorders, *Psychiatry Research*, 136(2–3), 153–162.

Cure, S., Chua, W., Duggan, L., and Adams, C. (2005). Randomised controlled trials relevant to aggressive and violent people, 1955–2000: A survey, *British Journal of Psychiatry* 186, 185–189.

Department of Health (2009). *Best Practice in Managing Risk: Principles and Evidence for Best Practice in the Assessment and Management of Risk to Self and Others in Mental Health Services*. London: Department of Health.

Deutsche Gesellschaft für Psychiatrie, Psychotherapie und Nervenheilkunde (German Association for Psychiatry and Psychotherapy) (DGPPN) (2009). *Praxisleitlinien in Psychiatrie und Psychotherapie (Guidelines in Psychiatry and Psychotherapy)*.

Douglas, K. and Skeem, J. (2005). Violence risk assesment: Getting specific about being dynamic, *Psychology, Public Policy and Law*, 11(3), 347–383.

Elbogen, E., Mercado, C., Scalora, M., and Tomkins, A. (2002). Perceived relevance of factors for violence risk assessment: A survey of clinicians, *International Journal of Forensic Mental Health*, 1(1), 37–47.

Elbogen, E. B., Mustillo, S., van Dorn, R., Swanson, J. W., and Swartz, M. S. (2007). The impact of perceived need for treatment on risk of arrest and violence among people with severe mental illness, *Criminal Justice and Behavior*, 34(2), 197–210.

Farrington, D. P. (2006). Key longitudinal-experimental studies in criminology, *Journal of Experimental Criminology*, 2, 121–141.

Farrington, D. P. (2007). Origins of violent behaviour over the life span, in D. J. Flannery, A. T. Vazsonyi, and I. D. Waldman (eds), *The Cambridge Handbook of Violent Behaviour and Aggression*. Cambridge: Cambridge University Press, pp. 19–48.

Farrington, D. P. and Coid, J. W. (eds) (2003). *Early Prevention of Adult Antisocial Behaviour*. Cambridge: Cambridge University Press.

Farrington, D. P., Jolliffe, D., and Johnstone, L. (2008). *Assessing Violence Risk: A Framework for Practice*. Paisley: Risk Management Authority.

Friedman, R. A. (2006). Violence and mental illness – how strong is the link?, *New England Journal of Medicine*, 355(20), 2064–2066.

Friedman, S. H. and Loue, S. (2007). Incidence and prevalence of intimate partner violence by and against women with severe mental Iilness, *Journal of Women's Health*, 16(4), 471–480.

Gadon, L., Johnstone, L., *et al.* (2006). Situational variables and institutional violence: A systematic review of the literature, *Clinical Psychology Review* 26, 515–534.

Gannon, T. A., Ward, T., Beech, A. R., and Fisher, D. (eds) (2007). *Aggressive Offenders' Cognition*. Chichester: John Wiley & Son Ltd.

Garrido, V. and Morales, L. A. (2007). *Serious (Violent and Chronic) Juvenile Offenders: A Systematic Review of Treatment Effectiveness in Secure Corrections*. Philadelphia, PA: Campbell Collaboration Reviews of Intervention and Policy Evaluations (C2-RIPE), available at www.campbellcollaboration.org/doc-pdf/Garrido_seriousjuv_review.pdf.

Geen, R. (2001). *Human Aggression*. Buckingham: Open University Press.

Greendyke, R. and Kanter, D. (1986). Therapeutic effects of pindolol on behavioral disturbances associated with organic brain disease: A double-blind study, *Journal of Clinical Psychiatry*, 47, 423–426.

Harper, G. and Chitty, C. (eds) (2005). *The Impact of Corrections on Re-offending: A Review of 'What Works'*, 3rd edn, Home Office research Study 291. London: Home Office Research, Development and Statistics Directorate.

Hollis, V. (2007). *Reconviction Analysis of Interim Accredited Programmes Software (IAPS) Data*. London: Research Development Statistics, National Offender Management Service.

Jones, P., Barnes, T., Davies, L., Dunn, G., Lloyd, H., Hayhurst, K., Murray, R., Mrakwick. A., and Lewis, S. (2006). Randomized controlled trial of the effect on quality of life of second- vs first-generation antipsychotic drugs in schizophrenia. Cost utility of the latest antipsychotic drugs in schizophrenia study (CUtLASS 1), *Archives of General Psychiatry*, 63, 1079–1087.

Krahe, B. (2001). *The Social Psychology of Aggression*. Hove: Psychology Press.

Krakowski, M., Czobor, P., Citrome, L., Bark, N., and Cooper, T. (2006). Atypical antipsychotic agents in the treatment of violent patients with schizophrenia and schizoaffective disorder, *Archives of General Psychiatry*, 63, 622–629.

Leitner, M., Barr, W., McGuire, J., Whittington, R. and Jones, S. (2006). *Systematic Review of Prevention Strategies for the Forensic Mental Health Population at High Risk of Engaging in Violent Behaviour*. Final Report to National Forensic Mental Health R&D Programme, Liverpool.

Leucht, S., Corves, C., Arbter, D., Engel, R., Li, C., and Davis, J. (2009). Second-generation versus first-generation antipsychotic drugs for schizophrenia: A meta-analysis, *Lancet*, (3), 31–41.

Lieberman, J., Stroup, S., and McEvoy, J. E. A. (2005). Clinical antipsychotic trials of intervention effectiveness (CATIE) investigators. Effectiveness of antipsychotic drugs in patients with chronic schizophrenia, *New England Journal of Medicine*, 353, 1209–1223.

Lipsey, M. W. and Wilson, D. B. (1998). Effective intervention for serious juvenile offenders: A synthesis of research, in R. Loeber and D. P. Farrington (eds), *Serious and Violent Juvenile Offenders: Risk Factors and Successful Interventions*. Thousand Oaks, CA: Sage Publications, pp. 313–345.

Lipsey, M. W., Landenberger, N. A., and Wilson, S. J. (2007). *Effects of Cognitive-Behavioral Programs for Criminal Offenders*. Campbell Collaboration Systematic Review, available at http://db.c2admin.org/doc-pdf/lipsey_CBT_finalreview.pdf.

Loeber, R., Farrington, D. P., Stouthamer-Loeber, M., and White, H. R. (2008). *Violence and Serious Theft: Development and Prediction from Childhood to Adulthood*. New York and London: Routledge.

McGuire, J. (2004). *Understanding Psychology and Crime: Perspectives on Theory and Action*. Maidenhead: Open University Press/McGraw-Hill Education.

McGuire, J. (2008). A review of effective interventions for reducing aggression and violence, *Philosophical Transactions of the Royal Society B*, 363, 2577–2597.

Messner, S. (2003). Understanding cross-national variation in criminal violence, in W. Heitmeyer and J. Hagan (eds), *International Handbook of Violence Research*. Dordrecht: Kluwer Academic, pp. 701–716.

Moffitt, T. E. (1993). Adolescence-limited and life-course-persistent antisocial behavior: A developmental taxonomy, *Psychological Review*, 100, 674–701.

Moffitt, T. E. (2003). Life-course-persistent and adolescence-limited antisocial behaviour: A 10-year research review and a research agenda, in B. B. Lahey, T. E. Moffitt, and A. Caspi (eds), *Causes of Conduct Disorder and Juvenile Delinquency*. New York and London: Guilford Press, pp. 49–75.

Monahan, J., Steadman, H., Silver, E., Appelbaum, P., Robbins, P., Mulvey, E., Roth, L., Grisso, T., and Banks, S. (2001). *Rethinking Risk Assessment: The MacArthur Study of Mental Disorder and Violence*. New York: Oxford University Press.

NICE (2005). *Clinical Practice Guidelines for the Violence: The Short Term Management of Disturbed / Violent Behaviour in Psychiatric In-Patient Settings and Emergency Departments*. London: National Institute for Health and Clinical Excellence.

NICE (2009). *Core Interventions in the Treatment and Management of Schizophrenia in Primary and Secondary Care (Update)*. London: National Institute for Health and Clinical Excellence.

Novaco, R. W. (2007). Anger dysregulation, in T. A. Cavell and K. T. Malcolm (eds), *Anger, Aggression and Interventions for Interpersonal Violence*. Mahwah, NJ: Lawrence Erlbaum, pp. 3–54.

Olweus, D. (1979). Stability of aggressive reaction patterns in males: A review, *Psychological Bulletin*, 86, 852–875.

RMA (2006). *Risk Assessment Tools Evaluation Directory*. Paisley, Scotland, Risk Management Authority.

Roberts, D. (2008). *Human Insecurity: Global Structures of Violence*. London: Zed Books.

Schomerus, G., Heider, D., Angermeyer, M., Bebbington, P., Azorin, J.-M., Brugha, T., and Toumi, M. (2008). Urban residence, victimhood and the appraisal of personal safety in people with schizophrenia: Results from the European Schizophrenia Cohort (EuroSC), *Psychological Medicine*, 38, 591–597.

Scott, C. L. and Resnick, P. J. (2006). Violence risk assessment in persons with mental illness, *Aggression and Violent Behavior*, 11(6), 598–611.

Shaw, J., Hunt, I. M., Flynn, S., Meehan, J., Robinson, J., Bickley, H., Parsons, R., McCann, K., Burns, J., Amos, T., Kapur, N., and Appleby, L. (2006). Rates of mental disorder in people convicted of homicide: National clinical survey, *British Journal of Psychiatry*, 188(2), 143–147.

Silver, E. (2006). Understanding the relationship between mental disorder and violence: The need for a criminological perspective, *Law and Human Behavior*, 30(6), 685–706.

Silver, E., Felson, R., *et al.* (2008). The relationship between mental health problems and violence among criminal offenders, *Criminal Justice and Behavior*, 35, 405–426.

Steadman, H. J., Mulvey, E. P., Monahan, J., Robbins, P. C., Appelbaum, P. S., Grisso, T., *et al.* (1998). Violence by people discharged from acute psychiatric in-patient facilities and by others in the same neighbourhoods, *Archives of General Psychiatry*, 55, 393–401.

Staub, E. (1989). *The Roots of Evil: The Origins of Genocide and Other Group Violence.* New York: Plenum Press.

Staub, E. (2003). *The Psychology of Good and Evil: Why Children, Adults and Groups Help and Harm Others.* Cambridge: Cambridge University Press.

Swanson, J. W. (1994). Mental disorder, substance abuse, and community violence: An epidemiological approach, in J. Monahan and H. J. Steadman (eds), *Violence and Mental Disorder: Developments in Risk Assessment.* Chicago, IL: University of Chicago Press, pp. 101–136.

Swanson, J. W., Swartz, M. S., van Dorn, R. A., Volavka, J., Monahan, J., Stroup, T. S., McEvoy, J. P., Wagner, H. R., Elbogen, E. B., Lieberman, J. A., and the CATIE investigators (2008). Comparison of antipsychotic medication effects on reducing violence in people with schizophrenia, *British Journal of Psychiatry*, 193(1), 37–43.

Tremblay, R. E. (2000). The development of aggressive behaviour during childhood: What have we learned in the past century?, *International Journal of Behavioral Development*, 24, 129–141.

Tremblay, R. E. (2003). Why socialisation fails: The case of chronic physical aggression, in B. B. Lahey, T. E. Moffitt, and A. Caspi (eds), *Causes of Conduct Disorder and Juvenile Delinquency.* New York & London: Guilford Press, pp. 182–224.

Tuddenham L. and Logan, J. (2005). Psychotropic drugs given for aggressive incidents in a special hospital, *Journal of Forensic Psychiatry and Psychology*, 16(1), 85–91.

Vogel, V. de, Vries, Robbé M. de, Ruiter, C., and Bouman, Y. (under review). Assessing protective factors in forensic psychiatric practice: Introducing the SAPROF, *International Journal of Forensic Mental Health.*

Volavka, J. and Nolan, K. (2008). Methodological structure for sggression research, *Psychiatric Quarterly*, 79(4), 293–300.

Waller, J. (2007). *Becoming Evil: How Ordinary People Commit Genocide and Mass Killing*, 2nd edn. Oxford: Oxford University Press.

Yang, M., Wong, S. C. P., & Coid, J. (2010). The efficacy of violence prediction: a meta-analytic comparison of nine risk assessment tools. *Psychological Bulletin*, 136, 740–767.

Zumkley, H. (1994). The stability of aggressive behavior: A meta-analysis, *German Journal of Psychology*, 18, 273–281.

6

Suicide and Homicide by People with Mental Illness: A National Overview

Kirsten Windfuhr and Nicola Swinson

Introduction

One of the principles of developing best practice in mental health services is keeping up to date with current, high quality research and translating the findings into service improvements. This chapter provides readers with current findings from the National Confidential Inquiry into Suicide and Homicide by People with Mental Illness (hereafter referred to as the Inquiry) and discusses how these findings are translated into mental health practice and policy.

The Inquiry is a unique research project that collects detailed data on a national clinical population. It has made a significant contribution to the knowledge base about the risk of suicide and homicide in people receiving mental health care in the United Kingdom. This chapter is designed to provide a broad overview of the work of the Inquiry. The first two sections describe the background and methodology of the Inquiry. The third and fourth sections discuss the main findings as they relate to suicide and homicide in persons who had been in contact with mental health services in the 12 months prior to death/homicide. The findings are based on our most recent report for England and Wales, *Avoidable Deaths* (Appleby *et al.*, 2006). The next two sections discuss how the findings of the Inquiry have been translated into recommendations to impact on clinical practice and mental health policy. Each section addresses how these recommendations impact on managing the risk of self-harm and violence and relate to *Best Practice in Managing Risk* (Department of Health, 2009). Reference to the wider research literature on suicide and homicide is also made. The chapter ends with a brief account of future research directions.

Self-Harm and Violence: Towards Best Practice in Managing Risk in Mental Health Services, First Edition.
Edited by Richard Whittington and Caroline Logan.
© 2011 John Wiley & Sons, Ltd. Published 2011 by John Wiley & Sons, Ltd.

How the Inquiry was Established

The Inquiry was established at the University of Manchester in 1996, after having previously been based in London. It was initially set up following concerns about patient and public safety expressed by the Royal College of Psychiatrists and the Government about homicides by people in contact with mental health services (Robinson and Bickley, 2004). In particular, criticisms of the Christopher Clunis case (Ritchie and Lingham, 1994) played a significant role in the development of the Inquiry.

Around the same time, the Department of Health instituted targets to reduce the incidence of suicide in England (Department of Health, 1992), and the development of a knowledge base of suicide risk in people in the care of mental health services became part of the remit of the Inquiry. Suicide prevention has increasingly become a government priority in England since this time (Department of Health, 1999a, 1999b), most clearly demonstrated by the launch of the suicide prevention strategy in 2002 (Department of Health 2002). People with mental illness represent one of the most important high risk groups, as their suicide rate is 5- to 15-fold higher compared with the general population (Harris and Barraclough, 1997).

The broad aims of the Inquiry are to:

- collect national data on all suicide and homicide cases, by people in contact with psychiatric services;
- recommend changes to clinical practice and policy that will reduce the risk of suicide and homicide; and
- disseminate the findings.

How Does the Inquiry Work?

Inquiry methodology: suicide

The stages of data collection for the suicide Inquiry are shown in Figure 6.1. There are three main stages to data collection for suicide: the collection of national suicide data irrespective of receipt of mental health care; the identification of individuals in recent contact with mental health services (within 12 months); and the collection of detailed sociodemographic and clinical data about these individuals (see Windfuhr *et al.*, 2008 for a detailed account of the methodology).

Information about all those receiving a coroner's verdict of suicide or undetermined death ('open verdict') at inquest is provided to the Inquiry from national sources. It is convention to include deaths by suicide and open verdicts in suicide research as most open verdicts are thought to be suicide cases (Linsely, Schapira and Kelly, 2001; O'Donnell and Farmer, 1995). National suicide statistics in the United Kingdom (i.e., Office for National Statistics) are also based on this inclusive definition of suicide (i.e., suicide and open verdicts) (C. Rooney, personal communication, 14 February 2006).

Once the national suicide data are received by the Inquiry, data on each individual are submitted to our administrative contacts within each mental health hospital throughout the United Kingdom. Our contacts identify which individuals had contact with mental health services in the 12 months prior to suicide. Cases in which there has been contact become 'Inquiry cases'.

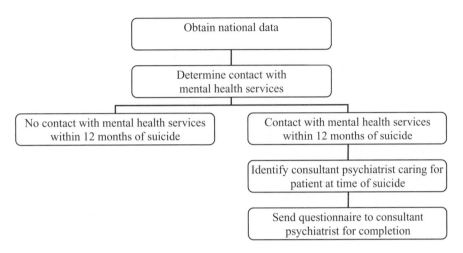

Figure 6.1 The stages of data collection for cases of suicide.

For all Inquiry cases, the clinician who had been caring for the patient prior to suicide is identified and sent a questionnaire. This clinician, or someone from the mental health team, is asked to complete the detailed questionnaire on the care that their patient received prior to their suicide.

Inquiry methodology: homicide

The stages of data collection for the homicide Inquiry are shown in Figure 6.2. Information on all homicides occurring in the general population is obtained from the Home Office Homicide Index in England and Wales, and from national data providers in Scotland and Northern Ireland. Additional information on all individuals notified to the Inquiry, such as previous offences or aliases, is also collected from other agencies.

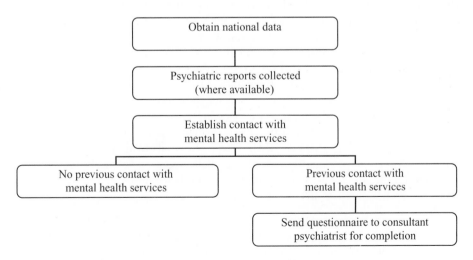

Figure 6.2 The stages of data collection for cases of homicide.

As in the collection of suicide data, details for each homicide perpetrator are submitted to our administrative contacts within every mental health hospital nationally. However, unlike suicide Inquiry cases, we collect data on homicide perpetrators who had (1) any lifetime contact with mental health services, and (2) contact within 12 months of the offence. These individuals become 'Inquiry cases', although only those with recent service contact (e.g., within 12 months of offence) are analysed as the main Inquiry case sample. For all Inquiry cases, the clinician, or other member of the mental health team who had been caring for the patient prior to the offence, is identified and sent a detailed questionnaire to complete.

For the remainder of this chapter, we will use the term 'suicides' or 'suicide deaths' and 'homicides' or 'homicide perpetrators' to describe suicide and homicide by individuals in the general population. We will use the term 'patient suicides' or 'patient homicides'/'patient perpetrators' to refer to 'Inquiry cases' (i.e., suicide and homicide occurring in the 12 months prior to death/homicide).

Suicide Inquiry Findings

For the reporting period of Avoidable Deaths (amounting to 4 years 9 months, 2001–2004) (Appleby *et al.*, 2006), the Inquiry was notified of 23,477 suicide deaths occurring in the general population, corresponding to an average annual rate of 10.2 per 100,000 population in England and Wales.

Suicide deaths were predominantly male (N = 17,434; 74%) and suicide was most common in the 25–44 year age group. Of all suicide deaths, the most common methods of suicide were hanging/strangulation (N = 9,059), self-poisoning (N = 6,088), and jumping or multiple injuries (N = 2,285), which together accounted for 74% of all suicide deaths.

Patient suicides

There were 6,203 patient suicides identified in the time period of the report, representing 27% of all suicide deaths. The 27% reported for the years 2001–2004 is slightly higher than the 24% reported in the previous Inquiry report (Appleby *et al.*, 2006). Rates of contact in the Inquiry sample for England and Wales appear to be similar to rates of contact in the year before suicide in the rest of the United Kingdom (Scotland: 28%; Northern Ireland: 28%) (Appleby *et al.*, 2001, 2006). These rates of contact are also broadly in line with the wider literature on mental health service contact in the year prior to suicide (Luoma, Martin, and Pearson, 2002).

The social and clinical characteristics of these patient suicides are shown in Table 6.1. Briefly, patient suicides are characterized by features of social isolation and adversity (e.g., living alone, unemployed/long-term sick leave). Behavioural and clinical characteristics of this group include a history of self-harm and substance misuse, and severe mental illness (e.g., schizophrenia, affective disorder).

Inquiry suicide patient sub-groups

The Inquiry looks at specific sub-groups of Inquiry cases. In the following section, the specific characteristics of these patient sub-groups will be described, including inpatients,

Table 6.1 Social and clinical characteristics of all patient suicides

	No. (6,203)	%	(95% CI)[a]
Demographic features			
Age: median (range)	43 (10–95)	—	—
Male	4,107	66	(65–67)
Ethnic minority[b]	423	7	(6–8)
Not currently married	4,219	69	(68–71)
Unemployed	2,377	40	(39–41)
Long-term sick[c]	1,085	18	(17–19)
Living alone	2,604	44	(42–45)
Homeless	130	2	(2–3)
Priority groups			
Inpatients	856	14	(13–15)
Post-discharge patients	1,271	24	(23–25)
Receiving care under enhanced CPA	2,118	35	(34–36)
Missed last contact	1,523	29	(28–30)
Non-compliance in last month	813	14	(13–15)
Clinical features			
Primary diagnosis:			
Schizophrenia and other delusional disorders	1,145	19	(18–20)
Affective disorder (bipolar disorder and depression)	2,821	46	(45–47)
Alcohol dependence	491	8	(7–9)
Drug dependence	206	3	(3–4)
Personality disorder	518	8	(8–9)
Any secondary diagnosis	3,298	54	(53–55)
Duration of history (under 12 months)[d]	1,212	20	(19–21)
Over five previous admissions	931	15	(14–16)
Last admission was a re-admission	586	16	(15–18)
Behavioural features			
History of self-harm	4,124	68	(67–69)
History of violence	1,291	22	(21–23)
History of alcohol misuse	2,631	44	(42–45)
History of drug misuse	1,789	30	(29–31)
Contact with services			
Last contact within 7 days of death	2,955	49	(47–50)
Symptoms at last contact[e]	3,759	63	(62–65)
Estimate of immediate risk: low or none[f]	4,984	86	(85–87)
Estimate of long-term risk: low or none[f]	3,368	59	(58–61)
Suicide thought to be preventable	1,017	19	(18–20)

Source: Reproduced by permission of NPSA.

[a] Ninety-five percent confidence intervals are included for all estimates in the tables, indicating the accuracy of each estimate by showing the range of values within which the true figure is likely to lie. See *Avoidable Deaths* (www.manchester.ac.uk/nci) for a full account of methodological procedures.

[b] Patients from an ethnic minority group included patients who were Black African, Black Caribbean, Indian/Pakistani/Bangladeshi, Chinese, White, Mixed Race, and other ethnic groups not already listed. Ethnic minorities make up approximately 8% of the general population. Ethnic minorities are neither over- or under-represented among patient suicides.

[c] Long-term sick is generally defined as anyone in receipt of sickness benefit. The clinician determined whether the patient had been long-term sick.

[d] Duration of history (under 12 months) refers to those patients for whom the time period since the clear onset of their primary diagnosis was under 12 months.

[e] Symptoms at last contact refers to whether the respondent felt that the patient had communicated any of the following behaviours or thoughts during their last contact with mental health services: emotional distress, depressive illness, deterioration in physical health, delusions or hallucinations, hostility, increased use of alcohol, increased use of other substances, recent self-harm, hopelessness, suicidal ideas.

[f] Respondents were asked to estimate the patient's risk *at their last contact* with mental health services. For both long term and immediate risk, respondents were asked whether the patient's risk was thought to be: none, low, moderate, or high.

patients recently discharged, patients subject to the Care Programme Approach (CPA), patients who were non-compliant with drug treatment, patients with a dual diagnosis, and older patients.

Suicide risk factors for inpatients and post-discharge patients will also be described. The Inquiry is a large case-series of all patient suicide deaths. This study design can describe the sample, but aetiological conclusions regarding specific risk factors – or factors associated with increased risk of patient suicide – cannot be drawn from such a study design. A study design which can address the more specific question about what factors increase the risk of suicide among inpatients, for example, is the case-control study. Put simply, an individual who died by suicide (i.e., a case) is matched with an individual who was also an inpatient, but did not die (i.e., a control) and equivalent information is collected on each of the patients to identify specific factors associated with risk of suicide.

Inpatients In the period of the report, there were 856 inpatient suicides, representing 14% of Inquiry cases. The socio-demographic and clinical characteristics of inpatients were similar to the Inquiry sample as a whole, although they were a more morbid group of patients (e.g., high rates of schizophrenia, history of self-harm, violence and multiple previous admissions to an inpatient unit). Over an eight-year period from 1997 to 2004, there was a significant decrease in the number and proportion of inpatient suicide deaths (1997: 222 (17%) versus 2004: 155 (11%)). Rates of inpatient suicide deaths followed a similar pattern during that time period, with inpatient suicide deaths falling from 1.41 to 1.02 per 100,000 bed days between 1997/8 and 2002/3 (a 28% reduction). The magnitude of the decline varied between 9% and 28% depending on the denominator data used to calculate rates (Kapur *et al.*, 2006).

Hanging and strangulation were the most common methods of suicide overall (N = 377; 44%), with 75% (N = 188) of all inpatient deaths on the ward dying by these methods. Of those suicides that occurred on the ward, the most common ligature type was a belt; the most commonly used ligature point was a hook or a handle. Although hanging and strangulation were common, the number of deaths using this method declined significantly over the eight year period from 1997 to 2004, equating to a fall of 51%. This may in part be the result of recommendations made in 2002 to remove specific ligature points (Department of Health, 2000b), and continued vigilance about the removal of other potential ligatures and ligature points. (See 'Recommendations' section below for a comprehensive discussion.)

There appeared to be heightened periods of risk for inpatients. Fifteen percent (N = 117) of inpatient suicides took place within the first week of an admission while 35% (N = 292) occurred during the period of discharge planning. Suicide was more common in the evening and at night for those patients who died on the ward, although this was not statistically significantly different from other times of day.

Twenty-two percent (N = 185) of inpatient suicides were under non-routine observation. Eighteen inpatient cases (3%) died while under one-to-one observation. There were 227 (27%) inpatients who absconded prior to suicide. Of those who absconded, 44% (N = 96) died either during the first week of admission or during the period of planning discharge.

In a recent case-control study of 222 inpatient suicide deaths matched with living inpatients (Hunt *et al.*, 2007), three independent risk factors were identified: male sex, a primary diagnosis of affective disorder, and previous self-harm. Inpatients who died by

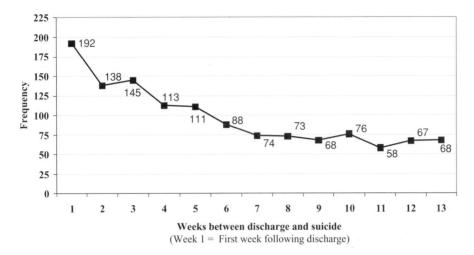

Figure 6.3 Number of patient suicides per week following discharge. Reproduced by permission of NPSA.

suicide more often had multiple risk factors compared with control patients: 71% had two risk factors (compared with 35% of control patients) and 13% had all three risk factors (compared with 5% of control patients). Further, characteristics such as unemployment, living alone and substance misuse, often associated with suicide deaths in the general population, were not associated with this clinical sample, suggesting differences in the risks associated with suicide in the general and mental health population.

Community patients There were 1,271 patients who died within three months of discharge from an inpatient unit, representing 20% of all Inquiry cases. Compared with all patient suicides, community patients were less likely to die by self-poisoning and more likely to die by jumping/multiple injuries. There was no clear trend in the number of post-discharge suicide deaths although there is a suggestion that the rate may have increased slightly (Kapur *et al.*, 2006).

Suicides were most frequent in the first three weeks after discharge from hospital (N = 475) representing 14% of all community suicide deaths and 37% of all post-discharge suicide deaths (see Figure 6.3). Of the 475 cases that occurred in the first three weeks, 192 (40%) occurred in the first week, with the highest figures occurring in the first four days (N = 110; 57%). Of the 475 cases, 46% died before their first follow-up in the community. One feature that distinguished these early post-discharge deaths from the post-discharge sample as a whole was that they were more likely to have discharged themselves from the inpatient unit. Encouragingly, however, the proportion that died before follow-up in the community has declined since the previous report (Appleby *et al.*, 2001) where 68% had died prior to their first community follow-up appointment. This may be in part the result of Inquiry findings showing the first week following discharge to be a significant period of risk, and subsequent recommendations suggesting follow-up within 7 days of discharge from hospital (Appleby *et al.*, 2001) (see 'Recommendation' section below for a comprehensive discussion).

In a case-control study (see above for a description of this methodology) of recently discharged patients carried out by the Inquiry (Hunt *et al.*, 2009), risk factors associated with post-discharge patient suicides included male sex, history of self-harm, primary diagnosis of affective disorder, recent last contact with mental health services, missed last appointment, patient initiated last discharge, symptoms of suicidal ideation at last contact, and co-morbidity. Cases of suicide were significantly more likely to have multiple risk factors compared with control patients.

Use of the Care Programme Approach (CPA) There were 2,118 cases receiving care under enhanced CPA at the time of death, corresponding to 35% of the Inquiry sample. This is a decrease from the 47% in the previous reporting period. One-quarter of patients under CPA were inpatients (N = 531; 25%). Just over one-third had been discharged into the community in the previous three months (N = 572; 36%). Of those who died in the community and were receiving care under enhanced CPA (N = 1,587), 91% had been admitted previously; 25% had been under the Mental Health Act at their last admission. Nearly all discharged patients had been allocated a key worker (98%). In 81% of all patients under CPA, a date had been set for the next review, and in 99%, a follow-up appointment had been arranged.

Despite receiving care under enhanced CPA, one-fifth had been non-compliant with treatment in the month prior to suicide (20%) and just over one-quarter (27%) had missed their final contact with services. One-third (32%) of patients were seen within 24 hours of death, and in 58% of these, the key worker had been present at the appointment. There was a notable absence of the use of CPA for high risk patients. One-third of patients with schizophrenia (35%) and two-thirds of patients with affective disorder (66%) had not been receiving care under CPA despite presenting with features of social isolation, long-standing illness, a history of self-harm and non-compliance with treatment (see 'Recommendations' section for a comprehensive discussion about the underuse of CPA).

Non-compliance Of all Inquiry cases, 813 (14%) had been non-compliant prior to suicide. Of this group, 276 (39%) also missed their final appointment with services. This is substantially lower than in the previous reporting period, where 929 (22%) of Inquiry cases had been non-compliant in the month before suicide.

Non-compliant patients were more likely than other Inquiry cases to be male and present with features of social isolation (e.g., living alone) and adversity (e.g., unemployment). Clinically, they had higher rates of severe and enduring mental illness, violence, substance misuse, and co-morbidity. Of all non-compliant patients, 169 (21%) had co-occurring schizophrenia and substance misuse problems. Forty-six percent of non-compliant patients were also deemed to require care at the higher levels of CPA. Compliance with medication was encouraged in 73% of cases, an increase from the 62% previously reported (Appleby *et al.*, 2001). Non-compliant patients with schizophrenia (N = 165; 83%) were encouraged to comply with treatment via face-to-face meetings, while families were contacted in 63% of cases.

Dual diagnosis There were 1,659 Inquiry cases with severe mental illness and substance misuse or dependence problems, corresponding to 27% of the Inquiry population. This is a slight increase from the 23% previously reported (Appleby *et al.*, 2001). Hanging and strangulation, and self-poisoning were the most common methods of suicide, together accounting for 65% of cases. Compared with other Inquiry cases, service users with a dual diagnosis had higher rates of previous self-harm and violence, long-standing illness, and

Table 6.2 The number and percentage of patients in specific patient sub-groups.

Patient group	N	%
Inpatients	856	14
Post-discharge patients	1,271	20
Patients subject to CPA	2,118	35
Non-compliant patients	813	14
Patients with a dual diagnosis	1,659	27
Older patients	740	12

Source: Reproduced by permission of NPSA.

multiple admissions to an inpatient unit. They were also more likely to be an inpatient at the time of death, receiving care under higher levels of CPA and non-compliant with medication. Thirty-two percent of patients with a dual diagnosis, who were living in the community, had missed their final contact with services.

Older people There were 740 suicides over 65 years, corresponding to 12% of the Inquiry sample. Older patient suicides were more often female (N = 326; 44%), white (N = 692; 95%) and married (N = 287; 39%) compared with the rest of Inquiry cases. Hanging and strangulation (30%) and self-poisoning (28%) were the most common methods of suicide. They were less likely than younger Inquiry cases to have a history of behavioural problems (i.e., history of self-harm violence, substance misuse), to be receiving care under the higher levels of CPA, to have been non-compliant or missed contact with mental health services. However, they were more likely than younger Inquiry cases to have had contact with mental health services in the week prior to death, to have reported deterioration in physical health, and to have demonstrated evidence of depressive illness. The most common adverse life events reported for the three months prior to suicide included physical health problems and bereavement.

Summary: Patient suicide sub-groups The size of the patient sub-group is shown in Table 6.2.

Although patient suicides can be characterized by some common features, suicide deaths in specific patient sub-groups are also characterized by distinct features and risk factors. Some guidance has already been developed on the basis of Inquiry findings to help prevent suicide in these specific patient populations (e.g., inpatients). However, further research determining the features of patient sub-groups is needed to continue to develop specific recommendations to help reduce the occurrence of suicide.

Critical risk factors and risk management: considerations for suicide

Immediate and long-term risk assessment[1] at final contact with services is shown in Figure 6.4. High immediate and high long-term risk was identified in very few cases where suicide occurred (N = 106; 2%, N = 520; 9%, respectively). The majority of those who went on to commit suicide were judged to be at low or no immediate and long-term

---

[1] Risk of immediate and long-term risk are based on clinical judgement.

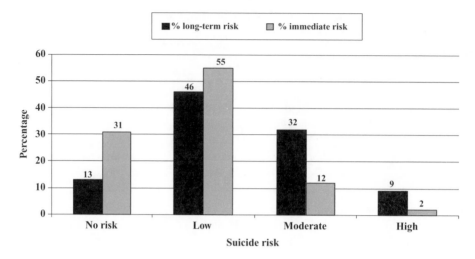

Figure 6.4   Mental health teams' estimation of suicide risk at last contact. Reproduced by permission of NPSA.

risk (86% and 59%, respectively). The pattern of risk assessment was similar for patients seen in the week prior to suicide.

Risk was more likely to be deemed high or moderate based on clinical features (e.g., non-compliance), rather than social or behavioural features (e.g., marital status, substance misuse).

Clinicians were asked about their views on preventability.[2] Respondents reported that suicide could have been prevented in 1,017 (19%) cases, slightly fewer than the 21% in the previous report. Specific patient characteristics were associated with assessment of preventability. Specifically, suicides in patients with severe mental illness, patients with affective disorder, inpatients, patients with demonstrable symptoms of mental distress at the final contact with services, and young patients (i.e., under 25 years) were judged as more preventable than the Inquiry sample as a whole. Suicides in patients with drug dependence were viewed as least preventable by clinicians.

Respondents' views on preventability varied depending on the specific patient subgroup. For example, respondents viewed inpatient suicides as more preventable than the Inquiry sample as a whole. The most common suggestions made by respondents to reduce the likelihood of inpatient suicide included better supervision and better compliance with treatment. Staff factors included better training, increased staff numbers, and better staff communication. Problems with ward design and problems with observation of other patients were also cited. Of all inpatient groups, patients who had absconded were viewed by respondents as the most preventable patient suicides. Risk was more often viewed as moderate or high although these cases were seen as no more or less preventable compared with other Inquiry cases. Further, for patients subject to CPA, risk was more

---

[2] Respondents were asked two questions pertaining to suicide prevention: (1) 'In your opinion, could the suicide have been prevented?' and (2) 'Which of the following would have made suicide significantly less likely at that time' followed by 18 suggestions, with space to include any other suggestions that had not already been listed. Respondents were asked to answer yes or no to the first question and yes or no to options presented in question 2. For a sample questionnaire, see www.manchester.ac.uk/nci.

often viewed as moderate or high although these cases were seen as no more or less preventable compared with other Inquiry cases.

Alternatively, the most preventable suicide cases could reasonably be defined as those individuals who were in closest proximity to services, in particular those individuals whose risk was evident but they did not receive the care commensurate with their assessed level of risk. For example, some inpatients died by suicide while under close observation, while other patients who had recently been discharged from an inpatient unit died by suicide before their first follow-up appointment with services. In some patient suicides, the patient had been subject to CPA, but there had been no assertive attempt by services to engage clients following a missed appointment. Viewed in this way, we can determine the number of most preventable patient suicide deaths. The number of suicide cases that may have been preventable equate to 349 (41%) inpatients, 255 (22%) post-discharge patients, and 504 (12%) community suicides. Based on this definition of preventability, 1,108 (18%) potentially preventable patient suicides (233 per year) were identified. Notably, both the calculation of preventability based on this definition, and respondents' views (previous paragraph) corresponded well (18% and 19%, respectively).

Homicide Inquiry Findings

The Inquiry was notified of 2,670 homicide convictions in the general population for the reporting period of Avoidable Deaths (4 years 9 months, 1999–2003) (Appleby *et al.*, 2006), corresponding to an average annual rate of 1.23/100,000 population in England and Wales (Appleby *et al.*, 2008).

Homicide perpetrators were characterized by male sex (90% of all perpetrators were males) and young age (median: 28 years). Victims were also often young and male (55%) and were most often acquaintances of perpetrators, particularly among males. However, 20% of victims (N = 435) were unknown to the perpetrator, or, so-called stranger homicides. Perpetrators of stranger homicides were more likely to be young males and the method of homicide was likely to be by hitting or kicking. These perpetrators were less likely to have mental illness or contact with mental health services than other homicide perpetrators. In line with this, Shaw *et al.* (2004) reported that, while there has been a rise in stranger homicides in the last few decades, there has been no equivalent rise in the number committed by people with mental illness. As such, the introduction of community care has not increased the risk to the general public.

Patient homicides

There were 249 (9%) homicides by patients (i.e., Inquiry cases, that is, individuals who had contact with specialist mental health services in the 12 months prior to the homicide). This equates to 52 patient homicide cases per year, which has remained stable since 1997. The social and clinical characteristics of these cases are shown in Table 6.3.

Patient homicide perpetrators were suffering from severe mental illness in 45% of cases (affective disorders or schizophrenia), and 52% had a secondary diagnosis. Substance dependence, personality disorder, and affective disorder were the most common secondary diagnoses. Substance misuse occurred in 85% of patients (N = 167), while 29% (N = 73) had a dual diagnosis (severe mental illness and substance misuse/dependence). Patient

Table 6.3   Social, clinical, offence characteristics and final outcome in court for patient homicides.

	No. (249)	%	(95% CI)
Demographic features			
Age of perpetrator: median (range)	31 (15–80)	—	—
Male suspect	216	87	(82–91)
Ethnic minority	44	19	(14–25)
Not currently married	165	71	(64–76)
Unemployed	143	62	(55–68)
Long-term sick	27	12	(8–17)
Living alone	82	37	(31–44)
Homeless	12	6	(3–9)
Priority groups			
Receiving care under enhanced CPA	67	27	(22–33)
Missed contact	90	39	(33–46)
Non-compliance	53	25	(19–32)
Clinical features			
Primary diagnosis (lifetime)			
Schizophrenia and other delusional disorders	74	30	(24–35)
Affective disorder (bipolar disorder and depression)	37	15	(11–19)
Alcohol dependence	36	14	(10–19)
Drug dependence	28	11	(7–15)
Personality disorder	42	17	(12–22)
Lifetime mental illness	240	96	(93–98)
Mentally ill at the time of offence	87	48	(40–55)
Offence variables			
Age of victim: median (range)[a]	38 (0–86)	—	—
Male victim	149	60	(53–66)
Victim was a stranger	24	11	(7–16)
Victim was a family member	42	17	(12–22)
Victim was a current or former spouse/partner	69	28	(22–34)
Victim was an acquaintance	70	28	(23–34)
Blunt instrument used	26	10	(7–15)
Final outcome			
Murder	102	41	(35–47)
Manslaughter section 2 (diminished responsibility)	37	15	(11–20)
Manslaughter (other including provocation, self defence)	104	42	(36–48)
Disposal			
Prison	170	68	(62–74)
Hospital order	71	29	(23–35)
Non-custodial	11	4	(2–8)

Source: Reproduced by permission of NPSA.

[a] The ages ranged from 0 to 86. There were 110 (4%) victims who were less than 1-year-old.

homicide perpetrators were often characterized by enduring mental illness (longer than five years) although 32% (N = 38) had never had an admission to hospital. This suggests that there is a significant proportion of perpetrators who did not have severe mental illness, conventionally defined. The commonest method of homicide was by the use of a sharp instrument, and victims were most often family members or spouses/partners (former or current).

Homicide perpetrator sub-groups

Although homicide perpetrators may share common characteristics, some sub-groups of homicide perpetrators who are mentally ill are also characterized by specific features. Three sub-groups of perpetrators are described below: perpetrators with a primary diagnosis of schizophrenia, perpetrators with a primary diagnosis of personality disorder, and perpetrators with alcohol and drug misuse problems.

Schizophrenia In total, 141 (5%) individuals had a primary diagnosis of schizophrenia, corresponding to approximately 30 cases per year. Of these, 74 (52%) had been in recent contact with mental health services (within 12 months) (i.e., patient homicide perpetrators). Eighteen patient perpetrators (13%) with schizophrenia had been in contact, but not within one year. Forty-nine individuals (35%) had never had contact with mental health services.

Patient homicide perpetrators with a primary diagnosis of schizophrenia were characterized by a history of drug misuse (N = 47; 72%); just under half of all patients had a history of alcohol misuse (N = 30; 50%). Forty-seven (57%) patients had a previous history of violence. Over two-thirds of patients were subject to CPA. Just under one-half of patient perpetrators (N = 31; 46%) were non-compliant with medication in the month preceding the offence while 26 (40%) missed their final contact with services. At the time of the offence, 51 (80%) patient perpetrators were mentally ill, with 48 (81%) psychotic at the time of the offence.

Personality disorder Of all patient perpetrators notified to the Inquiry, there were 146 (5%) individuals with a primary diagnosis of personality disorder, in the absence of severe mental illness. Of these, 42 (29%) had been in contact with mental health services within 12 months. Sixty-three perpetrators (43%) had never had contact with mental health services, and the remaining 41 (28%) had been in contact with mental health services, but not within one year of the offence.

Of patient perpetrators with a primary diagnosis of personality disorder, over half (N = 23; 55%) had a secondary diagnosis, predominantly substance misuse. A history of substance misuse was present in 33 (97%) patients while 32 (80%) had a history of self-harm. Eighteen (45%) patients had previous convictions for violence. Eight (19%) individuals with a diagnosis of personality disorder were receiving care under the highest levels of CPA. Six were non-compliant with treatment in the month prior to the offence, while 13 had missed their final contact with services.

History of alcohol and drug misuse There were 123 (21%) patient perpetrators with a history of alcohol misuse – individuals who had been in contact with services in the 12 months prior to homicide. Of those in contact within 12 months, 31 (25%) had been receiving care under higher levels of CPA, 48 (42%) had missed their final contact with services and 29 (27%) had been non-compliant with treatment in the month preceding the offence.

There were 122 (20%) individuals with a history of drug misuse who had been in contact with services in the 12 months prior to the homicide. Of those in contact within 12 months, 41 (34%) had been under higher levels of CPA, 51 (47%) had missed their final contact with services and 33 (32%) had been non-compliant with treatment in the month preceding the offence.

There was an increasing trend in substance misuse between 1997 and 2003.

Critical risk factors and risk management: considerations for homicide

Of the 249 patient perpetrators, immediate risk was judged high or moderate in 25 cases. Long-term risk was judged high or moderate in 62 cases. Patient perpetrators with severe mental illness and a history of serious violence were more likely than other patients to be viewed at high or moderate risk at last contact with services (N = 8; 22%).

Clinicians were asked about their views on the preventability of homicide by patients. Clinicians felt that there were some homicides that may have been prevented (N = 41; 21%), including those by 23 (56%) patients with schizophrenia, by 6 (15%) with multiple admissions, and by 25 (61%) patients who had previously been detained under the Mental Health Act. The factors that clinicians felt could have made homicide less likely included better patient compliance, closer contact with patient's family, closer supervision, and improved staff communication and training.

As with patient suicides, the most preventable homicides by patients could also reasonably be considered to be homicides perpetrated by patients who were in the closest proximity to services and who did not receive care commensurate with their level of risk (e.g., patients who committed homicide while under close observation while an inpatient, patients who committed homicide before their first follow-up appointment with services, patients with severe mental illness and a history of violence who were not subject to the CPA). Viewed in this way, we could identify 34 (14%) patient homicides – seven per year – that may have been preventable (including inpatients, post-discharge patients, and community patients).

Summary

The number of patient homicides has remained stable across the period of the study (N = 52). Mental illness was common although approximately one-third had never had an admission to hospital, suggesting that a substantial proportion of perpetrators did not have severe mental illness (as conventionally defined).

Patient homicide perpetrators may share some common features although patient sub-groups may also be characterized by specific factors. Further research into the general characteristics of homicide perpetrators and the specific characteristics of patient perpetrator sub-groups will help to develop guidance, with the aim of reducing the occurrence of homicide.

Recommendations

Since its inception, the Inquiry has made recommendations aimed at mental health services to help inform service provision and clinical practice. These recommendations (Appleby *et al.*, 2001) have formed a safety checklist for mental health services, incorporated into the National Suicide Prevention Strategy (NSPS) (i.e., '12 points to a Safer Service'). Inquiry work has also resulted in the inclusion of safety standards adopted as part of the evidence on clinical safety on which the National Service Framework (NSF) (Department of Health, 1999b) Standard 7 (suicide prevention) was based, and clinical recommendations which were included in the NHS plan (Department of Health, 2000a) (e.g., assertive outreach teams, and improving access to services for families and patients in crisis). The findings from this recent report underline the importance of certain key areas in relation to decreasing the likelihood of suicide and homicide occurring. These recommendations can be used to help services develop strategies to manage the risk of suicide and homicide in the patients of mental health services.

Absconding from inpatient wards

In line with previous research (Powell *et al.*, 2000), our findings showed that suicide risk increases during an inpatient admission. In our sample, 27% of inpatient suicides occurred when the patient had left the ward without permission, predominantly during periods of heightened risk (i.e., in the first week of admission, during the period of planning discharge). Services can reduce the risk of patients absconding through addressing the physical security of the ward, such as monitoring and controlling ward entry and exit through the use of swipe cards or CCTV. An awareness of the increased risk of patients absconding when the ward environment is disturbed is required. Further, although certain risk factors are common to many patients, an appreciation of individual level risk factors and triggers can help staff to identify when a patient's risk of absconding may increase.

Safety on inpatient wards

Inquiry recommendations have impacted on inpatient deaths – a decrease of 30%, equating to 67 fewer deaths per year (Appleby *et al.*, 2006). Further, recommendations on the removal of ligature points adopted in the Chief Medical Officer's Report (Department of Health, 2000b), have contributed to the decline in deaths by hanging. Overall, deaths by hanging have decreased by 51% since the inception of the Inquiry. The fall in inpatient suicides is encouraging, in particular the fall in suicides by hanging. Nonetheless, self-strangulation remains the commonest method of suicide on mental health wards, accounting for 75% of suicides. Clinical services and estates departments must continue to be vigilant about potential ligature points and ligature types, removing them where possible or ensuring that they are inaccessible.

Nonetheless, over one-fifth of inpatient suicides – 185 cases – occurred in patients under observation at the time of death, of which 18 (3%) were under close observations (i.e., one-to-one). Clearly there is a need to address observation protocols. Given the long gaps that occur in intermittent observations, patients deemed at high risk should be managed on close observations. Furthermore, if intermittent observations are considered suitable for a particular patient, they must be closely adhered to. Close observations can sometimes appear unduly intrusive to service users, particularly if distressed. Therefore, ensuring that observing staff interact with the service user concerned in a meaningful and therapeutic way can ensure that the process is beneficial, not only in managing risk but also in engaging service users in their care and facilitating progress.

Transition from inpatient ward to the community

Previous research has shown the period following discharge into the community to be a period of increased suicide risk (Ho, 2003). There is evidence to suggest that the suicide rate is over 100 times that of the general population in the first month after discharge, with the rate of suicide remaining elevated at around 30 to 60 times the general population rate for one year (Goldacre, Seagrott, and Hawton, 1993). In line with this, our findings showed that suicide cases were most frequent in the week following discharge, with the highest number occurring in the first few days. Of all post-discharge suicide, 22% occurred before the first follow-up by services.

There is clearly a need for intensive support in the community early on in the post-discharge period. Measures that could be implemented to manage the transition from ward to community more safely include immediate follow-up, particularly for those individuals with the highest risk or who are receiving care under CPA, and access to crisis services. A discussion with the patient about their individual risk factors is also important. Care plans need to consider the impact of these stressors, and clearly identify actions that can help to minimize their impact on the individual. Risk fluctuates during the period of planning discharge and needs to be regularly assessed and monitored, both before and after discharge has occurred.

Individuals who initiate their own discharge are at increased risk of suicide in the community, and require care which is commensurate with this, including adequate support arrangements in the community. The discharge of a patient can be a worrying and difficult time for families and carers and they should be involved in care planning (see also Chapter 3). This should include an assessment of their needs and a plan for managing those identified, with points of contact should they require additional support.

Use of CPA and management of risk

The Care Programme Approach (CPA) is an assessment framework designed for mental health services. It was introduced in 1991 (Department of Health, 1990) to ensure that patients with the highest level of need and at highest risk receive the most appropriate package of care. However, 436 patients who died by suicide and 18 homicide perpetrators had high levels of need and risk, but were not under CPA. Individuals not under CPA who died by suicide were characterized by severe mental illness and a history of either self-harming behaviour or recent detention under the Mental Health Act. Similarly, perpetrators not under CPA were characterized by severe mental illness and a history of violence or recent detention under the Mental Health Act. These patients constituted 39% and 53% of the most preventable suicides and homicides, respectively. This is a clear illustration of the underuse of CPA in people at high risk.

Further, there were individuals with high levels of need and risk who, although receiving care under the CPA, did not always receive sufficiently intensive care. For example, in 68 patients who died by suicide and in six who committed homicide, non-compliance with medication or disengagement from services did not elicit active attempts by services to encourage compliance or re-engage with services. It is, however, encouraging to note that although 14% of patient suicides and 25% of patient homicides were preceded by non-compliance with drug treatment, this number appears to be falling.

We can only speculate as to why CPA is underused. It may be that historical evidence of risk is not always available or checked (i.e., a violent incident several years ago) or that risk factors are common and are therefore not always acted upon. It is clear, however, that there is a need for robust use of the CPA, with care at the level required to provide treatment and manage risk. The CPA process needs to be more closely aligned to the management of risk, with comprehensive assessment of risk being carried out at CPA reviews. Necessary intervention if a patient's risk increases, such as non-compliance with medication or disengagement from services, should be clearly specified in the care plan, with nominated individual actions. The care plan should be developed in conjunction with the service user and their carers, ensuring that requirements of the patient are explicit to everyone involved. This should identify individual risk signatures and ensure that interventions are appropriate to individual needs. In addition to working with families, the use of home visits and close supervision may help prevent disengagement from services. In patients with a history of disengagement, the use of assertive outreach teams has been shown to help in maintaining contact with patients (Eagles *et al.*, 2003).

Guidelines reforming the CPA have recently been published (Department of Health, 2008). These focus on clarifying the underlying principles of the CPA, clearer links with risk management and a single level of CPA, equivalent to enhanced CPA with standard CPA being determined locally. To aid in ensuring that those at high risk, and in greatest need, are cared for under the CPA, the CPA has been redefined with the identification of key groups. These groups include people with severe mental illness or severe personality disorder and parenting or significant caring responsibilities, those with dual diagnosis (substance misuse), a history of violence or self-harm or who are in unsettled accommodation.

To improve care for those identified at high risk and on the CPA, guidelines include regular reviews of care pathways to improve continuity of care and to ensure that crisis and contingency planning, including risk assessment and management, are integral to care planning, with the use of risk assessment tools where appropriate.

Dual diagnosis

Dual diagnosis of schizophrenia and drug/alcohol problems increases the risk of both suicide and violence. Our findings showed that 27% of suicides and 36% of homicide perpetrators had a dual diagnosis. This patient group continues to be catered for poorly within general adult mental health services and greater consideration needs to be given to tackling the increased risk of patients with a mental illness and co-morbid substance misuse problem. This group is not infrequently stigmatized as being challenging and difficult, which can exacerbate difficulties in engagement. These difficulties can be minimized by utilizing a structured approach to assessments and, when required, support from equality and diversity resources within the organization. A team approach to care planning and frequent supervision of practitioners is also essential (Department of Health, 2009).

All staff within mental health services should have training in the detection and management of substance misuse. A collaborative approach, with engagement and involvement of the service user, carers and the clinical team, is critical in this service user group. This should involve working together with individualized support and, ideally, the service user taking a lead role in care planning, thus ensuring that needs are best met and that the most useful support mechanisms can be put in place (Department of Health, 2009).

Where possible, dual diagnosis services should be developed more comprehensively. However, in the absence of such dedicated services, there needs to be improved collaboration and joint working between general adult mental health and substance misuse services. This should include information sharing, jointly developed care plans and clear, explicit referral criteria for both services to ensure that these patients do not fall between the care of different services. An integrated approach to dual diagnosis has been shown to lead to improvements in engagement with patients, their psychotic symptoms, their need for admission to hospital, and their quality of life (Drake *et al.*, 1997).

All patients with severe mental illness and destabilizing substance misuse problems require intensive care and support and should receive care under the CPA to facilitate this. Recent guidelines reviewing the CPA process (Department of Health, 2008) explicitly include dual diagnosis patients as requiring assessment, with a view to caring for them under the provisions of the CPA.

Suicide in older people

The characteristics of older suicide cases differed from younger patients in a number of ways and suicide prevention strategies aimed at this age group must reflect these differences. Physical illness, recent bereavement and affective disorder are more significant for older adults, while schizophrenia and substance misuse are less common. Reducing suicide risk in older individuals should include good clinical care, with an awareness of the potential for the onset of mental illness during physical illness and after bereavement. Over two-thirds of older people had an affective disorder and there is a need to ensure detection and adequate treatment of depression in the elderly. The absence of any other features, such as substance misuse, suggests that standard therapies may be effective in managing affective disorders in this population.

Preventability and predictability

The Inquiry collects data on clinicians' views regarding preventability of suicide and homicide. Clinicians felt suicide could have been prevented in approximately one-fifth (19%) of suicide cases and in one-fifth of homicide cases (21%). Preventability was associated with factors such as proximity to care, multiple admissions to an inpatient unit, and detention under the Mental Health Act. Diagnostically, those with severe mental illness were seen as more preventable than those with alcohol or drug dependence. Factors that teams thought would decrease the likelihood of the suicide or homicide included closer supervision, better compliance with medication, closer contact with the family and carers and better staff training.

Arguably, patients who are in the closest proximity to care and at identifiably high risk may be most preventable, including those who were inpatients, recently discharged, had severe mental illness, had a history of violence or self-harm, were detained under the Mental Health Act, were non-compliant with treatment, or had disengaged with services. Viewed in this way, 18% of suicide and 14% of homicide cases could have been prevented.

Assessing the risk of suicide and violence amongst service users can be difficult; the low base rate of both is compounded by the high prevalence of factors increasing risk such as male gender, personality disorder and substance misuse. Management of risk necessarily involves better overall clinical care with appropriate and robust use of the CPA. Regular comprehensive assessment of risk should take place involving relevant tools where appropriate as an aid to decision-making, as outlined in the Best Practice guidance (Department of Health, 2009). Risk management through early intervention at the first signs of relapse or increased risk, alongside collaborative working with service users to understand individual risks, is, however, an achievable goal for services.

Future Directions

The Inquiry continues to provide definitive figures, and identify temporal trends in suicide and homicide. Where possible, we aim to do this in relation to Inquiry recommendations. For example, a continuing piece of work the Inquiry is undertaking is the investigation of the relationship between mental health service configuration and suicide rates. Specifically, this study examines the relationship between the implementation of Inquiry recommendations by mental health trusts, in relation to changes in suicide rates overall, and by individual trusts.

The case-series design of the Inquiry has limitations. For example, the data are based on clinical judgement and not standardized interviews (although a review of Inquiry methods in 1999 suggests that the Inquiry methodology is robust; Appleby *et al.*, 1999). Further, although the study design can provide data on the antecedents of suicide and homicide in mental health patients, it cannot identify specific factors associated with risk of suicide or homicide. To address this limitation, the Inquiry also conducts studies (as described in the previous sections of this chapter) using other methodologies (e.g., case-control studies), to identify the specific factors associated with risk (see Hunt *et al.*, 2007).

As well as employing different study designs, the Inquiry investigates other adverse outcomes in mental health patients. For example, the focus of the Inquiry to date has been on perpetrators of homicide who have been in the care of mental health services. However, less well understood is the likelihood of individuals with mental illness becoming a victim of homicide. The available evidence suggests that people with mental illness are at elevated risk of becoming a victim of homicide, with risk increasing in specific diagnostic and demographic groups (Hiroeh *et al.*, 2001). Given the public perception of the mentally ill as violent, this is a timely study to highlight the increased vulnerability of patients with mental illness to becoming victims of homicide themselves.

Taken together, the work of the Inquiry will continue to provide definitive figures on risk of suicide and homicide in mental health patients, to help inform service development, clinical practice and mental health policy.

Acknowledgements

Professor Louis Appleby is the Director of the Inquiry and the National Director for Mental Health in England. Funding for the work of the National Confidential Inquiry into Suicide and Homicide by People with Mental Illness (Inquiry) in England and Wales is provided by the National Patient Safety Agency (NPSA). We acknowledge the help of district directors of public health, health authority and trust contacts, the Office for National Statistics and consultant psychiatrists and other clinicians for completing the questionnaires.

References

Appleby, L., Shaw, J., Amos, T., McDonnell, R., Harris, C., McCann, K., Bickley, H., Parsons, R., Kiernan, K., and Davies, S. (1999). *Safer Services: Report of the National Confidential Inquiry into Suicide and Homicide by People with Mental Illness*. London: Stationery Office.

Appleby, L., Shaw, J., Sherrat, J., Amos, T., Robinson, J., McDonnell, R. *et al.* (2001). *Safety First: Five-year Report of the National Confidential Inquiry into Suicide and Homicide by People with Mental Illness*. London: Department of Health.

Appleby, L., Shaw, J., Kapur, N., Windfuhr, K., Ashton, A., Swinson, N., *et al.* (2006). *Avoidable Deaths: Five Year Report by the National Confidential Inquiry into Suicide and Homicide by People with Mental Illness, 2006*, available at www.manchester.ac.uk/nci.

Appleby, L., Shaw, J., Kapur, N., Windfuhr, K., Ashton, A., Swinson, N., *et al.* (2008). *The National Confidential Inquiry into Suicide and Homicide by People with Mental Illness: Lessons for Mental Health Care in Scotland*, available at www.manchester.ac.uk/nci.

Department of Health (1990). *The Care Programme Approach for People with a Mental Illness, Referred to Specialist Psychiatric Services*. HC(90)23/LASSL(90)11. London: Joint Health and Social Services Circular, Department of Health.

Department of Health (1992). *The Health of the Nation: Strategy for Health in England*. London: HMSO.

Department of Health (1999a). *Saving Lives: Our Healthier Nation*. London: Stationery Office.

Department of Health (1999b). *National Service Framework for Mental Health*. London: Department of Health.

Department of Health (2000a). *The NHS Plan: A Plan for Investment, a Plan for Reform*. London: Department of Health.

Department of Health (2000b). *An Organisation with a Memory*. Report of an expert group on learning from adverse events in the NHS chaired by the Chief Medical Officer. London: Department of Health.

Department of Health (2002). *National Suicide Prevention Strategy for England*. London: Department of Health.

Department of Health (2008). *Refocusing the Care Programme Approach: Policy and Positive Practice Guidance*. London: Department of Health.

Department of Health (2009). *Best Practice in Managing Risk: Principles and Evidence for Best Practice in the Assessment and Management of Risk to Self and Others in Mental Health Services*. London: Department of Health, available at www.dh.gov.uk/publications.

Drake, R. E., Yovetich, N. A., Bebout, R. R., Harris, M., and McHugo, G. J. (1997). Integrated treatment for dually diagnosed homeless adults, *Journal of Nervous and Mental Disease*, 185, 298–305.

Eagles, J. M., Carson, D. P., Begg, A., and Naji, S. A. (2003). Suicide prevention: a study of patients' views, *British Journal of Psychiatry*, 182, 261–265.

Goldacre, M., Seagrott, V., and Hawton, K. (1993). Suicide after discharge from psychiatric care, *Lancet*, 342, 283–286.

Harris, E. C. and Barraclough, B. (1997). Suicide as an outcome for mental disorders, *British Journal of Psychiatry*, 170, 205–287.

Hiroeh, U., Appleby, L., Mortensen, P. B., and Dunn, G. (2001). Death by homicide, suicide and other unnatural causes in people with mental illness, *Lancet*, 358, 2110–2112.

Ho, T. P. (2003). The suicide risk of discharged psychiatric patients, *Journal of Clinical Psychiatry*, 64, 702–707.

Hunt, I., Kapur, N., Webb, R., Burns, J., Robinson, J., Turnbull, P., Shaw, J., and Appleby, L. (2007). Suicide in current psychiatric inpatients: A case-control study, *Psychological Medicine*, 37, 831–837.

Hunt, I., Kapur, N., Webb, R., Robinson, J., Burns, J., Shaw, J., and Appleby, L. (2009). Suicide in recently discharged psychiatric patients: A case-control study. *Psychological Medicine*, 39, 443–449.

Kapur, N., Hunt, I., Webb, R., *et al.* (2006). Suicide in psychiatric inpatients in England. 1997 to 2003, *Psychological Medicine*, 3610, 1485–1492.

Linsely, K. R., Schapira, K., and Kelly, T. P. (2001). Open verdict v. suicide – importance to research, *British Journal of Psychiatry*, 178, 465–468.

Luoma, J. B., Martin, C. E., and Pearson, J. L. (2002). Contact with mental health and primary care providers before suicide: A review of the evidence, *American Journal of Psychiatry*, 159, 909–916.

O'Donnell, I. and Farmer, R. (1995). The limitations of official suicide statistics, *British Journal of Psychiatry*, 166, 458–461.

Powell, J., Geddes, J., Deeks, J., Goldacre, M., and Hawton, K. (2000). Suicide in psychiatric hospital inpatients: Risk factors and their predictive power, *British Journal of Psychiatry*, 176, 266–272.

Ritchie, J., Dick, D., and Lingham, R. (1994). *Report of the Inquiry into the Care and Treatment of Christopher Clunis.* London: Stationery Office.

Robinson, J. and Bickley, H. (2004). The role of the National Confidential Inquiry in relation to suicide prevention, in D. Duffy and T. Ryan (eds), *New Approaches to Preventing Suicide: A Manual for Practitioners.* London: Jessica Kingsley.

Shaw, J., Amos, T., Hunt, I., Flynn, S., Turnbull, P., Kapur, N., and Appleby, L. (2004). Mental illness in people who kill strangers: Longitudinal study and national clinical survey, *British Medical Journal*, 38, 734–737.

Windfuhr, K., While, D., Hunt, I., Turnbull, P., Lowe, R., Burns, J., *et al.* (2008). Suicide in juveniles and adolescents in the United Kingdom, *Journal of Child Psychology and Psychiatry*, 49, 1155–1165.

7

Evidence and Principles for Service User Involvement in Risk Management

Helen Gilburt

Introduction

Risk management in psychiatry has traditionally been seen as an organizational requirement, undertaken by clinicians, to highlight and prevent the risky behaviour of people
with mental health problems. As such, practices and policies have grown up centred
on the expertise and experiences of the clinicians involved and a growing body of research on risk and effective prevention and management strategies. Although the focus of
assessment, service users have and continue to play little or no role in risk management.

This chapter discusses the involvement of service users in risk management. The chapter is divided into three sections: the first section addresses user involvement, its origins,
and importance in the provision of mental health care and services; the second section
discusses the current position of user involvement in risk assessment and management
and common arguments for and against involvement; and the final section focuses on
practical examples of how clinicians can improve practice through user involvement and
the means for doing this.

The chapter provides evidence-based guidance derived through research and practice.
It aims to bring together the views and experiences of service users and practitioners,
introducing new ways of working for both parties and strengthening the interaction
between patient and clinician through improved risk management practices. In addition
to service users and carers, service managers may find this chapter useful in managing
services with increasingly diverse and dual roles. A number of examples of the application
of involvement models are explored here along with frameworks on the basis of which
involvement can be fostered.

Self-Harm and Violence: Towards Best Practice in Managing Risk in Mental Health Services, First Edition.
Edited by Richard Whittington and Caroline Logan.
© 2011 John Wiley & Sons, Ltd. Published 2011 by John Wiley & Sons, Ltd.

Introduction to User Involvement

The evolution of user involvement

The rise of consumerism, choice, and the recognition of the rights of individuals to be involved in the care they receive has led to an increased interest in user involvement in all aspects of health care. User involvement sits at the heart of government legislation on the provision of health services including mental health and has been identified as key to the modernization of the NHS (Department of Health, 2004). Often seen as 'experts by experience', service user involvement has been seen to benefit the development and running of health services, the provision of care, and the research undertaken and reported in a growing body of literature.

Despite this, user involvement is by no means uniform across different health specialities. The power balances that affect all relationships between providers and consumers of health services have proved to be a hurdle to service user involvement in a number of circumstances, this being perhaps most apparent in mental health. Rush (2004) argues that assumptions of dangerousness and irrationality about people with mental health problems creates an unresolved tension between the role of health professionals in, on the one hand, managing risk and treatment and, on the other hand, considering service users as equal partners. As such, user involvement in mental health remains at times contentious and moves to involve service users in mental health care, from service development through to decisions about an individual's care, have been inconsistent.

Types of user involvement

One way of resolving the tensions between service users as experts and partners and service users as passive recipients of care has been through the identification of levels of involvement. Models of involvement have been derived predominantly from studies of citizenship and involvement in systems of wider society, the most widely recognized being Arnstein's 'Ladder of Citizen Engagement' (Arnstein, 1969) (see Figure 7.1).

Arnstein describes degrees of involvement in terms of the participation of citizens in wider society, but this model has been used to describe levels of involvement in many different situations including research and health care provision. At the bottom of the ladder, there are citizens, be they members of a group or users of a service, who have little or no power. The bottom two rungs of the ladder describe involvement in terms of being manipulated or being educated. Arnstein sees people at these two levels as non-participants, because they have no power to influence the process or the decisions made as part of the process. The middle three rungs of the ladder are often identified as forms of tokenism. As such participants may receive information and have a voice and be heard, but they have insufficient power to ensure that their views will be taken into account. Inherent in these initial levels of engagement is the consideration of the power differential between two parties or groups. These three levels describe processes in which there is an unequal balance of power. Within the context of clinician–patient relationships, most often the clinician is the dominant power holder as the provider of care or containment. Arnstein argues that it is only when power is shared or there is a switch in the dominant power holder that true participation is achieved. The top three rungs of the ladder describe such situations in which partnership enables negotiation, compromise between

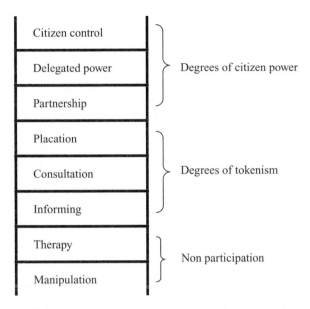

Figure 7.1 Arnstein's ladder of citizen engagement. (Reprinted by permission of the publisher (Taylor & Francis Group, www.informaworld.com).)

participants, and, for those who traditionally have been less empowered, the opportunity to obtain the majority of decision-making or managerial power.

Although this model has been the most prominent for the last 40 years, it has been criticized more recently as being too simplistic, particularly with reference to the involvement of patients in health services and decision-making processes. Tritter and McCallum (2006) argue that Arnstein's ladder implies that the best measure of participation is where service users are in control of the decision-making process, however, there are many instances where shared control, and at times control held by practitioners, may be preferable to service users. The ladder also implies that the power lies with one or the other of the participants and precludes the possibility that different views and opinions may exist. An analysis of this position is that, in facilitating user involvement, practitioners must be mindful of the level of participation that a service user wishes in addition to the recognition that multiple perspectives may exist. Negotiation of differences of opinion is the key to facilitating effective user involvement.

A model more often utilized in discussions of public involvement in the National Health Service is that proposed by Hanley *et al.* (2003). The model presents a more positive view of participation than Arnstein's and sidesteps those who set out to involve service users tokenistically (McLaughlin, 2009). Lying on a continuum, the model identifies three levels of involvement: consultation, collaboration and citizen control, each of which will now be discussed.

Consultation and collaboration

The concepts of consultation and collaboration are two dimensions of participation that have emerged as beneficial in the implementation of user involvement in research (Hanley *et al.*, 2003). Both involve practitioners and service users working together and the recognition of expertise on the side of each of the participants. Each represents a medium where participants with differing perspectives, training, and expertise can come together, the outcomes of which can be seen to meet at least some of the needs of all parties involved.

Consultation has been one of the most commonly adopted methods regarding the commissioning and restructuring of health services. In some areas, it is not only good practice but a legal requirement in which the views of service users must be taken into account. At the consultation level, service users are consulted about an issue with no sharing of power. Consultation represents a simple and easy way to involve service users. However, one of the main downfalls of this approach is that although service users may review or give an opinion on a topic or aspect of care, with the exception of legal contexts, they do not have to be adopted. This level of involvement can be perceived as tokenistic because clinicians maintain ultimate control (Trivedi and Wykes, 2002). With recognition of the differential expertise and knowledge of the parties involved, positive outcomes can be derived, both in terms of service users 'being heard' and clinicians obtaining further information as well as being able to assess potential peaks and pitfalls using a consultative approach.

Collaboration exists in the middle ground between consultation and citizen control and represents a form of partnership working. It is a process widely adopted across business, government, and academia. At its simplest, collaboration is about working together. It, therefore, implies both difference and commonality. Collaboration is about relationships – working together and not just alongside where, most commonly, parties aim to achieve a common goal (Meads and Ashcroft, 2005). The initial keys to collaboration involve bringing interested parties together, providing an understanding of the project or problem, and defining the desired results. Communication is a fundamental consideration in collaboration in which trust and mutual respect are important factors in its success. Crucially, the ability of both parties to negotiate and come to a mutual agreement enables a decision that benefits from the input of all parties to be reached and one in which each party has a vested interest. The outcomes of partnership relationships characterized by collaboration and negotiation indicate a number of benefits over traditional relational styles in which power is held predominantly by the professional. They are associated with higher uptake of medication (Day *et al.*, 2005; Fenton, Blyler, and Heinsson, 1997), lower hospitalization rates (Priebe and Gruyters, 1993), better prediction of inpatient violence during hospitalization (Beauford, McNeil and Binder, 1997), and improved outcomes such as quality of life, symptoms and functioning in depression (Zuroff *et al.*, 2000), schizophrenia (Svensson and Hansson, 1999), and case management (Crane-Ross, Lutz and Roth, 2006). This process of collaboration with service users has been most often situationally defined, with guidance developed on partnership working in research (Hanley *et al.*, 2003) and the provision of education and training (Harper, Goodbody, and Steen, 2003; Repper, 2000). Within care provision, perhaps one of the most promising areas addressing collaboration with service users is that of shared decision-making, which will be discussed in greater detail in the section 'Implementation of User Involvement', below.

Citizen control

Consumerist-focused approaches emphasize the importance of service user involvement in health care provision, yet there has been some resistance to the investment that this entails (Kirkpatrick, 2006). More democratic approaches, such as those driven by the civil rights movements in mental health, have challenged approaches to service user involvement that do not establish equality between participants. They have opted for service user-controlled endeavours. Two areas in which service user-controlled endeavours are becoming increasingly prominent are service user-led research and service user-run services. Both can be seen to evolve from structures in which service users were typically the subject of research or treatment with little or no power. Challenges in positivist dialogues on the nature of knowledge have seen service user experiences become increasingly important and service user-led services are beginning to flourish. Perhaps one of the most long-established and widely known user-led services is the alcohol treatment service, Alcoholics Anonymous. Service user-led services have shown that they can provide equal if not better treatment services for people with mental health problems from community support through to inpatient facilities (Greenfield *et al.*, 2008). This remains an exciting area of development, which many envisage will continue to grow.

Summary

This section has provided a brief introduction to service user involvement drawing from the literature and experience that has developed from the fields of academic research, service development, and service provision. It has introduced some frameworks for considering degrees of service user involvement and some exciting developments in each of these areas. But what of service user involvement in risk management? The next section discusses the status of user involvement in risk assessment.

User Involvement and Risk Management

Risk assessment, government and policy

Mental health policy has enabled the development of community services over the past 30 years with the cumulative effects becoming more noticeable over the past 10 years. In addition, a significant outcome of the ensuing media attention of incidents involving people with mental illness in the community in the 1990s has been a growth in the area of risk assessment and management (Hanily, 1999). The role of risk assessment and management is ultimately to reduce the likelihood of adverse events, which, in turn, benefits both service users, practitioners, and the public. Many argue that in the case of mental health, government pressure and legislation has led to a change in the climate of psychiatric services, which have inevitably become risk orientated (Petch, 2001). The development of a risk averse culture in the NHS has led to staff having to cope with increased attribution of blame and low staff morale, resulting in problems with recruitment and retention in services (Health Select Committee, 2000; Szmukler, 2000) (see also Chapter 11). As services move from a primary objective of providing better health outcomes for patients to public safety (Holloway 1996), what voice do service users have in the ascertainment of risk and resulting management plans that ultimately affect their lives and, in some cases, their liberty?

Government policy on user involvement in health provision does not exclude risk assessment and management but actively advocates it. Policy guidance and legislation in England and Scotland state that 'service users should be involved in the process of risk assessment and management' (Department of Health, 1999; Scottish Executive, 2000). This is further reflected in the first of the *Best Practice* guidelines (Department of Health, 2009; see below)

Best Practice point 1

Best practice involves making decisions based on knowledge of the research evidence, knowledge of the individual service user and their social context, knowledge of the service user's own experience and clinical judgement.

Why involve my patient in risk management?

A good and justifiable risk management plan is one built on the best evidence, information, and clinical judgement available. There are three parties involved in risk management: the clinical team, those who have information about the patient such as carers, and the patient him- or herself. As such, the best decisions about risk management involve obtaining information from, and sharing it with, all three parties. Increased service user involvement at the assessment phase provides enhanced information while involvement in formulation and transparency in decision-making maximizes accountability to service users, providing a greater than otherwise chance of keeping them engaged in interventions and risk management arrangements (Logan, 2003).

> Patients involvement in the process of risk formulation is likely to improve the value of the assessment. (Kumar and Simpson, 2005)
> In the work of forensic and general adult psychiatrists is the need to involve patients in their own risk assessment, if they are expected to understand why interventions are necessary. (Kumar and Simpson, 2005)

The therapeutic value of allowing service users to become involved in their own care and treatment not only has implications for risk management but for the wider provision of health care, which should be considered (Boevink, 2000; Davidson, Lawless and Leary, 2005; Hickey and Kipping, 1998). A literature review of user involvement in mental health care indicates benefits including a better quality of care, greater treatment compliance, improved health, and higher levels of patient satisfaction (Stringer *et al.*, 2008).

Involving service users in discussion and decisions around risk management has an increasing importance in meeting the government agenda of personalized services. To address the competing agendas of avoidance of adverse risk and the increasing demand for personalized services (which may be less subject to regulation and so potentially more risky), service managers can work with users to develop a common understanding of the measurement, recording, and reduction of risk (Scottish Executive, 2006).

Finally, within health policy, the gradual move towards greater access to patient information and e-communication in health may have further implications for service user involvement in risk assessment. In a discussion paper addressing risk communication in mental health using electronic systems, Langan (2009) reminds professionals that rights and safeguards around the handling, exchange of, and access to, information contained in the Data Protection Act (1998) and Freedom of Information Act (2000) promote routine sharing of health and social care information with service users. Guidance reinforcing this highlights that where information is stored with a marker indicating the increased likelihood of violence, the service user should be informed of the fact, the rationale for using the marker, and when it will be reviewed or removed (Information Commissioner's Office, 2006). The guidance indicates that where the service user is not informed, this should be in extreme cases only.

Service user involvement in risk assessment: Langan and Lindow

While both research and policy promote the involvement of service users in risk assessment and management, there exists a dearth of information as to how this should be done and the implications of doing so. Besides the numerous case studies of services developing involvement, perhaps one of the only documents to address service user involvement in risk assessment is that of Langan and Lindow (2004).

This piece of research evolved from concerns that the voices of people who were considered to pose a risk to others were absent from research, policy, and practice. In working with a small group of such service users and members of their care team, they provide a valuable insight into the perceptions of the risks posed by and to service users, the process of risk assessment, and the help provided in managing risk and its usefulness. One of the outcomes of the research was a set of guidelines, informed by service users about the management of risk to others among mental health service users living in the community.

Knowledge and involvement in risk management

Langan and Lindow (2004) found that it was uncommon for mental health service users to be involved in risk assessment and management or to know that risk assessments were being conducted on them (see also Chapter 2). Frank discussion about risk between professionals and service users appeared rare. Audits undertaken by the Mental Health Act Commission found that, despite guidance that care plans should be shared and signed by service users, it was extremely rare for risk assessments to be so signed, a further indication of a lack of service user involvement in care planning and risk assessment (Mental Health Act Commission, 2006). Although this research took place some time ago, a review of policy and research indicates that little has changed since (Langan, 2008).

> We may not be as open about our risk assessments as we need to be. (quote from psychiatrist interviewed by Langan and Lindow, 2004)

A number of authors have suggested reasons for the lack of user involvement in risk assessment. The dual roles of containment of risk and promotion of service user involvement are often contradictory (Rose *et al.*, 2004). While the former reinforces professional power, control, and expertise, the latter involves recognition of shared expertise and power-sharing in decision-making, which some professionals may think risky and preclude user involvement (Langan, 2008). Interviews conducted with professionals indicate some of their fears and reservations about making risk assessment more transparent and increasing the involvement of service users (Langan and Lindow, 2004). Some expressed concern about the impact on service users of being assessed as posing a risk and the consequences of being assigned stigmatizing labels to the service user's identity. A few thought that openness might prompt disengagement, particularly where the service user did not agree with the professionals' views about risk. Many were concerned about the risks to personal safety if they were to tell a service user that professionals considered them to pose a potential risk to other people, although we will see that this is commonplace within forensic mental health services. In contrast, such fears do not always represent reality and involving service users in risk management can sometimes have surprising outcomes:

> And I think that it's interesting that, since we did the risk assessment, he's been much better with us ... You know, I sometimes think it may have improved his relationship with us. (Langan and Lindow, 2004)

For those who do wish to work more collaboratively with service users, there is very little literature on how to do this and many professionals lack confidence or experience in discussing risk openly with service users (Langan and Lindow, 2004).

Service user's perceptions of risk

A common barrier to involving patients in risk assessment is a professional's fear of service users who lack insight, leading them to underestimate or be unaware of the risks they may pose and the situations in which harmful outcomes might occur. While some service users are unable to accept that they may be dangerous, Langan and Lindow's interviews show that many others are equally able to recognize the risk they have presented and continue to present to others and themselves.

> You know when I start getting towards the point when I, myself, am getting violent ... I don't know what I would do with myself if I had hit X. You know, even if the injuries hadn't been severe, I still don't know what I what I would have done with myself. (Langan and Lindow, 2004)

For many, acknowledgement of risk led to deeply distressing feelings about their behaviour when unwell. Yet many responded with an expressed need to work with the professionals supporting them in order to reduce the likelihood of them acting in ways that put themselves and other people at risk. As such, many service users are keen to play a role in their own risk assessment and management.

Accurately assessing and recording risk

Risk assessment is dependent on accurate information about mental state, past and present risk behaviours, triggers, protective factors, social functioning and social circumstances (Langan and Lindow, 2004). It is argued that the involvement of service users is central to obtaining accurate information on each of these aspects in formulating a risk management plan.

Risk contains elements which are both static and dynamic. While static elements, such as a history of suicide attempts, may present a person at a higher risk level, rarely do people present as a risk all of the time. Developed through studies of specific populations, actuarial methods of risk assessment based on static risk assessment provide evidence of the probability of risk behaviours. However, one-dimensional models employing static risk factors alone are inadequate in risk prediction. Multidimensional information in which context is an integral consideration in risk assessment can enable greater prediction in terms of imminence and severity of violence (Michie and Cooke, 2006). Dynamic factors, unlike static factors, are dependent on the here-and-now situations in which service users find themselves. Their predictive value is relevant to the short-term rather than long-term probability of risk. This understanding of day-to-day changes in the status of dynamic factors requires more significant involvement with services users (Langan and Lindow, 2004).

Service user involvement and the understanding of contextual factors also have an important role to play in the risk management of people from black and minority ethnic communities. Studies of violence based predominately on Caucasians of European heritage have led to concern that a lack of cultural sensitivity and awareness may play a role in the over-representation of ethnic minorities in forensic settings. In a qualitative study of Australian indigenous offenders, anger was widely expressed but had a number of culturally specific meanings, not all related directly to risk of violence (Day *et al.*, 2006). The authors highlight the importance of context in understanding risk factors in ethnic minority populations.

Risk formulation: strengths and protective features

Although service users may present a number of risks to self and to others in particular contexts, often these can be avoided. A recognition of service users' strengths alongside possible problems that they might encounter and with which they might present is an invaluable tool in risk management. This is reflected in point 4 of the *Best Practice* points reproduced below.

Best Practice point 4

Risk management must be built on a recognition of the service user's strengths and should emphasize recovery.

There is widespread recognition that service users are experts, with an in-depth knowledge of living with a mental health problem (e.g., Chief Medical Officer, 2001). As experts in their own illness and individual journey through the mental health system, the experiences of service users are an important resource that can help improve care planning (Tait and Lester, 2005) and can be integral in understanding what factors lead to an episode of illness and which factors helped them recover. Borrill (2000) emphasizes the way in which users can predict when they are about to become unwell and formulate appropriate responses at an early stage. Such approaches are embraced in the use of wellness action plans, joint crisis plans, and advance directives, which will be discussed in section three.

Risk management strategies

Despite recognition of contexts in which risk may be heightened, and the triggers and factors that protect against such risks, risk is an inevitable part of life. One of the products of risk management in mental health has been a predominance of contributions by practitioners suggesting that risk is something best managed by professional experts (Ryan, 2000). Much of this focuses on high risk but low frequency events. In the fields of health and social care, where a great deal of risk assessment and management in day-to-day life is undertaken by non-professionals, including service users and informal carers, this represents an important and largely omitted source of information (Manthorpe and Alaszewski, 1998). Ryan (2000) argues that since what we perceive frequently dictates what we do, often despite evidence to the contrary, understanding what service users perceive as risk is the prerequisite for understanding how risks are identified and then managed.

In a qualitative study of perceptions of risk, a wide range of risks were examined with service users and their risk management experiences explored (Ryan, 1998). The study found that many of these risks were routinely dealt with on a daily basis and, therefore, many of the strategies employed by users were not given much consideration. However, other risks produced a wide range of responses. Ryan identifies two models of service user strategies: proactive risk management and passive risk management. Proactive strategies exist where the user makes a conscious and premeditated effort to deal with a particular risk. These were often risks they faced or posed as a result of their illness and service users were frequently seen to take the initiative in managing the risk using the experiences they had gained from living with their illnesses. Many of the strategies that users found easiest to identify were those that managed violence to other people or violence to themselves. The principal characteristic that appears to be most strongly associated with this model is the length of illness experience; those with lengthy illness experiences were likely to have a larger number of strategies for coping with changing risk. A further characteristic relating to this model was that of insight; where service users understood and accepted their illness, they appeared more capable of proactively managing risk. Decision-making characteristics which were associated with this model of risk management included learning from previous experiences to influence future strategies and calling upon other people to assist in the management of risk.

In the second model, service users responded passively to risk events that occurred and in some circumstances they did not do anything at all. Virtually all the examples of passive risk management obtained from service users were concerned with low consequence risks. None was concerned with the risk of violence to others or self. Service users with brief or lengthy illness experiences adopted passive strategies. However, those service users with less insight were more likely to adopt passive strategies or to have no strategy at all. The risks commonly managed through this model were vulnerability including disempowerment, and self-harm.

Summary

With risk management being an important consideration in the provision of care and treatment provision for people with mental health problems, the studies of Langan and Lindow (2004) and Ryan (2000) highlight not only the relevance and importance of risk management to service users, but also the potential benefits of involving service users in the process of risk assessment and management.

It can be seen that service users have an interest in, and knowledge of, the risk factors posed and faced by people with mental illness. Furthermore, research demonstrates that they have a considerable array of methods for dealing with the range of risks they face as a result of their illness, which many use proficiently. It is also clear that service users have significant insights and skills that could be allied to those of mental health professionals to improve risk management in general.

Professionals could improve their own formal risk management by both learning from users about the risks they perceive, how users manage risks, and by helping service users to develop their skills further in this area. Exploring ways that this could be achieved could truly involve mental health service users whilst at the same time enabling them to take greater control of their lives (Ryan, 2000).

Current lack of service user involvement in risk management may represent not only professional attitudes to expertise, insight, and management of people with mental health problems, but also a lack of skills and confidence in working collaboratively with service users. Effective training may address some of these deficiencies, enabling clinicians to become more capable of effecting user involvement in daily practice including risk management (Stringer *et al.*, 2008).

The next section aims to provide some examples of the implementation of user involvement in the provision of care and treatment. Examples will include the process of shared decision-making, the use of risk management measures in which user involvement plays an integral role, crisis planning, and the emergence of the recovery model as a framework for effecting user involvement risk management.

Implementation of User Involvement

Investing in relationships to manage risk

Therapeutic relationships remain at the heart of the effective provision of mental health care. The ability to establish a therapeutic relationship is one of the most important competencies; the clinician–patient relationship is one that affects every aspect of the clinical process and the quality of care given. In the context of risk assessment, there is extensive evidence that the quality of the therapeutic alliance is one of the most significant factors in assessing risk in suicidality (Bongar *et al.*, 1989), as well as assessing potential for violence in those at risk to others (Beauford, McNeil and Binder, 1997). In terms of outcomes, the therapeutic alliance has a strong positive impact on suicidal ideation of patients as well as a positive impact on reducing future displays of violence. Overall, the therapeutic relationship is an important and reliable predictor of patient outcome in mainstream psychiatric care.

A large proportion of the research on therapeutic relationships has been undertaken in psychotherapeutic settings. Studies of the factors associated with therapeutic alliance teach us much about forming relationships with patients to engage in consultation and collaboration in risk management. Key components of the therapeutic alliance include the relationship and bond between the therapist and client, and a consensus between the therapist and client regarding the goals of treatment (Bordin, 1979, 1994). Such components are not a simple function of a relationship but as we will see demand skills and the development of competencies much like any other clinical process.

A number of therapist factors are known to affect – positively and negatively – the formation and maintenance of the therapeutic alliance (Ackerman and Hilsenroth, 2003). Therapist factors which *positively* affect the formation and maintenance of the therapeutic alliance include:

- being flexible and allowing patients to discuss issues which are important to them;
- being respectful;
- being warm, friendly and affirming;
- being open;
- being alert and active;
- being able to show honesty through self-reflection;
- being trustworthy. (Ackerman and Hilsenroth, 2003)

Therapist factors which *negatively* affect the formation and maintenance of the therapeutic alliance include:

- being rigid;
- being critical;
- making inappropriate self-disclosure;
- being distant;
- being aloof;
- being distracted;
- making inappropriate use of silence. (Ackerman and Hilsenroth, 2001)

The building and maintenance of a therapeutic alliance is an active process requiring ongoing self-reflection. The development of therapeutic relationships requires a number of skills, which must be invested in as with any other area of professional development (Ackerman and Hilsenroth, 2003).

Key skills in the development of a therapeutic alliance are the ability to:

- listen to the patient in a sensitive, supportive, and non-judgemental way, conveying a comfortable attitude when the client describes their experience;
- make sure that the patient is clear about the rationale for the offered treatment;
- gauge whether the patient understands the treatment rationale and to respond to any concerns openly and non-defensively to resolve uncertainty;
- help the patient express concerns or doubts about the treatment and/or their clinician, especially related to mistrust or scepticism;
- help the patient articulate their treatment goals and maximize the congruence between the aims of patient and clinician. (Ackerman and Hilsenroth, 2001, 2003)

In Langan and Lindow's (2004) work on risk assessment, the role of the therapeutic relationship is particularly highlighted by service users. A good relationship within which a service user's qualities were valued was important in discussing risk, as were sensitivity and timing. They also highlighted the value of holistic approaches to risk assessment, considering not just mental state and behaviour but all risks that the person may be experiencing; for example, those arising from lack of work, poverty, stigma, discrimination, or racism, as well as the risks of suicide and self-harm. Where the patients' strengths and abilities were valued, they had a good relationship with a professional that had developed over time. Also, where the support offered was what the person wanted rather than being imposed, negotiation and the reaching of common ground in establishing a risk management plan was more likely.

The therapeutic relationship in practice: risk assessment and management of self-harm

Self-harm confers a considerable risk of completed suicide and is one of the most common reasons for admission to hospital (National Institute of Clinical Excellence (NICE), 2004). The experience of care for people who self-harm has often been identified as unacceptable, with attitudes among those responsible for providing services being highlighted as being of importance in ensuring appropriate management of this patient group. NICE guidelines highlight the value of several of the factors identified by Ackerman and Hilsenroth (2001, 2003) in providing care to people who self-harm. Key priorities include treating people who have self-harmed with care, respect and privacy, taking into account the distress a patient may be experiencing. Increasingly, guidance on the treatment of self-harm calls for a comprehensive assessment of needs, a process Slade (1994) argues should arise from negotiation between service users and staff. In assessing risk and needs, health care workers should work to understand and engage the service user. Since the use of risk assessment scales is recommended in only the most severe cases, the importance of developing a therapeutic alliance in a full assessment is of utmost importance.

Shared decision-making

One of the most common and increasingly popular forms of collaboration between clinicians and patients in health services is that of shared decision-making. The last decade has seen a substantial move towards empowering the users of health care services in the United Kingdom, through the promotion of choice and shared decision-making (Breeze, 1998). Shared decision-making is presented as one effective method of developing government mandated patient-centred care and constructing management plans that best meet the needs of the patient.

Shared decision-making is built upon the notion that there are two experts in the consultation room: the patient and the provider. In shared decision-making, the clinician considers the care of a service user, the problems faced, and a number of possible solutions. Providers have expertise in the science-informed processes of medical diagnosis and treatment. Patients have the expertise by virtue of the lived experience of their disorder, and their intimate knowledge of what gives their life value, meaning, purpose, and quality. Ideally, both knowledge domains are bridged through the process of shared decision-making, as both parties strive for agreement on what the problem is and what the outcomes of treatment should be (Deegan, 2007; Deegan and Drake, 2006).

During the process of shared decision-making, the clinician must both explore the service user's views of the problem and illness as well as the possible care options available. The clinician is required to act as a source of unbiased information and expertise for the patient in making a decision. They must create an atmosphere in which the patient feels comfortable expressing his or her views and in which they will be listened to. The patient must be able to outline what he or she feels is important and, if necessary, the clinician must actively seek out the patient's values. The values must be made explicit because this helps the patient him- or herself clarify what is important, and it emphasizes that the clinician is interested in their opinion. Finally, the clinician must negotiate with the patient what the objectives of the care are and which options are most appropriate for that patient. In practice, clinicians must be open to a number of options, be honest with the patient, be prepared to state their preferred option and why, answer any questions the patient has, discuss the patient's preferred option, and negotiate towards a final decision.

Mental health, like other areas of medicine, is moving towards shared decision-making (Adams and Drake, 2006). Many of these studies have taken place with community-based populations. However, a study of shared decision-making for inpatients with schizophrenia showed that the process was feasible for most patients, and those patients that took part felt more involved in their care and treatment (Hamann *et al.*, 2006). In terms of outcomes of shared decision-making in mental health, studies show improved patient satisfaction (Malm *et al.*, 2003; Swanson *et al.*, 2007), treatment compliance, and clinical outcomes (Ludman *et al.*, 2003; von Korff *et al.*, 2003). While obstacles such as time constraints still remain (Gravel, Legare, and Graham, 2006), evidence suggests that this model of communication can be a beneficial tool in increasing user involvement in decisions involving treatment and care.

Shared decision-making in practice: Joint crisis plans

Risk management has had a predominately paternalistic decision-making approach. That is, risk management has been the role of the professional required often to make a decision based on the best interests of the patient. However, as a challenge to the emphasis of the professional as expert and ultimate decision-maker, an alternative approach has been gaining ground encompassing shared decision-making and is proving to be a useful tool with favourable outcomes acceptable to all parties. In the process of risk assessment and management, the use of joint crisis plans (JCPs) in mental health has demonstrated the value of collaborative working.

Starting as a service user-led self-advocacy initiative, crisis cards have been used in the voluntary sector since 1989. They offer service users the ability to record their wishes, needs, and concerns should they experience a mental health crisis. Since their advent, a number of variations have arisen and the scope of the cards has widened in a number of instances to incorporate not just preferred care during a crisis but active exploration of preventative strategies based on strengths-led approaches and greater involvement of the care team.

The JCP as pioneered by Sutherby *et al.* (1999) represents an advanced form of crisis card incorporating preventative strategies, crisis care, and practical considerations for during a crisis. It incorporates elements of the strengths-based approach and shared decision-making involving the clinical team and service user working in partnership facilitated by an independent JCP facilitator.

In practice, the development of a JCP involves the service user, clinical team – usually psychiatrist and care coordinator – a carer, and an independent facilitator. The plan is developed over a period of three meetings. In the first meeting, the facilitator meets with the service user and their care coordinator to introduce the plan and what will be involved.

The service user is encouraged to take the blank plan away and discuss with friends and family. The plan is formulated in the second meeting. At this meeting care coordinator, psychiatrist, service user, and carer reflect on previous crises to establish how to approach crises in the future. Led by the facilitator, participants are encouraged to be open about risk, including risk factors leading to relapse, as well as staff, patient and carers' perceptions of risk during crises, and how to avoid and also how to deal with adverse risks during crises. Contrary to traditional crisis planning, in which the professionals take the lead and whose decisions ultimately result in the plan, during the JCP process the group as a whole aim to arrive at a number of decisions regarding crisis planning that are acceptable to all parties. Where there are differences of opinion, the role of the facilitator is to offer possible options for each party and facilitate agreement. If no agreement can be reached, then this is reflected in the crisis plan with the service user's views and preferred option recorded.

While JCPs are in their infancy, early results show that they are acceptable to service users and that they may also prove to be valuable aids in involving service users in care and facilitating partnership working around areas of risk. The outcomes for service users utilizing a JCP are also favourable. In a randomized controlled trial of service users with relapsing psychotic illness, those using crisis cards had fewer compulsory admissions and treatment (Henderson *et al.*, 2004). Further trials are underway to establish long-term outcomes and wider applications of this model.

Recovery: a framework implementing user involvement in risk management

Recovery has been a movement in mental health for some time. It has grown from strength to strength in the United States, Australia, and New Zealand and has taken root in the United Kingdom to a more limited extent. It is an approach that recognizes that people with mental illness may experience symptoms throughout their life, but that this need not impinge on their ability to live full and fulfilling lives. Recovery is not the absence of illness – an absolute recovery – but a recovery from the often overwhelmingly negative and disabling effects of mental illness. Instead of becoming passive subjects of illness and recipients of care, recovery supports service users in taking control and striving for meaningful lives. Recovery-orientated services work collaboratively with service users to identify their strengths, enhance skills, deal with losses, as well as find meaning in illness, developing hope along the way for a positive future. Central to their role in recovery, recovery-orientated services support people 'to do', or 'do with' professionals rather than professionals 'doing to' patients.

Recovery serves as strong model for enhancing user involvement in risk management, both in theory and in practice. User involvement and empowerment is at the heart of the recovery model. While the recovery model is too vast to explore here in full, this section presents how some of some of the central premises of risk management are addressed within a recovery framework.

Fostering collaborative relationships in recovery

As we have identified, successful risk assessment and management along with user involvement are hinged on the facilitation of effective relationships. Recovery-focused mental health services are underpinned by a focus on relationships. Slade (2009) characterizes clinician–patient relationships into three categories: 'real relationships'; 'partnership relationships'; and 'detached relationships'. They exist not as separate entities but lying on a spectrum. In traditional mental health services, there is an emphasis on professionalism often exemplified by the detached relationship category. In detached relationships discourse is driven by the clinician's agenda and, in practice, power is held by the clinician. Within recovery-orientated services, there is a move towards partnership relationships and, in some instances, real relationships. Partnership relationships represent the centre of the spectrum and involve collaboration and joint working, recognizing each person as experts in their area, while real relationships are those in which both parties involved exhibit genuineness – being yourself – and realism, in this context perceiving another not through a clinical lens but as another person. Within traditional mental health services, real relationships are often seen as unprofessional, while in the right circumstances, these are legitimized in recovery-focused services.

Partnership relationships predominate in recovery-focused services. Two key differences between partnership and detached relationships have been identified: power and listening. In a partnership relationship, the ultimate decision-maker is the patient other than where legal issues override. Partnership relationships in such services involve a change in role and focus for both staff and service users. The particular role that the clinician takes, which is prominent in the recovery approach, is that of coach. Coaching involves empowering patients to take personal responsibility, focusing on the process of recovery, that is, how the person can live with mental illness and its effects rather than just on treating mental illness. The clinician uses their skills in supporting strengths rather than focusing on deficits and so develops self-management. Ultimately, they work towards the goals of the patient rather than the clinician, using the skills of the clinician, and above all developing a relationship in which both participants must make an active contribution. Listening as a skill is a key component in this process. Listening here is not centred as in detached relationships on achieving a diagnosis or formulation to fit a person but in deriving a patient-centred understanding of what their goals are, be it to avoid hospitalization or to get back to work, and how to achieve these. It is a process in which the patients' values, preferences and strengths are established.

Dealing with risk

Risk-taking plays an important contribution to recovery. Taking risks is a necessary part of being human; as Deegan (1992) has suggested, people need to have 'the dignity of risk' and 'the right to fail' in order to learn from their own mistakes. Recovery-focused services classify risk into two distinct entities: harmful risks and positive risk-taking. Harmful risk relates to behaviours that are illegal or not socially sanctioned. Positive risk relates to behaviours which involve the person taking on challenges leading to personal growth and development (Slade, 2009). In an increasingly risk averse society and with mental health professionals as purveyors of personal and public safety, often the boundaries between harmful risk and positive risk-taking can become blurred and professionals can err on the side of over-protectionism.

In its advocacy of power sharing and collaborative working with service users, it is not surprising that one of the main concerns facing the recovery model is that recovery increases professionals' and providers' exposure to risk and liability (Davidson *et al.*,

2006). Yet Davidson argues that advocates of recovery approaches actively embrace the appropriate use of risk assessment and management. They welcome it on the condition that, in the majority of cases, when people are found not to pose serious or imminent risks to themselves or others, they are allowed to make their own choices and, by necessity, their own mistakes through positive risk-taking. Thus, although a recovery orientation might in fact increase risk, it is primarily the person's access to opportunities for taking risks that needs to be increased, not necessarily the provider's or the community's exposure to risk.

Positive risk management is very much a focal point for recovery-focused mental health services – and the *Best Practice* guidance exemplifies this in the second of its guidelines. Such services identify both recovery goals as well as treatment goals and the utilisation of positive risk-taking is used as a means to developing strategies for avoiding harmful risk and strengthening the patient's ability to deal with such risk.

Best Practice point 2

Positive risk management as part of a carefully constructed plan is a required competence of all mental health practitioners.

Slade (2009) identifies a number of steps taken in the approach to risk management by recovery-focused services, which highlight the role of the service user as central to the process:

- Audited and organizationally-supported systems are used to assess, develop, and document actions focused on reducing harmful risk. The service user understands that these treatment goals are necessary for the professional – it is not necessarily done for the consumer. The development of treatment goals is led by the professional.
- Audited and organizationally-supported systems are used to assess, develop, and document actions involving positive risk-taking in the service of recovery goals. The professional understands that this is about the recovery goals of the service user – it is not necessarily agreed with by the professional. The development of recovery goals is led by the service user.
- There is a greater focus on positive risk-taking than on avoiding harmful risk, because this is what develops risk self-management skills.
- Actions to reduce harmful risks are as far possible decided collaboratively with the service user. Differences are discussed openly, and where treatment goals need to be set because of level of risk, this is acknowledged and explained, and a consensual middle ground sought. (Slade, 2009)

Risk management focusing entirely on identifying and avoiding negative risk factors as well as reinforcing an illness identity can disempower patients from taking an active role in controlling potential risks. As such the role risk management plays within a recovery-focused service is not only focused on deficits and disease, although the understanding and open discussion of these is important, but also on positive risk-taking. Traditionally, positive risk-taking has focused on the strengths approach and coping strategies but in a recovery-focused service this is taken beyond into an exploration of the dreams, goals, and aspirations of the patient.

The recovery-focused approach may appear in direct opposition to many of the central facets of risk management. Care may move from a focus on medication management and compliance to one focused on patients' goals. Medication then becomes a positive option in maintaining a life worth living rather than the central premise of the treatment itself. The outcomes for recovery-focused management of risk are hopeful. In sharing and taking control, service users must face difficult realities of illness and risk and work positively to overcome these. An openness on the part of clinicians of treatment goals and increasing focus on positive risk-taking and management can impact on the reduction and management of harmful risk through increasing patient self-efficacy and skills in self-management and taking responsibility for their own actions (Slade, 2009). A focus on the wider goals and dreams further encourages a patient to engage and take responsibility for their health and wellbeing in achieving these aspirations.

Integrating recovery approaches and risk management in forensic mental health

An area in which the recovery model is gaining interest is in forensic mental health services. One reason for this may be the recognition of the importance of the promotion and preservation of hope in the development of therapeutic environments in secure forensic services (Mental Health Commission, 2006), a central facet of the recovery model. By definition, forensic patients often represent high risk requiring relationships in which staff are highly skilled in containing and preventing risk-related behaviours. In the face of such risk, practitioners have embraced the recovery approach in working to foster responsibility both for index offences and for risk management in forensic patients.

One primary difference between forensic and adult mental health services is a fundamental shift in responsibility for high risk behaviours. Professionals initially take a paternalistic approach, with patients often held by community supervision orders and a need to attend treatment as determined by the court. Clinicians recognize that for the majority of clients, it is impossible to provide this level of supervision in the long term. As such, developing a joint understanding of risk and risk management between the clinical team and service user is an integral role of forensic services. Often the first step is the service user taking responsibility for their index offence and working with the clinical team to develop a greater understanding of events leading up to and precipitating episodes at which the service user has posed a high risk. This requires professionals to be open and frank regarding risk with service users.

Recovery approaches are also prominent in developing and implementing risk management processes. Working in partnership to identify strengths is an important factor in empowering service users to manage risk. The exploration of service users' goals can also encourage and drive increasing self-management. Goals have been recognized to be of importance for the development and maintenance of hope (von Roenn and von Gunten, 2003). The goals identified by a service user, particularly one within forensic services and subject to high levels of monitoring may be incongruous initially with perceived levels of risk. However, the role of the professional is to work creatively to foster responsibility and encourage positive risk management. As such, the team may work collaboratively with the service user to identify a series of goals, gradually building skills in self-management and leading to the achievement of greater wishes and dreams.

While the majority of patients in mental health services have not committed offences during periods of mental illness, many of the principles managed by forensic mental health services remain the same. There is a need to move from high levels of containment with low risk to positive risk management enhancing self-management skills in which gradually harmful risk behaviours associated with mental illness are managed and staff are more able to take a step back in responsibility for such patients. The recovery model is proving to provide a framework for engagement and the development of service user skills in achieving this.

Summary

In the third section of this chapter, practitioners and service users have been provided with a number of potential models of practice in which service user involvement in risk assessment can be enhanced. Consultative relationships have been championed in the model of shared care that is being increasingly recognized as a model of good practice in the provision of health care. This has been developed to enhance the process of risk assessment through joint crisis plans and shown to have many of the favourable outcomes of shared care in other areas of health provision. The recovery model provides a framework in which skills such as consultation and collaboration can implemented. Its growing use in mental health services, in which risk management remains an integral role, encourage a move towards greater involvement of services users in their care. The creative use of clinical skills in recovery not only seeks to reduce risk behaviours but to encourage empowerment of service users in the skills of self-management and increased growth through goal-orientated positive risk management. Perhaps most importantly, this section reminds us that underpinning each of these models is the central point that effective service user involvement and, indeed, effective risk assessment and management, cannot occur without attention to the building of therapeutic relationships.

Conclusion

Risk management has been, and is likely to remain, a central function of mental health services. While the importance of, and evidence base for, service user involvement has been growing to form an important marker of good practice, this is has largely alluded risk management. The overwhelming emphasis on risk management in the role of the clinician, the unsubstantiated fears of professionals, and a lack of guidance on implementation has led to the exclusion of service users in decisions about their risks of harm to others and themselves. Ultimately, this affects their treatment, care, and in some cases, their freedom and human rights.

This chapter presents some of the wider arguments behind user involvement, its importance in health service provision, and models of involvement. Using an evidence base derived from research studies and wider literature, a case is proposed for service user involvement as a whole and specifically within the process of risk assessment. The literature shows that the role of user involvement in risk assessment is not only ethical, but essential in the accurate measurement and management of risk. User involvement not only strengthens risk formulation, but for staff hit by increasing pressures and limited funding, a culture in which staff accept complete responsibility for risk management is at the least unfeasible and at the most dangerous in itself. User involvement in risk assessment should no longer be seen as a mark of policy guidance, not only identified as best practice, but essential to the practice of risk management.

The chapter concludes with a number of examples of user involvement put into practice. Built on the foundations of effective therapeutic relationships, collaborative working practices such as shared decision-making, with existing strong footings in other health care arenas, are introduced to the forum of risk management. The recovery model is further presented as a framework in which such relationships can be developed. Presenting a major paradigm shift from traditional mental health service provision, it focuses on service user identified goals with the professional utilizing their skills and knowledge to fulfil these. Recovery reframes risk management from its current emphasis as mediator of public health concerns to that of facilitating growth in individuals, potential for self-management, and development of enhanced quality of life through positive risk management. It offers an increasingly robust evidence base in which to facilitate user involvement in risk management along with tools and skills fundamental to the practice of mental health care provision.

The outcomes for user involvement in risk management are gradually becoming apparent, such as developing stronger relationships between service providers and service users, increasing engagement, and enhancing the process from assessment through to management. Perhaps some of the most influential evidence is to come from services that manage service users who present some of the highest risks. Built on a process of accepting responsibility, developing an understanding of risk and the learning of self-management skills in the management of that risk, forensic services present one of the most exciting and forward thinking forums for the increased involvement of service users in risk management. Early indications are that user involvement will soon no longer be good practice, but will form the fundamentals of risk management across modern day mental health services.

References

Ackerman, S. J. and Hilsenroth, M. J. (2001). A review of therapist characteristics and techniques negatively impacting the therapeutic alliance, *Psychotherapy*, 38, 171–185.

Ackerman, S. J. and Hilsenroth, M. J. (2003). A review of therapist characteristics and techniques positively impacting the therapeutic alliance, *Clinical Psychology Review*, 23, 1–33.

Adams, J. R. and Drake, R. E. (2006) Shared decision-making and evidence-based practice, *Community Mental Health Journal*, 42, 87–105.

Arnstein, S. (1969). A ladder of participation, *Journal of the Royal Planning Institute*, 35(4), 216–224.

Beauford, J. E., McNeil, D. E., and Binder, R. L. (1997). Utility of the initial therapeutic alliance in evaluating psychiatric patients' risk of violence, *American Journal of Psychiatry*, 154, 1272–1276.

Boevink, W. (2000). Ervaring, ervaringskennis, ervaringsdeskindegheid (Experience, experience-based knowledge, lay experts), *Deviant*, 26, 4–9.

Bongar, B., Peterson, L. G., Harris, E. A., and Aissis, J. (1989). Clinical and legal considerations in the management of suicidal patients: An integrative overview, *Journal of Integrative and Eclectic Psychotherapy*, 8, 53–67.

Bordin, E. S. (1979). The generalizability of the psychoanalytic concept of the working alliance, *Psychotherapy: Theory, Research and Practice*, 16, 252–260.

Bordin, E. S. (1994). Theory and research on the therapeutic working alliance: New directions, in A. O. Horvath and L. S. Greenberg (eds), *The Working Alliance: Theory, Research and Practice*. New York: Wiley-Interscience, pp. 13–37.

Borrill, J. (2000). Developments in treatment for people with psychotic experiences. *Updates*, 2 (9). London: Mental Health Foundation.

Breeze, J. (1998). Can paternalism be justified in mental health care?, *Journal of Advanced Nursing*, 28(2), 260–265.

Chief Medical Officer (2001). *Expert Patients Programme*. London: Department of Health.

Crane-Ross, D., Lutz, W., and Roth, D. (2006). Consumer and case manager perspectives of service empowerment: relationship to mental health recovery, *Journal of Behavioural Health Services and Research*, 33(2), 142–155.

Davidson, L., Lawless, M. S., and Leary, F. (2005). Concepts of recovery: Competing or complementary?, *Current Opinion in Psychiatry*, 18(6), 664–667.

Davidson, L., O'Connell, M., Tondora, J., Styron, T., and Kangas, K. (2006). The top ten concerns about recovery encountered in mental health system transformation, *Psychiatric Services*, 57(5), 640–645.

Day, A., Davey, L., Wanganeen, R., Howells, K., DeSantolo, J., and Nakata, M. (2006). The meaning of anger for Australian Indigenous offenders: The significance of context, *International Journal of Offender Therapy and Comparative Criminology*, 50(5), 520–539.

Day, J. C., Bentall, R. P., Roberts, C., Randall, F., Rogers, A., Cattell, D., Healy, D., Rae, P., and Power, C. (2005). Attitudes towards antipsychotic medication: The impact of clinical variables and relationships with health professionals, *Archives of General Psychiatry*, 62(7), 717–724.

Deegan, P. E. (1992) Recovery: The lived experience of rehabilitation, *Psychosocial Rehabilitation Journal*, 9(4), 11–19.

Deegan, P. E. (2007). The lived experience of using psychiatric medication in the recovery process, and a shared decision-making program to support it, *Psychiatric Rehabilitation Journal*, 31(1), 62–69.

Deegan, P. E. and Drake, R. E. (2006). Shared decision-making and medication management in the recovery process, *Psychiatric Services*, 57, 1636–1639.

Department of Health (1999). *Effective Care Co-ordination in Mental Health Services: Modernising the Care Programme Approach, 16736 HSD*. London: Department of Health.

Department of Health (2004). *Patient and Public Involvement in Health: The Evidence for Policy Implementation*. London: Department of Health.

Department of Health (2009). *Best Practice in Managing Risk: Principles and Evidence for Best Practice in the Assessment and Management of Risk to Self and Others in Mental Health Services*. London: Department of Health, available at www.dh.gov.uk/publications.

Fenton, W. S., Blyler, C. R., and Heinssen, R. (1997). Determinants of medication compliance in schizophrenia, *Schizophrenia Bulletin*, 23(4), 637–651.

Gravel, K., Legare, F., and Graham, I. D. (2006). Barriers and facilitators to implementing shared decision-making in clinical practice: a systematic review of health professionals' perceptions, *Implementation Science*, 1, 16.

Greenfield, T. K., Stoneking, B. C., Humphreys, K., Sundby, E., and Bond, J. (2008). A randomized trial of a mental health consumer-managed alternative to civil commitment for acute psychiatric crisis, *American Journal of Psychology*, 42(1–2), 135–144.

Hamann, J., Langer, B., Winkler, V., Busch, R., Cohen, R., Leucht, S., and Kissling, W. (2006). Shared decision-making for in-patients with schizophrenia, *Acta Psychiatrica Scandinavica*, 114(4), 265–273.

Hanily, F. (1999). Policy and legislation in the management of crisis and risk, in T. Ryan (ed.), *Managing Crisis and Risk in Mental Health Nursing*. Cheltenham: Stanley Thornes.

Hanley, B., Bradburn, J., Barnes, M., Evans, C., Goodare, H., Kelson, M., Kent, A., Oliver, S., Thomas, S., Wallcraft, J., and Steel, R. (2003). *Involving the Public in NHS, Public Health, and Social Care Research: Briefing Notes for Researchers.* Eastleigh: INVOLVE.

Harper, D., Goodbody, L., and Steen, L. (2003). Involving users of services in clinical psychology training, *Clinical Psychology*, 21, 14–19.

Health Select Committee (2000). *Provision of NHS Mental Health Services*, Fourth Report. London: The Stationery Office.

Henderson, C., Flood, C., Leese, M., Thornicroft, G., Sutherby, K., and Szmukler, G. (2004). Effect of joint crisis plans on user of compulsory treatment in psychiatry: Single blind randomised controlled trial, *British Medical Journal*, 329(7458), 136–138.

Hickey, G. and Kipping, C. (1998). Exploring the concept of user involvement in mental health through a participation continuum, *Journal of Clinical Nursing*, 7(1), 83–88.

Holloway, F. (1996). Community psychiatric care: from libertarianism to coercion. 'Moral Panic' and mental health policy in Britain, *Health Care Analysis*, 4, 235–243.

Information Commissioner's Office (2006). *Data Protection Good Practice Guide: The Use of Violent Warning Markers.* London: Information Commissioner's Office.

Kirkpatrick. I. (2006). Taking stock of the new managerialism in English social services, *Social Work and Society*, 3(3), 14–24.

Kumar, S. and Simpson, A. I. F. (2005). Application of risk assessment for violence methods to general adult psychiatry: A selective review of the literature, *Australian and New Zealand Journal of Psychiatry*, 39(5), 328–335.

Langan, J. (2008). Involving mental health service users considered to pose a risk to other people in risk assessment, *Journal of Mental Health*, 17(5), 471–481.

Langan, J. (2009). Mental health, risk communication and data quality in the electronic age, *British Journal of Social Work*, 39(3), 467–487.

Langan, J. and Lindow, V. (2004). *Living with Risk: Mental Health Service User Involvement in Risk Assessment and Management.* Bristol: Policy Press.

Logan, C. (2003). Ethical issues in risk assessment practice and research, in G. Adshead and C. Brown (eds), *Ethical Issues in Forensic Research.* London: Jessica Kingsley.

Ludman, E., Katon, W., Bush, T., Rutter, C., Lin, E., Simon, G., von Korff, M., and Walker, E. (2003). Behavioural factors associated with symptom outcomes in a primary care-based depression prevention intervention trial, *Psychological Medicine*, 33, 1061–1070.

Malm, U., Ivarsson, B., Allebeck, P., and Falloon, I. R. H. (2003). Integrated care in schizophrenia: A 2-year randomized controlled study of two community-based treatment programs, *Acta Psychiatrica Scandinavica*, 107(6), 415–423.

Manthorpe, J. and Alaszewski, A. (1998). Special issue on risk: Editorial, *Health and Social Care in the Community*, 6, 1–3.

McLaughlin, H. (2009). Keeping service user involvement in research honest, *British Journal of Social Work*, Online, 1–18, available at doi:10.1093/bjsw/bcp064.

Meads, G. and Ashcroft, J. (2005). *The Case for Interprofessional Collaboration: In Health and Social Care.* Oxford: Blackwell.

Mental Health Act Commission (2006). *In Place of Fear? 11th Biennial Report 2003–2005.* London: The Stationary Office.

Michie, C. and Cooke, D. J. (2006). The structure of violent behaviour: A hierarchical model, *Criminal Justice and Behavior*, 33(6), 706–737.

National Institute of Clinical Excellence (NICE) (2004). *Self-harm: The Short-term Physical and Psychological Management and Secondary Prevention of Self-harm in Primary and Secondary Care.* London: NICE.

Petch, E. (2001). Risk management in UK mental health services: An overvalued idea?, *Psychiatric Bulletin*, 25, 203–205.

Priebe, S. and Gruyters, T. (1993). The role of the helping alliance in psychiatric community care: A prospective study, *Journal of Nervous and Mental Disease*, 181, 552–557.

Repper, D. (2000). Adjusting the focus of mental health nursing: Incorporating service users' experiences of recovery, *Journal of Mental Health*, 9(6), 575–587.

Rose, D., Fleischmann, P., Tonkiss, F., Campbell, P., and Wykes, T. (2004). *User and Carer Involvement in Change Management in a Mental Health Context: Review of the Literature*. Report to the National Collaborating Centre for NHS Service Delivery and Organisation R&D. London: Department of Health.

Rush, B. (2004). Mental health service user involvement in England: Lessons from history, *Journal of Psychiatric and Mental Health Nursing*, 11(3), 313–318.

Ryan, T. (1998). Perceived risks associated with mental illness: Beyond homicide and suicide, *Social Science and Medicine*, 46, 287–297.

Ryan, T. (2000). Exploring the risk management strategies of mental health service users, *Health, Risk and Society*, 2(3), 267–283.

Scottish Executive (2000). *Risk Management, Report of the Mental Health Reference Group*. Edinburgh: Scottish Executive.

Scottish Executive (2006). *Changing Lives: Report of the 21st Century Social Work Review*. Edinburgh: Scottish Executive.

Slade, M. (1994). Needs assessment: Involvement of staff and users will help meet needs, *British Journal of Psychiatry*, 165, 293–296.

Slade, M. (2009). *Personal Recovery and Mental Illness*. Cambridge: Cambridge University Press.

Stringer, B., van Meijel, B., de Vree, W., and van Der Bijl, J. (2008). User involvement in mental health care: the role of nurses. A literature review, *Journal of Psychiatric and Mental Health Nursing*, 15(8), 678–683.

Sutherby, K., Szmukler, G. I., Halpern, A., Alexander, M., Thornicroft, G., Johnson C., and Wright, S. (1999). A study of 'crisis cards' in a community psychiatric service, *Acta Psychiatrica Scandinavica*, 110(1), 56–61.

Svensson, B. and Hansson, L. (1999). Therapeutic alliance in cognitive therapy for schizophrenic and other long-term mentally ill patients: Development and relationship to outcome in an in-patient treatment programme, *Acta Psychiatrica Scandinavica*, 99(4), 281–287.

Swanson, K. A., Bastani, R., Rubenstein, L. V., Meredith, L. S., and Ford, D. E. (2007). Effect of mental health care and shared decision-making on patient satisfaction in a community sample of patients with depression, *Medical Care Research and Review*, 64(4), 416–430.

Szmukler, G. (2000). Homicide inquiries. What sense do they make?, *Psychiatric Bulletin*, 24, 6–10.

Tait, L. and Lester, H. (2005). Encouraging user involvement in mental health services, *Advances in Psychiatric Treatment*, 11, 168–175.

Tritter, K. Q. and McCallum, A. (2006). The snakes and ladders of user involvement: Moving beyond Arnstein, *Health Policy*, 76, 156–168.

Trivedi, P. and Wykes, T. (2002). From passive subjects to equal partners: Qualitative review of user involvement in research, *British Journal of Psychiatry*, 181, 468–472.

von Korff, M., Katon, W., Rutter, C., Ludman, E., Simon, G., Lin, E., and Bush, T. (2003). Effect on disability outcomes of a depression relapse prevention program, *Psychosomatic Medicine*, 65(6), 938–943.

von Roenn, J. H. and von Gunten, C. F. (2003). Setting goals to maintain hope, *Journal of Clinical Oncology*, 21(3), 570–574.

Zuroff, D. C., Blatt, S. J., Sotsky, S. M., Krupnick, J. L., Martin, D. J., Sanislow, C. A. III., and Simmens, S. (2000). Relation of therapeutic alliance and perfectionism to outcome in brief treatment of depression, *Journal of Consulting and Clinical Psychology*, 68(1), 114–224.

Part III
Practice

8

Guidelines and Standards for Managing Risk in Mental Health Services

Caroline Logan, Norbert Nedopil and Thomas Wolf

Introduction

Best Practice in Managing Risk (Department of Health, 2007a, 2008a) is a set of aspirational guidelines for practitioners in mental health services who work with clients who are at risk of harming themselves or others. This document, prepared after an extensive consultation process for the National Mental Health Risk Management Programme, endeavours to promote high standards in clinical risk assessment and management practice based on evidence of what works with at-risk users of mental health services. Why are practice guidelines required in this area?

The implementation of best clinical practice in managing risk may be limited by a lack of clarity or certainty about the risks posed by complex clients and about the most appropriate – effective, proportionate – course of action in the event that risks to self or others become raised, such as when the client is acutely unwell or in crisis. Best clinical practice may also be limited by anxiety about how one's professional work will be judged by others in the event of scrutiny, such as after a serious untoward incident (SUI). However, the costs of anything less than best practice with such clients are potentially very high in terms of the physical and psychological health and the financial and legal security of all those involved, from the client to his or her personal and professional carers, mental health services as a whole, and the public at large. Practice guidelines can help practitioners recognize and be clear on the contentious issues that might be raised in the care of service users at risk, putting them in a better position to understand and manage risk and minimize or prevent harmful outcomes of any kind. The *Best Practice in Managing Risk* guidance was intended to fulfil that role.

Best Practice in Managing Risk was put together to provide practitioners in England with the means of both understanding better the risks posed by their clients and acting appropriately on their identification. However, the principles of clinical guidance in relation to at-risk clients are very far from being solely an English or even British interest.

Self-Harm and Violence: Towards Best Practice in Managing Risk in Mental Health Services, First Edition.
Edited by Richard Whittington and Caroline Logan.
© 2011 John Wiley & Sons, Ltd. Published 2011 by John Wiley & Sons, Ltd.

The professional and legal requirement to provide guidance on the care and management of clients at risk is very widespread. Indeed, a great deal of excellent work conducted outside of Britain informed the justification and the basis for the *Best Practice* guidance. Therefore, one objective of this chapter is to review some of that work in order that the *Best Practice* guidance can be seen in an international context of guidance on clinical risk assessment and management. However, *Best Practice* also emerges from a long and respected tradition of evidence-based clinical practice – the 'new knowledge regime in health services' (Tannenbaum, 2005, 163). Therefore, a second objective of this chapter is to highlight the key principles of evidence-based practice (EBP) in order to demonstrate how the *Best Practice* guidance has attempted to embody them.

This chapter will begin with an overview of EBP and the relevance of clinical guidelines to this philosophy of client care. It will then describe a pair of linked symposia that took place at the annual meeting of the International Association of Forensic Mental Health Services in Montréal in 2007. All the authors of this chapter participated in these symposia, which addressed directly the desirability of establishing standards and guidance in clinical risk assessment and management – and the costs of doing so – as well as the similarities and differences in guidance across jurisdictions and national borders. The chapter concludes by bringing both EBP and clinical risk assessment and management together in a brief discussion about the *Best Practice* principles.

Evidence-Based Practice and the Role of Clinical Guidelines

Introduction

Over 300 clinical practice guidelines relating to mental disorder are listed by the American National Guideline Clearing House (www.guideline.gov). In England and Wales also, much mental health best practice guidance has been published by the Department of Health since the establishment of the National Service Framework for Mental Health in 1999 (Department of Health, 1999). Recent examples include guidance for mental health nurse training (Department of Health, 2006), medium secure services (Department of Health, 2007b), supported decision-making (Department of Health, 2007c), crisis services (Department of Health, 2007d), support, time, and recovery worker competencies (Department of Health, 2008b), as well as best practice in managing clinical risk (Department of Health, 2008a). In addition, the National Institute for Health and Clinical Excellence (NICE) issues practice guidelines relating to a number of mental health problems (Rawlins, 2004), several touching on the issue of clinical risk (e.g., guidelines on antisocial personality disorder; NICE, 2009). Why issue practice guidelines? Do practice guidelines really lead to better mental health care?

Evidence-based practice and clinical guidelines

The term *clinical guidelines* refers to the synthesis of empirical evidence on a particular subject into an accessible and practical form in order to facilitate improved – relevant, effective, efficient, equitable, consistent, and quality – health care (Timmermans and Mauck, 2005). Traditionally, guidelines are derived through an approximation to the following process. First, a representative committee of experts in a particular field is selected by an authoritative governing body and invited to define the subject and the audience for a new set of practice guidelines. Secondly, the committee retrieves, evaluates, and synthesizes the published evidence available on the subject, identifying the best studies using strict protocols on research method and summarizing the risks and benefits of each of the treatments or interventions described. In most instances, the empirical evidence does not cover all the areas that need to be covered by a set of clinical guidelines and the consensus views of the experts involved are incorporated using a variety of recognized structured means (Raine, Sanderson and Black, 2005). Thirdly, on the basis of the observations made about each piece of evidence regarding interventions or the consensus views of experts, the committee prepares a coherently sequenced set of practice recommendations – guidelines – for a range of decision-making situations where an intervention is required. Finally, the guidelines are published and the intended audience notified of their existence through various professional forums (e.g., special meetings, conferences, journals, and letters) and mainstream media outlets (e.g., news items, newspaper articles; Dobrow *et al.*, 2006; Geddes, 2005; Timmermans and Mauck, 2005).

The phenomenon of clinical guidelines has emerged from evidence-based medicine (EBM) (Sackett *et al.*, 1996). EBM has become very influential over the last two decades and underpins the practice of virtually all medical – and allied – professionals (Sackett *et al.*, 2000). Indeed, EBM is now more widely referred to as EBP and the literature on this approach to health care is now considerable across a number of clinical fields (Geddes, 2005; Tannenbaum, 2005); its popularity has been likened to a 'revolution . . . [asserting] the supremacy of data over authority and tradition' (Patterson, 2002, 71). The popularity of EBP is grounded on the premise that the carefully scrutinized evidence upon which clinical guidelines are derived maximizes the validity and reliability of decision-making based on those guidelines. That is, a set of clinical guidelines will recommend procedure A (e.g., pressurized, metered-dose inhaler spacers) in response to condition B (asthma) because the best quality research evidence indicates that procedure A is the most effective at generating the outcome of choice (i.e., better symptom control) of all the procedures examined (Powell *et al.*, 2001). Therefore, a practitioner's decision to implement procedure A with a service user with condition B means that the good evidence on which the clinical guidance was based underpins his or her choice.

Clinical guidelines may be differentiated from *standards*; guidelines are aspirational, designed to raise the quality of practice voluntarily, while standards are obligatory and must be followed. Standards may describe a legal or professional obligation to perform in a particular way in a particular setting, thus ensuring a minimum standard of acceptable practice in a particular area. For example, in Scotland, the Risk Management Authority (RMA) oversees the implementation of a new sentence called an Order for Lifelong Restriction (OLR). A convicted person is given this sentence when the high court is satisfied that he or she poses a high risk of violence in the absence of restrictions. The Criminal Justice Act (Scotland) 2003 stipulates that risk assessment reports, on the basis of which the judge makes a decision about whether to sentence the defendant to an OLR, must be carried out in a particular way. Therefore, the RMA prepared a set of standards and guidelines for risk assessment – and subsequently risk management – for so sentenced offenders (www.RMAscotland.gov.uk), which accredited assessors must follow.

Therefore, both standards and guidelines are intended to promote as well as enhance the quality and the evidence base for clinical practice across the range of health care activity (Geddes, 2005; Timmermans and Mauck, 2005; Woolf *et al.*, 1999). In doing so, in declaring what good – or best – practice should look like, a number of outcomes ought to ensue. First, standards and guidelines should reduce inconsistencies between practitioners and between services; they should improve both the validity and the reliability of decision-making resulting in broadly comparable decisions even across a range of disparate services. Thus, maverick or high risk practice based on minimal evidence or poorly informed professional practice is discouraged. Secondly, standards and guidelines help practitioners through the assessment process and make them aware of the obligations they have to those to whom they answer, namely their patients and their carers, their professional bodies, their employers, and the courts. Consequently, standards and guidelines help novices to understand the requirements of particular forms of intervention sooner than they might otherwise have done. Standards and guidelines also help more experienced practitioners to continue to practice according to what the literature recommends are the most up-to-date procedures.

Thirdly, standards and guidelines promote and encourage a shared language and understanding about the problem under consideration. As a result, when practitioner X talks about condition Z and practitioner Y also talks about condition Z, they both know they are talking about the same condition because definitions have been agreed in the published guidelines that underpin their practice. Fourthly, standards and guidelines enable deciding bodies like courts or other decision-making or review panels to judge the quality of the work provided to them by the practitioners who are meant to be compliant with those standards and guidelines. Thus, poor quality work may be more easily differentiated from good quality work because standards and guidelines make clear what good quality work should look like and practitioners not meeting the standards described may be subject to sanction. However, the opposite also holds true: practitioners operating in accordance with the required standards and recommended guidelines will be afforded their protection in the event of scrutiny or investigation. Finally, standards and guidelines are intended to be accessible to service users and carers as well as to practitioners and other formal agencies. As a result, they ensure that service users and carers have the opportunity to become better informed about – and more involved in influencing – the treatment and care choices available to them, the quality of the care they can expect to receive, and their opportunities and scope for complaint in the event that such standards and guidelines are not upheld.

Therefore, standards and guidelines enhance the quality and transparency of decision-making, both by practitioners and those who act on their practice, such as the courts. They also improve transparency and accountability by making it clear who is responsible for what aspect of care and why. Standards and guidelines ensure that the basis for judgements and decision-making is more evidentially sound and free from bias than might otherwise have been the case. A means of promoting good clinical governance, standards and guidelines are rational policies that drive caring organizations to be seen to provide the best available interventions to all their clients.

The problem with clinical guidelines

However, standards and guidelines are not endorsed universally; not everyone thinks they are a good thing or that the quality of health care is improved as a result of their existence. Tannenbaum (2005) reviews a number of concerns. First, standards and guidelines describe the minimum requirement for quality care in a particular area. Thus, it has been suggested that they promote 'good enough' practice rather than best practice and that they dumb down health care to the minimum achievable standard rather than promote its enhancement to the highest standard possible. Secondly, practitioners have a professional requirement to maintain up-to-date, evidence-based clinical practices. The very existence of standards and guidelines implies that practitioners do not adhere to this professional requirement – or that they cannot be trusted to do so without being obliged to – the implication of which can be insulting to those who do so willingly. Thirdly, the proliferation of standards and guidance from areas of uncommon practice, where the description of recommended procedures and interventions can be welcome, into areas of more established routine practice can mean that basic clinical tasks are increasingly subject to minute regulation, which some practitioners regard as an impediment to autonomous professional practice. Fourthly, the evidence base on which standards and guidelines are founded privileges some evidence over others – that from randomized controlled trials (RCTs), for instance, over less rigorous forms of treatment outcome research. This is a problem in mental health care where both financial support for research and the capacity to undertake RCTs specifically is limited and this form of study is not always desirable (e.g., because of the prioritization of reliability over validity, efficacy over effectiveness, and the favouring of manualized treatment interventions such as behavioural and cognitive interventions; Tannenbaum, 2005).

Finally, it is a significant achievement to derive and publish a set of standards or guidance in any area of health care. However, ensuring that they remain up-to-date and reflect the most recent research evidence is a significant undertaking further to the development of the guidance in the first instance. Consequently, standards and guidelines age, leaving practitioners unsure whether they are still relevant and, indeed, what guidance they should follow in the increasingly busy and often conflicting standards and guidance marketplace. Thus, standards and guidelines may restrict or freeze clinical practice rather than regulate and enhance it, limiting practice development and innovation rather than supporting it.

There is available an abundance of overlapping, conflicting, and poorly constructed guidance of variable quality, and their collective usefulness has been questioned (Timmermans and Mauck, 2005). Practitioners struggle to identify good from bad guidance and the literature on the evaluation of clinical guidelines is in its infancy. While clinical guidelines are a good idea in principle, it is thought that few lead to consistent changes in the behaviour of care providers (Timmermans and Mauck, 2005). Barriers to compliance include lack of awareness of the existence of guidelines, disagreement over the recommendations made, and the desire for autonomy and discretion in professional practice rather than regulation and uniformity. Consequently, professionals treat many practice guidelines more as options than as true standards to adhere to, and professional organizations do not enforce adherence to guidelines or reward guideline-following behaviour (Timmermans and Mauck, 2005).

Concluding comments

EBM and EBP more generally, from which clinical guidelines have largely emerged, assumes practitioners will take a rational approach in which science alone will convince them to change and improve their practice. However, the implementation of clinical guidelines and standards of practice has not been as good as expected and the limited efforts made to date to evaluate their impact have shown limited positive change (Perleth, Jakubowski, and Busse, 2001). Therefore, much remains to be done to persuade practitioners of the rationality of guidelines – and guideline-makers of the real needs of practitioners and the clients they serve. This is especially the case in the clinical risk assessment and management field to which we now turn.

Standards and Guidance in Clinical Risk Assessment and Management: An International Perspective

Introduction: Montréal 2007

The International Association of Forensic Mental Health Services (www.iafmhs.org) was established in Vancouver in 2001, where its inaugural meeting was held the same year. Conferences are held annually, rotating between North America, Europe, and Australia. In June 2007, the annual meeting took place in Montréal. At this meeting, two linked symposia took place, one directly following the other, the titles of which were *Standards of Risk Assessment: How appropriate are they really? Part I* and *Part II*.

The first symposium was chaired by Norbert Nedopil and compared standards and guidelines for risk assessment practice published in Germany (described by Thomas Wolf), Scotland (described by Roisin Hall), Switzerland (described by Volker Dittmann), and Canada (described by Christopher Webster) in terms of their legal, psychiatric, and psychological perspectives. (The *Best Practice* guidance was still in development at the time these symposia took place and so was not included.) The purpose of this first symposium was to raise awareness of some of the standards and guidelines in existence and to examine their usefulness in guiding practice in clinicians and criminal justice systems across these different jurisdictions. Caroline Logan chaired the second symposium. Here, themes emerging from the earlier symposium were identified and discussed in a debate centring on the following general questions: (a) what do we mean when we talk about standards and guidelines in clinical risk assessment and management?; (b) are standards and guidelines in risk assessment a help or a hindrance to clinicians?; and (c) is there any other way of improving practice in clinical risk assessment and management apart from using standards and guidelines? Debate was energetic, and a number of relevant observations and views emerged. The following sections summarize the answers to the three questions addressed at the debate using examples given in the first of the two symposia.

What do we mean when we talk about standards and guidelines in clinical risk assessment and management?

Best Practice in Managing Risk (Department of Health, 2007a, 2008a) is one example of a set of guidelines intended to encourage practitioners and services to raise the quality of their practice in respect of clients at risk of harming themselves or others. This guidance makes recommendations about the nature and purpose of clinical risk assessments undertaken in mental health services, the involvement of multiple practitioners as well as service users and their carers, and about their review and change in response to effective – or indeed, ineffective – risk management. The Scottish Risk Management Authority (RMA) has also published a set of standards and guidelines for risk assessment (RMA, 2005) and a separate set covering risk management (RMA, 2007). These standards and guidelines are intended to ensure that accredited risk assessors and those in prisons and forensic psychiatric hospitals preparing risk management plans, undertake their work in respect of those subject to an OLR sentence in accordance with the exact legal requirement. The standards and guidelines make recommendations about the nature and frequency of contact with the person subject to risk assessment, the approach to be taken in the risk assessment, and the format of the report to be prepared for the court and for the agency charged with the task of subsequent risk management planning. In a number of other countries, similar practice requirements have been issued to aid the work of clinical services and the courts – and judges in particular – who have to make decisions about restricting the liberty of at-risk individuals as a way of managing their risks and justifying the action taken.

In Germany, for example, an interdisciplinary taskforce of renowned judges from the High Court of Appeals (the *Bundesgerichtshof* or BGH), mental health professionals, prosecutors, and defence lawyers prepared a set of minimal requirements for the risk assessments submitted to the German courts for consideration in sentencing and preventative detention hearings. Why? Over the past few years, there has been much discomfort among judges (especially those in the Courts of Appeal), as well as forensic experts and practitioners, because many expert reports[1] have been of poor quality, especially those involving juvenile defendants. Indeed, a considerable number of these poor quality reports lead to strongly criticized court decisions, mostly because the reports on which the decision were based at least in part contained unstructured and unsound judgements. Therefore, in 1999, the BGH ruled in a principal decision what structured or approved assessment methods had to be used for such expert reports and, with advice from experienced forensic mental health professionals, they established a number of questions that had to be answered by the experts within their reports. Following this ruling, a group of judges from the BGH, in addition to a number of senior forensic experts and clinicians, some Federal prosecutors and experienced judges and defence lawyers, gathered as a task force in order to establish a set of 'minimal requirements' (MR) for expert reports addressing the issue of the criminal responsibility of offenders (Bötticher *et al.*, 2006).

The group collected and for the first time systematized all court decisions pertaining to risk assessment. The MR eventually prepared were formulated for psychiatric and psychological experts providing reports for the courts. A year later, they established MR for all steps in the judicial procedure, from sentencing to release, either from prison or from a forensic hospital, on the nature of the expert's engagement with the client, and on the choice and use of clinical risk assessment tools. The MR are not legally binding – experts do not have to comply with them if there are good reasons not to do so and these reasons are explained – but they have had a great deal of impact because of the moral authority of their authors and the encouragement given to all German courts to apply them. The careful application of MR protects the expert from accusations of

---

[1] The expression 'expert report' is used here in accordance with the language of the European Court of Human Rights; expressions like 'expert testimony' or 'expert witness' do not seem to be quite correct because according to German law an expert cannot be a witness and vice versa.

wrongdoing or negligence; a report on future risk not adhering to the MR can lead to the practitioner being charged with a crime if the offender or patient in their care is violent following an incorrect assessment of low risk.[2] Thus, MR in Germany help practitioners to write informative reports relevant to the purpose of the court and they help the court to understand the opinion of the expert; they clearly distinguish between the responsibilities of the judge and those of the expert, and they make it easier for the court to select and guide the expert. Regular reviews of expert reports and their compliance with the MR ensures that standards of practice are both maintained and enhanced across the national pool of expert practitioners. In addition, even though judges are not bound to follow the MR as they endeavour to uphold the law, when they make decisions about detention or release from preventive detention, these decisions will be questioned by the Courts of Appeal if the MR were not applied. This creates considerable pressure on judges when they have to argue against applying the MR and so most of them will apply the MR rather than risk being over-ruled.

Therefore, the MR have a significant impact on the practice of experts in Germany and on the legal decisions that follow from the reports that are prepared in accordance with them. Other international examples of risk assessment requirements in North America and Australia can be found in Eaves *et al.* (2000) and McSherry and Keyzer (2009), respectively. These locally relevant standards of practice are underpinned by the requirements of the agencies receiving expert reports in addition to good and empirically informed professional practice in respect of key stages in the clinical risk assessment and management process.

Are standards and guidelines in clinical risk assessment and management useful?

The answer to this question appears to be that it depends. Specifically, the answer depends on how the term 'useful' is defined. Evidence-based standards and clinical guidelines carry a great deal of moral authority (Tannenbaum, 2005); why would one wish to practice in a way other than that recommended by the evidence of one's expert peers? However, the moral authority of practice guidelines in the clinical risk assessment and management field is undermined when the evidence base is compared with that of guidelines developed in the health care field. The volume of good quality research comparing risk assessment techniques is rather small (Leitner, Barr and Hobby, 2008; Leitner *et al.*, 2006); risk assessment tools vary considerably in terms of the evidence on which they are based and the evidence gathered subsequently on their use demonstrating their reliability and validity. Further, there is disagreement in the risk assessment field as to the approach to take – actuarial or structured professional judgement. This disagreement is very interesting but it has lead to deep divisions among researchers and practitioners on whether the focus should be on the prediction of future harm or its prevention and how prediction can – or cannot – aid in the identification of effective prevention strategies (e.g., Buchanan, 2008; Harris and Rice, 2007; Hart, Michie and Cooke, 2007). Research into the prediction of future harm still dominates the empirical literature

---

[2] In 2004, the BGH upheld a verdict that sentenced a psychiatrist to a term in prison, because he allowed three days leave of absence to a patient on the basis of a faulty risk assessment. The patient raped and killed two women during this leave. The psychiatrist was found guilty of involuntary manslaughter.

(e.g., studies examining the predictive validity of risk assessment tools), yet practitioners invariably see their duty as being to *prevent* harmful outcomes. Unfortunately, research on the prevention of harm is limited because it is problematic to measure what has been prevented (e.g., violence) and then to attribute its non-occurrence to specific interventions (e.g., participation in a violence reduction programme). Consequently, a comparatively weak empirical evidence base underpins standards and guidelines in the clinical risk assessment and management field compared with standards and guidelines in general health care.

However, while there are problems with the evidence base for risk assessment and management, there is a great deal of evidence that is relevant to clinical practice with at-risk individuals. Earlier chapters in this book have expertly reviewed the evidence on risk factors for harm to both self and others. On the basis of this and other evidence from systematic reviews and large-scale studies of the outcomes of interest (e.g., Monahan *et al.*, 2001), our knowledge and understanding of harmful behaviour has never been greater. Therefore, while aspects of the evidence base for clinical guidelines in the risk field are weak, it is not uniformly so. In addition, risk assessment and management practice has implications across a range of domains that do not lend themselves to the easy collection of data or an RCT. Further, clinical guidelines in the risk field as elsewhere do not relate simply to evidence-based clinical practice (Raine, Sanderson and Black, 2005). Instead, they range across service organization and delivery, multidisciplinary team working, the positive engagement of service users as partners in their care, responsive risk management, formulation-based risk management, and providing the information required by bodies tasked with making the fairest, most justifiable, and most proportionate responses to the risks presented by individuals. As in the example given above, of the minimum requirements for expert reports in German courts, standards and guidelines in clinical risk assessment and management take many forms and cover many very relevant issues. The diversity of the evidence base for these guidelines should be regarded as more a strength than a weakness. The direct comparison of clinical guidelines in the risk field with those in other areas of EBP should be undertaken with caution and with a full awareness of what is in fact required by those in need of useful guidance.

Is there any other way of improving practice in clinical risk assessment and management apart from using standards and guidelines?

Standards and guidelines are a key way in which research findings – and best practice recommendations – are communicated to practitioners tasked with the job of implementing the most effective and justified interventions (Reed, McLaughlin and Newman, 2002). Standards and guidelines lead practitioners from the task of the risk assessment and management of complex cases to the outcome of clearly communicated and relevant observations and recommendations, to be acted upon by bodies legally empowered to do so (Hart and Boer, 2010). Is there a better system of informing practitioners of all kinds – responsible clinicians, psychologists, nurses, social workers, probation officers, the police, solicitors, judges – of their obligations to service users and their carers as well as each other? We think not. Indeed, we regard the existence of standards and guidelines in the clinical risk assessment and management field to be critical and perhaps more so than in other fields because the need for clarity and authority in this conflicted area is greater than in most others. In which case, how can the current system of establishing standards and guidelines of practice in the risk field be improved?

First, research on risk factors – and increasingly, protective factors – must continue. Specifically, research must examine the functional relationship between these variables identified as risk (and protective) factors and harmful behaviour rather than simply their correlation. It is not enough to know that, for example, personality disorder is frequently present in individuals who are harmful towards themselves and others – why is this correlation frequently observed and what is the underlying mechanism of the link (Logan and Johnstone, 2010)? In addition, how do protective factors operate to limit the harmful potential of risk factors? The manual of the Structured Assessment of Protective Factors (SAPROF) (de Vogel *et al.*, 2009) speculates in detail about what this relationship might be. Empirical research should now attempt to model these potential relationships.

Secondly, research of a qualitative as well as a quantitative nature is also required into the use of the structured professional judgement (SPJ) approach. SPJ is a very practitioner-based approach to clinical risk assessment and management (e.g., Hart and Boer, 2010) where prevention of harm rather than its prediction is the target. Risk assessment tools, like the HCR-20 violence risk guide (Douglas and Reeves, 2010; Webster *et al.*, 1997) and the Risk for Sexual Violence Protocol (RSVP) (Hart and Boer, 2010; Hart *et al.*, 2003), represent highly specific empirically supported practice guidelines that reflect the opinions and recommendations of their authors rather than the official position or policy of a professional body or agency. Future research needs to focus on the supported or structured decision-making process prescribed here rather than the capacity of SPJ tools to predict harmful outcomes, which is not in fact what they were intended to do.

Thirdly, in order to create well-supported, realistic, acceptable, comprehensive, and comparatively brief clinical guidelines, input is required from multiple stakeholders over a protracted consultation period (Curry, 2000). Consequently, more time and effort needs to be put into the real involvement of service users and carers in the design of clinical guidelines in relation to risk and in related activities such as teaching and training. Finally, more attention must be given to the implementation of standards and guidelines into the practice of those for whom they are intended. Built into this implementation process should be measures of adherence to guidelines, their impact on service provision and the service user experience, as well as the regular review of the scientific literature and update of the guidance as required (Timmermans and Mauck, 2005; Vlayen *et al.*, 2005).

Therefore, there is little realistic viable alternative in this era of evidence-based practice than to persevere with standards and guidelines. Greater stakeholder involvement, time, and resources for their development and implementation can contribute to the preparation of a useful set of guidelines; 'rather than a final product that spontaneously propels change by the force of rationality, the [clinical] guideline becomes then a scientific rallying point in a comprehensive organizational process of change' (Timmermans and Mauck, 2005, 26).

Concluding comments

Two linked symposia at the International Association of Forensic Mental Health Services conference in Montréal in 2007 generated much thought and opinion on the matter of clinical risk assessment and management and its regulation by standards and clinical practice guidelines. This section has tried to summarize what emerged during those three or so hours of discussion and to put it into the context of what this area of work aspires to, namely, evidence-based practice. Standards and guidelines in the risk field are positive and a help more than a hindrance to the work of busy practitioners of all kinds. They assist practitioners to know what best to do in difficult circumstances with at-risk clients, and they help clients to know what to expect of the services engaged with them. However, a powerful conclusion of the symposia was the importance of implementing standards and guidance in practice. Therefore, the implementation of the *Best Practice* guidance in England is considered next.

Implementing Best Practice in Managing Risk

The principles of best clinical practice

Best practice has been defined as 'the "best way" to identify, collect, evaluate, disseminate, and implement information about as well as to monitor the outcomes of health care interventions for patients/population groups and defined indications or conditions' (Perleth, Jakubowski and Busse, 2001, 237–238). Best practice requires knowledge and continuous progress in our understanding of the efficacy, effectiveness, cost-effectiveness, appropriateness, safety, social and ethical value, and quality of health care interventions as the basis for recommendations to practitioners about practice improvements, which are delivered in the form of health technology assessments, evidence-based medicine, and clinical practice guidelines (Perleth, Jakubowski and Busse, 2001). Therefore, the basic aim in best practice in health care is to link research findings as closely as possible with both practice and policy as well as outcome measurement and monitoring (Perleth, Jakubowski, and Busse, 2001).

Best Practice in Managing Risk (Department of Health, 2007a, 2008a) embodies the principles of best practice in health care as described by Perleth and colleagues. The process of developing this guidance involved a systematic review of the evidence for self-harm and violence (also vulnerability to exploitation and harm and self-neglect) and the generation of an expert consensus view about clinical risk assessment and management practice. In addition, it involved the systematic (and independent) examination of the technical performance, clinical efficacy and effectiveness, cost and cost-effectiveness, organizational impact, and the legal and ethical aspects of the application of risk assessment tools. The clinical practice guidelines that evolved from this work – *Best Practice in Managing Risk* – are, and remain, intended to improve effectiveness in mental health care, especially in relation to clinical risk, and to be an instrument for quality assurance for practitioners, the services they work for, and the service users and carers with whom they work.

The development of the *Best Practice* guidance

Best Practice in Managing Risk comprises several sections compiled using different methods of evidence gathering. The main part of the guidance is the section on the 16 *Best Practice* principles (see Box 8.1). The 16 principles were developed using a nominal group technique involving professional experts and by using a Delphi technique with service users and a focus group of carers (see Raine, Sanderson and Black, 2005). The subtle and complex processes involved in doing risk management are not so amenable to the research methods that rate highly in the standard hierarchy of evidence (e.g., the RCT);

in the absence of such 'high-quality' evidence, the consensus group was thought to be the only real alternative to distilling knowledge and expert experience on best practice. Consequently, the information sources underpinning the section on the 16 principles were a combination of empirical evidence, the consensus views of experts, including service users and their carers, and policy documents. Three meetings took place, with attendance ranging from seven to ten at each meeting, and frequent consultations were held by email and telephone with the national expert advisory group, which numbered 30 in total.

Box 8.1: The 16 *Best Practice in Managing Risk* principles

Introduction

1. Best practice involves making decisions based on knowledge of the research evidence, knowledge of the individual service user and their social context, knowledge of the service user's own experience, and clinical judgement.

Fundamentals

2. Positive risk management as part of a carefully constructed plan is a required competence for all mental health practitioners.
3. Risk management should be conducted in a spirit of collaboration and based on a relationship between the service user and their carers that is as trusting as possible.
4. Risk management must be built on a recognition of the service user's strengths and should emphasize recovery.
5. Risk management requires an organizational strategy as well as efforts by the individual practitioner.

Basic Ideas in Risk Management

6. Risk management involves developing flexible strategies aimed at preventing any negative event from occurring or, if this is not possible, minimizing the harm caused.
7. Risk management should take into account that risk can be both general and specific, and that good management can reduce and prevent harm.
8. Knowledge and understanding of mental health legislation is an important component of risk management.
9. The risk management plan should include a summary of all risks identified, formulations of the situations in which identified risks may occur, and actions to be taken by practitioners and the service user in response to crisis.
10. Where suitable tools are available, risk management should be based on assessment using the structured clinical (or professional) judgement approach.
11. Risk assessment is integral to deciding on the most appropriate level of risk management and the right kind of intervention for a service user.

(continued)

Working with Service Users and Carers

12. All staff involved in risk management must be capable of demonstrating sensitivity and competence in relation to diversity in race, faith, age, gender, disability and sexual orientation.

13. Risk management must always be based on awareness of the capacity for the service user's risk level to change over time, and a recognition that each service user requires a consistent and individualized approach.

Individual Practice and Team Working

14. Risk management plans should be developed by multidisciplinary and multi-agency teams operating in an open, democratic, and transparent culture that embraces reflective practice.

15. All staff involved in risk management should receive relevant training, which should be updated at least every three years.

16. A risk management plan is only as good as the time and effort put into communicating its findings to others.

The guidance – *Best Practice in Managing Risk: Principles and Evidence for Best Practice in the Assessment and Management of Risk to Self and Others in Mental Health Services* – was eventually produced in June 2007. It was made available online and advertised nationally through a combination of health care and professional networks. The framework of 16 principles is intended to underpin best practice across all mental health settings and, helpfully, provided comprehensive information about a set of evidence-based risk assessment tools that could be used to structure the usually complex task of risk management. The philosophy underpinning the principles is one that balances need for care against need for risk management, and that emphasizes positive risk management, collaborative working with the service users and others, the importance of recognizing and building on the service user's strengths, and the organization's role in risk management as well as that of the practitioner.

The recommendation of the guidance was that organizations (e.g., NHS trusts), care teams and individual practitioners should benchmark their current practice against the 16 principles set out in the guidance, and consider ways of embedding these principles in their daily clinical practice. They were also invited to consider the list of risk assessment tools described in the guidance and to examine if and how their practice could be improved by the incorporation of one or more of the tools into their risk assessment and management activities.

Implementing the *Best Practice* guidance

Recognizing the importance of implementation as a critical process in the development of clinical practice guidelines (Perleth, Jakubowski and Busse, 2001), the Department of Health initiated a six-month project to support the implementation of the guidance across England following their online publication in June 2007. This project was led by the same group that had led on the development of the guidance. The objectives of the implementation project were to publicize the guidance as widely as possible and to provide practical support to mental health trusts across England in the development of their local clinical risk assessment and management practice.

The implementation project consisted of three stages. In the first stage, a national communication framework for the *Best Practice* guidance was developed in the form of a website (www.managingclinicalrisk.nhs.uk). In the second stage, two conferences were organized, one in London and the other in Liverpool, to publicize the guidance and to provide examples of its local implementation. Many of the contributors to this book contributed to these conferences. In the third stage, support was offered to seven mental health trusts across England, selected on the basis of their size, range of services, and geographical location, in their implementation of the *Best Practice* guidance. A workshop was arranged in each trust to which directors of service and heads of specialty were invited.

All the workshops began with an introduction to the *Best Practice* guidance. Those attending were then invited to gather into small groups and to rate their own Trust using the Implementation Toolkit. In this Toolkit, which is available at the above website, each one of the principles is listed and suggestions are provided for some of the ways that mental health trusts can demonstrate evidence of the best practice described. Those attending the workshop were then invited to make ratings on the basis of the extent to which they thought their Trust could evidence each kind of best practice. A rating of '2' for each of the 16 principles suggests that a Trust can evidence the highest level of practice in the area described. A rating of '1' suggests that practice is good or that there is some evidence of best practice but that there is room for improvement. A rating of '0' suggests that work is in progress and that best quality practice is in development. Following this rating exercise, there was a feedback session in which those attending were asked to describe and justify the ratings given by their group for their Trust. Any differences between groups were also discussed and in this way consensus ratings for each Trust on each of the 16 *Best Practice* principles were agreed. These consensus ratings, together with all the information gathered about the Trust at the workshop, were then compiled into a report, which contained an action plan for moving the Trust toward best practice – where it was identified that improvements were indeed required. (A template of the action plan, with some examples of best practice and developing practice, and some examples of the actions suggested in one or more of the Trusts taking part in this exercise, is also available on the *Best Practice* website.) The Implementation Toolkit thus underpinned a self-assessment exercise in which Trusts were helped to think of developments and improvements in local practice. Trusts were not compared with one another using the Toolkit – it was intended simply as an instrument to aid self-scrutiny and subsequent planned action to improve practice. Following this implementation exercise, the *Best Practice* guidance was updated (to include a more detailed account of the implementation project) and made available in hardcopy only (Department of Health, 2008a).

Lessons learned

Efforts to implement *Best Practice* in some of the seven trusts participating in the process described above are described in more detail in the case studies that feature in the later chapters of this volume. What these case studies describe are very unique – locally sensitive – implementation arrangements. Overall, the implementation process highlighted four key lessons about implementing practice guidelines. First, there is a very great desire for guidance in the area of clinical risk assessment and management – from practitioners working with service users, from service managers, and from service users and their carers. Far from dumbing down practice, those attending the implementation workshops (and the two conferences) appeared to welcome a systematic approach to extracting practical guidance from the morass of evidence on clinical risk assessment and management. The workshops described above were very intense events involving a great deal of animated discussion and debate, which highlighted strengths but also weaknesses in local areas, some hitherto unknown or unappreciated by those present. Workshops could easily have taken longer than the half-day allocated in order to cover adequately the perspectives of practitioners, managers, and service users and carers. In addition, reports of the workshop proceedings and action plans for positive change were intended to provide suggestions for a practical way forward for Trusts in areas highlighted as underperforming – but they could easily have been far longer and more specific than they were. The nature and volume of interest in the *Best Practice* guidance was unforeseen. Therefore, the second point is that implementing practice guidelines in areas where they are required is at least as labour-intensive as preparing the guidance in the first place and time and resources should be allocated accordingly. Thirdly, as can be seen in the case studies that follow in this volume, implementation of practice guidelines is so locally specific that their overall evaluation is somewhat problematic. This is to be expected but unfortunate in terms of improving the evidence base for the effectiveness of guidelines themselves. Finally, while there is a paucity of RCTs in the clinical risk assessment and management field, there is still a wealth of evidence on the basis of which to provide useful guidance on best practice at this time. A critical task will be to update this guidance with new evidence as it emerges.

Conclusions

This chapter began with an overview of EBP and the relevance of clinical guidelines to this philosophy of client care. A pair of linked symposia that took place at the annual meeting of the International Association of Forensic Mental Health Services in Montréal in 2007 was then described, which addressed directly the desirability of establishing standards and guidance in clinical risk assessment and management – and the costs of doing so. The chapter concluded by bringing both EBP and clinical risk assessment and management together in a discussion about the *Best Practice* guidance and justifying their relevance to current practice. The case is made for the existence and perpetuation of guidance in the clinical risk assessment and management field.

References

Bötticher, A., Kröber, H. L., Müller-Isberner, R., Böhm, K. M., Müller-Metz, R., and Wolf, T., (2006). Mindestanforderungen für Prognosegutachten, *Neue Zeitschrift für Strafrecht (NStZ)*, Heft 10.

Buchanan, A. (2008). Risk of violence by psychiatric patients: Beyond the 'actuarial versus clinical' assessment debate, *Psychiatric Services*, 59, 184–190.

Curry, S. J. (2000). Organisational interventions to encourage guideline implementation, *Chest*, 118 (8), Suppl. 2, 40S–46S.

Department of Health (1999). *A National Service Framework for Mental Health: Modern Standards and Service Models*. London: Department of Health, available at www.dh.gov.uk/prod_consum_dh/groups/dh_digitalassets/@dh/@en/documents/digitalasset/dh_4077209.pdf.

Department of Health (2006). *Recruitment and Retention of Mental Health Nurses: Good practice guide*. London: Department of Health, available at www.dh.gov.uk/prod_consum_dh/groups/dh_digitalassets/@dh/@en/documents/digitalasset/dh_4133979.pdf.

Department of Health (2007a). *Best Practice in Managing Risk: Principles and Evidence for Best Practice in the Assessment and Management of Risk to Self and Others*. London: Department of Health, available at webarchive.nationalarchives.gov.uk/+/www.dh.gov.uk/en/publicationsandstatistics/publications/publicationspolicyandguidance/DH_076511 and www.managingclinicalrisk.nhs.uk.

Department of Health (2007b). *Best Practice Guidance: Specification for Adult Medium-Secure Services*. London: Department of Health, available at www.dh.gov.uk/prod_consum_dh/groups/dh_digitalassets/documents/digitalasset/dh_078050.pdf.

Department of Health (2007c). *Independence, Choice and Risk: A Guide to Best Practice in Supported Decision-Making*. London: Department of Health, available at www.dh.gov.uk/prod_consum_dh/groups/dh_digitalassets/@dh/@en/documents/digitalasset/dh_074775.pdf.

Department of Health (2007d). *Guidance Statement on Fidelity and Best Practice for Crisis Services*. London: Department of Health, available at www.dh.gov.uk/prod_consum_dh/groups/dh_digitalassets/@dh/@en/documents/digitalasset/dh_063017.pdf.

Department of Health (2008a). *Best Practice in Managing Risk: Principles and Evidence for Best Practice in the Assessment and Management of Risk to Self and Others*. Revised document. London: Department of Health.

Department of Health (2008b). *Support, Time and Recovery (STR) Workers: Learning from the National Implementation Programme*. London: Department of Health, available at www.dh.gov.uk/prod_consum_dh/groups/dh_digitalassets/@dh/@en/documents/digitalasset/dh_081753.pdf.

Dobrow, M. J., Goel, V., Lemieux-Charles, L., and Black, N. A. (2006). The impact of context on evidence utilization: A framework for expert groups developing health policy recommendations, *Social Science and Medicine*, 63, 1811–1824.

Douglas, K. S. and Reeves, K. A. (2010). Historical-Clinical-Risk Management-20 (HCR-20) Violence Risk Assessment Scheme: Rationale, application, and empirical overview, in R. K. Otto and K. S. Douglas (eds), *Handbook of Violence Risk Assessment*. New York: Routledge.

Eaves, D., Douglas, K. S., Webster, C. D., Ogloff, J. R. P., and Hart, S. D. (2000). *Dangerous and Long-Term Offenders: An Assessment Guide*. Burnaby, BC: Simon Fraser University, Mental Health, Law, and Policy Institute.

Geddes, J. (2005). Evidence-based practice, in A. James, A. Worrall, and T. Kendall (eds), *Clinical Governance in Mental Health and Learning Disability Services: A Practical Guide*. Royal College of Psychiatrists, London: Gaskell.

Hart, S. D., Kropp, P. K., Laws, D. R. Klaver, J., Logan, C., and Watt, K. A. (2003). *The Risk for Sexual Violence Protocol: Structured Professional Guidelines for Assessing Risk of Sexual Violence*. Mental Health, Law and Policy Institute. Vancouver, Canada: Simon Fraser University.

Hart, S. D., Michie, C., and Cooke, D. J. (2007). Precision of actuarial risk assessment instruments: Evaluating the 'margins of error' of group vs individual predictions of violence, *British Journal of Psychiatry*, 190, 60–65.

Hart, S. D. and Boer, D. P. (2010). Structured professional judgement guidelines for sexual violence risk assessment: The Sexual Violence Risk-20 (SVR-20) and the Risk for Sexual Violence

Protocol (RSVP), in R. K. Otto and K. S. Douglas (eds), *Handbook of Violence Risk Assessment*. New York: Routledge.

Leitner, M., Barr, W., Jones, S., McGuire, J., and Whittington, R. (2006). *Systematic Review of Prevention and Intervention Strategies for Populations at High Risk of Engaging in Violent Behaviour*, Final Report, National Forensic Mental Health R&D Programme, University of Liverpool, June.

Leitner, M., Barr, W., and Hobby, L. (2008). *Effectiveness of Interventions to Prevent Suicide and Suicidal Behaviour: A Systematic Review*. Edinburgh: Scottish Government Social Research, available at www.scotland.gov.uk/Resource/Doc/208329/0055247.pdf.

Logan, C. and Johnstone, L. (2010). Personality disorder and violence: Making the link through risk formulation. *Journal of Personality Disorders*, 24, 610–633.

McSherry, B. and Keyzer, P. (2009). *Sex Offenders and Preventative Detention: Politics, Policy and Practice*. Leichhardt, NSW: The Federation Press.

Monahan, J., Steadman, H. J., Silver, E., Appelbaum, P. S., *et al.* (2001). *Rethinking Risk Assessment: The MacArthur study of mental disorder and violence*. New York: Oxford University Press.

National Institute for Health and Clinical Excellence (NICE) (2009). *Antisocial Personality Disorder: The NICE Guideline on Treatment, Management and Prevention*, National Clinical Practice Guideline No. 77. London: British Psychological Society and Royal College of Psychiatrists, available at www.nice.org.uk/nicemedia/live/11765/43046/43046.pdf.

Patterson, K. (2002). What doctors don't know (almost everything). *New York Times Magazine*, 5 May, 71–72.

Perleth, M., Jakubowski, E., and Busse, R. (2001). What is 'best practice' in health care? State of the art and perspectives in improving the effectiveness and efficiency of the European health care systems, *Health Policy*, 56, 235–250.

Powell, C. V., Maskell, G., Marks, M., South, M., Robertson, C., and Lenney, W. (2001). Successful implementation of spacer treatment guideline for acute asthma, *Archives of Disease in Childhood*, 84, 142–146.

Raine, R., Sanderson, C., and Black, N. (2005). Developing clinical guidelines: A challenge to current methods, *British Medical Journal*, 331, 631–633.

Rawlins, M. (2004). NICE work: Providing guidance to the British National Health Service, *New England Journal of Medicine*, 351, 1383–1385.

Reed, G. M., McLaughlin, C. J., and Newman, R. (2002). American Psychological Association policy in context: The development and evaluation of guidelines for professional practice, *American Psychologist*, 57, 1041–1047.

Risk Management Authority (RMA) (2005). *Standards and Guidelines for Risk Assessment*. Paisley, Scotland: Risk Management Authority, available at www.rmascotland.net/viewfile.aspx?id=138.

Risk Management Authority (RMA) (2007). *Standards and Guidelines: Risk Management of Offenders Subject to an Order for Lifelong Restriction*. Paisley, Scotland: Risk Management Authority, available at www.rmascotland.net/ViewFile.aspx?id=264.

Sackett, D. L., Rosenberg, W. M. C., Muir Gray, J. A., *et al.* (1996). Evidence-based medicine: What it is and what it isn't, *British Medical Journal*, 311, 71–72.

Sackett, D. L., Straus, S. E., Richardson, S., *et al.* (2000). *Evidence-Based Medicine: How to Practice and Teach EBM*, 2nd edn. New York: Churchill Livingstone.

Tannenbaum, S. J. (2005). Evidence-based practice as mental health policy: Three controversies and a caveat, *Health Affairs*, 24, 163–173.

Timmermans, S. and Mauck, A. (2005). The promises and pitfalls of evidence-based medicine, *Health Affairs*, 24, 18–28.

Vlayen, J., Aertgeerts, B., Hannes, K., Sermeus, W., and Ramaekers, D. (2005). A systematic review of appraisal tools for clinical practice guidelines: Multiple similarities and one common deficit, *International Journal for Quality in Health Care*, 17, 235–242.

Vogel, V. de, Ruiter, C. de, Bouman, Y., and Vries Robbé, M. de (2009). *SAPROF: Guidelines for the Assessment of Protective Factors for Violence Risk.* Utrecht: Forum Educatief.

Webster, C., Douglas, K., Eaves, D., and Hart, S. (1997). *HCR-20: Assessing Risk for Violence*, 2nd edn. Vancouver, BC: Mental Health, Law and Policy Institute, Simon Fraser University and the British Columbia Forensic Psychiatric Services Commission.

Woolf, S. H., Grol, R., Hutchinson, A., Eccles, M., and Grimshaw, J. (1999). Potential benefits, limitations, and harms of clinical guidelines, *British Medical Journal*, 318, 527–530.

9

Organizations, Corporate Governance and Risk Management

Ben Thomas

Introduction

Previous chapters in this part have considered government policy initiatives relating to harmful behaviour by the users of mental health services, including the National Suicide Strategy. Implementation of these 'top-level' initiatives is the responsibility of the organizations that make up the NHS. It is also the responsibility of these organizations to manage risk, provide safe care, and to protect people who use their services and staff from harm. In addition, it is widely acknowledged that errors and adverse events that result in harm are much more likely to result from systems failures within an organization rather than the poor performance of an individual.

This chapter will be of interest not only to NHS managers, but also practising clinicians as it explains the organizational responsibilities involved in the management of risk, providing safer mental health services, and managing harmful behaviour. These responsibilities include compliance with legislation, the provision of a safe environment, adequate staffing levels, competent staff, and well maintained equipment. It also includes an effective risk management system, incorporating complaints procedures, litigation, claims handling, and financial risk. While the policy framework described here is that which operates in England, many of the issues will be relevant to organizations and individuals in other countries.

From April 2010, risk management responsibilities will form part of the new mandatory registration requirements on quality and safety. The new system of regulation requires all providers of certain health and adult social care activities (including specialist mental health services) to register with the Care Quality Commission (CQC) in order to provide services. The registration requirements on quality and safety are described in more detail under the section discussing the work of the CQC.

In addition to legislative requirements, there are extensive national policies and guidance available to help organizations ensure service users are treated and cared for in

Self-Harm and Violence: Towards Best Practice in Managing Risk in Mental Health Services, First Edition.
Edited by Richard Whittington and Caroline Logan.
© 2011 John Wiley & Sons, Ltd. Published 2011 by John Wiley & Sons, Ltd.

high quality services that respect and promote users' safety, privacy, and dignity. This chapter examines how such policies and guidance are translated and implemented locally. It recognizes that knowing what to do does not always translate into doing the right thing. The chapter explores the ways in which organizations can support staff in making the best decisions around risk and thus drive up standards across the board. In doing so, the chapter also describes the work of other organizations, particularly independent agencies and the 'arm's lengths' bodies of the Department of Health, in supporting policy implementation, decision-making and monitoring services. These organizations include the NHS Litigation Authority (NHSLA), the CQC, including the Mental Health Act Commission, and the National Patient Safety Agency (NPSA).

Drawing on the work of the NPSA in the area of risk management, the chapter also outlines how organizations can integrate risk management and carry out proactive risk assessments and minimize harm to service users and staff. In discussing what organizations do to minimize risk, various theoretical positions are considered. The chapter concludes by examining the role of national guidelines and proposes that complying with current guidance and putting into practice what we know works will assist organizations in managing risk.

In examining organizational issues, the first part of the chapter recognizes the complexity of modern mental health services and examines the need to embed best practice. It discusses the importance of partnership working and the culture of mental health organizations.

Embedding Best Practice

Managing harmful behaviour in mental health services is a complex business, both for individual practitioners and for organizations as a whole. Modern mental health services often comprise of large numbers of staff working in a variety of settings and specialities, covering expansive geographical areas. These areas may well include a mix of rural, urban and inner city areas. The staff employed often come from different cultures and belong to a variety of professional groups, each with its own socialization process. Such organizations present managers with many challenges. On the one hand, they are accountable for the delivery and monitoring of safe, high quality services and, on the other, they have to ensure that patients have choice, that clinicians lead change locally, and that staff are empowered and encouraged to be creative and innovative (Department of Health, 2008).

Partnership Working

In recent years, mental health services have adopted a much more systemic approach to managing and delivering services, including robust clinical and corporate governance arrangements. It is recognized that there are multifactorial aspects involved in mental health care; services need to work in partnership with a variety of stakeholders, including social care services, local authorities, criminal justice agencies, and others, to deliver high quality and safe care (Department of Health, 2009). Such partnerships require a sharing of perspectives, shared values, purposes and practices, and a common language. Mental health services also require frameworks, tools, and national guidance to assist services in developing effective partnerships, and shared governance in the areas of risk and patient safety. The *Good Practice Guidance: Independent Investigation of Serious Patients Safety Incidents in Mental Health Services* (NPSA, 2008) is an example of such guidance.

Risk is an important part of the wider spectrum of comprehensive mental health service delivery. Managing risk is about integrated, multidisciplinary, multi-agency discussion and coordination, promoting involvement of service users and carers, and valuing colleagues across all sectors. The precursor to the CQC, the Healthcare Commission (HCC), along with a number of independent investigations, has identified the patient safety problems that occur between one service boundary and another. They report that effective partnership working is essential with formalized integrated risk management and governance arrangements to ensure patient safety is not compromised (HCC, 2008b).

Organizational Culture

The NHS is in a constant state of change. In recent years, much attention has been given not only to structures and processes, but also to the culture of mental health organizations. Creating a safer organization where risk assessment and management are high priorities requires leadership and a commitment from all staff. A safer organization requires a culture that values safety, where all staff are aware of what can and does go wrong, and where the management of risk is uppermost in their mind. It is well recognized that transforming services, especially bringing about cultural change and implementing safer practice, often requires different implementation strategies and stakeholder involvement. However, the implementation of new ways of working is normally successful if four conditions are present. These conditions are:

- the provision of evidence for the need to change;
- clearly defined goals for change;
- the creation of interest and energy for change; and
- consistent and continuous leadership support.

This approach to service transformation and the implementation of safer practice is emphasized in *High Quality Care for All: NHS Next Stage Review* (Department of Health, 2008). The review highlights the value of empowering patients by giving them greater choice, more rights, and more control over health and care. It recognizes that health care is delivered in a team, that there is a need for a shared endeavour, and a requirement to give frontline NHS staff the freedom to use their talents.

Having briefly highlighted some of the complexities of mental health services the next section looks at the type and scale of risks within mental health organizations. The section examines the organizational systems that have been set up to protect the safety of people who use services and their staff and promote improvements in both safety and quality. These systems include clinical and corporate governance and the distinction between the two is drawn. Finally, the section discusses the requirements under the Health and Safety at Work Act 1974 and the Manslaughter and Corporate Homicide Act 2007.

Assessing, Preventing and Managing Harmful Behaviours: The Size of the Problem

The assessment and management of harmful behaviours are a continual challenge to mental health services. For example, the HCC's 2007 National Audit of Violence pointed to an increase in the frequency and severity of violent incidents over the previous 12 months:

- 51% of nurses and 43% of patients reported feeling upset or distressed in mental health settings;
- 73% of nurses and 31% of patients had been threatened or felt unsafe; and
- 45% of nurses and 15% of patients had been physically assaulted.

The HCC reported similar findings in their *Count Me in 2008* census (HCC, 2008a), which found that almost one in eight mental health service users (12%) had experienced a physical assault while an inpatient in either the NHS or an independent organization in England and Wales. The survey of mental health staff showed that one in five had experienced physical violence and one in three had experienced bullying, harassment, or abuse from service users or their relatives during the previous 12 months.

A 2009 survey of mental health acute inpatients, which collected responses from 7,500 people from 64 trusts, showed that less than half (45%) said that they always felt safe in hospital. Thirty-nine percent of people said that they 'sometimes' feel safe and 16% that they did not feel safe (CQC, 2010).

Over 22,000 patient safety incidents involving disruptive and aggressive behaviour are reported to the NPSA's Reporting and Learning System from mental health services every year. In addition, there are over 18,000 incidents reported involving self-harming behaviour. All mental health organizations have implemented local systems for collecting data on patient safety incidents. The collection of such data forms part of an organization's clinical governance remit. The White Paper, *A First Class Service: Quality in the New NHS* (Department of Health, 1998) defines clinical governance as:

> A framework through which NHS organizations are accountable to for continuously im-
> proving the quality of their services and safe-guarding high standards of care by creating an
> environment in which clinical care will flourish. (Department of Health, 1998, 33)

All NHS organizations must fulfil their clinical governance responsibilities, which are underpinned by the statutory duty of quality introduced in the Health Act 1999. Clinical governance requires Boards to be assured that the organization has in place, systems, and processes to support staff and corporate accountability for the delivery of safe, high quality, patient-centred care within a reporting and learning culture.

Corporate governance is defined as the system by which organizations direct and control their business. It includes systems, processes, accountabilities, and decision-making. Together clinical and corporate governance are essential for all mental health organizations to achieve quality and safer services and deliver appropriate standards of care. Central to the structure of clinical governance are clear policies aimed at assessing and managing risk, including clinical risk. Risk management has emerged as a concept in mental health services providing a means of reasoned decision-making (Alaszewski, 2000). NHS mental health trust boards are required to set the direction for effective local risk management, including systems and structures supported by an organizational risk management strategy and policy. Such a strategy and the policies they translate into must be an integral part of the organizational culture, values, and performance standards.

Corporate governance includes effective health and safety management. Under the Health and Safety at Work Act 1974, employers have a number of legal responsibilities. Health and safety law states that organizations must:

- provide a written health and safety policy (if they employ five or more people);
- assess risks to employees, customers, partners, and any other people who could be affected by their activities;
- arrange the effective planning, organization and control, monitoring and review of preventive measures;
- ensure they have access to competent health and safety advice; and
- consult employees about the risks at work and current preventive and protective measures.

Failure to comply with these requirements can have serious consequences for both organizations and individuals. Sanctions include fines, imprisonment and disqualification.

The Corporate Manslaughter and Corporate Homicide Act 2007

Further requirements to ensure that organizations manage health and safety adequately are made under the Corporate Manslaughter and Corporate Homicide Act 2007. This Act emphasizes the need for all NHS Trusts and Primary Care Trusts (PCTs) to have robust risk assessment and management systems in place and to review regularly these procedures to ensure compliance. An organization will be guilty of an offence under the Act if the way in which its activities are managed or organized causes a death and amounts to a gross breach of duty of care to the deceased. A substantial part of the failure within the organization must have been at senior level. These include people who make significant decisions about the organization at both the centralized headquarters level as well as those in operational management. The Ministry of Justice suggests that the Act provides organizations with an opportunity to ensure they are taking proper steps to meet current legal duties. These include organizations satisfying themselves that systems and processes for managing health and safety are adequate.

There are a number of national agencies in England that support organizations in managing, reducing, and monitoring risk with the aims of improving safety for people who use their services and for their staff. The following section describes the work of these national agencies.

The Role of the National Patient Safety Agency

The National Patient Safety Agency (NPSA) was established in 2001 following the publication of *An Organization with a Memory* (Department of Health, 2000) and the Government's response, *Building a Safer NHS for Patients* (Department of Health, 2001). It is a Special Health Authority set up to facilitate learning from patient safety incidents across the NHS in England and Wales. The NPSA (2010) defines a patient safety incident as 'any unintended or unexpected incident that could have or did lead to harm for one of more patients receiving NHS-funded health care'. This definition is intended to include errors in treatment or care that did not harm patients, including situations where the problem was identified and put right so the patient was not affected. Reported patient safety incidents are classified according to the degree of harm caused ranging from no-harm to death.

The NPSA helps the NHS learn from things that go wrong and seeks ways to prevent their reoccurrence thereby improving patient care. It does this through the analysis of patient safety incidents, identifying themes and trends and feeding back to the wider NHS. It also identifies solutions working in partnership with other NHS organizations that can be implemented locally to build a stronger culture of safety. The principles of building a patient safety culture are outlined in the NPSA's publication *Seven Steps to Patient Safety* (NPSA, 2004). This document promotes the need to be open and fair and encourages the sharing of information. It takes a systems approach with an emphasis on understanding the 'how' rather the 'who' when an incident happens.

Detecting and analysing safety hazards and risks through effective reporting systems is the cornerstone of patient safety. The NPSA collects patient safety incidents through the Reporting and Learning Systems (RLS). Most NHS organizations in England and Wales are connected to the RLS and by the end of 2009, the RLS had received over 4 million patient safety incident reports. Despite this wealth of information, the *Safety First* report (Department of Health, 2006b) criticized the RLS for not delivering high quality, routinely available information on patients, trends, and underlying causes of harm to patients. Unfortunately, despite the large number of reports, there were few examples where actionable learning for local NHS organizations had resulted. Since the *Safety First* report, the NPSA has sought ways to improve both the collection of data and ways to help frontline staff to improve patient safety, for example, by identifying new methods of rapid reporting of most serious incidents and the improvement of feedback reports to NHS organizations.

Integrated Risk Management in Organizations

In 2004, the NPSA provided guidance to assist mental health organizations build on the integrated governance approach and to develop integrated risk management systems. The NPSA defines integrated risk management as the process of identification, assessment, analysis, and management of all potential risks, including harmful behaviours, and patient safety incidents, such as self-harm and violence. It applies to all mental health services at every level. Thorough assessment of risks will help mental health trusts to set their priorities and improve decision-making with an optimal balance of risk, benefit, and cost.

When changes in service reconfiguration, expansion, development, and clinical governance are considered, organizational risk management is a key component of any project design. Organizational risk management involves the following key elements:

- collating all sources of information related to risk and safety, for example, 'reactive data' (such as patient safety incidents, clinical litigation claims, complaints, and health and safety incidents) and 'proactive data' (such as the results of risk assessments);
- consolidating all the assessments of all types of risks for an organization at every level;

- incorporating all risks into an organization's risk assessment programme and risk register; and
- providing a consistent approach to the training, management, analysis and investigation of all potential risks and actual incidents.

A risk register is a database in which the results of all of an organization's risk assessments are collated. It is used as a form of audit to monitor how organizations manage their risks. The risk register should be both updated on a regular basis to show the effects of this management and reviewed on a regular basis. An integrated risk management strategy enables an organization to plan more effectively through having a better understanding of what could be done to avoid, control, or reduce the effects of the risks identified. The information captured through incidents, their investigations and the findings of risk assessments can be used to develop future business and strategic plans and improve the safety and the quality of the care provided. The benefits of integrated risk management for mental health organizations are outlined in Box 9.1.

Box 9.1: Benefits of integrated risk management for mental health organizations

- Increases awareness of risk so that the overall scale and nature of risk to individual service users can be efficiently and effectively assessed and managed.
- Provides a systematic and consistent approach to the identification, analysis, and investigation of all risks, that is, through root cause analysis (RCA) and/or significant event audit (SEA), which can be used for complaints and claims as well as incidents.
- Assists organizations to comply with all relevant national standards, as well as clinical governance, Clinical Negligence Scheme for Trusts (CNST), Risk Pooling Scheme for Trusts (RPST), Welsh Risk Pool (WRP), and Health and Safety Executive (HSE) requirements.
- Helps organizations plan for uncertainty and cope with the impact of unexpected events, which increases service user and public confidence.

(Adapted from *Seven Steps to Patient Safety: The Full Reference Guide*, NPSA, 2004)

According to the NPSA integrated risk management is important for several main reasons. First, it is now well recognized that mental health care involves a wide range of risks and that any development, change or innovation brings new risks as well as rewards. For example, the introduction of specialist community teams has introduced a number of new interfaces and with them the increased risks associated with different referral criteria which may delay transfer and receiving appropriate services.

Secondly, although many people regard patient safety incidents as random occurrences or unpredictable events beyond effective control, the majority of patient safety incidents occur in systematic and recurrent patterns. For example, recommendations made continually in independent inquiries include poor risk assessment and deficiencies in the transfer of vital information between agencies (National Confidential Inquiry into Homicides and Suicides by People with Mental Illness (NCISH), 2009).

Thirdly, mental health services are continuously changing, which can cause the identified risks to change over time. If these organizations systematically identify, assess, learn from, and manage all risks and incidents at every level, they will be able to reduce potential and actual risks and identify opportunities to improve health care and patient safety across the whole organization. For example, the introduction of community care resulted in some organizations being over-zealous with the reduction of inpatient beds that had to be reinstated later. Today services are planned in a much more systematic way to reflect the needs of the local population. Any proposed reduction in beds and development of community services includes public consultation and negotiation with the PCT to ensure appropriate services are provided.

Fourthly, integrated risk management not only focuses on the reduction or mitigation of risk, but supports and fosters innovation so the greatest returns can be achieved with acceptable results, costs and risks. An integrated system aims to balance risks with likely impact and possible outcomes. For example, many new buildings have not only incorporated anti-ligature collapsible rails to prevent suicides by hanging, but have introduced other anti-ligature measures such as sensor taps in bathrooms (see also Chapter 6). Integrated risk management is also an essential component of good overall management and provides a focus for building improved organizational resilience and flexibility in the face of uncertainty. Organizational resilience is defined as the system's resistance to its operational risks.

Finally, integrated risk management supports better decision-making through a solid understanding of all known risks and their likely impact. In the absence of effectively integrated risk management processes, the weaknesses and vulnerability of procedures, practices, or policy changes are not identified and so cannot be managed or controlled. This can compromise patient safety and result in delivery of care without well-considered contingency plans. For example, all mental health organizations have produced preparedness plans, including the possibility of staff shortages in the event of an influenza pandemic.

What should organizations do?

Mental health organizations need to be clear about their role and responsibilities with regards to risk management. The Trust Board and senior management need to show their commitment to risk management and that they are confident that the systems, policies, and staff employed are operating effectively and focused on key risks. The *Integrated Governance Handbook* highlights the need for Boards to both concentrate on strategic and important matters and to be certain that all risks are effectively controlled and managed (Department of Health, 2006a). The Trust Board seeks assurance that the organization has implemented an effective system of internal controls including robust risk management arrangements as part of its integrated governance arrangements. Integrated governance is defined as: 'Systems, processes and behaviours by which trusts lead, direct and control functions in order to achieve organizational objectives, safety and quality of services and in which they relate to patients and carers, the wider community and partner organizations,' (Department of Health, 2006a). This is done through implementation of a risk management strategy and an assurance framework (Department of Health, 2002). To demonstrate this there is a requirement that all NHS chief executives sign a Statement of Internal Control, which forms part of the statutory accounts and annual report. In addition to receiving progress reports on the Board Assurance Framework, Trust Boards need to be alerted to any risks that are not being effectively managed. A key governance principle involves establishing a system and an infrastructure where managing risk is debated in an open, transparent, and honest manner. This enables those responsible for making decisions to have access to all the available evidence.

It is recommended that mental health organizations have an appropriate infrastructure in terms of committee and individual responsibilities to carry through the overall policy and strategy around risk management. A risk management or governance committee, constituted as a Trust Board sub-committee usually acts as the coordinator and filter for the risk assessment processes. As part of their structures many mental health trusts and PCTs employ a central team of experts in all types of risk headed up by a risk manager. These include a health and safety manager, an infection control team, fire safety and manual handling, preventing and managing violence, medicines governance, medical devices, safeguarding children/adults and IT. The central team is responsible for coordinating all the activities associated with clinical and non-clinical risk including collating all information relating to risks such as patient safety incidents. In large organizations the central team may provide support to other local risk management groups and ensure that staff receive training in risk assessment, risk management, the reporting of incidents and their investigation using root cause analysis (RCA). The central team is often linked to external risk management networks, for example, regionally at Strategic Health Authority level. Information gathered from local experience is shared and used to improve safety and reduce risk.

It is essential that Boards receive regular reports providing assurances on the management of risks including trends, their potential impact, the likelihood that they will happen, and forecasts about future possible risks in order to anticipate changes in demand and performance. Exception reporting, focusing on any significant risk to the organization, also provides the Board with efficient oversight. The *Assurance Framework* (Department of Health, 2002) provides a simple framework for reporting key information to Trust Boards. It identifies the main risks where there are inadequacies in the operation of controls or where the organization has insufficient assurances about them. It also provides structured assurances about where risks are being managed effectively and therefore allows Boards to make efficient use of their resources and address the risks identified in order to improve the safety and quality of care.

Achieving Integrated Risk Management

Seven Steps to Patient Safety: The Full Reference Guide (NPSA, 2004) suggests that the most effective, integrated risk management system must be woven into normal working processes and existing decision-making structures and processes. To achieve an integrated risk management approach, mental health organizations must:

- have a system in place reporting when things go wrong and ensuring that lessons are learned following investigation;

- ensure that risk is actively managed and appropriately communicated throughout the organization;
- use existing multidisciplinary groups to discuss risk management in the organization or practice;
- provide appropriate training to ensure that all staff understand risk management and patient safety and are aware of the local processes used to inform practice;
- promote and support an open and fair culture;
- achieve compliance with external accreditation, for example, the different levels under the NHSLA accreditation scheme;
- establish a risk register;
- ensure staff use the organization's reporting system;
- ensure there is regular feedback to staff about reported patient safety incidents in the form of a newsletter or other means of communication, which also contain details of action being taken to prevent re-occurrences;
- review aggregated risk management data and risk assessments and use tools (such as failure modes and effects analysis (FMEA) to help forecast possible problems and contingency planning;
- review RCA investigations;
- establish a system to review, update and disseminate clinical policies and procedures to promote and support best practice; and
- ensure appropriate systems are in place for sound governance arrangements.

Organizational risk assessment

Integrated risk assessment involves both the integration of different assessment approaches and assessing as many risks as possible, for example, environmental dangers in ward design and equipment and the organization of the delivery of nursing care and the interventions used. Integrated risk assessment is a process that helps organizations understand the range of risks they face (both internally and externally), the level of their ability to control those risks, the likelihood of the occurrence of these risks, and their potential impact on the organization. An integrated risk assessment helps mental health organizations obtain an understanding of their risk management capacity, practices, and culture. It helps refine practices so they become safer and more resilient. Integrated risk assessment assists in achieving strategic and operational targets set by external stakeholders. Integration and management of all risks will assist mental health organizations to comply with their clinical governance targets, risk accreditations such as CNST, RPST, WRP, and the HSE requirements. Integrated risk assessment and management also ensures that lessons are learnt and shared within and across the organization.

Risk assessments should be conducted with staff for whom the risks are relevant. For example, board and management teams will need to advise on strategic risks, while clinical teams will need to be involved when assessing an individual patient's care or a procedural risk in their department. All parties affected by risks, including patients and the public, can also be involved in the decision process where possible. Each service should take ownership of their own risks and feed these into a risk register for the organization. The risk assessment process is then used to develop local plans and as evidence for service development.

Organizational risk assessment tools There are a number of tools available to identify potential safety incidents, technical hitches, problems, complications and sometimes disasters. These include:

- risk matrix;
- probabilistic risk assessment (PRA); and
- failure modes and effects analysis (FMEA).

A brief description of these organizational risk assessment tools is given below, but a full description is provided in *Seven Steps to Patient Safety: The Full Reference Guide* (NPSA, 2004).

Risk matrix This is a commonly used tool in organizational risk assessment. It is used to map risks against likelihood of occurrence and severity of impact, combining judgements with numerical analysis. A risk matrix can be used to assess patient safety incidents that have already happened and those that have been prevented, as well as potential future risks. The risk matrix should be used by clinical and managerial staff together to assess local incidents and risks. The risk matrix for risk managers and *Healthcare Risk Assessments Made Easy* can be accessed at www.npsa.nhs.uk.

Probabilistic risk assessment PRA examines incidents and their contributory factors and determines the likelihood of the event occurring. PRA involves a mixture of quantifying risks and judgement, and applies tools such as event tree analysis. Event tree analysis is an approach which maps out the different paths and factors that can lead to an event occurring. It also uses fault tree analysis. Fault tree analysis is an extension of the event tree, which shows the cumulative effects of the faults within a system. The assessment defines the nature and size of the risks and weighs these against the benefits of reducing or eliminating them, as well as the costs of achieving this. A decision is then taken on how best to manage the risk. An overview of PRA can be found in the *Risk Assessment Programme Overview*, which can be accessed at www.npsa.nhs.uk/nrls/improvingpatientsafety/patient-safety-tools-and-guidance/risk-assessment-guides.

The PRA approach works out the likelihood of each outcome and what could be done to reduce that likelihood. It attempts to quantify the potential risks by scoring the likelihood of a particular risk or incident actually happening, including a consideration of the frequency with which it may arise. To help with this quantification, incident data can be assessed along with expert estimation of how often a process could fail, for example, a doctor making a prescription error, or by undertaking a clinical audit of the process to demonstrate actual failure rates, for example auditing medication charts.

Once a risk has been identified, the risk matrix is used to estimate the chances of an incident occurring or re-occurring, taking into account the measures in place to prevent it. The chances of occurrence are rated from highly unlikely to very likely, helping an organization to think about ways to reduce risk further and the urgency with which they need to do so. The matrix is then used to assess the actual or potential consequences of the risk to patients. Incidents that have no impact on patients are registered as 'not harmful' or 'low risk'; the most serious incidents, which could potentially cause death, are ranked 'extreme risk'.

Failure modes and effects analysis FMEA is widely used in industry and has been adapted as a tool for risk assessment in health care in the United States (Joint Commission on Accreditation of Healthcare Organizations, 2005). It is a proactive tool that helps to evaluate a process or a new product or design of service to identify potential points of failures and the effect these failures could have on individuals and/or the organization. The actions that need to be taken to prevent an incident can then be prioritized.

The seven stages of an FMEA, its benefits and examples of its use, are provided in the NPSA's *Risk Assessment Programme Overview* available at www.npsa.nhs.uk/nrls/improvingpatientsafety/patient-safety-tools-and-guidance/risk-assessment-guides.

The NHS Litigation Authority

This section describes the role of the NHSLA which was set up in 1995 to assist NHS organizations fund the cost of clinical negligence claims. It is a Special Health Authority and administers the Clinical Negligence Scheme for Trusts (CNST), a risk pooling scheme. Membership of the scheme is voluntary and open to all NHS Trusts, Foundation Trusts, and PCTs in England. Funding is on a pay-as-you-go non-profit basis, and organizations receive a discount on their scheme contributions where they can demonstrate compliance with the relevant NHSLA risk management standards. An example of a litigation claim is provided in Box 9.2.

Box 9.2: Example of a litigation claim

Savage v. South Essex Partnership NHS Foundation Trust (2008)

Mrs Savage was detained under Section 3 of the Mental Health Act 1983. She was treated for paranoid schizophrenia on an open ward. She absconded and jumped in front of a train, suffering fatal injuries. Her daughter brought a claim not for negligence, but rather under Article 2 of the European Convention on Human Rights (right to life). Following a preliminary issue trial on the proper test in law to establish a breach under Article 2, the High Court held that it was at least one of 'gross negligence', that is, conduct such as to allow a charge of manslaughter to be brought. However, on 20 December 2007, the Court of Appeal overturned this ruling. It decided that the claimant must demonstrate that at the material time, the Trust knew or ought to have known of the existence of a real and immediate danger to the life of the patient and that it failed to take measures within the scope of its powers which, judged reasonably, might have been expected to avoid that risk. On 10 December 2008, the House of Lords dismissed the appeal by South Essex Partnership NHS Foundation Trust finding that, where there was a real and immediate risk of a patient detained in a mental hospital committing suicide, there is obligation on the medical authorities to do all that could be reasonably expected of them to prevent them doing so.

(See http://lawreports.co.uk/WLRD/2008/HLPC/dec0.5.htm.)

The NHSLA standards and assessment process are designed to provide a structured framework within which to focus effective organizational governance and risk management activities to deliver quality improvements in the safety of service users, staff, and others in contact with the organization such as volunteers and visitors. They are also meant to encourage and support organizations in taking a proactive approach to improvement, reflect risk exposure, and empower organizations to determine how to manage their own risks.

Overall, the NHSLA standards and assessment process are intended to contribute to embedding risk management into the organization's culture, reducing the number of adverse incidents and the likelihood of recurrence, and thereby the level of claims. They also assist in the management of adverse incidents and claims and provide assurance to the organization, other inspecting bodies, and stakeholders, including service users.

Assessments against the NHSLA standards are used by the CQC to inform the registration process for NHS Trusts.

The progression of organizations through the NHSLA standards is logical and follows the development, implementation, monitoring, and review of policies and procedures. Table 9.1 provides an example of a criterion in the NHSLA Risk Management Standards for Mental Health and Learning Disability Trusts at each of the three levels. Compliance

Table 9.1 Example of a criterion in the NHSLA: Risk Management Standards for Mental Health and Learning Disability Trusts 2010/11.

Standard 1 – Criterion 1: Risk Management Strategy

The organization has an approved risk management strategy that is implemented and monitored.

Level 1   Minimum requirements

1.1.1   As a minimum, the approved documentation must include a description of the:
   a. organizational risk management structure detailing all those committees/sub-committees/groups which have some responsibility for risk
   b. process for board or high level committee review of the organization-wide risk register
   c. process for the management of risk locally, which reflects the organization-wide risk management strategy
   d. duties of the key individual(s) for risk management activities
   e. authority of all managers with regard to managing risk
   f. process for monitoring compliance with all of the above.

Level 2   Minimum requirements

2.1.1   The organization can demonstrate compliance with the objectives set out within the approved documentation described at Level 1, in relation to the:
   • process for the management of risk locally, which reflects the organization-wide risk management strategy.

Level 3   Minimum requirements

3.1.1   The organization can demonstrate that it is monitoring compliance with the minimum requirements contained within the approved documentation described at Level 1, in relation to the:
   • process for the management of risk locally, which reflects the organization-wide risk management strategy.

   Where the monitoring has identified deficiencies, there must be evidence that recommendations and action plans have been developed and changes implemented.

with Level 1 demonstrates that the process for managing risks has been described and documented. Compliance with Level 2 demonstrates that the process for managing risks, as described in the approved documentation, is in use. Evidence must be provided for a number of departments and/or staff groups and/or service users and carers. The evidence may include completed risk assessments, records such as patient safety incident reports, training programmes and safety improvement action plans which have been implemented. Level 3 compliance demonstrates that the process for managing risk, as described in the approved documentation, is working across the entire organization. Where failings have been identified, action plans must have been developed and changes made to reduce risks. Monitoring is normally proactive and designed to highlight issues before an incident occurs. This should consider both positive and negative aspects of a process.

The Role of the Care Quality Commission

The CQC is the independent regulator of all health and adult social care in England. The precursor of the CQC was the Healthcare Commission, which was set up in 2004 to improve how health care is regulated in England. The CQC regulates all health and adult social care services in England, regardless of whether or not they are provided by the NHS, local authorities, private companies, or voluntary organizations. The CQC also protect the interests of people held under the Mental Health Act.

The CQC makes sure that essential quality standards are being met everywhere that care is provided from hospitals to private care homes, and they aim to improve standards. They promote the rights and interests of people who use services and they have a wide range of powers to take action if services are unacceptably poor. The CQC's main activities include the following:

- the registration of health and social care providers to ensure they are meeting common quality standards;
- the monitoring and inspection of all health and adult social care services;
- the use of their enforcement powers, such as fines and public warnings or closures if standards are not being met;
- the improvement of health and social care services by undertaking regular reviews of how well those who arrange and provide services locally are performing and special reviews on particular services, pathways of care, or themes, where there are particular concerns about quality; and
- the reporting of the outcomes of their work so that people who use services have information about the quality of their local health and adult social care services, to help those who arrange and provide services to see where improvement is needed and to learn from each other about what works best.

Review of Mental Health Services

In 2008, the HCC published its findings on the quality and safety of care provided by NHS acute inpatients and psychiatric intensive care units in England. The HCC focused particularly on whether admission was appropriate, therapeutic, and safe for service users. This was the largest review of acute inpatient mental health services and for the first time provided a national picture of the safety of 69 NHS Trusts. The report highlighted those trusts that were rated as 'weak' on the criteria relating to safety and pointed out that insufficient attention was given to sexual safety.

What the HCC assessed

The mental health assessment framework has a number of criteria, including one that looked at the infrastructure in place to promote safety. Box 9.3 illustrates the assessment undertaken.

Box 9.3: Is there an infrastructure in place that promotes safety?

- Trust current assessment level for CNST demonstrating the level of effectiveness with regard to risk management.
- Proportion of clinical and administrative staff who report having received training in how to prevent or handle violence and aggression to either staff, patients or service users in the last 12 months (HCC survey of staff, 2006).
- Proportion of clinical staff who report having received training in assessing use of alcohol and drugs, and how to handle patients who are drunk or under the influence of drugs (HCC survey of staff, 2006), constructed by combined indicators using:

    (a) the proportion of clinical staff who report having received training in how to ask service users about their use of alcohol or drugs (including illegal drugs); and
    (b) the proportion of clinical staff who report having received training **in** how to handle patients who are drunk or under the influence of drugs (including illegal drugs).

- Proportion of bank and agency nursing staff from 1 October 2006 to 31 March 2007 (bespoke data collection).
- Proportion of service users for whom a range of risk assessments have been completed (bespoke data collection), constructed by audit of the following issues:

    (a) risk of sexual vulnerability;
    (b) identification of predatory behaviour, potential to abuse or offend; and
    (c) patterns of substance misuse.

- Proportion of ward-based nursing staff (qualified and unqualified) trained in sexual safety awareness from 1 April 2005 to 31 March 2007 (bespoke data collection).

The findings from the HCC review

The review found marked differences in standards between Trusts and sometimes between wards within the same Trust. The HCC found no Trust that scored 'excellent' on all four of the criteria. In addition only 19% of Trusts had achieved CNST Level 1, which indicates that risk management systems and processes have been implemented in practice, and assessment of risk of sexual vulnerability was the least likely of the risk assessments to be completed. Around one in nine Trusts was rated as 'weak' on providing individualized care; and no Trust was rated as 'excellent' for the effectiveness of its care pathway from admission to discharge.

Based on these findings, the HCC identified a number of key areas for improvement. These included taking steps to minimize violence and aggression using approaches that have been proven elsewhere, promoting a more positive therapeutic environment and better engagement with service users, promoting sexual safety and sexual health, ensuring risk management systems are implemented in practice, and looking at ways to minimize the likelihood of patients going missing.

The HCC report reinforced the responsibility of all mental health trusts to minimize risk, to provide safe care and to protect both people who use their services and their staff from harm. From 2010, alongside its quality improvement function the CQC will operate a new system of mandatory registration for providers of health and adult social care in England. This includes mental health trusts. It will be illegal for any body not registered with the CQC to provide health and adult social care services that comes within the scope of registration. There are a number registration requirements relating to quality and safety. Examples of these are listed in Box 9.4.

Box 9.4: Examples of registration requirements on quality and safety

- care and welfare of service users;
- assessing and monitoring the quality of service provision;
- safeguarding vulnerable adults;
- cleanliness and infection control;
- management of medicines and medical devices;
- meeting nutritional needs;
- safety and suitability of equipment;
- respecting and involving services users; and
- consent to care and treatment.

The registration requirements set out essential levels of quality and safety. They are broad categories and will be underpinned by guidance that is under development by the CQC, who will legally enforce registration requirements. Failure to comply may result in conditions on registration, suspension, and/or fines up to £50,000.

Organizational Characteristics that Influence the Capacity to Deliver Effective Risk Management

Having outlined a number of national agencies who support organizations in managing, reducing, and monitoring risk with the aims of improving safety for people who use their services and their staff, the next section examines some of the characteristics of organizations that may have an impact on their ability to do so adequately.

Organizational responsibility and supporting care teams

As discussed at the beginning of the chapter, it is important that an organization develops and promotes a safety culture. An increasing body of knowledge has identified some of the core aspects of organizations that are relevant to safety within health care (Hoff *et al.*, 2004). These include sufficient staffing levels, the competencies of staff, strong visible leadership, fair management, and adequate supervision, together with teamwork, good communication channels, procedures and equipment. West (2005) suggests that by monitoring these aspects through staff and service user surveys, managers can identify which areas to focus attention on and target resources to reduce risk and errors. A study by Vincent (2001) identified organizational problems, including poor communication, supervision, and deficiencies in training that were likely causal factors in a serious patient safety incident on a psychiatric ward (Vincent, 2001).

West (2005), who identified the following four characteristics, has identified other organizational characteristics that may be intrinsic to its level of risk and danger:

1. the division of labour in complex organizations;
2. structural holes in communication networks;
3. diffusion of responsibility; and
4. environmental or other pressures that deflect organizations from their main task.

These are discussed fully below.

Division of labour According to West (2005), this is the most fundamental characteristic of organizations. As mentioned previously, as mental health services become much more specialized and compartmentalized, then the risks of managing harmful behaviour increase due to the need for more communication, monitoring, coordination, and cooperation.

To reduce the complexity that exists in modern health services requires the standardization and formalization of tasks. For example, in hospitals standardization could include keeping resuscitation trolleys stored in the same position and stocked in the same way. In community care, standardization in ways of working could include caseload numbers, standardized referral criteria, handovers, and the use of health and safety policies such as 'lone working'.

Formalization refers to the extent to which roles, rules, and procedures are applied within an organization. In an attempt to reduce variation in standards of care, formalization has been introduced by means of operating procedures, guidelines, and protocols. West (2005) suggests that the tendency towards formalization is demonstrated by the growth of the 'guideline movement'. For example, preventing and managing violent and aggressive behaviour is a common occurrence for staff in mental health organizations. From an organizational perspective, it is imperative that there is a policy based on available evidence, national guidance and sound clinical principles that ensures service users receive the most effective and humane care possible and that staff are not harmed. A further discussion on the use of clinical guidelines is provided later in the chapter and elsewhere in Chapter 8.

Structural holes in communication networks   The barriers to communication in mental health services have been discussed previously. These barriers are erected by the hierarchical nature of health care organizations, by the importance of professional allegiances, and by inter-agency working. West (2005) suggests that a system of 'checks and balances' goes someway towards promoting safety and reducing risk so that important actions are not the sole responsibility of one individual. For example, powerful drugs are always checked by two people. Other models of communication to improve safety are beginning to emerge such as the 'Concord collaborative care model' (Morath and Turnbull, 2004).

Diffusion of responsibility   The diffusion of responsibility within complex organizations often makes it difficult to determine who is responsible for what. In mental health care, mistakes are often associated with a particular clinical decision, for example, the decision to discharge someone into the community or to reduce the level of someone's observation. Unfortunately, those involved in direct clinical care are therefore more vulnerable to blame than are people in other positions and at other levels in the hierarchy. For example, there may be managerial pressure put on psychiatrists to discharge patients and free up beds, or to reduce observation levels due to the cost implications of employing extra nurses. West (2005) suggests that decisions at higher levels within an organization are much less clear-cut and because the repercussions of these decisions may not manifest for some time, they may be difficult to track. For example, a manager may defer preventative maintenance on buildings to reduce costs, but as the building continues to be used over time, it becomes more unsafe. Blurred lines of responsibility within an organization are not conducive to creating a safety culture. The Corporate Manslaughter Act now addresses this somewhat by making individual directors responsible,

The environment of an organization   West (2005) suggests that the organizational literature is full of examples of how organizations set up for one purpose come to strive for other very different goals. It is apparent that mental health services are extremely vulnerable to wider socioeconomic and political pressures that can divert time and attention into goals that are not directly related to patient care. One of the biggest threats to the goals of providing care and treatment is the need for organizations to remain economically viable. Achieving financial targets can mean trade-offs between competing goals and managers have a difficult task juggling business activities with striving for quality and safer services.

Training

All professional staff are expected to keep up-to-date with their knowledge and skills. However, there is also an organizational responsibility to ensure that staff are adequately trained in relation to harmful behaviour and that their competencies are maintained through the regular provision of training and up-dating. The competencies required may include the ability to assess the patient, to assess the environment, the use of techniques to de-escalate the situation, and the use of restraint, seclusion, rapid tranquillization, and observation. There are a number of clinical risk assessment tools to assist staff in identifying potential risks and which offer a link between risk assessment and management of aggression. Despite the development of structured and standardized clinical risk assessment tools, cynicism around their usefulness still exists, for example, Morgan (2007) in a briefing paper for the Royal College of Psychiatrists suggests that their dominance may distort clinical priorities and lead to defensive practice. The Mental Health Act Commission, on the other hand, is in favour of organizations using the new guidance produced by the Department of Health in 2007 as the basis for practice in this area.

In 2006, the Court of Appeal held Nottinghamshire Healthcare NHS Trust liable for injuries inflicted by a patient on six staff members at Rampton Hospital when a patient attacked one member of staff and injured five others who went to restrain her. At the time, the Trust had not implemented the 'Tilt' Safety and Security Directions (Department of Health, 2000), which had by then come into force, and the court found that this was relevant since, had they been implemented the patient would have been in more secure surroundings and not at liberty to assault the staff. The Trust proposed that any breach in its duty of care towards its staff should be tested according to the Bolam principles (*Bolam v. Friern*, 1957), which is to say on a test of whether it could be shown that no responsible body of clinicians would have failed to confine the patient. The judge accepted that the duty of care towards staff must take into account that sometimes a competing duty of care is owed to the patient. However, if the Trust could take precautions so as not to expose its employees to unnecessary risks and still not be in breach of its duty to a patient then it might well be in breach if it failed to take these precautions.

According to the Mental Health Act Commission, such rulings may be interpreted by already risk-averse service managers as an additional liability for staff safety that further promotes defensive practices, including greater confinement and control of patients at the expense of opportunities for patients to exercise limited freedom and regain their autonomy. In considering risk to self, staff, and others, risk aversion must always be considered. Overstated risks can lead to unnecessary exclusion from services, stigmatization, and a breakdown in the relationship between service users and the mental health team (see also Chapter 11).

Clinical Guidelines and Risk Management

The final section of this chapter examines the use of clinical guidelines in improving risk management in organizations and promoting the safety of people who use their mental health services and their staff. As stated in the introduction, despite the number of policies and guidance available there is no guarantee that knowing what to do is always translated into doing the right thing.

The use of clinical guidelines to improve risk management and service user safety

Generally, most national guidelines and policies highlight the action required both at an organizational level and at an individual practitioner level. For example, the NICE (2005) guidance on the short-term management of violence identified the need for organizations to have an integrated approach for adult psychiatric wards with a clear organizational strategy and policy supported by management. Organizations are expected to adopt national guidelines and policies locally and adapt them to local circumstances. Many NHS Trusts publish their policies on their websites.

Policies and guidelines are generally regarded as supportive and helpful with the main aim of reducing variations in clinical care. Organizations are expected to facilitate the implementation of guidelines from NICE and their monitoring as well as implementing policies, rapid responses, and alerts from other NHS bodies. Recognition that issuing policies and guidance will not necessarily change clinical behaviour means that much more attention is now given to implementation strategies that support practitioner acceptance and adoption.

Mental health organizations can use clinical guidelines to improve clinical effectiveness and safety, by using guidelines as tools within planned quality improvement activities and by making them readily available and accessible for all clinical staff in their day-to-day practice and as part of their continuing education and training. Practically, mental health organizations will be able to implement and support only a limited number of clinical practice guidelines at any one time. Therefore, organizations need a process by which they can set and pursue their clinical priorities. These often reflect national priorities as discussed previously, or they can be set at a local level, particularly if there has been an identified clinical theme or trend, such as an increase in people going missing from acute psychiatric wards or an inappropriate variation in performance and expenditure, such as length of stay under certain clinicians or re-admission rates. Such criteria raise questions about service delivery and health outcomes and the availability of guidelines to address the problem.

The introduction of clinical practice guidelines to improve the safety of service users needs to take into account the characteristics of the organization, including its culture, its leadership style, and its ability to adapt to change. Large and complex mental health trusts will require different strategies of implementation to PCTs. Many large organizations introduce clinical practice guidelines by using a controlled pilot study method. This means introducing the guidelines in a particular area for a set period and then evaluating their introduction. Following successful introduction, the guidelines are introduced into the next area or rolled out more widely across the organization.

Not only do clinical practice guidelines take resources to develop, but more importantly, they cost time and money to disseminate, implement, and sustain. Commitment of required resources needs to be a corporate decision with a worked out communication, implementation, spread, and sustainability plan including timeframes, training requirements, replacement costs, and monitoring requirements. To assist organizations in this process the NPSA has produced *Closing the Gap: Toolkit for Improving Implementation of Safer Practices* (2008), which can be obtained from www.npsa.nhs.uk.

The benefits of implementing NICE guidance for organizations are well documented, including meeting the *Standards for Better Health*, conforming to the NHSLA risk management standards and enabling organizations to meet the requirements of the NHS operating framework. However, sometimes organizations may disagree with national policy and recommendations or with clinical guidance and decide not to implement them. If this is the case, the organization should do so only through a mechanism of due process that is required in public law for the accountability of the reasonableness of such a decision (Samanta and Samanta, 2004). According to Daniels and Sabin (1997), four factors need to be taken into account to demonstrate an organization's accountability for the reasonableness of such a decision. First, decisions in areas covered by NICE guidelines and their rationale should be publicly accessible to the local population. Secondly, the rationale must be based on evidence and reason, and the principles that all fair-minded parties, including managers, clinicians, and service users can agree upon, are relevant to the decision. Thirdly, there must be an appeals mechanism to challenge any decision, including the opportunity for revising any decision taken by the organization in the light of further evidence or arguments. Fourthly, organizations that take a decision to deviate from specific NICE guidelines are expected to regulate the process to ensure that the first three conditions are met.

Conclusion

This chapter has examined the role and responsibilities of organizations in the management of risk relating to harmful behaviours. It has explored the ways in which organizations can support staff in making the best decisions around risks and, thus, not only improve standards across the board, but also save lives. One of the key ways to achieve these goals is to integrate and actively manage risk across the organization. The chapter has outlined proactive risk assessments and the role of external review by independent agencies in identifying and managing clinical and non-clinical risk and improving the safety of service users and staff.

Organizational responsibility for safety includes the implementation of government policy and national guidance. Organizations have to prioritize and determine the relevance of the guidance to the local situation. Management has a key role to play in prioritizing and supporting staff to implement the changes required. At an organizational level, it is necessary to review services and practice in relation to national guidance and advice and implement the best available recommendations. This means identifying the changes that need to be made, explaining to staff why change is required, and then identifying what differences and benefits have been achieved as a result of the changes implemented. Even when there is strong public opinion and national guidance, it is not always easy to implement and bring about change.

At an organizational level, management, including the executive board, must take responsibility for safety and the management of risk and these should be high on the agenda of all Board and management meetings. To show that the management of risk is a priority and that the organization is committed to improvement, managers and leaders must be visible and active in leading risk management activities and involving staff. Most of the risks involved in mental health care, such as self-harm, absconding, and disruptive behaviour, have complex systemic causes that may require actions by an individual clinician, by a team, and at an organizational level. Complying with current guidance and putting into practice what we know works is the first step. Proactively anticipating risk and preventing harm, particularly in areas that are prone to such problems, is the second step. Mental health organizations are in a fortunate position in that we often know what we need to do in order to assess and manage harmful behaviour. Creating safer care for service users is not the sole responsibility of those who deliver care. The creation of safer care for service users also includes systematic design and decision-making from the executive board and throughout the organization.

References

Alaszewski, A. (2000). *Managing Risk in Community Care.* Edinburgh: Baillere Tindell.

Care Quality Commission (2010) *National NHS Patient Survey Programme: Mental Health Acute Inpatient Service Users Survey 2009.* London: CQC, available at www.cqc.org.uk/ PatientSurveyMentalHealth2009, accessed 23 February 2010.

Daniels, N. and Sabin, J. (1996). Accountability for reasonableness, *British Medical Journal,* 312, 15553–15554.

Department of Health (1998). *A First Class Service: Quality in the New NHS.* London: Department of Health, available at www.open.gov.uk/doh/newnhs/quality.htm.

Department of Health (2000). *An Organisation with a Memory: Report of an Expert Group on Learning from Adverse Incidents in the NHS Chaired by the Chief Medical Officer.* London: The Stationary Office.

Department of Health (2001). *Building a Safer NHS for Patients.* London: Department of Health, available at: www.dh.gov.uk/en/Publicationsandstatistics/Publications/Publications PolicyAndGuidance/DH_4006525.

Department of Health (2002). *Building the Assurance Framework: A Practical Guide for NHS Boards.* London: Department of Health, available at www.dh.gov.uk/en/Publicationsandstatistics/ Publications/PublicationsPolicyAndGuidance/DH_4093992?IdcService=GET_FILE&dID= 28278&Rendition=Web, accessed June 2008.

Department of Health (2006a). *Integrated Governance Handbook: A Handbook for Executives and Non-executives in Healthcare Organisations.* London: Department of Health.

Department of Health (2006b). *Safety First: A Report for Patients, Clinicians and Healthcare Managers.* London: Department of Health.

Department of Health (2007). *Best Practice in Managing Risk: Principles and Guidance for Best Practice in the Assessment and Management of Risk to Self and Others in Mental Health Services.* London: Department of Health, available at www.dh.gov.uk/en/publicationsandstatistics/ publications/publicationspolicyandguidance/DH_076511.

Department of Health (2008). *High Quality for All.* London: Department of Health.

Department of Health (2009). *New Horizons: A Shared Vision for Mental Health.* London: Department of Health.

Healthcare Commission (HCC) (2006). *NHS National Staff Survey 2006,* available at www.cqc.org.uk.

Healthcare Commission (2008a). *Count Me in 2008: Results of the 2008 National Census of Inpatients in Mental Health and Learning Disability Service in England and Wales.* London: Commission for Healthcare Audit and Inspection.

Healthcare Commission (2008b). *Learning from Investigations.* London: Healthcare Commission.

Healthcare Commission and the Royal College of Psychiatrists (2007). *The National Audit of Violence (2006–2007).* Final Report: Working age adult services, available at www.rcpsych. ac.uk/PDF/Iremovd-WAA%20Nat%20Report%20final%for%20Leads%2010%2012.pdf.

HMSO (1974). Health and Safety at Work Act 1974, available at www.opsi.gov.uk/acts/ actsq974a/pdf/ukpga_19740037_en.pdf.

HMSO (1999). Health Act 1999, available at www.hmso.gov.uk/acts/acts1999/19990008.

HMSO (2007). Corporate Manslaughter and Corporate Homicide Act 2007, available at www.opsi.gov.uk/acts/acts2007/pdf/ukpga+20070019_en.pdf.

Hoff, T., Jameson, L., Hannan, E., and Flink, E. (2004). A review of the literature examining linkages between organizational factors, medical errors, and patient safety, *Medical Care Research and Review,* 61 (1), 3–37.

Ministry of Justice (2007). *Understanding the Corporate Manslaughter and Corporate Homicide Act 2007,* available at www.justice.gove.uk.

Morath, J. M. and Turnbull, J. E. (2005). *To Do No Harm.* San Francisco, CA: John Wiley & Sons.

Morgan, J. F. (2007). *Giving up the Culture of Blame: Risk Assessment an Risk Management in Psychiatric Practice.* Briefing Document for the Royal College of Psychiatrists, February 2007.

National Patient Safety Agency (NPSA) (2004). *Seven Steps to Patient Safety: The Full Reference Guide.* London: NPSA.

National Patient Safety Agency (NPSA) (2008). *Good Practice Guidance: Independent Investigations of Serious Patient Safety Incidents in Mental Health Services.* London: NPSA, available at www.npsa.nhs.uk.

National Patient Safety Agency (NPSA) (2010). Available at www.npsa.nhs.uk/nrls/reporting/what-is-a-patient-safety-incident, accessed 23 February 2010.

National Institute for Health and Clinical Excellence (NICE) (2005). *NICE CG25: The Short Term Management of Disturbed/Violent Behaviour in Inpatient Psychiatric Settings and Emergency Departments.* Available at http://guidance.nice.org.uk/CG25/niceguidance/pdf/English.

NCISH (2009). *National Confidential Inquiry into Homicides and Suicides by People with Mental Illness, Annual Report: England and Wales.* University of Manchester, NCISH.

NHS Litigation Authority (2003). *CNST and RPST Risk Management Standards.* Available at www.nhsla.com, accessed June 2004.

Samanta, A. and Samanta, J. (2004). NICE Guidelines and law: Clinical governance implications for trusts, *Clinical Governance: An International Journal*, 9(4), 212–15.

Vincent, C. (ed.) (2001). *Clinical Risk Management. Enhancing Patient Safety*, 2nd edn. London: BMJ Books.

West, E. (2005). Sociological contribution to patient safety, in K. Walshe and R. Boaden (eds), *Patient Safety: Research into Practice.* Maidenhead: Open University Press.

10

Formulation in Clinical Risk Assessment and Management

Caroline Logan, Rajan Nathan and Andrew Brown

Introduction

In preceding chapters, self-injury and violence have each been considered in some detail. The nature of the risks to be managed and the risk factors associated with the occurrence of self-injury and violence have been explored and options for organizational responses to manage the risks assessed have been discussed. The perspectives of service users at the receiving end of clinical risk assessment and management practices as well as the perspective of carers responsible for a relative or friend at risk have also been examined. In addition, the practice of positive risk management has been scrutinized; that is, the practice of making accountable decisions to take risks with clients who have a history of harmful behaviour towards themselves or others based on a good understanding of the behaviour in question and on a collaborative relationship between the client and his or her clinical team. These are all essential considerations in any discussion about risk assessment and management in clinical settings. Formulation is also an essential clinical task and this is the focus of the present chapter, specifically formulation in the context of clinical risk assessment and management. Risk formulation is the process of deriving a shared understanding of future risk potential – in relation to risk of harm to self or others – based on an understanding of relevant past behaviours (risk assessment), which then acts as a bridge to hypotheses about change (or risk management). Often excluded from discussions about the clinical risk assessment and management process, an examination of risk formulation is thought by the present authors to be essential in this practical guide for those delivering and receiving care.

This chapter will begin with an overview of the task of clinical risk assessment. Commonly used approaches and tools intended to help the practitioner understand the risks presented by an individual client will be described. The practice of clinical risk management will then be reviewed. This section will be somewhat brief as the literature on risk management is minimal, despite the ubiquity of its practice. The links between

Self-Harm and Violence: Towards Best Practice in Managing Risk in Mental Health Services, First Edition.
Edited by Richard Whittington and Caroline Logan.
© 2011 John Wiley & Sons, Ltd. Published 2011 by John Wiley & Sons, Ltd.

risk assessment and risk management will then be explored in the context of a discussion about formulation – specifically, risk formulation. The chapter will conclude with a brief case study in which the risks presented by a fictitious service user are described and the risk assessment, formulation, and management plan summarized in order to illustrate the practice recommended.

Clinical Risk Assessment and Management: An Overview

In the last 20 or so years, the process of risk assessment has been advanced considerably by the development of evidence-based standardized measurement guides. Such guides – or instruments or tools – are based on research identifying the variables or risk factors most frequently associated with the harmful outcome of interest (e.g., a history of violence is strongly associated with future risk of violence and is, therefore, a risk factor for this outcome). Thus, a key characteristic of these guides is the provision of a list of risk factors that are linked to the undesirable outcome to be managed (e.g., violence). In practice, clinicians are required to examine each risk factor and indicate via a pre-set rating, whether the factor is present or not, and, if present, the extent to which it is present (e.g., partially, definitely). Further, the clinician is required to provide examples or evidence to support his or her rating of a risk factor as present. Once all risk factors have been examined, the clinician is then usually required to make some form of overall judgement about the client's future risk of the harmful outcome – usually a statement or prediction about the likelihood of the harmful outcome occurring again in the future – on the basis of which a risk management plan is prepared. Examples of some of the early risk assessment guides, which emphasized this simple risk assessment method, are the *Violence Risk Appraisal Guide* (VRAG) (Quinsey *et al.*, 1998, 2006; Webster *et al.*, 1994), the *HCR-20* (Webster *et al.*, 1997), the *Static-99* (Hanson and Thornton, 1999), and the *Risk Matrix 2000* (RM2000) (Thornton *et al.*, 2003). The Care Programme Approach (CPA) also encourages risk assessment via the use of checklists of risk factors and summary judgements of likelihood intended to aid case prioritization (Department of Health, 1998, 2008).

Thus, the use of such risk assessment tools in routine practice requires clinicians to explicitly examine risk in a way that draws on the research findings, particularly with regard to factors that appear to be correlated with, or are predictive of, the harmful outcome under consideration. In this way, assessments can be said to have an evidence base and a violence risk assessment tool will be different in some major respects from a suicide risk assessment tool because the evidence base is different. The evidence base underpinning judgements about risk is good and a considerable improvement on un-structured judgements about risk, which were pervasive before such practices as outlined above were implemented. It has been argued that an assessment of the likelihood of an undesirable outcome (e.g., violence), which is based on factors that have an empirically demonstrated association with that outcome, improves the reliability and validity of the assessment of risk (e.g., Quinsey *et al.*, 2006).

However, there are two problems with this approach. First, while the identification of the risk factors that are present in the individual client is a critical early step in the whole risk assessment and management process, this step can come to dominate the clinicians' perspective (the so-called anchoring or adjustment bias). When this step is reduced to its most basic, the focus is simply on whether each of a list of risk factors is present or absent with little further thought given to *understanding* how these factors have developed and how they interact with one another – and the environment – to create the potential for harmful behaviour in the client at any one point in time. The application of this type of brief, stripped-down risk assessment process – more like a risk screen than a risk assessment – is often derided as contributing to a 'tick-box culture', where the throughput of clients takes precedence over the quality of the engagement with them and the whole process of risk assessment is grossly oversimplified.

Secondly, while standardized approaches to the assessment of risk improve the accuracy of the prediction of risk within clinical groups (Buchanan, 2008), the prediction of the risks posed by individual clients remains elusive if not impossible to determine (Hart, Michie and Cooke, 2007). Instruments that purport to estimate the probability of a client engaging in harmful behaviour, in fact, record only the frequency with which individuals with some similar characteristics engaged in the harmful behaviour under scrutiny (as evidenced by, for example, criminal convictions or completed suicides). Such instruments do not predict the probability with which a particular client will engage in that harmful behaviour in the future. This limits the application of these tools considerably and questions the value of attempting to quantify risk. Further, it raises questions about just how valid are assessments of risk based on the application of risk prediction tools.

Unfortunately, advances in the process of clinical risk assessment stalled somewhat due to this focus on risk factors and on predicting harmful outcomes. Indeed, for a lengthy period during the last two decades, attention to risk prediction became almost an academic necessity and the issue of prevention was overlooked both empirically and practically. However, this situation is changing now and support is increasing for the use of approaches to clinical risk assessment and management that encourage the collection and synthesis of information in a methodical and, more importantly, consistent and meaningful way (Carroll, 2007). Risk formulation is – and should be – at the core of this development (Kumar and Simpson, 2005).

In 2003, the *Risk for Sexual Violence Protocol* (RSVP) (Hart *et al.*, 2003) was published. This marked a significant turning point in the risk field. First, it exemplified a structured professional (or clinical) judgement approach, emphasizing understanding and prevention rather than prediction, and it directly linked risk assessment and risk management. The worksheet accompanying the RSVP guides the practitioner through each stage, from start to finish. Specifically, practitioners are encouraged to record evidence for and against the risk factors identified in the literature as potentially important to risk of sexual violence. Risk factors are described in the RSVP manual, ensuring consistency in the evaluations made across time and among practitioners. Next, practitioners are asked to rate the relevance of each of the risk factors that are present to the individual client's risk of future sexual harm. Thus, the assessment is both evidence-based and specific to the client. The findings of the assessment stage are then examined in detail and a risk formulation derived by exercising a combination of decision theory and scenario planning. This involves speculating about possible futures in which an act of sexual harm may occur, then identifying how and why they might come about based on the practitioner's understanding of the risk factors most relevant to that client's risk and the reason why the client might decide to be sexually harmful again in the future. The underlying mechanism of the client's risk is therefore exposed by the formulation process, which in turn acts as a platform for the preparation of a risk management plan. This was the first time that risk assessment was so explicitly linked to risk management, and that risk formulation was identified as a critical stage in proceedings.

The second way in which the publication of the RSVP led to a shift in the risk field was because it led to the revision of the worksheet of the much more popular HCR-20 risk assessment guide (Webster *et al.*, 1997) into a very similar format to that used in the RSVP, which has resulted in more widespread exposure to this approach. While not universally accepted – many practitioners still prefer to use the HCR-20 and its original very brief worksheet as just a checklist of risk factors – the new worksheet and its more delineated method is, nonetheless, contributing to the way in which risk is being discussed and communicated, and how the practice of risk assessment and management is being taught.

A third point is worth making. While instruments have not always directed the attention of practitioners to protective factors – those characteristics of the person or the situation they are in that mitigate or moderate risk potential (de Vogel *et al.*, 2009) – it is, nonetheless, implicit in the structured professional judgement approach that protective factors are identified and enhanced just as risk factors are identified with a view to diminishing their influence on the individual's behaviour. While protective factors were flagged up in instruments that preceded the RSVP (for instance, in the *Structured Assessment of Violence Risk in Youth* (SAVRY); Borum, Bartel and Forth, 2006), their integration into formulation became integral to the structured professional judgement approach from the publication of the RSVP onwards (e.g., the *Short-Term Assessment of Risk and Treatability* (START); Webster *et al.*, 2004).

Thus, the emphasis on prediction, which encouraged a dissatisfying 'tick-box' approach to complex and influential risk assessments, is gradually being overtaken by an approach emphasizing understanding and prevention. In the structured professional judgement approach, risk assessment may be defined as the estimation of an individual's risk potential based on our understanding of the balance between certain conditions that we assume to be risk factors and certain other conditions that we assume to be protective factors, all of which have relevance to the harm potential of the client in question. Risk management – the objective of which is the prevention of the harmful outcome being considered, or at the very least, the minimization of that harm – is the purpose of the assessment. Formulation will be discussed shortly, but what exactly do we mean when we talk about risk management?

Risk management is action taken to prevent or limit potentially harmful outcomes. Unfortunately, risk management per se has been subject to only a fraction of the research to which risk assessment has been subject (Risk Management Authority, 2007). Nonetheless, in the structured professional judgement approach, risk management is clearly defined. Risk management originates in an understanding about individual risk (the risk formulation) and consists of three essential components – treatment interventions, supervision, and monitoring – and an additional optional process of victim-safety planning, valuable when previous harmful activity has targeted a specific victim such as an intimate partner who may be targeted again (Hart *et al.*, 2003).

In terms of risk management, treatment is the implementation of strategies to moderate risk factors or enhance protective factors (Hart *et al.*, 2003). Treatments broadly include psychological therapies (e.g., cognitive-behaviour therapy), psychosocial interventions (e.g., therapeutic community), and psychotropic medication (e.g., clozapine) for conditions such as major mental illness and personality disorder that assessment has linked to the client's risk of harm. Therefore, treatment is the action recommended to repair or restore deficits in adjustment and functioning, thus modifying risk factors relevant to harm potential. However, treatment can also act to enhance the functioning of protective factors; training in thinking skills and in interpersonal problem-solving may result in a less impulsive or reckless individual better able to avoid situations or manage incidents that triggered harmful behaviour previously.

Supervision is a different risk management strategy from treatment because it targets the environment in which the individual is based rather than the individual him- or herself, although the objective of reducing the influence of risk factors and enhancing the role of protective factors remains the same. In risk management terms, and in structured professional judgement terms in particular, supervision refers to the restrictions imposed on the client's activities, movements, associations, or communications in order to limit his or her access or exposure to risk factors (Hart *et al.*, 2003). Examples of supervisory strategies may include limiting access to potential victims (e.g., children), random drug testing to limit access to substances that impair thinking and problem-solving and reduce the effectiveness of prescribed medications, or restriction orders to discourage communication with former victims. Supervision also refers to enhancements to the individual's lifestyle that are reasonably supposed to improve the operation of protective factors (Hart *et al.*, 2003). Examples of the ways in which supervision may work supportively include the development of occupational and recreational skills and activities – to assist in the provision of daily structure, purpose, and routine, and in the case of employment, financial reward and security also – and regular access to social support, such as through weekly visits from a community psychiatric nurse.

Monitoring as a risk management activity refers to the identification of early warning signs of a relapse to harmful activity and the dissemination of that information to all those involved in managing the client's risk of harm alongside guidance on what to do when such signs are observed (Hart *et al.*, 2003). Monitoring differs from supervision because it focuses on surveillance rather than controlling, managing, or limiting the client's activities and is, therefore, considerably less intrusive. Derived from the risk assessment, and ideally from detailed discussions with the client and his or her carers, monitoring information communicated to others should include what the earliest warning signs are of an increasing risk of relapse to harm, then what the signs are that might follow if those are overlooked, as well as the not so early warning signs that risk is significant, escalating, and imminent. In addition, the monitoring component of a risk management plan should also contain information about what to do – and critically, what not to do – when early warning signs are detected. For example, social isolation and the avoidance of eye contact in someone with a history of schizophrenia, which assessment suggests is linked directly to risk of violence, may constitute very early warning signs that risk may be increasing. Similarly, carrying a weapon in case of attack in someone already very paranoid might suggest risk of violence is more imminent and severe in its possible consequences for a victim.

Finally, victim safety planning refers to the action recommended to keep a possible future victim safe. Such a person may be identifiable because they have been victimized by the client in the past (e.g., an intimate partner). Alternatively, threats have been made against them or they are likely to be working closely with the client (such as a community psychiatric nurse or responsible clinician), a scenario that may have resulted in conflict and heightened risk of harm in the past.

In conclusion, the clinical risk assessment and management field has undergone a great many developments in the last 20 years. An initial emphasis on risk prediction has given way to a greater emphasis on risk assessment and management, and risk formulation is increasingly recognized as the critical process that links one activity with the other (Kumar and Simpson, 2005). However, it is a good deal easier to measure what has happened than what has been prevented and empirical research in the risk field continues to refer to the prediction of harmful outcomes. In clinical settings, among practitioners tasked with the management of clients with a history of violence or self-injury, the requirement to predict harm is greatly outweighed by the requirement to prevent it from happening. Therefore, this section has outlined the structured professional judgement process and its two essential elements of risk assessment and risk management. The following section turns to risk formulation, a key clinical process in the prevention of harmful outcomes.

General Principles of Clinical Formulation

Formulation provides an evidence-based explanation of a person's difficulties. Formulation draws on a broad range of literatures, theories, and findings to knit together experiences and explanations in order to tell a coherent story about how and why a person has behaved in a particular way in the past and how and why and in what context they might do so again in the future. Formulation is not a new phenomenon. On the contrary, it is established as a routine part of therapeutic interventions (Persons, 1989). Formulation-based approaches to understanding and managing a range of psychopathologies and problems are commonplace within the clinical literatures (e.g., see Johnstone and Dallos, 2006). It is widely recognized that formulation is the critical task that underpins the safe management of complex clients (Davidson, 2006), and is responsible for providing an evidence-based understanding of a client's problem ensuring the most appropriate and proportionate responses to the risks assessed (Tarrier, 2006). Despite its common use elsewhere (Bruch and Bond, 1998), and its recommended use in the risk field (Kumar and Simpson, 2005), formulation has yet to become an established part of the risk assessment and management process. This section draws on the available literatures and proposes that a formulation-based approach (Table 10.1) might provide a way forward for managing the complexities of clients at risk.

The first stage in preparing a formulation is to generate a detailed description of the presenting problem (e.g., violence or self-injury) – or problems (e.g., violence combined with substance dependence, relationship conflict, problem-solving difficulties) – in the form of a list (Persons, 1989). Problem description as the primary stage in formulation ensures that the focus of the work being undertaken is not lost, invaluable when problems are many and inter-related in complex ways: 'The list of behavioural difficulties serves a variety of purposes such as structuring the clinical interview, specifying the range of problems the individual is experiencing, and, most importantly, providing the therapist with information for generating hypotheses' (Meyer and Turkat, 1979, 262). The collaboration of the client in the generation of a problem list – and the identification from this list of the chief complaint – is strongly recommended (Persons, 1989) in order to promote engagement and enhance the effectiveness of the interventions that follow by ensuring they are sensitive to the problems subjectively described (Lane, 1990).

The second stage in preparing a formulation is to explore and identify the range of factors contributing to – if not causing – the presenting problems by testing hypotheses about what these components are and how they inter-relate. For example, Young, Klosko, and Weishaar (2003) recommend the assessment of early maladaptive schemas (related to, for example, autonomy, connectedness, worthiness, and limits/standards) because of their relevance to a range of the presenting problems commonly seen in mental health

Table 10.1 Seven stages of formulation development.

1	List and describe the presenting problem(s) (e.g., depressed mood, substance dependence, relationship conflict) and identify the chief complaint (e.g., depressed mood).
2	Identify (a) contributing or causal factors relevant to the chief complaint (e.g., interpersonal problem-solving difficulties, childhood abuse and neglect), and (b) the protective factors that have ceased to be effective at the time of presentation (e.g., social support, employment).
3	Delineate the mechanism whereby components generate the presenting problem (e.g., childhood abuse and neglect → maladaptive beliefs or schema → poor relationship management → depressed mood → substance dependence, which compounds poor relationship management and the client's experience of depressed mood).
4	Define the developmental origins of these components (e.g., experience of childhood abuse and neglect distorted the client's beliefs about him- or herself and created a range of expectations about him- or herself in relation to others that others have difficulty understanding and managing).
5	Identify triggers that activate this mechanism to create the chief complaint at any one time (e.g., the client's partner stays out late without telling him where she or he is or with whom).
6	Identify maintenance factors (e.g., fear of being alone because being alone recreates intolerable feelings reminiscent of those experienced in childhood).
7	Prepare hypotheses about (a) problem recurrence, (b) interventions required, and (c) anticipated obstacles to effective intervention.

Source: *Personality Disorder and Violence: Making the Link Through Risk Formulation*, Logan and Johnstone (2010). Copyright Guilford Press. Reprinted with permission of the Guilford Press.

settings (e.g., depression). Presenting problems are individually scrutinized using functional analysis in the first instance, where the stimulus, response and consequences are identified and explored with the client (Bruch, 1998). An additional and sometimes overlooked part of this second stage of formulation is to identify protective factors (such as employment or social support), the positive influence of which have somehow ceased to be effective in moderating the negative influence of causal or contributing factors, thus encouraging the appearance of presenting problems and in the ways observed.

The third stage in preparing a formulation is the development of an explanation for the process or the *mechanism* whereby contributory factors – negative and positive – have interacted with one another over time to generate the presenting problem(s). This is a critical stage. Hypotheses are generated about possible mechanisms and tested through discussions with the client and others as well as through formal assessment and observations. Subsequently, the fourth stage is to explore the developmental origins of the key contributory factors, a process also accomplished through hypothesis testing with the client in conjunction with information obtained from collateral sources. A detailed history is obtained for each of the presenting problems in order to better comprehend their genesis and their persistence over time as well as to access more of the underlying mechanism of their operation. In order to change behaviour in a meaningful way, its aetiological determinants require exploration: 'every behavioural problem is examined from its very first occurrence through all changes in its development to the present' (Turkat, 1986, 124). Information about the origins of presenting problems dovetails with the process of identifying the main contributing or causal factors (Bruch, 1998).

In the fifth stage of formulation preparation, triggers are identified – those situations or processes (such as the client having a row with his partner or experiencing disrespect from a work colleague) that activate an acute phase of the presenting problem, thus creating a deterioration leading to an unacceptable level of psychological distress (Persons, 1989). Subsequently, in the sixth stage, those processes of learning and reinforcement that have operated across the lifespan to create and maintain presenting problems, making them hard to change, are identified and incorporated into the evolving view about the underlying mechanism of the presenting problem. The assessment of the consequences of problems and the self-preserving or self-soothing responses made to them by the client provides clarification about operant-maintaining factors in the short- and the long-term (Bruch, 1998).

The final stage in formulation development is the preparation of hypotheses regarding what interventions are required – the strategy, tactics and methods of their administration (Tarrier, 2006) – and how such interventions might operate to reduce the severity of the presenting problem as it is now understood. Hypotheses about appropriate interventions should be accompanied by a plan of action as to how they might be delivered and when, and how barriers or obstacles to positive change might be overcome. Ideally, hypotheses are confirmed or disregarded as untenable on the basis of the systematic exploration of treatment options with the client (Turkat, 1985). This collaboration with the client is integral to comprehensive information-gathering and preparation for change at this stage (Bruch, 1998). Indeed, Tarrier (2006) queries how informed consent for assessment and treatment can be given by a client in the absence of such a collaborative approach.

A clinical case formulation that has been developed rigorously in accordance with the seven stages described above (see also Table 10.1 for a summary) may be presented in clinical settings in a number of different ways. A narrative case formulation summarizes in writing the findings of each of the stages. Such narrative case formulations may be extensive, and appropriately so in some settings or circumstances (e.g., following admission to an inpatient service or at the commencement of an outpatient therapeutic engagement), taking up a significant part of the report describing the therapist's engagement with the client. Alternatively, they may be brief, offering a more limited examination of one of the presenting problems rather than all those on the problem list. Alternatively still, reports may provide only recent evidence of change – or the absence of change – and revisions to formulations developed earlier and in a more elaborate way, a format suitable for treatment progress reports. Clinical case formulations may also be presented diagrammatically (e.g., formulations in cognitive analytic therapy; Ryle and Kerr, 2003), sketching out the presenting problems, the components and their mechanism of operation, and proposing the means of their development and maintenance. Such diagrammatic representations of clinical case formulations offer the same facility of exposing the workings of the presenting problem and offering the means of determining their resolution with the additional advantage of brevity and immediate accessibility, which clients may appreciate.

Risk Formulation in Practice

Clients who are not well understood – clients whose actions defy understanding and for whom a formulation cannot easily be prepared or is limited in range and scope – are not risk managed with focus, clarity of objectives, or confidence (Reid and Thorne,

2007), and restrictive practices are more likely to prevail in such instances. However, how the process of formulation may be achieved in clients with complex presentations and a history of harming themselves or others, how the needs of the client may be rationally balanced against the requirement to keep him or her and others safe, has hitherto not been clearly defined. This is problematic because, in the absence of clarity about what is expected and how it may be achieved, the formulation process can be contaminated by error (Eells, Kendjelic and Lucas, 1998; Nezu and Nezu, 1989; Persons, 1989; Tarrier, 2006) and the risk management actions that follow therefore built on foundations that limit transparent, accountable, and ethical practice. As a consequence, practice can vary hugely depending on the experience and confidence of the practitioner and a lack of clarity and agreement regarding the functional link between presenting problems and harmful outcomes persists. Thus, while clinical case formulation is regarded as an essential task, it is a task frequently undertaken without confidence except by more competent and experienced practitioners of particular therapeutic approaches and the widespread use of formulation remains more science fiction than science fact (Bieling and Kuyken, 2003).

Kuyken (2006) proposes a set of evidence-based guidelines for generating 'good enough' formulations for cognitive-behaviour therapy. Such guidelines are intended to assist in the generation of formulations that would improve cognitive-behaviour therapy (CBT) practice by linking theory, research, and intervention, to normalize problems and increase empathy, organize complex information, and enable quality supervision. Such guidelines are also intended to generate formulations capable of helping practitioners thereafter to select and sequence appropriate interventions, to appreciate a client's preferred way of changing, to identify 'therapy interfering behaviours', and to enable the simplest and most cost-efficient interventions (Kuyken, 2006, 14). These guidelines are a useful starting point for ensuring 'good enough' – if not better – *risk* formulations.

Kuyken (2006) proposes first that initial contacts with the client and with collateral sources of information should be an opportunity to generate provisional hypotheses, which will be scrutinized further by all opportunities arising subsequently and by all those involved in the preparation of the formulation and in its translation into practice. Thus, in a risk assessment, information should be collected from multiple sources allowing it to be cross-referenced and verified. In order to maximize opportunities to develop a rapport with the client, information gathering from files and collateral sources should commence prior to first contact between the client and the practitioner.

Secondly, information gathering frameworks such as evidence-based risk assessment guides (e.g., the HCR-20) and structured assessments of other potentially relevant factors (e.g., major mental illness) provide a basis both for collecting information about predisposing risk and protective factors. Such structured assessments also create opportunities for collaboration with the client – and others – through the emphasis on rapport-building. In addition, the use of assessment tools enhances the connection between the hypotheses derived and tested and the existing theory and literature on the subjects of interest, which enhances the anchoring of hypotheses and the eventual formulation on published evidence.

Thirdly, hypotheses may be tested through exploration with the client but also through investigation with others who know the client well, thus affording a triangulation procedure with credible information taking precedence over that which is not corroborated. However, Kuyken (2006) suggests that involving the client in a risk formulation from the very beginning of the process may not always be a good thing. Research emerging from the CBT literature (Chadwick, Williams and Mackenzie, 2003; Evans and Parry, 1996) suggests that clients are frequently positive about some aspects of involvement in formulation development (e.g., they gained a better understanding of themselves, the therapist listened to them, clarity about the way forward through therapy). Such clients also reported negative views of other aspects of the process (e.g., feeling overwhelmed, frightened by the inferences being made, being reminded of distressing events). Kuyken likened the collaboration of clients in the generation of formulations to the assistance offered by a navigator to a driver: 'a navigator who shares the whole road map with the driver may hinder rather than help the driver keep on track because the driver is given information not directly relevant to the current task and the amount of information may be overwhelming' (Kuyken, 2006, 30). The nature and extent of client cooperation on risk formulation awaits exploration.

Fourthly, practitioners must understand the impact of factors known to affect their judgement. For example, practitioners' reasoning about the presenting problems of their clients may be adversely influenced by cognitive short-cuts or heuristics. One example is bias arising from representativeness – the tendency to see aspects of the presenting problem as representative of a certain class of problems, leading to the potential for incorrect judgement based on too little information and, therefore, inappropriate treatment. Another example is bias arising from the ready availability of certain kinds of salient information or experience, which is utilized in the current case incorrectly. Finally, anchoring or adjustment bias is when the practitioner is overly influenced by their initial judgements about a case such that he or she ignores subsequent evidence suggestive of a different explanation.

Fifthly, practitioners should prepare a formulation that identifies the key components of risk – predisposing risk and protective factors, precipitating factors or triggers, and any relevant maintenance or perpetuating factors – and propose an explanation for how these factors developed over time and inter-relate to create elevated risk potential. Contributing to this process should be functional analyses of instances of harmful conduct in the past, in order to identify the most critical factors and then develop proposals for a risk management plan that addresses each of the relevant factors in a hierarchical and systematic way. Practitioners should then test this formulation with colleagues who know the client well and work with him or her also, such as the membership of a multidisciplinary team. The final stage is to prepare the formulation either in a narrative or diagrammatic form for discussion with the client.

Sixthly, interventions suggested by the formulation should be identified where priority is given to triggers in order to moderate risk potential at the earliest time. Interventions should cover the key areas of treatment, supervision, and monitoring processes, and victim safety planning responses if necessary. The prepared formulation is then revised on the basis of evidence of the success – or otherwise – of the various interventions attempted. Practitioners ought to be more willing to question their opinions in the face of new evidence, and should adopt a continuing stance of curiosity in relation to understanding the client.

Kuyken (2006) makes clear that in CBT and elsewhere, much research remains to be done to establish the value of formulations in relation to the outcomes eventually achieved. Further, expertise in formulation appears to improve their reliability and it is assumed their validity also. A key requirement for implementing clinical case – and risk – formulations is having the time and resources to invest in rapport building with the client, in motivating him or her to engage sufficiently, to conduct assessments, to consult with others, and to sample evidence contained in multiple places and cross-reference or triangulate it with information from elsewhere. Moreover, an additional requirement is demonstrable knowledge and competency in evaluating risk, violence and self-injury, and mental health needs in general in order to know the value of what is observed on assessment and its relevance to the formulation in development. These requirements may not be present in all practitioners or the mental health settings in which they work. However, team work, peer review, clinical supervision, and opportunities for continuing professional development may ensure these requirements are broadly met.

While risk formulation is a critical process in bringing together disparate elements of the individual, his or her developmental history, and aspects of their situation, what is weak in the guide to risk formulation just proposed is Kuyken's recommended top-down theory to provide the evidence base for the work that follows. Theories address aetiology and change potential and process. While many theories of violence and self-injury exist, they are varied in focus (psychological, social, and biological theories; social learning theories; psychoanalytic theories; and feminist theories to suggest only a few) and supported by differing amounts of empirical research, both in terms of their explanatory power and their role in effecting change. The structured professional judgement approach to risk assessment and management is not a theory about risk. Instead, it is a valuable practical framework for coordinating risk information. However, a 'theory-knitting' process, where theories of harmful behaviour and the decisions individuals make to be harmful are integrated to produce a more unified and deep explanation for its origins and maintenance, such as that described by Ward, Polaschek and Beech (2006) in the field of sexual offending, may have some merit as a way forward. A theory-knitting strategy could allow the integration of the best existing ideas in the domains of risk and violence and self-injury within a new framework. Such an endeavour could both improve our understanding of harmful behaviour as a whole and support the role of risk formulation in preventing the recurrence of harm. The development of theory on risk is awaited.

Concluding Comments on Risk Formulation

In conclusion, formulation is a critical process in clinical case management with clients who are complex in their presentation and potentially harmful towards themselves and others (Davidson, 2006). In such cases, formulation enables the bringing together of disparate assessment findings and creates a platform on the basis of which interventions – including their nature, mode of delivery, and sequence – can be jointly agreed, commenced, and evaluated. This collaborative engagement with the client is fundamental to the purpose and the value of formulation and the interventions that follow from it (Tarrier, 2006). However, when cases are very complex, when the cooperation of clients cannot be guaranteed for whatever reason, when they present with multiple problems across several domains of functioning, and when risk of serious harm to self or others is real and substantial, the confidence of practitioners in the preparation and utilization of a valid and reliable formulation can diminish. Consequently, there is a risk that the formulation stage may be excluded just when its presence is potentially of most value. Guidance, such as that offered above and an awareness of the problems associated with deriving 'good enough' formulations has the potential to encourage their development despite any pressure to do otherwise, thus ensuring that risk management is inevitably based on an understanding of the underlying mechanism of the client's potential to cause harm.

Case Study

In order to illustrate the guidance on risk formulation given above, a case study is now presented. In this case, a fictional person is subject to a risk assessment in order to prepare a risk formulation and, subsequently, a risk management plan. The seven steps to formulation described above (and summarized in Table 10.1) underpin the evaluation described. Information about the fictional subject of the assessment – Mr Smith – is limited as the purpose of this section of the chapter is simply to describe an example of how formulation-based risk assessment and management could be presented. Real clinical reports would of course contain much more personal and rich detail.

Introduction

This case study is divided into four sections. In the first section, *the risks posed* by Mr Smith are set down. Mr Smith's history is not reviewed in full – only those aspects of his history that are relevant to this case study are described. (This first section covers stage 1 of the formulation development process described above and in Table 10.1). In the second section, *factors relevant to the risks posed* by Mr Smith are described where those factors thought to increase risk (risk factors) are described separately from those that are thought to moderate or reduce risk (protective factors). (This section covers stages 2, 5 and 6 from Table 10.1). In the third section of this case study, a *risk formulation* is described, that is, an account is given of how it appears that risk and protective factors interact over time to change risk. (This section covers stages 3 and 4 from Table 10.1). The case study concludes with a *risk management plan* in which treatment, supervision, and monitoring options are explored. (This plan covers stage 7 from Table 10.1).

Risk of what?

The primary concern regarding Mr Smith is his risk of harm towards others. He is presently in prison on remand on charges of common assault, but is likely to be released when he appears before the court because of the time already spent in prison. Specific concerns about risk of harm relate primarily to assaults on his peers and associates, which are especially likely when he is intoxicated, or acutely mentally unwell – or both. He has also been violent in the past towards his girlfriend. However, he is not currently in a relationship and has no contact with his ex-girlfriend.

A second and related risk is that of harm to himself, including suicide. Mr Smith has taken overdoses previously. In addition, he has demonstrated a reckless disregard for his own safety at times (e.g., when crossing busy roads), especially when distressed and/or intoxicated.

Factors relevant to the risks posed

Mr Smith has been assessed and his clinical records have been scrutinized. The *HCR-20 risk assessment guide* has been used as a framework for this case study because it ensures that all the potentially most relevant violence risk factors are examined.

In terms of predisposing risk factors or risk factors that are either static (historical and therefore unchanging) or dynamic (and therefore changeable) but stable, the following are relevant:

- Mr Smith has a complex combination of *mental health needs*, namely drug-induced psychosis, and a poor level of cognitive functioning suggestive of *learning difficulties*. In addition, he also has *clinically significant personality patterns* suggestive of dissocial, emotionally unstable (borderline), and paranoid personality disorders. Personality disorder symptoms encapsulate some key aspects of Mr Smith's current clinical presentation that cannot be better accounted for by either his major mental illness or his learning difficulties. Difficulties in each of these three areas are likely to be highly inter-related and the successful management of his ability to learn and his cognitive functioning may have a significant and positive effect on the management of the consequences of his personality difficulties and mental health problems.
- Linked to his learning difficulties and personality problems, but an additional and particularly pronounced risk factor, is *poor impulse control*. Directly linked to poor impulse control, are *problems with substance use*. Specifically, Mr Smith has used drugs and alcohol to cope with stress, which he experiences a great deal. Poor impulse control and problems with substance use, combined with emotional instability and poor stress management, suggest that *problems with planning* and *task (e.g., job) and relationship commitment* are likely to be very problematic for him, which they appear to be. *Treatment engagement* is likely to be a challenge to achieve because of the range of problems with which Mr Smith presents, his specific learning needs, and because of the more general problems he has with *compliance* and consistency.
- Mr Smith has a *history of violence*. In addition, his violent conduct towards others *commenced at a young age*, suggesting the incorporation of violent conduct into his repertoire of developing coping strategies at the expense of more adaptive ways of dealing with stress, frustration, and conflict with others. *Negative attitudes* that support the use of violence as a way of managing problems would appear to be present also.
- Mr Smith has relatively *poor insight* into his difficulties. That is, when not intoxicated, he can acknowledge the presence of difficulties in his life relating to his abuse of alcohol and drugs and his unstable lifestyle. However, when distressed or otherwise experiencing emotions with which he feels unable to manage, his insight diminishes and he seeks self-soothing ways of coping (e.g., drinking) as well as opportunities to identify, blame, and challenge others whom he sees as being responsible for the troubles that have befallen him. Problems with insight compound other problems the clinical team have experienced in getting Mr Smith to engage in treatment.

These risk factors are constantly or frequently present. What else has to be present, or what has to change in order to make risk both imminent and unacceptable? Precipitating risk factors – or triggers – which are external events or internal conditions that could precipitate a sharp increase in risk include the following:

- *Intoxication* appears to be a key trigger due to the dual role of substance use as a way of coping (badly) with problems that will not go away and as a way in which Mr Smith becomes disinhibited and less able to control his unstable emotions and suspicions about others.

- *Relationship conflict*, namely disagreements with others, frustration, feelings of disappointment or betrayal, feeling slighted or disrespected, can all act as ways in which conflict with others is initiated. In the main, aggression and violence follow quickly after being triggered, but occasionally harm towards others may be planned and executed at a later time.
- *Feeling under a lot of pressure* – too many people wanting too much from him all at once or feeling afraid for his own safety, even without justification – appears to result in intolerable levels of stress and the belief that he does not have the resources to deal with it. Unhelpful ways of coping, such as drinking, may follow generally accompanied by changes in his mood.
- *Low mood* and *feelings of hopelessness*, as well as *boredom*, may also make a contribution to triggering incidents of violence. Mr Smith has time to think about himself and his own needs, and is rarely distracted by constructive activity. The absence of *good social support* to help him in times of crisis – and at all other times – is also a problem.
- Most of these precipitating factors – or triggers – are currently being managed relatively well while he is in prison due to a combination of Mr Smith's efforts, those of staff, and his abstinence from drugs and alcohol. It appears Mr Smith's capacity to manage these triggers when support is not all around him is more limited.

What maintains or perpetuates his potential risk to others over time?

- Mr Smith is *socially isolated*, he has no close family members or intimates, and those individuals who are in any way close to him are not necessarily a good influence. This long-standing social isolation has engendered in him beliefs about himself that are negative and promote maladaptive ways of coping, which perpetuate these negative beliefs.
- Mr Smith has a *poor ability to solve problems*, which is linked to his generally poor coping ability and reliance on ways of coping that are emotion- rather than problem-focused.
- Mr Smith's *attitudes towards treatment* are inconsistent – sometimes he is willing to engage in treatment, but seems unable or unwilling at this time to commit to treatment in the medium- to long-term.

Mr Smith is certainly not always aggressive and violent when any or even all of the above risk factors are present. What helps? What moderates Mr Smith's risk to others?

- A *structured day*, that is, knowing what comes next, knowing where he stands, and knowing what the boundaries are.
- *Abstinence* from drugs and alcohol.
- *The availability of consistent and reliable support* from those around him.
- *Consistency* in his clinical management on a day-to-day basis.
- At the present time, other protective factors are unclear or unrealized. Protective factors are being provided by the environment in which he is currently resident – namely, prison.

Risk formulation

The majority of the concerns that others have about Mr Smith relate to his risk of violence towards others linked to symptoms of acute mental disorder (paranoid beliefs), intoxication, poor impulse control (linked to stress), and interpersonal conflict (threat, perceived insult). Victims in such a scenario are likely to be adults (he has little contact with children) and male when in a public area. His ex-partner has moved from the area, which has considerably reduced any risk to her, but any future partners could be at risk. However, of the scenarios envisaged in which violence towards others is a possible outcome, not all involve impulsive violence. Planned acts of violence appear to be more likely when alcohol and drugs are not involved. Interpersonal conflict (disrespect) seems to be a consistent factor, however, and planned acts of violence tend to be directed at those against whom Mr Smith holds a grudge.

Many risk factors are shared between Mr Smith's risk of harm to others and the risk of harm he poses to himself. However, what would appear to make risk of harm to self more likely is when strong feelings of hopelessness are present in addition to those identified above. He is more likely to feel hopeless when he self-reports feeling isolated or lonely, which is more likely to happen when there are any disruptions in his care, when an intimate relationship is faltering or has broken down, or when his closest associates are not available to him (e.g., because they have been imprisoned).

Where has this combination of risk factors come from? Why has Mr Smith become a potential risk to others? Mr Smith was taken into care when he was under five years of age when his mother, who had paranoid schizophrenia, was unable to look after him. He was periodically returned to his mother's care over the next six years until she died following an accidental drug overdose. Following his mother's death, Mr Smith was formally adopted by his maternal grandmother. However, he was difficult for her to control and he associated increasingly with his peers, notably a group of five to six young men, all older than him, who encouraged him to engage in fights and other acts of aggression on their behalf and who increasingly paid him for his efforts in cannabis, alcohol, cocaine, and crack. Therefore, violence became the currency by which he was accepted by others and the reason for his reward for services rendered – violence made him feel like he belonged and that he could have an influence in the world around him. Alcohol and drugs appear to have precipitated a first psychotic breakdown in his early twenties and this event made him feel the need to use violence more frequently because it exacerbated his feelings of paranoia. Inconsistent parenting and the trauma of the loss of his mother at a young age are still keenly felt and have significantly undermined his self-worth, enhancing his reliance on his peers, drugs, and violence and an enduring reluctance to change.

Options for risk management

Critical risk factors that, if managed, could become potent protective factors are *treatment engagement and compliance* and the *stabilization of his lifestyle*, in particular, a reduction in his reliance on – and use of – drugs and alcohol.

Therefore, *treatment* options should include: (a) approaches to improve Mr Smith's awareness of himself, his mental health, and his need for stability and support; (b) specifically, input that improves Mr Smith's motivation to abstain from alcohol and drugs; and (c) support for effective problem-solving and stress management should also be valuable. Treatment of this nature should be delivered through supportive contacts structured to ensure this form of preparation for more focused treatment (e.g., drug and alcohol rehabilitation, bereavement counselling, mood management, stress management, work around some of his antisocial attitudes and those attitudes that support the use of violence) when Mr Smith is in a better position to receive and benefit from it. The delivery of these forms of preparatory treatments should be through regular contact with mental health services. Mood stabilizers or other appropriate medication (e.g., chlorpromazine) may make a contribution to managing some of the symptoms of personality disorder, which could have a positive effect on his impulse control and the stability of his lifestyle. His compliance with medication would be an issue, as well as the risk of accidental – or deliberate – overdose. A referral to drug and alcohol services (and possibly assertive outreach) should be considered to facilitate some or all of the above recommendations.

Supervision options will include every possible move towards ensuring and encouraging compliance with drug and alcohol abstinence or at least moderate use, and supportive contacts/visits from mental health care staff. Drug and alcohol services would be able to assist with this. A structured daily living programme would be helpful too, to keep Mr Smith occupied and increase opportunities to improve his self-esteem and stabilize his lifestyle. A community treatment order could be recommended the next time he appears in court. Mr Smith is a MAPPA level 2 offender and this is an appropriate level of provision. The MAPPA facility should be used to ensure a coordinated approach from multiple agencies and to ensure that Mr Smith's potential risk to others is not underestimated for as long as critical risk factors are active.

Monitoring options should involve the close observation of changes in his drug and alcohol use, treatment engagement, and the stability of his lifestyle. Dramatic changes in any of these areas should prompt rapid action, as deterioration may be underway and risk of harm to others – and self – increased commensurately. Further, expressions suggesting an increased level of hopelessness should be monitored in order to track changes in his level of suicide risk. Fortunately, Mr Smith is often able and motivated to alert staff when he feels more at risk and working relationships with staff that enable this kind of communication to continue should be nurtured, especially when he returns to the community.

Final Conclusions

Formulation is an essential clinical task encapsulating the development of an understanding about the client's problems on the basis of which interventions are designed and explored, revised, and monitored. The principles of clinical case formulation described in this chapter provide a framework for formulating clients at risk. Consequently, the task of 'risk formulation' may be defined as the process of managing a client's future risk of harm based on a collaborative understanding of their past conduct – what appeared to contribute to it and how and why the potential for harm developed over time – and the circumstances in which and the reasons why harmful behaviour may recur. Risk assessment *without* formulation amounts to the mechanistic rating or scoring of risk factors identified by risk assessment tools; such assessments are devoid of the demonstration of any comprehension of the meaning or function of harmful behaviour for the client. Risk management in the absence of a formulation to drive it may mean that attention is paid to only select risk factors, and the adequacy of interventions in terms of how proportionate they are to the risks posed may not be known.

References

Bieling, P.J. and Kuyken, W. (2003). Is cognitive case formulation science or science fiction?, *Clinical Psychology: Science and Practice*, 10, 52–69.

Borum, R., Bartel, P., and Forth, A. (2006). *Manual for the Structured Assessment of Violence Risk in Youth (SAVRY)*. Odessa, FL: Psychological Assessment Resources.

Bruch, M. (1998). The UCL case formulation approaches, in M. Bruch and F. W. Bond (eds), *Beyond Diagnosis: Case Formulation Approaches to Cognitive Behaviour Therapy*. Chichester: John Wiley & Sons, Ltd., pp. 19–42

Bruch, M. and Bond, F. W. (eds) (1998). *Beyond Diagnosis: Case formulation approaches to cognitive behaviour therapy*. Chichester: John Wiley & Sons, Ltd.

Buchanan, A. (2008). Risk of violence by psychiatric patients: Beyond the 'actuarial versus clinical' assessment debate, *Psychiatric Services*, 59, 184–190.

Carroll, A. (2007). Are violence risk assessment tools clinically useful?, *Australian and New Zealand Journal of Psychiatry*, 41, 301–307.

Chadwick, P., Williams, C., and Mackenzie, J. (2003). Impact of case formulation in cognitive behaviour therapy for psychosis, *Behaviour Research and Therapy*, 41, 671–680.

Davidson, K. (2006). Cognitive formulation in personality disorder, in N. Tarrier (ed.), *Case Formulation in Cognitive Behaviour Therapy: The Treatment of Challenging and Complex Cases*. London: Routledge, pp. 216–237.

Department of Health (1998). *Modernising Mental Health Services: Safe, Sound and Supportive*. London: Department of Health.

Department of Health (2008). *Refocusing the Care Programme Approach: Policy and Positive Practice Guidance*. London: Department of Health.

Eells, T. D., Kendjelic, E. M., and Lucas, C.P. (1998). What is a case formulation? Development and use of a content coding manual, *Journal of Psychotherapy Practice and Research*, 7, 144–153.

Evans, J. and Parry, G. (1996). The impact of reformulation in cognitive-analytic therapy with difficult-to-help clients, *Clinical Psychology and Psychotherapy*, 3, 109–117.

Hanson, R. K. and Thornton, D. (1999). *Static-99: Improving Actuarial Risk Assessments for Sex Offenders*. User Report 99-02. Ottawa, ON: Department of the Solicitor General of Canada.

Hart, S. D., Kropp, P. K., Laws, D. R., Klaver, J., Logan, C., and Watt, K. A. (2003). *The Risk for Sexual Violence Protocol: Structured Professional Guidelines for Assessing Risk of Sexual Violence*. Mental Health, Law and Policy Institute. Vancouver, Canada: Simon Fraser University.

Hart, S. D., Michie, C., and Cooke, D. J. (2007). Precision of actuarial risk assessment instruments: Evaluating the 'margins of error' of group vs individual predictions of violence, *British Journal of Psychiatry*, 190, 60–65.

Johnstone, L. and Dallos, R. (eds) (2006). *Formulation in Psychology and Psychotherapy: Making sense of people's problems*. London: Routledge.

Kumar, S. and Simpson, A. I. F. (2005). Application of risk assessment for violence methods to general adult psychiatry: A selective review of the literature, *Australian and New Zealand Journal of Psychiatry*, 39, 328–335.

Kuyken, W. (2006). Evidence-based case formulation: Is the emperor clothed?, in N. Tarrier (ed.), *Case Formulation in Cognitive Behaviour Therapy: The Treatment of Challenging and Complex Cases*. London: Routledge, pp. 12–35.

Lane, D. (1990). *The Impossible Child*. Stoke-on-Trent: Trentham Books.

Logan, C. and Johnstone, L. (2010). Personality disorder and violence: Making the link through risk formulation. *Journal of Personality Disorders*, 24, 610–633.

Meyer, V. and Turkat, I. D. (1979). Behaviour analysis of clinical cases, *Journal of Behavioural Assessment*, 1, 259–69.

Nezu, A. M. and Nezu, C. M. (eds) (1989). *Clinical Decision-making in Behavior Therapy: A Problem-Solving Perspective*. Champaign, IL: Research Press.

Persons, J. B. (1989). *Cognitive Therapy in Practice: A Case Formulation Approach*. New York: W.W. Norton.

Quinsey, V. L., Harris, G. T., Rice, M. E., and Cormier, C. A., (1998). *Violent Offenders: Appraising and Managing Risk*. Washington, DC: American Psychological Association.

Quinsey, V. L., Harris, G. T., Rice, M. E., and Cormier, C. A. (2006). *Violent Offenders: Appraising and managing risk*, 2nd edn. Washington, DC: American Psychological Association.

Reid, W. H. and Thorne, S. A. (2007). Personality disorders and violence potential, *Journal of Psychiatric Practice*, 13, 261–268.

Risk Management Authority (2007). *Standards and Guidelines: Risk Management of Offenders Subject to an Order for Lifelong Restriction*. Paisley, Scotland: Risk Management Authority, available at www.rmascotland.net/ViewFile.aspx?id=264.

Ryle, A. and Kerr, I. (2003). *Introducing Cognitive Analytic Therapy*. Chichester: John Wiley & Sons, Ltd.

Tarrier, N. (2006). *Case Formulation in Cognitive Behaviour Therapy: The Treatment of Challenging and Complex Cases*. London: Routledge.

Thornton, D., Mann, R., Webster, S., Blud, L., Travers, R., Friendship, C., and Erikson, M. (2003). Distinguishing and combining risks for sexual and violent recidivism, in R. Prentky, E. Janus, M. Seto, and A. W. Burgess (eds), *Annals of the New York Academy of Science: Vol. 989. Understanding and Managing Sexually Coercive Behavior*. New York: New York Academy of Science, pp. 225–235.

Turkat, I. D. (1985). *Behavioral Case Formulation*. New York: Plenum.

Turkat, I. D. (1986). The behavioral interview, in A. R. Ciminero, K. S. Calhoun, and H. E. Adams (eds), *Handbook of Behavioral Assessment*, 2nd edn. New York: Wiley-Interscience, Inc.

Vogel, V. de, Ruiter, C. de, Bouman, Y., and Vries Robbé, M. de (2009). *SAPROF: Guidelines for the Assessment of Protective Factors for Violence Risk*. Utrecht: Forum Educatief.

Ward, T., Polaschek, D. L. L., and Beech, A. R. (2006). *Theories of Sexual Offending*. Chichester: John Wiley & Sons, Ltd.

Webster, C. D., Harris, G. T., Rice, M. E., Cormier, C. A., and Quinsey, V. L. (1994). *The Violence Prediction Scheme*. Toronto: Centre of Criminology, University of Toronto.

Webster, C., Douglas, K., Eaves, D., and Hart, S. (1997). *HCR-20: Assessing Risk for Violence*, 2nd edn. Vancouver: Mental Health, Law and Policy Institute, Simon Fraser University and the British Columbia Forensic Psychiatric Services Commission.

Webster, C. D., Martin, M. L., Brink, J., Nicholls, T. L., and Middleton, C. (2004). *Short-Term Assessment of Risk and Treatability (START)*. Hamilton and Port Coquitlam, Canada: St Joseph's Healthcare & Forensic Psychiatric Services Commission.

Young, J. E., Klosko, J. S., and Weishaar, M. (2003). *Schema Therapy: A Practitioner's Guide*. New York: Guilford Publications.

11

Evidence and Principles for Positive Risk Management

Paul Clifford

Introduction

The Department of Health best practice guideline, *Best Practice in Managing Risk* (Department of Health, 2007a, 5–6), lists the following 'fundamentals' of risk management:

- positive risk management as part of a carefully constructed plan is a required competence for all mental health practitioners;
- risk management should be conducted in a spirit of collaboration and based on a relationship between the service user and their carers that is as trusting as possible;
- risk management should be built on recognition of the service user's strengths and should emphasize recovery; and
- risk management requires an organization strategy as well as efforts by the individual practitioner.

Remarkably, the concept of 'positive risk management', unheard of until relatively recently, appears at the top of the list. Where has it come from and what does it mean? The concept can be understood as a product of several distinct strands of public policy. Concern about serious incidents involving users of mental health services has encouraged an emphasis on risk management in clinical practice in mental health services. However, at the level of day-to-day practice this has led to a danger of exaggerated public and media concern about relatively rare incidents leading to excessively risk-averse services in which documentation and defensive practice threaten to undermine a more positive emphasis on the service user's needs. On the more positive side, the Care Programme Approach has focused on the need for holistic assessment of needs and adequate care planning as the basis for service provision and the concept of 'recovery' has found acceptance. These themes symbolize the trend towards increased service user empowerment and recognition of the importance of collaborative engagement with both the service user and

Self-Harm and Violence: Towards Best Practice in Managing Risk in Mental Health Services, First Edition.
Edited by Richard Whittington and Caroline Logan.
© 2011 John Wiley & Sons, Ltd. Published 2011 by John Wiley & Sons, Ltd.

carers. Finally, the personalization agenda, initially within social care but increasingly across both health care and other areas of national policy, has highlighted the importance of individual service user outcomes, choice, and control. In this context, the concept of 'positive risk management' integrates the need for appropriate consideration of how best to minimize risk with a service user-oriented and empowering approach to service delivery.

So what is positive risk management? The Department of Health (2007a) guideline goes on, more specifically, to say:

> Positive risk management means being aware that risk can never be completely eliminated, and aware that management plans inevitably have to include decisions that carry some risk. This should be explicit in the decision-making process and should be discussed openly with the service user. Positive risk management includes:
>
> - working with the service user to identify what is likely to work;
> - paying attention to the views of carers and others around the service user when deciding a plan of action;
> - weighing up the potential benefits and harms of choosing one action over another;
> - being willing to take a decision that involves an element of risk because the potential positive benefits outweigh the risk;
> - being clear to all involved about the potential benefits and the potential risks;
> - developing plans and actions that support the positive potentials and priorities stated by the service user, and minimize the risks to the service user or others;
> - ensuring that the service user, carer and others who might be affected are fully informed of the decision, the reasons for it and the associated plans; and
> - using available resources and support to achieve a balance between a focus on achieving the desired outcomes and minimizing the potential harmful outcome. (Department of Health, 2007a, 10)

Positive risk management is thus an approach to risk that emphasizes the positive aspects of what can be achieved through risk management rather than simply the avoidance of undesirable consequences. While few could argue with the concept, the question for most practitioners is whether positive risk management requires substantial changes in existing practice. As with most interventions designed to enhance the service user's experience of mental health services, there will undoubtedly be a range of opinions. There will be those who argue that everyone is doing it already, that this is just new jargon for long-standing best practice. Others will argue that positive risk management requires a radical re-orientation in the way in which practitioners relate to service users and their carers. Finally, there will be those who suspect that there is probably an important point somewhere, but would like to understand a bit more about the practical implications.

This chapter is directed primarily towards the latter group. In order to focus on practical implications the next three sections follow the clinical process of risk assessment, risk decision-making in the context of care planning, and recording decisions in clinical documentation. These are followed by consideration of the organizational support required to move towards a positive approach to risk management.

Assessing Risk

The first stage of risk management is risk assessment. The use of standardized risk assessment tools has become commonplace over the past few years. If used correctly such tools help ensure that key risk factors are considered and consistent judgements based upon consideration of these are made. The manner in which risk assessments are framed can help support a positive approach. Two distinctions have become commonplace in the field of risk assessment:

- the distinction between actuarial approaches to risk assessment, in which the aim of the risk assessment is primarily to determine a likelihood of an adverse event occurring, and risk assessments based upon the use of structured clinical judgements, where the aim is to arrive at a considered, consistent judgement based upon consideration of the correct factors; and
- the distinction between static and dynamic risk factors, that is, between risk factors which can change over time and those which are fixed or historical.

The concept of positive risk management moves things on a little further and suggests the need for another important distinction, that between *underlying* risk and *contextual* risk. Underlying risk is the risk of an event occurring independently of the specific circumstances or state in which a person finds themselves. For example, an elderly frail person with a history of falls has a high underlying risk of falling again; or someone with a history of recurrent severe depression and suicide attempts has a high underlying risk of a further such attempt. In contrast, contextual risk is the risk of an event occurring judged *relative* to the specific circumstances in which the person finds themselves. So, if the elderly person is being pushed around in a wheelchair and adequately helped with transfers their contextual risk of falling may be low, despite the high underlying risk; similarly, if the person with a history of depression is currently being well monitored their contextual risk may also be low.

Traditionally, mental health risk assessment has focused on underlying (clinical) risk rather than contextual risk. Taking a more positive approach to risk management suggests that it might be useful to include the concept of contextual risk in risk assessments. This difference is illustrated in the two scales detailed in Table 11.1.

The scale on the left focuses on underlying clinical risk. In recording current risk status, the scale basically asks how 'active' the underlying risk is at present and what level of response is required. The level of risk is indicated by the urgency and level of intervention required to address it. The scale on the right also incorporates the concept of underlying risk. However, scale points 2–4 record the extent to which the current context adequately manages the underlying risk. This is helpful for positive risk management because it enables the consequences of positive risk decisions to be recorded explicitly. For example, if someone is being discharged home from an acute ward they will be moving from a situation equivalent to scale point 3 (risk managed with formal support) to one of situations 2–4 (hopefully 2 or 3). However, on the former scale there may be no change recordable because underlying clinical risk may not have changed. Similarly, if someone moves from reliance on mental health services to routinely monitor their mental state to a situation where they self-monitor, perhaps in conjunction with their family, then their score will change from 3 to 2. Again though, on the first scale no change would be recorded because the underlying risk, for example, of relapse has not changed.

Thus, a scale that contextualizes risk enables the recording of positive risk outcomes. Conversely, what one does not wish to occur is that a positive approach to risk management results in a managed risk becoming an under-managed risk – but if it does this negative risk outcome can also be recorded. For example, someone being accompanied on all walks in the community may successfully manage any risk associated with crossing

Table 11.1   Two methods of recording risk.

Underlying risk (Clifford 2003)	Contextual risk (FACE Recording & Measurement Systems 2009)
0 = No apparent risk: No history/warning signs indicative of risk.	*0 = No apparent risk*: No history/warning signs indicative of risk.
1 = Low apparent risk: No current indication of risk, but person's history and/or warning signs indicate possible risk. Required precautions covered by standard care plan, i.e., no special risk prevention measures or plan required.	*1 = Low apparent risk*: History and/or warning signs indicate possible underlying risk, but no specific current indication of risk. At most, information giving required, no special measures required.
2 = Significant risk: Person's history and condition indicate the presence of risk and this is considered to be a significant issue at present. Requires a contingency risk management plan.	*2 = Risk managed with informal support*: History and/or situation indicate the presence of significant risk, but this is satisfactorily managed by person, social network, and informal carer arrangements. Contingency arrangements may be advisable.
3 = Serious risk: Substantial current risk. Circumstances are such that a risk management plan should be/has been drawn up *and* implemented.	*3 = Risk managed with formal support*: History and/or situation indicate the presence of significant risk but this is managed at a reasonable and proportional level by person and existing formal and informal carer arrangements.
4 = Serious and imminent risk: Person's history and/or warning signs indicate the presence of risk and this is considered imminent. Highest priority to be given to risk prevention.	*4 = Under-managed risk*: History and/or situation indicate the presence of substantial risk and this is a significant issue at present. Current arrangements are inadequate or unsustainable. Action required to reduce risk/put alternative arrangements in place.
	5 = Serious and imminent risk: Urgent, immediate intervention required to reduce risk. Person/other at imminent and severe risk.

roads or untoward incidents with members of the public, for example. Withdrawal of such support may be a positive step in a person's move towards greater independence, but if it results in increased frequency of reported incidents or near misses then the risk might be appropriately described as having moved from being a formally managed risk to an under-managed risk, that is, the score will rise from 3 to 4 and therefore suggest the need for some further intervention.

An additional advantage of the second scale is that it explicitly includes consideration of the role of the person and their carers in the judgement of risk. The recording of actions that mitigate risk is integrated within the process of recording risk. Formalizing this inclusive approach may help ensure that the respective roles of all parties involved in decisions pertaining to risk are adequately taken into account.

Obviously, practitioners are perfectly capable of considering risk in context without using a scale that explicitly includes reference to it. However, the direct reference to context sharpens focus and avoids the ambiguity that is implicit in risk scales that do not make this reference. For example, is the murderer locked in a cell 'no risk' because he is locked in a cell, or is it rather that he is high risk – which is why he is locked in a cell? Both, obviously, but is it always clear which is being recorded? One final point about risk assessment is that the process and associated documentation can be used to introduce a more positive approach to risk. Risk assessment tools naturally focus on areas of concern. However, in order to ensure that all options are considered it may be useful to include a question such as 'Are there any areas where a more positive approach to risk may be beneficial?' that prompts practitioners to consider whether there are areas where an alternative approach to risk may be possible without compromising safety.

Taking Positive Risk Decisions

Having assessed risk, decisions then have to be made. This involves:

> weighing up the potential benefits and harms of exercising one choice over another . . . iden-
> tifying the potential risks involved, and developing plans and actions that reflect the posi-
> tive potentials and stated priorities of the service user. It involves using available resources
> and support to achieve desired outcomes, and to minimize potential harmful outcomes.
> (Morgan, 2004)

In making decisions, there has to be clarity about the decision-making process. Ideally the:

- team has to support the approach;
- service user should support the approach;
- service user's carers should support the approach; and
- service user's advocates should endorse the approach.

However, support for a decision is insufficient: it also has to be clear whose decision it is. Everyone may agree with a decision, but that does not mean they take equal responsibility for it or that they would all be held equally accountable in the event of something going wrong. This requires clarity about policy and ownership. So even where there is unanimous agreement the situation is not necessarily as straightforward as it might appear. Where there is disagreement things can become quite complex. Clarity over ownership of whatever decision is made becomes even more critical where there may be disagreement over a decision. Typically, a decision to cease taking medication is likely to be more controversial than a decision to reduce attendance at a day centre.

There has been relatively little research on the practical elements of positive risk management in mental health. However, positive risk management is in essence an approach to decision-making, and there are some instructive studies in person-centred decision-making in other areas of health care. One such area is advance care planning among patients about to receive treatments that could potentially lead to situations in which they are unable to take decisions and where someone else (e.g., a family member, referred to as a 'surrogate') may therefore have to so on their behalf. Such situations include those where serious medical complications may leave the person unconscious and decisions need to be made about prolongation of life or continuation of treatment.

It may also be that different types of decision-making process will be relevant to dif-ferent types of situation and also to different individuals. In a study that may have direct implications for mental health contexts, Graugard and Finset (2000) found that patients in general health care settings with a low baseline level of anxiety reported higher satisfaction with a patient-centred communication style, whereas those with high baseline levels of anxiety were less anxious after a more directive doctor-centred consultation. More generally, de Haes' (2006) review of decision-making research concluded that patients with lower education, a worse prognosis, and high levels of anxiety reported a lower preference for patient-centred approaches. Whether this is itself a function of lower expectations or lower perceptions of self-efficacy is an open question. Nevertheless, a possible implication is that being person-centred is not a matter of adopting a new style that is applied uniformly in all situations, but rather a matter of adopting the style most suitable to the individual person being interacted with.

Briggs *et al.* (2004) conducted a small controlled trial of 'patient-centred' advance planning, compared with a more traditional approach. Each patient received a 1-hour interview, which assessed the patient's understanding of their condition and prognosis and possible complications, provided information where necessary about this and advance planning, and described real treatment situations that might arise together with the related treatment choices the carer might be called upon to make. An interesting feature of this approach was that the carer/family member was engaged in the practitioner's 'assessment of the patient's illness representation'. That is, the carer was 'present as the interviewer carefully explored the patient's experiences, values, beliefs, and goals for living well'. This reportedly increased the carer's understanding of the service user's thinking, resulting in lowering of conflict. Briggs *et al.* (2004) reported three benefits of this approach (compared with a control group who did not receive this intervention): greater agreement between patients and surrogates; reduced experience of decisional conflict on the part of patients; and better quality of communication between professionals and patients.

Although one has to be cautious about over-generalizing from a single study in a different domain, the situation studied by Briggs *et al.* (2004) has many structural similarities to the mental health risk context. For instance, both involve acknowledgement of risks that many people would prefer not to have to contemplate. In addition, the risks in both contexts may be known at a population level, but can be difficult to assess accurately at the individual level. Furthermore, both involve three parties: the service user; the service user's family or informal carers; and care professionals.

In the mental health context, as in the more medical context referred to, the ideal outcome of a decision-making process is that a decision:

- is based on best evidence on likely outcomes;
- is based upon open consideration of the pros and cons of different courses of action;
- involves agreement by all parties as to the best course of action;
- minimizes the experience of internal conflict relating to the decision by each participant;
- involves clarity as to the role of the various participants in coming to the final decision; and
- involves clarity regarding ownership of the decision.

However, experience suggests that this open democratic ideal is not always achievable and there may, therefore, not be a single approach to decision-making that suits all situations or service users. As previously noted, the best way of being person-centred may vary from person to person (de Haes, 2006). For example, the service user who is conflicted about re-entering employment in case they break down or is anxious about moving away from their family, may be best served by a different approach to collaborative decision-making process to that of a service user who is very clear about their preferred outcomes.

Another way of thinking about good decision-making is to see it as supported decision-making. The Department of Health (2007b) guidance on supported decision-making, *Independence, Choice and Risk*, has this to say:

> The governing principle behind good approaches to choice and risk is that people have the right to live their lives to the full as long as that does not stop others from doing the same. Fear of supporting people to take reasonable risks in their daily lives can prevent them from doing the things that most people take for granted. What needs to be considered is the consequence of an action and the likelihood of any harm from it. By taking account of the benefits in terms of independence, well-being and choice, it should be possible for a person to have a support plan which enables them to manage identified risks and to live their lives in ways which best suit them. (p. 16)

Positive risk management is thus closely related to the concept of optimizing choice and control for the service user. This raises the ethical issue as to whether someone should be allowed to make unwise choices. Clearly, if someone lacks the capacity to fully understand the major implications of a choice, then this is different to someone who acknowledges the risks but decides to go ahead anyhow. Unfortunately, in practice many cases will fall in the grey area between these two. In such circumstances, there is a conflict: the natural protective instinct of the practitioner is to minimize risk, while the natural instinct of the service user may be to take the risk, even if they are perhaps slightly underestimating its severity or potential impact. In such circumstances, the practitioner needs to be able to be clear whether their view is, in fact, influenced by a natural desire to be protective of the service user, or the desire to be protective of themselves in the event of something going wrong. The tendency of the media to blame practitioners for the un-desirable actions of people suffering from mental illness naturally leads practitioners to be cautious about taking actions that might with hindsight be perceived as representing a failure to prevent a preventable incident, rather than a worthy attempt to give the service user licence to exercise their right to choice. This leads naturally to consideration of the question of responsibility for positive risk-taking. 'Positive risk-taking' in this sense will often amount not to a positive action, but rather a positive decision *not* to refrain from over-cautious behaviour. In theory, therefore, the responsibility for taking the positive risk should lie with the service user: that is after all the whole point, they are being allowed to exercise choice. In practice, however, many practitioners could be forgiven for being sceptical as to whether the media or their service managers would see it that way.

In sum then, clarity about ownership of decisions and the decision-making process is critical to positive risk management. This requires not just good intentions, but well-defined policies and lines of accountability that can be communicated clearly to the service user and the clinical team, and thereby provide a safe structure for balanced consideration of choices. If this is absent, it seems likely that either wrong choices will be made or teams will retreat into a more defensive approach.

Recording and Communicating Risk Decisions in the Care or Support Plan

Having made decisions, these need to be recorded in the care or support plan. It is increasingly seen as important that explicit reference to risks is made in a care or support plan, and that reference to these should be counterbalanced by a statement of strengths and mitigating factors.

The principle of emphasizing personal strengths when working with mental health problems is laudable, but there can be problems when putting it into practice. Too often statements of strengths read like special pleading and can have the opposite effect to that intended: rather than promoting a positive picture of the service user they can read more like damning someone with faint praise. This can be true especially in the assessment context, where the documented strengths can seem to fade in relation to the complexities of someone's needs.

Having said that, the move towards outcomes-focused care and support planning provides an opportunity to address this problem. Rather than trying to list someone's strengths in general, the care or support plan provides the opportunity to document how the service user will actively contribute to achieving specific preferred outcomes. This provides a more meaningful and realistic method of documenting strengths. In the context of positive risk management, this means documenting how the service user can help mitigate specific risks, whether it be through self-monitoring, active personal development, or simply turning up regularly to appointments.

Obviously if there is disagreement, this needs to be recorded. For example, if the views of carers are to be over-ridden on the grounds that they are being over-cautious, then this needs to be clearly documented and made clear to both the team and service user. This is not simply so that everyone is clear about who took the decision, it is also because disagreements should be reviewed: for example, it will be important to know at the next review whether the carer still disagrees with the decision in the light of what has occurred as a result of it.

An outcomes focus also places another useful slant on risk. The care and support plan should indicate any major risks in attempting to achieve a particular outcome (if any), and what the risks are to the achievement of that outcome and how these are being addressed. Obviously, copious documentation and a thorough health and safety analysis of every routine action is undesirable. Rather, within current documentation there should be greater emphasis on being explicit where there are major known risks, for example, of breakdown if the person goes back to work. This leads naturally into an approach based on identifying the system for monitoring risk and the contingency plan to be adopted should risk be heightened or adverse events begin to occur.

Positive Organizational Risk Management

'Positive risk management requires an organizational strategy as well as efforts by individual practitioners and clinical teams' (Department of Health, 2007a, 5). This means that positive risk-taking as a philosophy, along with its possible implications, needs to be endorsed and understood by the organization overall in both its positive and its negative aspects, as well as decisions being shared by the clinical team in relation to a particular individual. An inevitable consequence of taking more risks is that more things will go wrong. If no-one goes out for a walk, no-one will trip over a paving stone. It is this clash between the risk-averse tendencies of large organizations and the more person-centred tendencies of the practitioner that provides the greatest challenge. There are, however, some simple things that can be done to help resolve this tension.

Mental health services need to make clear that they support practitioners in taking a positive approach to risk. Risk would not be risk without risk. Risk means that things will sometimes go wrong, but an acceptance of this is not a justification for reducing vigilance or encouraging lax practice. At times the internal practices of mental health services reflect the culture of blame that appears to surround any incident involving mental health service users, rather than promoting honest inquiry into what has occurred and why, with no imputation of blame in advance of any investigation.

If clinicians are to become less risk averse they will need the support of their or-ganizations, but this is not sufficient to guarantee a more positive approach. Mental health services need to make available the time and resources to think through what is involved in developing routine practices that promote a positive approach. Equally important, they need to recognize that it is not only practitioners that need to change. Senior managers, clinical directors, and Trust Boards all need to change their attitudes and behaviour in ways that reflect a more positive and inclusive orientation.

The standard management approach to change is to embody desired changes in operational policies and revised procedures. Too often this is experienced by practitioners as the introduction of revised bureaucracy couched in shiny new buzzwords rather than as a real commitment to change. If things are to change at ground level proper thought needs to be given to the real challenges of positive risk management. An example of this is described by Kaliniecka and Shawe-Taylor (2008), who describe the introduction of a 'risk management panel' in a mental health trust to review cases. Participants found the panel helpful in affirming collective responsibility for risk management. Interestingly also, the majority of cases selected for presentation had diagnoses of personality disorder, perhaps indicating the cases that induce the most anxiety in practitioners.

More generally, the organization needs to encourage a culture where risk is reflected upon. This is a management responsibility and implies both providing a forum where risk management issues are discussed and also using information to think about risk. The response to 'the worst' happening needs to be debated and agreed in advance in collaboration with clinicians – personalization is a two-way street and has to involve a more inclusive relationship between managers and clinicians, not just between clinicians, service users, and carers. Changing the wording of policies is fine, but it has to reflect cultural change rather than lip service to the latest policy-speak.

The use of information to promote risk management is an example of such change. The recording and review of 'near misses', that is, situations where an adverse event nearly occurred, is routine in many industries and in other branches of health care, but such incidents are rarely reviewed in mental health services. Using the type of scales described above in Table 11.1, it would be straightforward to report upon risk outcomes; and simple measures of 'risk load' upon individual practitioners or teams would be straightforward to derive from information systems if the commitment was there. For example, the measurement of risk 'replacement rates' – that is, whether average level of risk across a team or for an individual practitioner was increasing or decreasing month on month – would provide an indicator of stresses and strains in the system.

Conclusion

This chapter has attempted to address the question to what extent does positive risk management require substantive changes in existing practice. It has been argued that positive risk management is an extension of current best practice, not something new or radical. However, it needs to be supported by modest but important shifts in both routine clinical practice and organizational management. As with all aspects of risk management, the challenge will be to ensure that these are not implemented simply as bureaucratic changes in documentation, operational policies and procedures but signal a real shift in the direction of more collaborative and innovative mental health services.

References

Briggs, L., Kirchoff, K., Hammes, S., Mi-Kyung, S., and Colvin, E. I. (2004). Patient-centered advance care planning in special patient populations: A pilot study, *Journal of Professional Nursing*, 20(1), 47–58.

Clifford, P. (2003). *The FACE Risk Profile*. FACE Recording and Measurement Systems Ltd, Nottingham.

de Haes, H. (2006). Dilemmas in patient centeredness and shared decision making: A case for vulnerability, *Patient Education and Counselling*, 62, 291–298.

Department of Health (2007a). *Best Practice in Managing Risk: Principles and Evidence for Best Practice in the Assessment and Management of Risk to Self and Others in Mental Health Services*. London: Department of Health, available at www.dh.gov.uk/publications.

Department of Health (2007b). *Independence, Choice and Risk: A Guide to Best Practice in Supported Decision Making*. London: Department of Health.

FACE (2009). The FACE Overview Assessment, in *The Core Assessment and Outcomes Package for Health and Social Care*. FACE Recording and Measurement Systems Ltd, Nottingham.

Graugard, P. K. and Finest, A. (2000). Trait anxiety and reactions to patient-centered and doctor entered styles of communication: An experimental study, *Psychosomatic Medicine*, 62, 33–39.

Kaliniecka, H. and Shawe-Taylor, M. (2008). Promoting positive risk management: Evaluation of a risk management panel, *Journal of Psychiatric and Mental Health Nursing*, 15, 654–661.

Morgan, S. (2004). Positive risk taking: An idea who's time has come, *Health Care Risk Report*, October, 18–19.

12

Encouraging Positive Risk Management: Supporting Decisions by People with Learning Disabilities* Using a Human Rights-Based Approach

Richard Whitehead, Ged Carney and
Beth Greenhill†

Introduction and Background

Traditional risk management focuses on assessing and managing 'threats' to the service user, their carers or community members. We argue in this chapter that using a human rights-based paradigm offers the potential to invert traditional approaches, and, through a process of enabling the rights of all affected by risk behaviours, may allow a more positive construction of the service user, their difficulties, and their ability to transcend them. We argue that a Human Rights-Based Approach (HRBA) offers one method for facilitating such 'positive risk management'.

This chapter presents recent developments in our service, building on 15 years' experience of moving people labelled with a learning disability (LD) and complex needs into the community. Our account is based on learning from many service users with whom we have made the journey from the pathologies and negative reputations of secure settings, to their leading *A Life Like Any Other* (House of Lords and House of Commons Joint Committee of Human Rights, 2008) as valued members of their communities. Although the account we present draws heavily on the legislative framework of the Human Rights Act (1998), specific to British Law, we believe, with adaptation, our approach may be transferable to other European countries within the framework of the European Convention of Human Rights (1950), or internationally, within the legal framework of the United Nations Declaration of Human Rights (1948) or the United Nations Declaration on the Rights of Disabled Persons (1975).

The HRBA to risk assessment and management discussed here was developed with a learning disability population. This immediately raises the question of whether this

---

* We are aware of the ongoing and contentious debate surrounding the use of 'learning difficulty' and 'learning disability'. For the purposes of this chapter we will be adopting the term 'learning disability' as set out in the Department of Health documents to which we refer.

† The authors would like to acknowledge the support of Amanda Roberts in the production of this chapter.

Self-Harm and Violence: Towards Best Practice in Managing Risk in Mental Health Services, First Edition.
Edited by Richard Whittington and Caroline Logan.
© 2011 John Wiley & Sons, Ltd. Published 2011 by John Wiley & Sons, Ltd.

approach can be applied with a mental health population, as the similarities and differences between these populations are open to debate. Services often emphasize differences to protect overstretched resources. For example 'learning disability' is a life-long label whereas psychiatric diagnoses of mental illness could be given at any point during a person's lifespan. One of the most pronounced differences when assessing risk in these populations is the higher risk of suicide in the mental health populations compared to that in the learning disability population. Other differences between these services centre around philosophy of care. In learning disability services person-centred approaches have been embraced over a number of years. Mental health services, up until recently, have been more dominated by the medical model.

We believe a HRBA for positive risk management is transferable to mental health settings. The approaches set out in *Best Practice in Managing Risk* (Department of Health, 2009b), such as involving the service user in a carefully constructed positive risk management plan, in a relationship that is trusting and valuing, within an overall organizational strategy, all dovetail perfectly with a human rights-based approach. Key concepts such as proportionality and balancing the rights of the service user when considering positive risk management should be integral to whichever service a person works in. Rather than ghettoizing services, the opportunity to share com-patible good practice between services and implement national guidelines should be encouraged.

In this section we discuss the background and context of our work developing a HRBA (Department of Health and British Institute of Human Rights, 2007) to positive risk management. The section 'A HRBA to Positive Risk Management' introduces the notion of human rights and key concepts involved in taking a HRBA. The section 'Moving from Assessment to Risk Management' describes the assessments, planning tools, and structures we have used to apply HRBAs in our service. 'The Transition to 'A Life Like Any Other' outlines practical issues in how to engage and support service users and staff once plans are developed. Finally, the Conclusion raises the obstacles we have encountered in trying to positively work with risk and proposes some solutions for overcoming any systemic problems. Case studies are used throughout to illustrate the approach in practice.

Human rights, people with learning disabilities and positive risk-taking: 'A life like any other'?

> We are disappointed that, at the start of the 21st century, almost ten years after the intro-duction of the Human Rights Act...the evidence convinces us that we need to emphasize that adults with learning disabilities have the same human rights as everyone else. (House of Lords and House of Commons Joint Committee on Human Rights, 2008)

The Joint Committee's report, quoted above, other reports such as *Death by Indifference* (Mencap, 2007), and the recent investigations into human rights abuses in Sutton and Merton (Healthcare Commission, 2007) paint a damning portrait of the lives of people labelled with learning disabilities in Britain today. Individuals with a learning disability (LD) are offered limited choices, with others placing restrictions on what they can do and, over the years, have been consistently one of the most devalued and oppressed groups in society (Sobsey, 1994).

Myths surrounding people with a learning disability also remain potent, shaping professional attitudes to risk for the people we serve. These myths find contemporary expression in either paternalism (the 'need to protect' adults who happen to have a learning disability), or in fear (the 'need to protect *from*' adults who happen to have a learning disability). Person-centred planning and 'social role valorization' (Goldiamond, 1974; O'Brien, 1987; Wolfensberger, 1972) have long challenged the tendency toward risk aversion, viewing it as denying learning disabled people the everyday opportunities from which we all grow and develop. It is this tradition that we have tried to follow by applying positive risk-taking through the vehicle of a HRBA, giving a method which we believe shows promise in positively managing risk with people of all abilities and diagnoses.

The origins of our work in using a person-centred approach to positive risk-taking, the precursor to the HRBA, emerged when a large local LD hospital closed in the early 1990s. In the early part of the twentieth century in the United Kingdom, at a government level, people with a learning disability were seen as a threat to society. This led to the incarceration of many people into institutions in a process which could be seen as a mass proactive strategy to manage the perceived risk to society. The institutions people were sent to could be described as a separate world with high walls to keep the 'threat' at bay. The *Politics of Mental Handicap* (Ryan and Thomas, 1987) describes how this segregation, rather than reducing the perception of risk, engendered fear of people with disabilities in the general population. From within the institutions, there is narrative evidence from people with learning disabilities indicating that risk aversive and degrading practices were used to manage perceived risk. For example, people had their teeth removed when being admitted to a hospital to prevent them from biting. The use of pain techniques to control behaviour also shows the aversive practices services used historically.

After initial successes in moving most people back into their communities, it became apparent a number of individuals remained in 'out-of-area' institutions. Often carrying negative reputations, supposedly dangerous and labelled with a range of psychopathologies, these people tended to live in secure settings a considerable distance from their home towns, for most of their lives.

Increasingly, commentators have recognized that 'out-of-area' placement of people with learning disabilities and complex needs has significant human rights implications (Bush, 2007). Many people who are moved away from their place of origin will experience this because ordinary community services feel unable to manage the levels of risk or challenge perceived to be involved in the person's behaviours (Mansell and Beadle-Brown, 2006). Despite being a Government priority for a number of years (Department of Health, 1992, 2009a; Reed Report, 1993), recent reports highlight that many people are still placed in long-term 'out-of-area' placements (Department of Health, 2007). Many people with complex needs do not give their informed consent to such moves and 'are at the greatest risk of being given anti-psychotic medication to control their behaviour' (Bush, 2007). There is a danger that for many people 'out of sight' becomes 'out of mind', with a concomitant increase in restrictive practice and human rights violations. As our local hospital prepared for closure, we explored how to support people back into their community using person-centred approaches, using a range of individualized packages of care or 'complex care packages'. 'Complex care packages' support people with complex needs; those identified as having high levels of behaviours risky to themselves or others, in their own community. The complex care pathway aims to secure a suitable supported placement for an individual within their city of origin, providing sufficient skilled support to enable, wherever possible, people with a disability to remain within their community, to benefit from being a member of that community, and to make a positive contribution. The pathway aimed to achieve this by balancing person-centred approaches and using positive clinical formulations. Historically, such packages of care have been funded jointly through pooled health and social services budgets and continuing health care monies.

One of the difficulties which began to occur was a polarization of clinical formulation and person-centredness within complex care packages. Increasingly, a clash of cultures appeared to emerge between the voluntary sector agencies providing direct support to service users, and the clinical practitioners involved. The current NHS climate of increased emphasis on risk assessment and public protection seems to produce an environment of professional risk aversion, with a reliance on the use of formal standardized assessments to establish levels of risk and appropriate interventions. Conversely, and perhaps in response to this shift in NHS practice, voluntary sector agencies seem to exclusively prioritize service user choice, without necessarily balancing this with the person's insight, experience, or understanding of the consequences of their choices. As an example, a service user diagnosed with pica was being supported to continually eat concrete on the grounds that he had 'chosen' to do so. The result was a risk-taking approach, at times, bordering on neglect and in which the rights of the service user were viewed as the only rights engaged in the decision. The challenge to clinical practitioners was to embrace risk and use individualized clinical judgement as a method to ensure safety rather than relying upon restrictive practice.

The HRBA seemed to offer a useful paradigm, allowing us to resolve some of these apparent tensions between person-centred approaches and clinical formulations. First, it contained the possibility of a positive, shared and inclusive language around risk with which all could engage. Significantly, at the same time, the language of human rights had become increasingly explicit in government policy. Secondly, because of its congruence with person-centred values, an HRBA appeared to be a 'good fit' across LD services of all levels. Thirdly, having the added weight of being universally applicable in law rather than best practice (Mansell and Beadle-Brown, 2006), the HRBA allowed us to consider the human rights issues for everyone involved in a person's care. Finally, the human rights paradigm seemed to provide an overarching framework linking new legislation (e.g., Mental Capacity Act, 2005) and the many other disparate ideas and assessments which may be needed to support someone with complex needs.

The Human Rights in Healthcare Project (Department of Health and British Institute of Human Rights, 2007) created an opportunity to adopt and develop use of an explicitly 'HRBA' in our practice as one of five pilot sites (Greenhill *et al.*, 2008). Through this project we were able to draw together several complimentary strands of current policy: the broad service user and carer inclusion agendas (Department of Health, 2008a, 2008b, 2009a), the emphasis on collaboration in the area of risk management (Department of Health, 2009b), the emphasis on reducing 'out-of-area placements' (Department of Health, 2007) and the increasing recognition of the needs to recognize the human rights of people with a learning disability (Department of Health, 2009a; House of Lords and House of Commons Joint Committee of Human Rights, 2008).

Our aim was to see if a HRBA to risk could deliver a robust process and clarify the concepts needed for positive risk-taking. In summary, the HRBA to risk assessment and management seemed to open more possibilities for risk balancing and to enable an environment in which positive risk management might take place.

A HRBA to Positive Risk Management

This section details the main points of the Human Rights Act (HRA) (1998), key concepts in a human rights-based approach and considers how these might apply to positive risk management.

Human Rights Act summary

The Human Rights Act (1998) incorporated into UK law most of the rights detailed in the European Convention on Human Rights. The European Convention is the main source of our legal human rights protection in the United Kingdom. Although its focus is on civil and political rights, it has strong significance within the context of health services because the rights it contains are defined broadly. The HRA imposes a direct legal obligation on NHS Trusts to ensure that we respect European Convention rights in all we do. The articles of the Human Rights Act are set out in Box 12.1.

Box 12.1: The rights contained in the Human Rights Act

Absolute rights:

- The right to life.
- The right not to be tortured or treated in an inhuman or degrading way.
- The right to be free from slavery or forced labour.

Non-absolute rights:

- The right to liberty.
- The right to a fair trial.
- The right to no punishment without law.
- The right to respect for private and family life, home, and correspondence.
- The right to freedom of thought, conscience, and religion.
- The right to freedom of expression.
- The right to freedom of assembly and association.
- The right to marry and found a family.
- The right not to be discriminated against in relation to any of the rights contained in the European Convention.
- The right to peaceful enjoyment of possessions.
- The right to education.
- The right to free elections.

Different types of human rights

As listed in Box 12.1, human rights can be most simply classified as *absolute rights* and *non-absolute rights*. Absolute rights can never be interfered with, in any way by any public authorities. This distinction is important when considering balancing rights associated with risk which we will explore below. The right to liberty (Article 5) is described separately.

Most rights in the HRA are non-absolute and have some degree of qualification. Non-absolute rights can be interfered with by NHS Trusts and social services if the decisions we make fulfil certain criteria. The interference must first be lawful and completed with reference to the appropriate legal frameworks. The interference must have a legitimate aim, being 'to protect the rights of others or for the wider good' and must be proportionate – 'appropriate and not excessive in the circumstances' (see Case Study 1 below). Finally, the interference must be balanced and take into account the rights of the service user, Trust staff, and the rights and general interests (e.g., national security and economic well-being) of the wider community of which both are a part. An example of a non-absolute right is the right to respect for private and family life, home, and correspondence.

The right to liberty (Article 5) can be 'limited in specific and finite circumstances' which are described within the HRA. For example, the right to liberty may be restricted to allow the legal detention of someone with mental health problems under the Mental Health Act.

What is an HRBA?

Key to making human rights real in risk management is an 'HRBA' built on a number of key principles (Department of Health and British Institute of Human Rights, 2007). In the context of positive risk management, this involves putting human rights and human rights principles at the heart of risk assessment and management planning. The rights implications of the service user's risky behaviours and the ways in which we try to manage them are made explicit. The HRBA emphasizes organizational leadership, and a commitment to empower staff and service users to be aware of and to achieve fulfilment of their human rights in practice. The process should meaningfully involve all key people, including the service user, so that risk management is optimally 'done with' rather than 'done to' service users. Accountability of the services involved and of the service user are seen as vital, although for the service user with a learning disability this raises some complex issues about capacity. The approach also highlights the need to 'pay attention to' social groups who may find it harder to access their rights, for example people with disabilities or those from different cultural backgrounds.

In essence, employing an HRBA should promote a shared sense of entitlement, encourage personal responsibility and uphold respect for the rights of others; while accounting for issues of equality and diversity. In work with people with a learning disability who may struggle with theory of mind and perspective-taking or may be used to occupying an infantilized social role, adopting a HRBA is likely to be an ongoing and developmental process, initially requiring significant environmental and relational 'scaffolding' (Vygotsky, 1978; Wood, Bruner and Ross, 1976) from support staff and professionals.

Proportionality

Proportionality is fundamental to positive risk management and an HRBA. In essence, a proportionate strategy is one that is 'appropriate and not excessive in the circumstances'

(Department of Health and British Institute of Human Rights, 2007). In practice, proportionality ensures that the infringement of a person's human rights is kept to a minimum and that interventions are always the *least restrictive strategy*. When considering if a strategy is proportionate the assessor should consider what will be left of the person's rights if the strategy is employed and whether an alternative strategy would be less drastic.

Proactive and reactive strategies

Accepting the principle of proportionality means that, in risk management, an emphasis on *proactive* rather than *reactive* strategies (LaVigna and Willis, 1995) is more likely to be consistent with the HRBA. The HRBA complements much other best practice in risk assessment and management, sharing an emphasis on carefully analysing the person's history and the context in which their difficult behaviours occur. Risk formulation (Department of Health, 2009b) involves gathering a detailed history and developing a formulation for situations in which risks may occur; and then identifying predisposing, precipitating, perpetuating, and protective factors (see also Chapter 10). Once predisposing and precipitating factors have been identified, the least restrictive option will often be to develop proactive strategies to address the cause of the person's behaviour.

It may take time for proactive strategies (e.g., psychological therapies) to have an impact on the person's behaviour. It may also take time for clinicians to understand the meaning of the person's behaviour in terms of communication. In this context, where reactive strategies are not being exclusively relied upon but have been developed as a short-term measure or in conjunction with proactive strategies, they are more likely to be human rights compliant.

Proactive strategies and human rights: Case Study 1 Shaun, a young man with 'autism' was reported by care staff to be trying to hit and bite them, usually in the mornings. Staff tried to manage Shaun's aggression reactively by using physical intervention techniques for extended periods of time. This risked violating Shaun's right not to be treated in an inhuman or degrading way.

After looking at when and why incidents occurred, staff realized Shaun would become aggressive when they were trying to assist him to get washed. After speaking to Shaun's mum, staff realized that, as a child, to wash him Shaun's mum had developed a highly structured shower routine which he was used to following every day. They proactively adopted this routine, Shaun's physical aggression reduced dramatically and his human rights were respected.

Reactive strategies, for example, as required medication or restraint, are much more likely to pose threats to people's human rights and a number of safeguards should be adhered to. Reactive strategies should be reviewed at regular specified intervals, they should use the least restrictive possible intervention, incorporating approved and accredited techniques, and should follow best practice and professional guidelines. Every effort should be made to explain reactive strategies to the person in an accessible format and, where possible, develop them with the service user (Department of Health, 2009b). If a service user has visits home to the family a version of these strategies should be developed with the family.

Balanced decision-making

The principle of proportionality leads to an additional aspect of risk assessment – 'balanced decision-making'. There are two important dimensions across which rights need to be balanced: the assessor should balance the potentially competing rights associated with the risk posed (for the person and others) and the strategy employed (for the person and others). In practice, this may mean trying to balance the service user's various rights. In particular, you may be trying to balance the rights involved in the person's risky behaviour against the rights involved in any management strategy you are proposing. The following example illustrates this point.

Balancing the rights in the risk and the rights in the strategy: Case Study 2 Melissa is a service user with a learning disability who seriously self-harms and leaves her care setting without support. When she leaves her carers, Melissa engages in risky sex with strangers. She has tried to take her own life on previous occasions when alone in the community. Melissa is on a section of the Mental Health Act.

Staff have placed restrictors on Melissa's window to prevent her from leaving her care setting. This interferes with Melissa's right to liberty, a limited right, but is done in order to protect her absolute right to life, which would be compromised by not employing a strategy. In this instance staff, are attempting to balance Melissa's right to life against her right to liberty. As Melissa is under a section of the Mental Health Act her right to liberty can legally be restricted.

In summary, we believe a HRBA to risk offers a unifying framework which can structure positive risk-taking and best practice (Department of Health, 2009b). We also believe the approach can guide a clear risk assessment and management process enabling practitioners to engage with the complexities of current legislation and relevant professional guidelines. By using this approach, relevant articles of the Human Rights Act are made explicit where they are relevant to the person's risk behaviours or risk management plans. This will necessarily involve highlighting different types of human rights. In using this approach, practitioners aim to involve the service user to the maximum of their ability. They will also need to consider any discrimination the person may experience in claiming their rights because of equality and diversity issues. The HRBA emphasizes a process of balanced decision-making concerning the rights of the person and the rights of their staff and their communities. It also emphasizes that proportionate interventions and acting proactively to prevent risk behaviour occurring in the first instance are more likely to be compatible with respect for the human rights of people with a learning disability.

In the next section we will outline the tools and structures we have used to deliver a HRBA to positive risk management with people who are supported in 'complex care packages'.

Moving from Assessment to Risk Management for 'A Life Like Any Other'

The process of facilitating a HRBA and positive risk-taking involves completing a number of core assessments in partnership with the person, their multi disciplinary or 'core team' and, where appropriate, any other key people (carers, family) in their life.

Establishing the core team

The core team coordinates the elements of the system working to support the person so they are cohesive at a number of different levels: strategic, service delivery, and individual. Ideally, the team is reasonably small, consisting of the Care Programme Approach (CPA) coordinator, social worker, key personnel currently supporting the person, an independent advocate, and the responsible clinician (RC) or clinical lead (an experienced Specialist Nurse Practitioner or Clinical Psychologist). Commissioners have a systemic overview which can be invaluable when joining all the pieces which need to be in place for a successful care package and should be regularly updated on progress.

The assessments described below are usually coordinated and completed by the responsible clinician and social worker and then authorized by the commissioners.

Getting to know the person

An HRBA to risk involves engaging with the person and making a detailed assessment of the meaning of their risks. Without knowing and understanding the person it is extremely difficult to gain a sense of their unique motivations, what their risk behaviours mean in the context of their history, and how their interpersonal style may affect engagement. In the absence of this understanding, developing appropriate strategies that support the person to feel, and be, safe, is unlikely and restrictive practices may ensue.

Throughout the assessment process, and again in keeping with the principles of an HRBA, the service user's involvement is encouraged as actively as possible. Initially, getting to know the person may draw on a number of service user tools (see below) depending on the person's ability to engage. It may also involve spending time talking with the person about their life; accompanying them on visits to local shops; visiting significant people and places; talking about risky behaviours; and planning the transition from long-term placements to an ordinary life. You should get a sense of the person's identity away from clinical labels. Overall, this process should give the clinician the sense of the person for whom the care plan is being designed.

In some cases, due to the level of risk, it may not be possible to create a 'getting to know you' process on an individual basis and practitioners may have to rely on the team supporting the person directly.

The person's ability to actively participate in collaborative change can often be gauged through the 'getting to know you' process, but may require more formal assessment. Optimally, the process will involve informed consent, depending on the person's capacity. The person's potential to engage collaboratively may well develop once good relationships and a 'secure emotional base' is established within the care package. Therefore, short- and long-term intervention strategies should be implemented which can be modified in the light of ongoing evaluation.

Service user tools for 'getting to know you' process

Essential Lifestyle Plan (ELP). The Essential Lifestyle Plan (Schmul and Anderson, 2001) is a person-centred tool through which the person and the people who are committed to him or her can explore and describe the most important things in a person's life. This is the cornerstone for developing appropriate support and services for an individual.

Staying well plan Staying well plans are completed with the service user. The plan highlights the person's sense of identified triggers for risk behaviours and their sense of any interventions they know to be helpful in reducing them.

Advanced statements This is defined as 'a statement (usually in writing) in which an adult whilst of sound mind sets out their wishes in relation to their care and treatment for the future when insight is reduced'. In our client group discussing proactive, reactive and relapse prevention strategies with the person can develop their insight and facilitate the service user's sense of 'being heard'.

Using advanced statements: Case Study 3 Marcus is a man labelled with a moderate learning disability and executive function difficulties. His periods of challenging behaviour involved assaults on staff. While Marcus was remorseful and wanted to change his behaviour after the incidents, staff found it difficult to work in partnership with Marcus during an incident. This led them to question whether Marcus should live in the community. Together, Marcus and his community nurse devised an Advanced Statement consisting of a four-level intervention strategy for staff to adopt when he was anxious. This included a protocol for PRN medication. Staff adopted the strategy, resulting in a reduction in the severity within each episode of challenging behaviour. Marcus continues to live in his own flat.

Human Rights Risk Screen Developed within our service (Lee *et al.*, 2008), this assessment involves service users, to the maximum of their insight and ability, in identifying their risk areas. The screen asks risk questions in accessible language (Clark, 2002) supplemented by pictures to promote service user inclusion (see Table 12.1).

The screen covers risks to self and risks to and from others. It also includes risks relating to the person's disability, ethnicity and culture, sexuality, and gender. For example, risks of racism to the service user from their community or of racist behaviour from the person towards their staff are highlighted and can be addressed.

Human rights issues inherent in each area of risk behaviour are made explicit. So, when considering self-harm, the screen prompts clinicians to question whether appropriate interventions are in place to avoid serious injury or death and to assess whether the person has access to suitable health care services for treatment that is in accordance with the right to life.

Table 12.1 Example item from the human rights risk screen.

(1-6) Deliberate self-harm	
I have hurt myself to cope with hard feelings.	I have used objects to cut/bruise myself. I have swallowed things. I have swallowed a substance. I have banged my head. I have bitten myself.
Cutting, head banging, biting, burning, risky behaviour, etc.	

Human Rights Joint Risk Assessment and Management Plan
(HR-JRAMP)

This document (Greenhill *et al.*, 2008), adapted from an original dissertation (Williams, Ferns and Riding, 1999), formulates a person's risk so potential support can be provided from a human rights perspective. It involves all the stakeholders from the core team and the information gathered from the person as part of the 'getting to know you' process.

The document involves compiling a 'critical event history', detailed analysis of the history, formulation and drawing this together into a management plan. The management plan itself consists of several components: clinical interventions, early warning signs, proactive and reactive strategies, human rights issues in the management plan, guidelines for support staff, and the service specification. Each of these steps are explained further below.

Critical event history The risk management process begins with the lead clinician compiling a 'critical event history' which draws on interviews, notes and reports, summarizing key events in a person's life. The first reported occurrence of a particular risk behaviour will often be of particular interest, perhaps representing the 'best solution' (Pitonyak, 2010) at that time for a person who may have had limited power and reduced problem-solving skills. When analysing documents the perspective of the author needs to be acknowledged; the person him- or herself may have different perceptions of and beliefs about events but these are rarely documented.

Analysis Once a detailed critical event history is compiled, the information about the person is analysed using an animistic approach examining 'social' factors (concerning the person's past and present social context), 'actuarial' factors (concerning their relative likelihood of experiencing risky events based on group membership), 'historical' factors (often a functional analysis of their history) and 'clinical' factors.

Clinical factors include the person's mental health, interpersonal issues and physical health. Since underlying physical health issues may often be a significant factor (Royal College of Psychiatrists, 2007) the assessment often incorporates a Health Action Plan, a comprehensive health assessment looking at all aspects of a person's mental and physical wellbeing. Other clinical assessments may include capacity assessments, psychometric measures, individualized community activity assessments, speech and language therapy assessment, occupational therapy assessment, and neuropsychological assessments.

Formulation The author then draws these four areas together in a formulation (Department of Health, 2009b). Formulation is a way of making sense of the person's behaviour and of drawing together all the information in a manageable format. Based on all the available evidence it aims to explain why a risk behaviour developed and its current function for the person (see also Chapter 9). Factors that are likely to maintain or alleviate the risk are also noted.

Using formulation: Case Study 4 According to records, Norman sustained a head injury playing on a building site as a child, following which he experienced uncontrollable aggressive outbursts. In a structured setting, Norman's outbursts decreased. Unfortunately, when on home leave aged 20, a sustained incident of aggression led to his admission into secure services. The threat of violence was very real in the institution and interventions were inconsistent. Punishment schedules, seclusion, physical restraint and mechanical restraints were used with Norman and, unsurprisingly, his violent behaviour escalated.

Careful analysis of patterns in Norman's risky behaviours suggested the following formulation. The main problems leading to aggression were significant difficulties in regulating his emotions, cognitive deficits preventing development of effective coping strategies and being dehumanized. Over time, the traumatic impact of restraints and seclusion meant Norman frequently misinterpreted others' actions as aggressive or threatening. In secure settings, Norman's behaviour always resulted in restraint, so he was unable to discriminate between innocuous approaches and threats. This, in combination with poor emotional self-regulation and poor inhibition led Norman to react with violence to any approach.

Management plan As far as possible the management plan should incorporate the person's own solutions, identified through the Keeping Me Safe and Well Screen, Staying Well Plan, the Advanced Statement, and Essential Lifestyle Plan.

Clinical interventions Clinical interventions should be formulation-driven, lending even complex multi-faceted plans an underlying coherence. Interventions will usually be at the level of the individual and at the level of the system.

The HR-JRAMP facilitates the use of a pan-theoretical and multi-therapeutic approach, where the therapeutic and systemic models most suitable for the needs of a particular service user can be applied to understand their difficulties. Adopting a 'pan-theoretical' approach with an individual with complex needs enables input at different therapeutic levels; staff teams may need systemic interventions, constructional behavioural approaches may be required for the person's challenges (Royal College of Psychiatrists, 2007), cognitive behavioural techniques may help the person learn increased self-control (Sternfert-Kroese, Dagnan, and Loumidis, 1997) and psychodynamic approaches (Sinason, 1992) may help to interpret underlying reasons for the person's distress. Accessible formulations can be developed for later use with the service user and their team. Increasingly, therapy is being seen as a valid treatment for people with a learning disability (Whitehouse *et al.*, 2006)

In addition, physical health issues need to be built into the clinical intervention.

Early warning signs and proactive and reactive strategies Early warning signs are indicators that a person may be becoming distressed. Every effort should be given to identify these in as much detail as possible. This is so relapse strategies can be put in place which may stop a person's behaviour escalating to the point where they find it distressing. The strategies should include any behaviours which have been identified by the service user in the 'Staying Well Plan'. Proactive and reactive strategies are then developed, again incorporating any insights gleaned from the service user through completing the Staying Well Plan.

Human rights issues in the management plan Once the management plan is complete, the interventions need to be reviewed using a human rights-based approach. Key considerations will be proportionality, which human rights are engaged and can they be interfered with, balancing the rights involved in the risk with those in the management strategy, legality, and best clinical practice, as discussed above in 'A HRBA to Positive Risk Management'. Human rights can provide a framework and motivation for making decisions about the type of service the person will receive. Each relevant service option is evaluated in terms of the risk profile and impact on the person's rights. So, this section will allow the assessor to consider whether a less restrictive community placement with a robust support framework is viable for the person rather than continuing in a secure setting.

Guidelines for support staff The formulation is operationalized in clear, accessible guidelines for support staff, enabling the staff team to work from it. Guidelines should be informed by all assessments, flow from the formulation and include proactive and reactive strategies, early warning signs, and relapse prevention strategies. They will also highlight the human rights considerations involved. Some examples might be interpersonal strategies for working with patterns of problematic interactions which the person has had throughout their life due to early experiences. Guidelines might include support for staff around abuse disclosure and training in procedures for the protection of vulnerable adults. Cognitive behavioural skill-based approaches looking at models of aggression may be incorporated. Tied in with all this would be a proactive approach of building meaningful activities in a person's life based on the ELP. Once things have stabilized for the individual a longer term goal would be to work around any underlying abuse issues identified.

Based on the clinical formulation, the HR-JRAMP will include a service specification, detailing the type of support the person needs, the number of hours required to support the individual and specification of levels of support during night and day. The specification will also usually include details of any legal framework relevant to the person. The housing specification is a key component, identifying the right type of housing and a good location for the person as there may be geographical areas to avoid or that are desirable. This will obviously need to incorporate any specific adaptations to housing the person has on the basis of physical disability or sensory impairment. Equally, in planning housing for a black or Asian service user consideration should be given to a placement in a multicultural area.

If an index offence was committed in an area to which the person wishes to move, careful consideration should be given as to whether it is safe for the individual to return. Clinicians also need to be sensitive to the needs of the victims and family. It is also important to be aware of staff prejudices and perceptions of people with negative reputations.

A compatibility profile within the HR-JRAMP helps establish desirable co-tenants for the person to live with which is crucial to the care package working effectively. For example, a service user who is quite intrusive and unable to settle at night is unlikely to get on well with someone who reacts violently when their personal space is invaded and their sleep disrupted. Factors to explore may include age, issues relating to the person's equality and diversity needs, attitudes, personality, and any specific triggers identified which obviously may lead to conflict.

Similarly, compiling staff profiles helps to establish characteristics which may optimally match those seen as most important by the individual. Again, this would include diversity issues, attitudes, and staff personality.

Choosing the right staff: Case Study 5 Naomi is a deaf woman, placed 'out-of-area' in a privately run institution because of 'challenging behaviour'. Staff relied on mechanical restraint to prevent her from gouging her face, which was lacerated and scarred from years of self-injury.

Naomi was supported to move back to her home city. The core team developed strategies to help 'fade out' the use of her mechanical restraints. Despite the best efforts of Naomi's staff, while her self-harm reduced, she became physically aggressive towards them, particularly when they talked to each other about day-to-day tasks within her home. She was taken to court over one assault.

An external psychologist, who used sign language, met Naomi and asked how staff could support her. Naomi took part in interviews to recruit new staff, who were all also members of the deaf community. With staff who could sign, Naomi was able to communicate and develop more meaningful relationships. She felt less 'different' and isolated. She has since been involved in providing deaf awareness and British Sign Language (BSL) training to professional staff.

The Transition to 'A Life Like Any Other': Obstacles, Challenges and Solutions to Delivering the HR-JRAMP

A number of problems can affect the process of moving people out. In this section we outline our experiences of challenges and solutions when planning with people to move into the community from secure provision.

The spiral of defensive risk management

A general culture of risk aversion, blame, and scapegoating can often lead to defensive practice (Department of Health, 2009b) with an emphasis more on policies and procedures than on the needs of the individual – so called 'tick-boxing'. Packages of care stagnate and people with a learning disability do not get the opportunities to take informed risks which are part of learning, living and 'every-day' life. In this culture, staff act on hypothetical fears about what 'might' happen rather than having an evidence-based approach to positive risk-taking. In our experience, once pockets of restrictive practice develop, the fear escalates and a spiral of restrictive practices occurs as staff lose their belief in the person and their faith in the person's ability to change. Staff become hypervigilant and negative, noticing yet more difficult behaviours as the person reacts to the constraints of restrictive practices such as restraint. In a number of local authorities, people are then moved out-of-area, which further damages their reputation and escalates staff fear and hypervigilance (Department of Health, 2007).

Containing structures and processes: developing the core team

Central to enabling positive risk management is the effective functioning of the core team (see 'Establishing the core team' above). It is crucial that an authority has suitable agencies to deliver care. Commissioners have a preferred list of provider agencies. A model that has worked locally for us is having an agency that was part of the same NHS management structures as the health professionals involved. Community Residential Services support many of our most complex cases and have close links to the community team. We also use voluntary agencies who have a demonstrated track record in working with people with complex needs and are accountable. It is important that any agency works closely with health workers to ensure that the HR-JRAMP is followed.

Once an appropriate agency has been identified, the process of transition to the community can begin. The agency should have shown a commitment to person-centredness and HRBAs during the selection process and, once appointed, will recruit the team leader first. During the transition to the community, weekly review meetings of the core team should take place. The core team then expands to include the team manager and area manager from the identified agency. It is important to establish partnership working with the team leader, liaising with and briefing them on assessments, formulation and interventions.

There are advantages in having small numbers of preferred providers with whom a close relationship can develop. Because of the high levels of training and close involvement of health professionals, support staff develop competencies in delivering human rights approaches and positive risk-taking. This should promote an open and honest culture, and a partnership through which a human rights framework can be properly embedded. Problems can be identified and resolved quickly and training deficits addressed. The health professional can have confidence that guidelines are being followed. This leads to the gradual handing over of clinical responsibility to the agency. If this relationship is not in place it is very difficult to maintain these packages in the community.

The service user's views are also raised at weekly meetings. If they are unable to attend, their views may be incorporated via accessible relapse or Staying Well Plans or through person-centred planning processes. We are hoping that 'Service User Consultants' who have been through the complex care pathway and are now settled in the community will be able to act as a voice for the person who does not want to participate themselves.

Direct care staff: individualized induction

Depending on the complexity of the service user's needs, induction training can vary, sometimes lasting up to 4 weeks in duration. In the initial stages, staff will need training in the guidelines developed in the HR-JRAMP, any specific interventions relevant to the service user (e.g., cognitive neurological rehabilitation) and training in human rights awareness. If the training includes building a developmental vision for the person, which incorporates a more sophisticated view of the person's human rights than simply focusing on choice, staff are less likely to polarize person-centred and clinical approaches. If an accessible formulation is shared, staff are more likely to interpret the person's risk behaviours meaningfully and consider what their own life experiences bring to the process in terms of their views on race, gender, criminal behaviour, class, sexuality, prejudice, etc., and how these might impact on their interactions with the service user.

Following the induction training, staff can work with existing staff in the institution and on outreach. Central to our approach is using non-aversive person-centred approaches with the commitment to move people back into the community. Although many inpatient settings hold similar views, many continue to rely on aversive interventions which necessitate extensive negotiation to move the process forward. Whilst working in a secure setting, members of the community team must be aware that the process belongs to the inpatient team, including the service user, until a person moves into the community.

Transition

The final part of the preparation for the move into the community is the transition timetable. This should be completed following the completion of all of the assessments. This is to ensure all the important pieces of work are completed before the move. The aim is to support the person through the transition at their own pace, with an awareness of particular challenges which might affect the person's broader access to their human rights. This may initially require the core team to proceed in ways which seem counter intuitive to a simple application of rights-based thinking.

For example, when the first tentative date for the move is made, ideally this would be shared with the service user. However, while it may seem contrary to rights-based approaches, we have often found it counterproductive to advise service users of a specific date as it may be put back a number of times due to the complexity of components to coordinate. In promoting human rights practice, consideration needs to be given to the specific needs of vulnerable groups. Service users with autism and who struggle with delay, and people with neuropsychological difficulties in planning, mental health issues which affect their toleration of change or cognitive difficulties in understanding the process of time, may understandably experience distress if the planned transition date does not go ahead. Where this distress is expressed behaviourally, and perhaps aggressively, the result can be that the move is suspended as staff 'lose their nerve' and feel it would not be safe for the service user to be moved. Another example is of the need to be sensitive to anniversaries or times of the year that have proved difficult for the service user in the past. Similarly, if a client has been an inpatient for a long period of time they are likely to be institutionalized. It is important to keep some of these institutional routines in place following the move. These can be gradually changed to more person-centred routines over the following months.

A low arousal approach needs to be taken on the day of the move. The proactive and reactive strategies need to be implemented consistently by staff following the move. The full programme of community activities can be phased in over the first month of the move.

Following the move into the community the overall aim is to enable the staff team to take over the care and to carry out the procedures independently with minimal health input. If a staff team can stay together and are still valuing the person they are supporting after two years, then in our experience even individuals with the most damaged backgrounds and negative reputations can improve significantly.

Maintaining 'a life like any other'

Regular, detailed reviews, training and supervision are essential in the first two years following the move into the community. We have speculated that the service user's relationship with the staff team, in line with attachment theory, is crucial for providing a safe emotional base from which to explore and develop in the world; in other words, to enable service users to learn from positive risk-taking.

Interpersonal patterns between staff and the person they are supporting and dynamics within the broader system, need to be contextualized in the formulation. If they are located here, rather than dismissed as 'attention seeking' or 'manipulative' behaviours they can be explored, This enables awareness of any damaging repeated patterns which occur and can be addressed through the plan of action.

Psychotherapeutic models may help frame systemic responses to the person if at this stage they cannot engage in one-to-one work. An example might be using a Cognitive Analytic Therapy (CAT) approach to understanding systemic dynamics through contextual reformulation (Ryle and Kerr, 2002) as illustrated in Case Study 6 below. Reflective practice can be introduced in staff team meetings so these patterns can be recognized and revised.

Working with the person's system: Case Study 6 With Olivia, a young woman with learning disability, we attempted to reformulate a functional analysis in CAT terms. Among Olivia's identified reciprocal roles (RRs) were 'rejecting/abandoning' – 'rejected/abandoned', and the fantasy of being 'ideally caring' – 'ideally cared for'. These interpersonal patterns originated from relationships with her parents and carers and emerged in Olivia's relationships with support staff, who found it hard to work with her without becoming 'burnt out'. Olivia longed for 'ideal/perfect care' in relationships with new staff. She tended to view new people as being able to provide her with 'magic solutions' to her difficulties, frequently telephoning them or requesting visits. Staff were either unable to meet this demand or did not live up to Olivia's expectations, resulting in her feeling let down. Olivia reacted by rebelling, taking risks, and trying to shock/scare others by self-harming across her throat and hitting others. As a result, the system around her set rigid limits to protect and manage her, leading to her feeling controlled. Olivia then became rejecting, intolerant, abandoning, and abusive towards them, leaving staff feeling hopeless and resentful.

Training using CAT 'as a consultative tool' (Ryle and Kerr, 2002) helped support staff understand why Olivia behaved in the ways she did and avoid collusion with her maladaptive roles. Olivia was able to co-deliver detailed training informing staff, in an accessible way, about helpful and unhelpful responses to her self-harm. This allowed her and her staff to 'exit' some of the damaging interpersonal processes they had been drawn into.

At regular core team meetings any difficulties can be addressed and related back to the formulation enabling staff to balance being either too risk averse or too risk-taking. Quite often guidelines and formulation may need adjusting in the light of practical experience. Consistency of approach and implementation of strategies can be monitored. Incidents can be analysed and given context as the individuals around the table would have a great deal of knowledge about the person. Staffing levels can be monitored to identify how many staff are leaving and available to provide training for new staff. Also practical difficulties around benefits and funding can be dealt with.

As the person's autonomy develops, Community Risk Assessments can be carried out by the team leader and brought to the meeting to be approved by the core team. It is important to feed back information to the community Responsible Medical Officer (RMO) to keep them abreast of the issues and to monitor the effect of medication. Depending on progress, weekly meetings can then become monthly, gradually devolving responsibility to the agency staff team.

Critical incidents

Inevitably there will be incidents as staff get to grips with complex care plans. Community outreach should be increased to enable testing out of proactive and reactive strategies.

These would be modified as more knowledge is acquired. Staff should be regularly debriefed to identify detailed inter- and intra-personal issues. Risk cannot be eliminated from all situations in a person's life, but services should adopt an informed risk-taking approach. If the core team model a 'no blame' learning culture, incidents can be used to consider how to improve the guidelines and to inform more detailed early warning signs and triggers. As with the development of strategies, where appropriate, the person's views on such incidents should be sought and can then also be part of the learning process and refinements to the formulation and strategies can take place. It is essential that a balanced view of incidents is taken on board by the core team.

Staffing levels should be regularly reviewed. If there have been no incidents at certain times then reductions could be tried. It is important that reduction in staffing is handled sensitively so plans can be developed with nightmare scenarios.

Leading your own 'life like any other'

At six months, input from the community health team should be reviewed. If the agency is developing competencies and taking informed, positive risks within the framework of the clinical formulation, input can be reduced. The whole point of the complex care process is to make the input of health professionals redundant, enabling the service user to move successfully into the community and hand the responsibility of support to the service user and their agency.

This is part of the structure that enables people with complex needs and negative reputations to lead 'a life like any other'. Prior to discharge agencies can suddenly identify a whole raft of difficulties which you were not aware of. We call this 'discharge anxiety' and it can usually be addressed with debriefing and ending sessions. A fast track re-referral process can be put in place so if any difficulties arise health staff can be contacted for immediate input. Whether the person still needs to be within the framework of the Mental Health Act (1983) needs to be reviewed.

Further systemic issues

Financial issues can be significant challenges in an increasingly fragmented and business-orientated NHS. Superficially, complex community care packages may not appear to be the cheaper option, until they are compared with the cost of expensive out-of-area placements, often in secure settings. A range of benefits and potential longer term outcomes need to be considered when moving someone into the community. Apart from the ethical and human rights benefits, it is likely that the economic benefit of moving someone into the community can be demonstrated after two years.

Without appropriate infrastructures of skilled agencies, experienced multi-disciplinary teams and decent housing, placements can easily fall apart. Health Authorities and Social Services need to commit to the move and to supporting people in the long term in the community. In our experience, good relationships with commissioners are essential for this process to work smoothly.

Working with the Mental Health Act can also pose challenges. An individual can be taken off their section by the review tribunals without the opportunity for adequate after-care planning. This has implications around the ability to utilize a Community Treatment Order for someone if they have been taken off a Mental Health Act, Section 3.

This emphasizes the need to plan discharge from the point of admission. There have been examples of people being released from prison with identified risk behaviours without adequate legal safeguards to ensure safe positive risk-taking.

Public perceptions and media coverage

Individuals are not always accepted into the community. A considerable minority of people still believe that people with a learning disability and/or mental health problems should be locked in institutions. If the media are also publishing stories involving individuals with mental health difficulties and risk then this can have a knock on effect on proposed moves of people with a learning disability back into the community.

Families and carers

A HRBA will include clear structures for families to raise informal concerns and, if necessary, make formal complaints so that the service is accountable and responsive. We would view this as an integral part of facilitating service users to claim their human rights. Most families are integral to the complex care pathway. Some families adopt a confrontational style in their interactions with services, usually following experiences of health and social services not meeting the needs of the person over the years. They may feel they have had little support from uncoordinated services. A collaborative approach, informing and involving the family at an early stage, can reduce difficulties. A number of initiatives, such as Partners in Policy Making, direct payments, and In Control have enabled families to feel their views are respected and work more effectively with the health and social care system. A very tiny minority of families may have members whose interests lie in sabotaging the person's recovery. Where this is the case vulnerable adult and safeguarding procedures may need to be invoked to protect the service user from further abuse.

Working with families and carers: Case Study 7 Bilal had severe learning disability and Down's syndrome. He was withdrawn from school following violent attacks on other children. His mother subsequently taught him at home.

Following a rise in violent attacks against family members Bilal was moved to a community placement. Activities were designed around his Essential Lifestyle Plan; Bilal's autonomy increased and violence decreased. Unfortunately, Bilal's placement broke down, with support staff citing the parent's daily criticisms of them as a major factor. A similar pattern occurred in two more placements.

Following a HR-JRAMP, key themes and patterns emerged. Bilal's mother was herself subject to considerable criticism from her family and social network, who assumed that any person with learning disabilities should be brought up by their own family. Shame was attached to outsiders taking over care and the family had unrealistically high expectations of agencies in caring for their son. When standards were not met, communication broke down between the family and the agency with the result that the family wished for Bilal to be moved. With each unsettling move, Bilal's challenges and distress increased as did his violence. His liberty was curtailed as people felt he was more of a risk.

Consideration of the relevant cultural and systemic issues allowed a package of care to be developed which maximized FREDA (Fairness, Respect, Equality, Dignity and Autonomy) principles. Without exploring these proactively, Bilal's rights would continue to be restricted and positive risk-taking could not progress as the process would keep repeating itself while his violence continued.

Conclusion

The approach we have described has worked within a learning disability context. Currently, our service has 14 people with complex needs in 'out-of-area' placements which is considerably lower than the national average (North West Training and Development Team, 2006). It has flourished as a result of good relationships between Health, Social Services, Commissioners and Provider Agencies. Over recent years this approach has faced a number of challenges which have been discussed above and which need to be considered when developing services.

This work is time consuming, requiring a service's most experienced clinicians to oversee the work. Within the current climate of setting targets for numbers of clients seen, being involved in this work for long periods of time could affect service reference costs, that is, services and individuals end up being seen as unproductive. With new government policies (Department of Health, 2007, 2009a) emphasizing the need to bring back people to their local communities, Key Performance Indicators (KPIs) should be discussed with Commissioners and the Strategic Health Authority so they reflect the work which is required and remain realistic. This should be then reflected in the KPIs.

As has been mentioned, taking a positive, albeit educated, risk, requires a professional to put their 'neck on the line' perhaps in the face of more conservative opposition. There is also the understandable fear of media scapegoating. That is why it is essential to have a very thorough assessment and multiprofessional agreement as to the course of action in combination with the service user. Without a supportive infrastructure the clinicians leading the positive risk-taking can feel very isolated. Collective responsibility is intrinsic to this approach.

Finally, people with a learning disability have been marginalized and denied their rights for too long. Labelled a 'risk' to society, placed in out-of-area institutions and ignored, the person becomes lost in the secure setting risk industry as society creates and then absolves itself of the person's difficulties. A HRBA puts the individual at the centre of their care so they are an ally in developing meaningful, holistic interventions, which manage risk effectively. This, we believe, respects human rights, creates opportunities for growth and meaningful community participation, and empowers people with a learning disability and complex needs to access 'A life like any other'.

References

Bush, A. (2007). Submission to the Joint Committee on Human Rights: The human rights of adults with learning disabilities – a call for evidence, *Clinical Psychology and People with Learning Disabilities*, 5, 16–20.

Clark, L. (2002). *Accessible Health Information: Project Report*, Liverpool Central PCT, available at www.leeds.ac.uk/disabilitystudies/archiveuk/Clark,%20Laurence/liverpool%20NHS.pdf, accessed 31 March 2010.

Department of Health (1992). *Services for People with Learning Disabilities and Challenging Behaviour or Mental Health Needs: Report of a Project Group*, Prof. J. L. Mansell, Chair. London: HMSO.

Department of Health (2007). *Services for People with Learning Disabilities and Challenging Behaviour or Mental Health Needs: Report of a Project Group*, Prof. J. L. Mansell, Chair. London: Department of Health.

Department of Health (2008a). *High Quality Healthcare for All. NHS Next Stage Review*, A. Darzi, Chair. London: Department of Health.

Department of Health (2008b). *New Horizons for Mental Health Commissioning – An Opportunity to Help Shape the Agenda*, J. Boyington, Chair. London: Department of Health.

Department of Health (2009a). *Valuing People Now: From Progress to Transformation – A Consultation on the Next Three Years of Learning Disability Policy*. London: The Stationary Office.

Department of Health (2009b). *Best Practice in Managing Risk: Principles and Evidence for Best Practice in the Assessment and Management of Risk to Self and Others in Mental Health Services*. London: The Stationery Office.

Department of Health and British Institute of Human Rights (2007). *Human Rights in Healthcare – A Framework for Local Action. Best Practice Guidance*, available at www.dh.gov.uk/en/Publicationsandstatistics/Publications/PublicationsPolicyAndGuidance/DH_088970, accessed 31 March 2010.

European Convention on Human Rights (1950). Available at www.hri.org/docs/ECHR50.html, accessed 31 March 2010.

Greenhill, B., Whitehead, R., Granell, M., Carney, G., Williams, J., Cookson, A., Chapman, F., Ward, E. L., and Lee, A. (2008). *The Human Rights Joint Risk Assessment and Management Plan (HR-JRAMP)*, available at www.dh.gov.uk/prod_consum_dh/groups/dh_digitalassets/@dh/@en/documents/digitalasset/dh_089266.pdf, accessed 31 March 2010.

Goldiamond, I. (1974). Toward a constructional approach to social problems: Ethical and constitutional issues raised by applied behaviour analysis, *Behaviourism*, 2, 1–84.

Healthcare Commission (2007). *Investigation into the Service for People with Learning Disabilities Provided by Sutton and Merton Primary Care Trust*. London: Healthcare Commission.

House of Lords and House of Commons Joint Committee on Human Rights (2008). *A Life Like Any Other? Human Rights of Adults with Learning Disabilities*. London: The Stationery Office.

Human Rights Act (1998). Available at www.opsi.gov.uk, accessed 31 March 2010.

LaVigna, G. W. and Willis, T. J. (1995). Challenging behaviour: A model for breaking the barriers to social and community integration, *Positive Practices*, 1, October, 1–2.

Lee, A., Kaur, K., Cookson, A., and Greenhill, B. (2008). *The Keeping Me Safe and Well Screen*. Available at www.dh.gov.uk/prod_consum_dh/groups/dh_digitalassets/@dh/@en/documents/digitalasset/dh_088787.pdf, accessed 31 March 2010.

Mansell, J. and Beadle-Brown, J. (2006). Person-Centred planning and person-centred action: A critical perspective, in P. Cambridge and S. Carnaby (eds), *Person-centred Planning and Care Management with People with Learning Disabilities*. London: Jessica Kingsley, pp. 183–197.

Mencap (2007). *Death by Indifference*. London: Mencap Publications, available at www.mencap.org.uk/document.asp?id=284, accessed 31 March 2010.

Mental Capacity Act (2005). Available at www.opsi.gov.uk/ACTS/acts2005/ukpga_20050009_en_1, accessed 31 March 2010.

Mental Health Act (1983) as amended by the Mental Health Act (2007) (3 November 2008). Available at www.opsi.gov.uk, accessed 31 March 2010.

North West Training and Development Team (2006). *Final Report on the Consultation of People with a Learning Difficulty and Mental Health Problems*, available at www.northwest.nhs.uk/document_uploads/Mental_Health_in_the_North_West/FinalReportonLDandMHconsultation.pdf, accessed 31 March 2010.

O'Brien, J. (1987). A guide to lifestyle planning, in B. Wilcox and T. Bellamy (eds), *A Comprehensive Guide to the Activities Catalogue*. Baltimore, MD: Paul Brookes Publishing.

Pitonyak, D. (2010). *Ten Things You Can Do to Support a Person with Difficult Behaviours*, available at www.dimagine.com/10%20Things.pdf, accessed 30 January 2010.

Reed Report (1993). *Review of Mental Health and Social Services for Mentally Disordered Offenders and Others Requiring Similar Services, Vol. 5: Special Issues and Differing Needs.* London: HMSO.

Royal College of Psychiatrists (2007). *Challenging Behaviour: A Unified Approach.* College Report No. CR144. London: Royal College of Psychiatrists.

Ryan, J. and Thomas, F. (1987). *The Politics of Mental Handicap.* London: Free Association Books.

Ryle, A. and Kerr, I. B. (2002). *Introducing Cognitive Analytic Therapy: Principles and Practice.* Chichester: John Wiley & Sons, Ltd.

Schmul, M. and Anderson, H. (2001). *A Guide to Essential Lifestyle Planning.* Accrington, Lancashire: North West Training and Development Team.

Sinason, V. (1992). *Mental Handicap and the Human Condition.* London: Free Association Books.

Sobsey, D. (1994). *Violence and Abuse in the Lives of People with Disabilities – The End of Silent Acceptance?* Baltimore, MD: Paul Brookes Publishing.

Sternfert-Kroese, B., Dagnan, D., and Loumidis, K. (eds) (1997). *Cognitive Behavioural Therapy for People with Learning Disabilities.* London: Routledge.

United Nations Declaration of Human Rights (1948). Available at www.un.org/en/documents/udhr, accessed 31 March 2010.

United Nations Declaration on the Rights of Disabled Persons (1975). Available at www2.ohchr.org/english/law/res3447.htm, accessed 31 March 2010.

Vygotsky, L. (1978). *Mind in Society: The Development of Higher Psychological Processes.* Cambridge, MA: Harvard University Press.

Whitehouse, R. M., Tudway, J. A., Look, R., and Kroese, B. S. (2006). Adapting individual psychotherapy for adults with intellectual disabilities: A comparative review of the cognitive-behavioural and psychodynamic literature, *Journal of Applied Research in Intellectual Disabilities*, 19, 55–65.

Williams, J. R., Ferns, C., and Riding, T. (1999). *Joint Risk Assessment and Management Plan (J-RAMP)* (unpublished: contact authors for details).

Wolfensberger, W. (1972). *The Principle of Normalisation in Human Services.* North York, Ontario: Canadian Association for the Mentally Retarded Publications Department (now called the Canadian Association for Community Living).

Wood, D., Bruner J., and Ross, G. (1976). The role of tutoring in problem solving, *Journal of Child Psychology and Psychiatry*, 1, 89–100.

Part IV

Implementation

Introduction to Case Studies

In the case studies that follow, clinicians in four quite different mental health NHS Trusts in England describe their efforts to move towards best practice in managing risk. The *Best Practice* guidance drove many of the developments and changes made. However, as will become clear, each organization took a very individual approach and brought their own particular experiences to bear on the innovations they each made. In *A Four-step Model of Implementation*, Geraldine Strathdee, Phil Garnham, Jane Moore, and Devendra Hansjee describe their introduction of changes to risk management procedures in a large general mental health trust in London and describe the four-step approach to implementation they followed. Next, Kate Hunt describes the innovations she and colleagues made in another general mental health trust in the south of England and discusses *Narrowing the Gap between Policy and Practice*. Following this, Louise Fountain and Patrick McKee describe a similar implementation project in south west England and outline their experiences, including the challenge for practitioners, of *Balancing Flexibility and Standards in Risk Management*. Finally, Lorna Jellicoe-Jones, Mark Love, Roy Butterworth, and Claire Riding describe their initiative to improve practice in accordance with the key principles in a medium secure unit in north west England in their chapter entitled *From Ticking Boxes to Effective Risk Management*.

These case studies are intended to demonstrate real-life efforts to make the transition from the principles, evidence, and guidelines discussed in earlier chapters of this volume to clinical practice by psychologists, psychiatrists, nurses, and occupational therapists who are motivated and supported to make where they can rational and pragmatic improvements in risk assessment and management processes within their organizations. All the authors of these case studies participated in the development of the *Best Practice* guidance and in the efforts that followed its publication to bring it to the attention of mental health trusts nationwide. Therefore, they represent a particularly motivated and committed group of people. But this does not make them unrepresentative nor their

Trusts dissimilar to most others across England. Further, the authors of all the case studies go to great lengths to make clear their processes of implementation, to identify the practice developments made with ease, and to highlight the barriers they encountered and how they were overcome. We commend these case studies to you and trust they will be a source of ideas and inspiration for developments in clinical risk assessment and management in your area too.

13

Case Study 1:
A Four-Step Model of
Implementation

Geraldine Strathdee, Phil Garnham, Jane Moore
and Devendra Hansjee

Introduction

This chapter is a case study describing how Oxleas NHS Foundation Trust has initiated the implementation of the recent Department of Health guidance, *Best Practice in Managing Risk* (Department of Health, 2007). The chapter presents the step-by-step approach Oxleas is taking in its journey to implement this guidance and improve clinical risk assessment and management practice overall. The organizational context is briefly described, followed by details of the stages of implementation and the challenges the facilitators encountered. A practical clinical case example of the Oxleas pilot stepped-care approach to risk management is presented. Finally, reflections on how the key challenges have been addressed and the processes implemented to overcome them are described. This chapter may be of interest to regulators and commissioners seeking to acquire governance structures that minimize risk to service users and providers of mental health services. This chapter may also be of interest to clinical and service managers and senior practitioners charged with developing service delivery care pathways to provide safe and effective clinical services and management practices.

The Case Study Context

Oxleas NHS Foundation Trust serves a diverse population of approximately three-quarters of a million people in the south east London boroughs of Bexley, Bromley, and Greenwich. The Trust is located in some of the most deprived areas in London, where at least 26 different languages are spoken. Oxleas employs approximately 2,000 members of staff and its services are spread across 76 hospital and community sites. Eight thousand service users per year, including children, working age adults, older adults, and people with learning disabilities use the Trust's services.

Self-Harm and Violence: Towards Best Practice in Managing Risk in Mental Health Services, First Edition.
Edited by Richard Whittington and Caroline Logan.
© 2011 John Wiley & Sons, Ltd. Published 2011 by John Wiley & Sons, Ltd.

The Step-by-Step Stages to Implementation

In this section, the communication strategy to raise awareness of the *Best Practice* guidance on risk is presented, in addition to a detailed description of the stages through which the guidance was implemented.

Stage 1: The governance and implementation system

Since 2007, Oxleas NHS Foundation Trust has worked on optimizing its systems for the implementation of emerging national policies, evidence-based practice including NICE guidelines, and other related quality and clinical effectiveness improvements. The Trust's clinical risk policy was identified as key to the development of a best practice pathway system. This system involved three components: the establishment of *governance arrangements*; the *implementation of the planning processes* required to build capacity and capability; and the identification of the *assurance processes* required based on our organizational culture of gathering objective information against which progress can be measured and the Trust Board assured. Figure 13.1 illustrates the three components of this pathway system.

Any trust's clinical risk policy needs to delineate safe clinical practice in all common areas of risk, including risk of harm to self and risk to and from others, risk of arson, falls, sexual vulnerability, and so on. In addition, such a policy needs to ensure that a managerial service delivery implementation pathway is in place to avoid a lack of capacity and competence in the workforce delivering safe care. In Oxleas, the Trust-wide Clinical Effectiveness Group (CEG) was identified as the most relevant steering group for the implementation of the clinical risk policy and, therefore, the *Best Practice* guidance. The membership and terms of reference for this group were reviewed as the

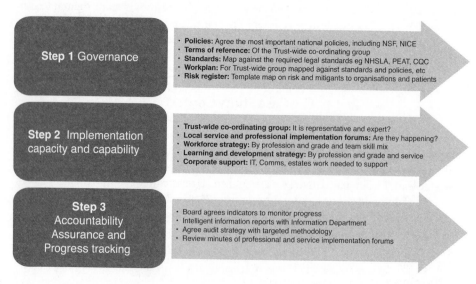

Figure 13.1   Clinical effectiveness in Oxleas: The three stages of the implementation method.

first stage in preparing to implement the guidance. The fact that this group comprises the clinical directors from all specialisms and the heads of profession, learning and development, and workforce indicated that an appropriate level of seniority and expertise were at hand to deliver effective implementation. The clinical risk policy requirements were mapped against the requirements of the main UK regulatory and governance organizations in order to ensure consistency and avoid duplication. These organizations included the national health care regulator, the Care Quality Commission, in addition to the National Patient Safety Agency, the Physical Environment Action Teams, the National Health Service Litigation Authority, and Monitor, which is the Foundation Trust Regulator.

The CEG serves as the co-ordinating central committee, which leads and receives feedback from each of the supporting area CEGs, which are chaired by the Clinical Directors. Each major service, including the Bexley, Bromley, and Greenwich working age adults services, the older people's services, the Children and Adolescent Mental Health Service, and learning disabilities services ensured that the emerging clinical risk policy and the associated *Best Practice* guidance was a standing item on the agenda for their regular meetings. This enabled the organization to prioritize and feed in local expertise and ideas at a local level. In addition, in a culture of learning from experience, the Trust-wide and local adverse incident management groups agreed to share lessons learnt from the previous three years of serious untoward incidents. Finally, the local public health reports, identifying suicide and adverse incident rates, were studied to benchmark our performance against that of comparable cluster groups; that is, those services across London that have similar levels of social deprivation and other sociodemographic indices that contribute to risk. Therefore, the widest possible range of skills and experience were tapped to inform the implementation process.

Summary of Stage 1

- The Trust responded to the Department of Health *Best Practice in Managing Risk* guidance (Department of Health, 2007) by reviewing its policy implementation processes.
- A three-stage pathway of establishing governance processes, implementation planning, and assurance was established to build capacity and competence with objective information to judge progress.
- The new clinical risk policy was subjected to this three-stage pathway process.

Stage 2: Developing the implementation plan

In line with the agreed Oxleas CEG implementation processes, the next stage was to develop an implementation plan for the Department of Health *Best Practice* guidance in order to build capability and capacity through benchmarking current practice, and to identify what workforce and learning and development strategies and corporate supports were needed to implement improved practices in relation to clinical risk. In order to develop the implementation plan, a workshop was held to discuss the *Best Practice* guidance and its implications for Oxleas. The 40 invited participants consisted of clinical and managerial staff at all levels and from all disciplines and directorates across the organization. Participants were asked to agree in priority order the essential steps to implementation of a revised and updated Trust clinical risk policy that would reflect the *Best Practice* guidance. The priorities agreed consisted of the following: delineation of the organization's principles of risk management; benchmarking existing processes and policies; modernization of the Trust clinical risk policies; and development of a learning and clinician decision-support programme.

Oxleas' principles of risk management The workshop participants concluded that it was essential that the Trust's attitude and culture towards risk be defined explicitly so that senior managers and clinicians worked in an understood and shared culture. Box 13.1 illustrates the principles that were developed in an iterative process, starting with the expressed views of the workshop participants, which were evolved through review and revision at each local and directorate CEG.

Box 13.1: The Oxleas' principles of risk management

- Oxleas staff aim to promote positive risk-taking and emphasize promoting safety for clients.
- We want to develop a shared understanding of risks and safety with our service users to support positive risk-taking and achieve our organizational aim of full social inclusion for our clients.
- Our risk policy has to be incorporated into routine clinical practice rather than be seen as an additional or parallel task.
- We need to develop processes in keeping with our electronic care records systems, as this is the primary clinical record (rather than parallel written records).
- We believe that risk/safety management consists of the three core elements of risk assessment, followed by risk minimization and risk management, and appropriate inter-agency risk-sharing.
- We want to develop a stepped-care approach to risk.
- We want to learn from our adverse and serious untoward incidents and incorporate the lessons into our practice.
- We work in close partnership with our community agencies, such as housing, criminal justice system, antisocial behaviour order unit, and other partners who have major risk management expertise also.

Benchmarking the use of risk processes across services in Oxleas In line with the action agreed at the workshop, the *Best Practice* guidance was sent out to all clinical teams for consideration. Teams were asked to describe to their local CEGs the risk assessment and management practices currently used in each team. Further, they were asked to describe their experiences with regard to the basic assessment and recording of risk using the newly implemented RiO (London) electronic care records risk assessment tool (specifically, the Assessment of Risk 1 or AOR1), and to describe their use of any additional expert risk

Table 13.1 The clinical supervisors' survey of care records in relation to risk.

Area	Risk assessments complete (%)	Risk assessment updated in last 6 months (%)	If there is major risk, is service user on enhanced CPA? (%)	If a risk has been identified, is it addressed in the care plan?	As a clinical supervisor, do you rate this plan as safe and showing good practice? (%)
Service A	92	67	68	81	52
Service B	93	79	80	78	59
Service C	76	63	89	52	32
Total	89	71	77	74	51

assessment tools. Finally, teams were encouraged to elaborate on their risk management and risk-sharing processes, both within teams and directorates, and with external partner agencies.

Table 13.1 shows a sample of the findings of a survey of 150 clinical supervisors in which they were asked to assess the completeness and quality of care records as they related to judgements about clinical risk. The findings of this survey indicate that, although most care records had a risk assessment completed, many were not recent. In addition, there was variation in the extent to which appropriate action had been taken in response to an identified risk. The national UK and Trust guidance recommends that service users with high levels of needs and clinical risk should be provided with an enhanced care plan using the Care Programme Approach (CPA). Such a care plan should address the identified risk and include a description of any relevant risk minimization interventions, developed in collaboration with the service user. Impressively, our clinical supervisors were, as always, keen to improve as evidenced by their own open assessment of quality of care plan delineated in the last column of the table.

The use of risk assessment tools and risk management partnerships Each directorate was asked to provide information on the use of assessment tools in addition to the basic AOR1. Table 13.2 shows some of the variation in tools and processes in use. The range of partnerships provided is not exclusive but indicates the range of external partners considered.

Summary of Stage 2

- A workshop of all levels of staff and management was held to ensure a wide range of engagement in the process of developing the new risk policy in line with the Department of Health *Best Practice in Managing Risk* guidance.
- Oxleas' key principles of risk management were agreed.
- An audit was undertaken into the views of clinical supervisors about care plans in order to benchmark practice standards.
- All directorates and services provided benchmarking information on their risk assessment and risk management processes, including the use of standardized assessment tools and risk-sharing with key community partner agencies.

Table 13.2   A sample of the specialized risk assessment tools in use in Oxleas.

Practice area	Tools	Common partner agencies
Forensic services	• Comprehensive history • *HCR-20* violence risk assessment guide • *Psychopathy Checklist Revised* (PCL-R) • Sexual violence risk assessments • Substance misuse assessment tools	• Multi-agency public protection panels (MAPPPs) • Probation • Criminal justice system
Complex needs	• Comprehensive history • Suicide risk assessment tools including *Beck Depression Inventory* • Substance misuse assessment tools • Concordance and side-effects of medication rating tools • Occasional use of *HCR-20* • Domestic violence assessments • NICE bipolar and sexual risk assessments	• Service users and carers • Locality high risk panels • Antisocial behaviour order teams • Appointeeship team • Third sector housing
Acute care and crisis home treatment teams	• NICE self-harm clinical guideline • Suicide assessments • NICE depression audit tool	• Users and carers • Accident and emergency
Older peoples' mental health services	• Depression assessments • NICE falls assessment and risk management tools	• Carers • Nursing and care homes • Day care services
Child and adolescent mental health service	• Child protection processes	• Local authority children in need and children at risk teams
Learning disability services	• Vulnerable adults processes	
Corporate departments (HR and the Estates Department)	• Criminal Records Bureau checking • Physical environment action team checks • Privacy and dignity self-assessments	
Cross-Trust organizational strategies for improving care and therefore risk	• 100% completion of *National Confidential Inquiry into Homicides and Suicides* questionnaires • Fourth best national performer in *Prescribing Observatory In Mental Health* prescribing standards	• Peer review accreditation systems

Stage 3: Modernizing the Trust's clinical risk policy

The Trust's clinical risk policy was modernized once agreement had been reached about the current standards of risk assessment, risk management, and risk-sharing. In 2002, the Trust had published a comprehensive 11-chapter risk policy book, on which subsequent risk training was based. Following the publication of *Best Practice in Managing Risk* in 2007 and the processes described in Stages 1 and 2 above, the CEG reviewed the existing policy and agreed that much of the basic guidance was still good, but that there was a pressing need to update the work. Since the original publication of the policy, the Trust had worked to achieve continual modernization. Key to risk management was the introduction in 2006 across the Trust of electronic care records. This innovation resulted in some major safety benefits, with accessible records wherever the service users presented. However, it also presented the Trust with the major challenge of entering the chronological risk data on to the new records and the disappointing removal of the Trust's own and preferred *Management of Risk* tool. In addition, key to effective risk management was the gradual introduction of assertive outreach, crisis resolution home treatment and early intervention psychosis teams, personality disorder day treatment services, and others.

Analysis of our *International Classification of Diseases* (ICD) multi-axial coding data for all those admitted to the Trust's acute beds showed that in 2000, 87% of people with acute psychosis were admitted to hospital. By 2008, this figure had reduced to 45%, with the remainder being treated in community and home settings. This change in focus and treatment delivery called for a very different approach to risk management. In addition, the publication and then gradual implementation into routine clinical practice of 28 clinical guidelines published by the UK National Institute of Health and Clinical Excellence (NICE) supported improved and more consistent practice – if the Trust could disseminate the learning. The Trust commitment to providing intelligent information reports meant that through the study of complaints, incidents, suicides and homicides, and our adverse incidents management group reports there was a better understanding of the key risk issues and needs. For example, the most prominent risk in our elderly population was falls, while in our acute inpatient units, the need to secure sexual safety was a priority.

One major finding of the workshop mentioned above, and the work carried out across the Trust subsequently, was the variation in standards of risk assessment and risk management across the organization. This situation was prioritized for attention. Consequently, the decision was made to update the Trust risk assessment and risk management policy book. Table 13.3 shows the agreed new content and structure.

In order to rewrite our policy book, a project manger has been appointed working under the supervision of two of the present authors (GS and PG). Clinical leaders have been nominated to write each chapter, using the consistent accessible headings for each area of risk indicated in Table 13.1. The idea is for each chapter to be approved by the CEG and for a best practice champion to be appointed to develop an e-learning programme for each risk area. As the Trust is dispersed across 76 sites and with approximately 500 staff to train, an online e-learning package, accessible from external sites, has been a major part of our learning and development strategy for mandatory training, and which we now want to expand for clinical effectiveness training.

Table 13.3 The new 2009/2010 Oxleas clinical risk policy and training guide.

Oxleas risk policies	Consistent risk policy format
Suicide	Who is at high risk – summary?
Severe self-neglect	How to assess risk
Harm from others	• When to assess
Harm to others	• What basic assessment is essential
	• What specialist tools are available on the new Trust Intranet?
	• Frequently asked questions
Dementia	What are the risk management strategies?
Driving	• In inpatient and in community settings
Falls	• Engagement strategies
Fire	• Practical interventions, including new teams and interventions
	• NICE evidence-based interventions
Mental capacity and consent	How to record on the RiO electronic care record
Learning disabilities	Oxleas stepped-care risk management process
Child protection	• Individual, team, directorate levels
	• External partners
Adherence to medication	What training is available?
	• Intranet assessment tools
	• Intranet best practice care plans
	• e-learning for each policy
	• Best practice trainers identified
	• Training in all continuing professional development and professional forums

Development of clinician decision-support systems One of our organizational priorities is to use technology to improve clinician knowledge and decision-support making. We were fortunate enough to be successful in our bid to become one of the National Information Prescription pilot sites for mental health (Office for Public Management, 2008); the provision of accessible information to all service users and their carers is seen as essential to modern clinical practice and to support self-management. As part of that work, we consulted widely with service users, carers, and staff and our Intranet service was re-designed as a consequence of the feedback obtained. The Intranet is now an accessible resource, providing information for service users and carers in multimedia formats, including brief and detailed written information on all conditions and treatment, as well as podcasts and video diary stories of recovery for those who find reading problematic. We also have a clinician decision-support section called 'evidence for practice', which assists decision-making on diagnosis, provides the best assessment tools for each condition, and makes available the *Best Practice* guidance and a range of relevant audit tools. As part of the implementation of our risk policy, we have added improved assessment tools to our evidence for practice assessment and outcome measurement library (Bhui, 2009). As part of the implementation of the new CPA, we have developed a best practice pathway to guide history-taking and risk assessment with subsequent consistent recording on to our electronic care record history and care plans. We are preparing good practice care plans as a training tool for clinicians. It is an organizational aim that we move to first-person singular care plans; that is, a care plan that is written collaboratively between the clinician and the service user which start with the word 'I'. This includes risk management planning further to drive personalized, informed, self-managing approaches to care, especially for those with longer term difficulties.

Summary of Stage 3

- Oxleas Trust decided to modernize its clinical risk policy in the light of the Department of Health *Best Practice in Managing Risk* guidance because an initial benchmarking exercise found standards of practice to be variable.
- Modernization took the form of the rewriting of the 11-chapter risk policy on all key risk areas, including risk to self and to and from others.
- Each chapter was written by a Trust clinician with expertise in the area and followed a structured format accessible to all levels of staff.
- The Trust agreed that working in partnership with service users to provide them with accessible multimedia information on their choices, their conditions and treatment was an essential core component of the new risk strategy.
- In order to make best practice supports such as diagnosis aids, assessment tools, and best practice guidelines easily available to support clinician decision-making, the Trust Intranet was completely redesigned.

Stage 4: Stepped-care approach

At the workshop held to agree the implementation process, which was described briefly in Stage 2 above, it was apparent that the Trust's clinical teams already use many processes to manage risk and to share expertise. Therefore, a stepped-care approach was implemented. The notion of stepped-care is to develop responses that are proportionate to the situation. Dwyer (2008) described a stepped-care model as one in which there are interventions of different levels of intensity available to the service user, and the service user's needs are matched with the level of intensity of the intervention. Service users move through less intensive interventions before receiving more intensive interventions (if they are necessary). There is careful monitoring of patient outcomes, allowing treatments to be 'stepped up' if required, and there are clear referral pathways between the differing levels of intervention with user involvement and self management at the heart of the approach.

Case Vignette

The Bromley Assertive Community Treatment (BACT) team utilizes the stepped-care approach to risk management. Figure 13.2 illustrates the processes they use and the following case study illustrates how this is applied to clinical practice.

SB is a 29-year-old man with a history of paranoid psychosis and substance misuse. He was referred to the BACT at the point when he was in danger of eviction due to his targeting of other vulnerable residents in his accommodation and his drug dealing.

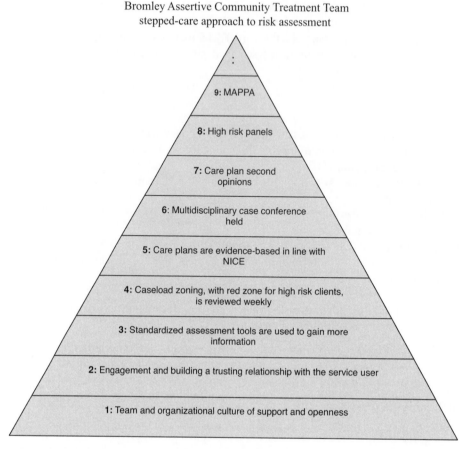

Bromley Assertive Community Treatment Team
stepped-care approach to risk assessment

:

9: MAPPA

8: High risk panels

7: Care plan second opinions

6: Multidisciplinary case conference held

5: Care plans are evidence-based in line with NICE

4: Caseload zoning, with red zone for high risk clients, is reviewed weekly

3: Standardized assessment tools are used to gain more information

2: Engagement and building a trusting relationship with the service user

1: Team and organizational culture of support and openness

Figure 13.2   The BACT stepped-care approach to risk assessment, risk management, and risk-sharing.

Step 1: Team and organizational culture of support and openness

The BACT is a multidisciplinary team working with 112 service users with complex needs (e.g., psychosis, substance misuse, personality development difficulties, neurocognitive deficits, and high risk profiles). The team uses a whole-team approach in which caseload zoning is a key tool to ensure that the whole team is aware of and knowledgeable about each service user and his or her risk profile.

Step 2: Engagement and building a trusting relationship with the service user

In order to build a trusting relationship, the team worked with SB to identify his needs. A new start in an environment free from the drug culture was high on SB's wish list.

Step 3: A comprehensive history and risk assessment was undertaken and documented

Contact was made with SB's family, his housing agency, and in-depth discussions were held with SB to ensure that we had a shared understanding with him of his history and formulation. He was supported to get a new flat, but soon afterwards complaints began to be made by his neighbours as he was observed bringing drug dealers on to the estate, and heard shouting every night until the small hours.

Step 4: Standardized assessment tools are used to gain more information when appropriate
Forensic colleagues supported us to undertake an HCR-20 violence risk assessment.
Step 5: Caseload zoning with red zone for high risk clients is reviewed weekly
SB was put in the red zone of the caseload zoning system and an intensive programme
to contact him daily was initiated. A thorough assessment through both meetings with SB
and email correspondence with his family, who were abroad, found that he was suffering
a drug-induced relapse of his paranoid psychosis. On the MAP and SADQ substance
misuse assessment scales, SB indicated that he was taking crack cocaine, amphetamines,
and ketamine daily. SB believed that he was not ill, but had a special mission to visit
his female neighbours, seeking companionship and money for drugs. SB was assessed as
presenting a danger to others and was admitted to the acute psychiatric unit. SB willingly
agreed to take antipsychotic medication, but was unable to understand why his tenancy
was at risk.
Step 6: Multidisciplinary case conference held to pull in expertise
*Step 7: Care plan second opinions from housing, antisocial behaviour order (ASBO) team,
and forensic experts*
Step 8: Local high risk multi-agency panels risk-sharing plans
The risk partnership and risk-sharing local arrangements were started and the housing
agency and local ASBO units were involved. The housing landlord was able to play back
to SB a loud noise nuisance recording made to show environmental noise pollution. SB
was genuinely distressed at the level of noise he had made. He did not, however, think
that he should alter his behaviour. ACT staff working with him identified that his key
career aims were to become an artist and he was supported to join an art group and art
course. The local ASBO team met with him to explain to him that his behaviour was
antisocial and was causing severe distress to vulnerable neighbours, especially females.
SB agreed to an appropriate behaviour commitment of not bringing drugs or alcohol
on to the estate late at night, not entertaining known drug dealers in his home, and not
shouting and knocking on the doors of vulnerable females on the estate. In parallel to the
local authority ASBO team, the ACT team were able to support SB with psychological
therapy, medication, and career development. The high risk panel locally were able to
support his commitment to appropriate behaviour by occasional visits from the local
community support officer who he came to know and see as supportive.

Challenges and Facilitators

The Oxleas plan to implement a new clinical risk policy, underpinned by the Department
of Health *Best Practice* guidance, is progressing and we expect full implementation for
our 1,600 clinical staff and 18,000 service users to take three to five years. Below we
describe the key challenges and facilitators.

The introduction of electronic care records, where well used, has been a great facilitator
in improving practice and the documentation of risk, and it has allowed 24-hour, seven-
day access to records, making service users and staff safer. The difficulty has arisen where
this new tool has been used, but not all relevant risk information entered. A continuing
challenge is for staff to understand that obtaining objective collateral information is vital
while negotiating patient confidentiality. Ensuring a consistent Trust-wide approach to
risk assessment and documentation also continues to present challenges, and the lack of

inclusion of our favoured risk management tool has meant that we need to find a way to replace this key clinician decision-support strategy.

The nature of modern mental health services, with large numbers of staff spread across dispersed sites is a challenge for learning and development departments. Our approach has been to engage clinicians in quality improvements; the project management support and time needed to do this is vital. Our Trust expert clinicians are working on the new policies and training programmes, but support from national e-learning training programmes for the key risks would significantly expedite our ability to train all staff to the highest standard. The best facilitator, however, is the attitude of openness and honesty of our staff who increasingly recognize where we need to improve and constantly strive to find a way to provide better care. Our service users and their carers who provide us with invaluable feedback are also key facilitators.

Conclusions and Recommendations

Our conclusions are that good risk assessment and risk management requires a whole systems and whole trust approach, with engagement from the front line right through to the Board in order that an organizational culture of safety is in place. We have found it vital to have a well communicated project plan with a feasible implementation timescale. There is still a great deal to do in Oxleas NHS Foundation Trust and supporting our service users with self-assessment and self-management tools remains a key priority.

References

Bhui, K., Dinos, S., and Khoshaba, B. (2009). *Outcomes Compendium: Helping you select the right tools for best mental health practice in your field.* London: Department of Health.

Department of Health (2007). *Best Practice in Managing Risk in Mental Health Services.* London: Department of Health.

Dwyer, S. (2008). *Primary Mental Health Care in New Zealand: Ministry of Health Update No. 3.* Wellington: Ministry of Health.

Office for Public Management (2008). *The Evaluation of Information Prescriptions: Final Report to the Department of Health.* London: Office for Public Management.

14

Case Study 2: Narrowing the Gap between Policy and Practice

Kate Hunt

Sussex Partnership NHS Trust was established in April 2006 following the merger of three predecessor organizations, and gained foundation trust status in August 2008. NHS foundation trusts are a new type of NHS trust in England, created to devolve decision-making from central government to local organizations and communities (Department of Health, 2005). Sussex Partnership provides specialist mental health, learning disability, and substance misuse services for a diverse population of approximately 1.5 million people, spread along an 80-mile coastal strip. At an organizational level, Sussex Partnership has a strong commitment to achieving excellence at all levels of mental health care and recognizes that ensuring best practice in managing risk is central to achieving this.

This chapter details how Sussex Partnership addresses best practice in clinical risk assessment and management, and some of the difficulties that we as a large organization have encountered in the process of implementing the principles outlined in *Best Practice in Managing Risk* (Department of Health, 2007). Starting with the governance of clinical risk, I will outline where this sits within Sussex Partnership NHS Trust and the importance of having integrated clinical and managerial leadership and clear lines of accountability. I will then outline our use of the *Best Practice in Managing Risk* Implementation Toolkit (Department of Health, 2008a) for developing an action plan for improving the quality of risk management. The remaining sections of this chapter focus on the development of the Trust's clinical risk policy, the Trust's training strategy, and the learning opportunities derived from reviewing Serious Untoward Incidents (SUIs) and case presentations to Risk Management and Review Panels. I will also outline the way in which a recovery approach provides a wider context for ensuring good practice and how future audits can be designed to monitor and improve practice.

Self-Harm and Violence: Towards Best Practice in Managing Risk in Mental Health Services, First Edition.
Edited by Richard Whittington and Caroline Logan.
© 2011 John Wiley & Sons, Ltd. Published 2011 by John Wiley & Sons, Ltd.

Governance

As with other trusts, clinical risk assessment and management in Sussex Partnership is part of a wider overall risk management strategy required by the NHS Litigation Authority (see also Chapter 9). The NHS Litigation Authority has been established to administer schemes in respect of managing claims for clinical negligence against NHS bodies (Department of Health, 2006). In February 2007, prior to the publication of *Best Practice in Managing Risk*, a clinical risk framework had been developed to ensure that the Trust as an organization created a safe and positive attitude to clinical risk. The principles on which the framework is based closely mirror the principles outlined in the *Best Practice in Managing Risk* document and it emphasizes positive risk management, organizational and management support, a focus on service users and carers, multidisciplinary teamwork, education and training, and supervision. This framework is delivered through our Integrated Health and Social Care Governance Structures, specifically through a Trust-wide Clinical Risk Group. The Clinical Risk Group was established in March 2007, and has representation from senior clinicians and managers across all care groups. A number of other Trust-wide groups inform the work of the Clinical Risk Group, including Trends and Lessons, which examines patterns emerging from the reporting of SUIs, and local Suicide and Homicide governance groups, which examine such incidents in detail.

The greatest challenge in taking forward the governance of clinical risk has arisen with respect to the Trust's post-merger clinical and managerial structure. This retained a locality focus in line with the three predecessor organizations and made it very difficult to establish clear leadership and direction. This situation has now resolved with the establishment of a Trust-wide care group structure, with each care group having multi-professional integrated governance teams and an identified lead for clinical risk tasked with ensuring the implementation of policy and lessons learnt from SUIs across the relevant care group. This also allows for a clearer accountability and reporting structure for front line clinicians and managers. In my view, clear and integrated clinical and managerial leadership is essential and a fundamental priority in improving the quality of clinical risk assessment and management.

The Use of the *Best Practice in Managing Risk* Implementation Toolkit

In November 2007, following the publication of *Best Practice in Managing Risk*, the Trust took part in a half-day workshop run by one of the authors of the guidance to discuss its implementation in Sussex Partnership NHS Trust. Essentially, key members of the Trust's Clinical Risk Group used the *Best Practice in Managing Risk* Implementation Toolkit (see Department of Health, 2008a) to rate the Trust's current practice on each of the 16 best practice principles and to identify key areas for development. The toolkit lists each of the 16 best practice principles and provides examples of how evidence of each principle may be demonstrated in practical terms. The group discussed the Trust's performance against the indicators for each principle and agreed a rating based on a coding system of green, amber, or red according to the extent to which they thought Sussex Partnership currently evidenced each principle. This proved to be an invaluable exercise, highlighting both areas of excellence and good practice, key areas for development in the short term, as well as impediments to developing best practice.

An area of identified excellence was that of the Trust's knowledge and understanding of mental health legislation as it is relevant to risk management, and good or very good practice in terms of demonstrable progress was identified in most other areas. Areas where more substantial improvements in practice were thought necessary included increasing the involvement of service users and carers and more extensive use of the structured professional judgement approach to risk assessment.

The group also identified a number of key impediments or issues that could be barriers to the further development of best practice. These included the fact that the Trust was at that time in a period of considerable ongoing change. In addition, the group suggested that improvements were necessary in the policy–practice link up, in availability of key resources, in the actual risk assessment process, in the consistency of good practice, in the involvement of service users and carers, and in the further development of staff skills and competencies.

Following the implementation workshop, the Trust Clinical Risk Group agreed that the development of a Trust-wide single policy for the assessment and management of clinical risk would be the first step in addressing the impediments identified and in ensuring fuller implementation of the principles outlined in the *Best Practice in Managing Risk* document.

Development of the Clinical Risk Policy

The development of the policy first required a review of all risk assessment and management tools and procedures being used across all care groups in Sussex Partnership, namely working age adults, children and adolescents, learning disability services, substance misuse, and older people, as well as across the care pathway from primary to secondary care, including inpatient care. It was very quickly apparent that there was considerable variation in the use of basic risk assessment tools, with different services and people using different forms and formats. To ensure consistency of standards, it was agreed that the priority was to harmonize the risk tools used in working age adult services. The challenge of this was to ensure we had clarity regarding which tool would be used in which setting, as well as clarity about when one would consider using a more comprehensive tool. We needed a brief screening tool that could be used in primary care settings and in the context of Increasing Access to Psychological Therapies (IAPT), in which contacts are often short and over the telephone. We also needed tools that were more comprehensive and suitable for use in complex cases and in secure forensic settings. The IAPT Programme was launched in 2007, and has been rolled out to increase access to services for people usually in primary care settings with minor or moderate common metal health problems, such as anxiety and depression (Care Services Improvement Partnership, 2007). Services are expected to see large numbers of referrals and the challenge has been to ensure that any concerns about clinical risk are noted and adequately assessed in a short time frame.

After considerable consultation, the Trust-wide Clinical Risk Group agreed on the tools to be used and renamed and amended the Care Programme Approach (CPA) risk tools we would use for working age adults. The CPA is a system of coordination and support to ensure a high quality of care for individuals receiving treatment and support from secondary mental health services (Department of Health, 2008b). In terms of the other care groups, we agreed to continue with the tools currently being used with a view to harmonization over the following year. This gentle pace of harmonization would fit in with further organizational changes planned, most notably that of the shift from a management structure related to three geographical localities to a single Trust-wide Care Group structure, as well as the introduction of CPA in Child and Adolescent Mental Health Services (CAMHS). We also agreed to work towards ensuring the adult tools covered the most relevant risk factors for older people.

The clinical risk policy was drafted by myself and ratified by our Trust-wide Policy and Professional Practice Group in January 2009 following extensive consultation, including focus groups, with a wide range and number of professionals, service users, and carers. The Policy and Professional Practice Group comprises the most senior members of the Trust, and the ratification of policies by this group is essential to ensuring accountability and good practice as all staff are required to adhere to policies as part of the terms and conditions of their employment. Policies ratified by this group are also published on the Trust website and are available in the public domain. The approval process requires evidence of extensive consultation, relevant National Policy and Guidance, and an Equality and Human Rights Impact Assessment.

The introduction of a Trust-wide policy on clinical risk has probably been the single most important driver in changing practice and raising standards, bringing together a number of requirements of the NHS Litigation Authority. The policy is substantially underpinned by *Best Practice in Managing Risk*. It includes the rationale, duties (responsibilities) of staff, the scope and principles of the policy, as well as clear detail as to the expected format of risk assessments, the process of risk assessment, the frequency of risk reviews, the communication of findings, training, supervision, standards, and audit. Details of the structured professional approach to risk assessment and management, risk tools, standards of practice, and a glossary of terms are in the appendices of the policy.

The Equality and Human Rights Impact Assessment that was undertaken on the policy highlighted the lessons from the Independent Inquiry into the Death of David Bennett (Norfolk, Suffolk, and Cambridgeshire Strategic Health Authority, 2003). David Bennett died in a medium secure unit after being restrained, and the Inquiry highlighted that a disproportionate number of people from black and minority ethnic communities are being detained under the Mental Health Act (1983) and are generally regarded as more aggressive, more dangerous, and more difficult to treat than are white people with similar problems. This will be a key issue in future audits of practice.

There has been extensive communication regarding the introduction of the policy, via electronic bulletins and in team meetings, and the author of the policy has been a contact point for staff if they have had any questions. From the feedback received, the key issue that has arisen relates to the need for training, especially with regards to 'formulation'. Formulation is the essential link between assessment and intervention or management of risk, and is critical for moving beyond the tick-box approach that has often dominated the process of risk assessment. A training strategy is in the process of being developed to ensure all clinical staff have the skills and competencies to undertake the assessments and management plans required. The training strategy is described below.

The policy is now due to be reviewed. I am the single point of contact for this policy. This has been an invaluable means of ensuring and coordinating feedback as to issues that have arisen in the process of implementing the clinical risk policy, ranging from the technical (e.g., accessing the policy from the intranet, uploading word documents onto the electronic CPA system) to the conceptual (e.g., need to clarify differences in requirements for different service areas).

Training Strategy

The training strategy has recently been drafted by myself and is due to be presented at the Trust's Learning and Development Group for approval. It is linked to the CPA training strategy, and will involve delivering a half-day essential training course to raise awareness about the *Best Practice in Managing Risk* guidance, the Trust's clinical risk policy, and basic skills in clinical risk assessment and management. A further half-day training will take place *in situ* with teams and all clinical staff to ensure policy–practice link up. This training will cover the process of undertaking multidisciplinary risk assessment and management planning and addressing risk issues common or more specific to each care group. More advanced or specialist training will be targeted for specific services and clinicians. In addition to this formal training, there will be training to teams regarding specific lessons from SUIs, and learning through Risk Management and Review Panels. This is described below.

The process of risk assessment and management will also be reviewed in an individual practitioner's supervision sessions and in other reflective practice opportunities.

Lessons from SUIs

The Trust-wide Trends and Lessons Group reports on all SUIs. Recurrent themes across SUIs are identified and reported through a monthly 'Risk and Safety Brief', which is sent to all staff via electronic mail. A training programme covering the lessons learned from SUIs is being rolled out for all clinical staff. This should endorse the process of ensuring strong links between policy and practice. A recent review of all the SUIs in Sussex Partnership in the past 12 months highlighted a number of key issues relevant to good practice in managing risk. Key issues included relevant risk factors being overlooked, a lack of multidisciplinary risk assessment and formulation, a risk management plan not being in place to meet identified risk, and no process of review following a change of circumstances. It is hoped that with the introduction of the Clinical Risk Policy all these issues will be better addressed in the future.

A recent example of drawing from the lessons learnt from SUIs followed on from a review of a service in which a service user violently attacked a member of the public. The risk assessment process and management plans were found to be lacking across a number of areas, including out-of-date and unsigned risk assessments, impoverished formulations, and lack of inter-agency communication. A small multidisciplinary team of senior clinicians attended all assertive outreach teams across the Trust to present the lessons learnt from this and other investigations. The training programme will include lessons learnt from this and a number of other SUIs.

Risk Management and Review Panels

Prior to the establishment of the Trust-wide Clinical Risk Group, local arrangements were already in place to ensure local support to teams through Risk Management and Review Panels (RMRPs). These panels were set up to act as an expert reference panel for clinical risk management across all care groups. Teams are asked to present their risk assessments and management plans for highly complex cases that have been difficult to contain at a service level.

A critical review of the presented information is undertaken using the principles and standards of risk assessment and management outlined in the Trust policy and the Root Cause Analysis tool developed by the National Patient Safety Agency as a diagnostic tool to investigate incidents (National Patient Safety Agency, 2009). This tool is routinely used in the Trust for SUIs and has proved to be extremely useful from a corporate and clinical perspective. We have found that the publication of *Best Practice in Managing Risk* and the introduction of the clinical risk policy have provided a much clearer framework for ensuring best practice, particularly with respect to ensuring 'defensible not defensive practice'. Moreover, the completion of the Root Cause Analysis tool, in effect, provides a 'reverse' Root Cause Analysis, ensuring 'controls' are in place relation to identified individual, team, and organizational risk factors.

The cases presented to the RMRP meetings are most often individuals about whom there is varied opinion as to degree of risk to themselves or others, or individuals for whom inpatient treatment is thought to be of little benefit, but discharging the individual back into the community is thought to present too much of a risk. From the cases presented over the past year, a number of key issues have become evident. First, documented evidence about the involvement of service users and carers in the development of risk management plans has often been absent. Their involvement in risk assessment and in the development of management plans requires a considerable shift in culture, a shift which embraces the concept of 'recovery'. The recovery approach is rapidly gaining ground in the development and delivery of mental health services and focuses on collaboration, partnership working, and self-directed care (Social Care Institute for Excellence, 2007). Although this approach specifically promotes creative or positive risk-taking over cautious risk assessment and restrictive risk management, it is clear that many staff feel anxious about talking with service users and carers about risk for fear of either upsetting people or increasing their risk. Staff training in the recovery approach is essential to overcome these barriers and our Trust has now developed a training strategy specifically focused on this (see below).

Secondly, it has become clear that staff often lack confidence in undertaking risk assessments and risk formulations and in developing risk management plans, despite evidence that the team's thinking around the case has been fairly complex and thorough. From the feedback received, the process of presenting at the RMRP meetings has been a valuable experience, increasing staff knowledge and confidence.

A third issue that has arisen has been in the context of varied opinion within a multidisciplinary team as to the most appropriate risk management plan. In one situation, following a case presentation by the care coordinator and team manager, the Panel recommended that the service user's medication was reviewed and that the service user should remain an inpatient while a comprehensive risk formulation was developed. The Responsible Clinician for the service user later expressed concern as to the Panel's opinion and role, and questioned whether the panel had the authority to overrule his wish to discharge the service user from inpatient services. The Responsible Clinician is a clinician who has the authority under the Mental Health Act 2007 to exercise various powers concerned with the circumstances under which a person with a mental health disorder can be detained for treatment without his or her consent or recalled for treatment following discharge into the community. Although potentially an area of conflict with respect to the Responsible Clinician's view and the view of the RMRP, this was resolved by clear communication and reference to the principles of *Best Practice in Managing Risk* and the Trust Policy.

The Recovery Approach

The Trust's development of its approach to risk management has taken place in the context of its commitment to recovery and wellbeing. This essentially places the person at the centre of decision-making about their care and aims to enhance personal autonomy and choice. It is clear that the extent to which the recovery approach is embedded into everyday practice varies across the Trust, and for some areas of service there is still a lot of work that needs to be done. This variation is thought to reflect the influence of individuals with a particular interest in recovery-orientated practice.

The Trust is currently mapping out the competencies of the recovery-orientated practitioner. These competencies will extend to teams against which to benchmark practice and will be used in staff development reviews and team away-days. The process of mapping staff competencies has highlighted the need to actively and meaningfully involve people in all aspects of their care, including shared responsibility for assessment of risk and risk-taking. It also recognizes the need to understand the importance of the service user's strengths and resources in developing care plans and risk management plans.

In addition, there is a recognized need to provide support for a cultural change and a training strategy for delivering recovery training to all clinical staff is currently in the process of being approved by the Trust.

Audit of Practice

The Trust conducts regular audits of CPA, including risk assessment and management. Until now, the standards for this audit have been broad and quantitative (e.g., is there a risk assessment and risk management plan), rather than qualitative (e.g., is there a risk formulation and identified protective factors) and the results of the audits have perhaps been overly positive. This came to light in the Service Review undertaken following the SUI described above. It emerged that the audit had been conducted prior to the introduction of the Clinical Risk Policy, such that the auditors did not have clear standards against which to assess the quality of the risk assessment and management plans. This certainly highlights the need for clear standards if we want to ensure governance of practice and evidence of high quality.

Therefore, a sample of the risk assessment process and management plans relating to a number of service users were reviewed by clinicians in some depth using the *Best Practice in Managing Risk* principles as a benchmark and then compared with the results of the audit of risk management practice for the Service. This more in-depth review highlighted considerable variation in the process and content of risk assessment and risk management plans. In future, the standards against which to benchmark practice and conduct an audit will draw on the standards outlined in the Clinical Risk Policy, which as I have said is substantially underpinned by the principles outlined in the *Best Practice in Managing Risk* document.

Summary and Conclusions

Sussex Partnership's commitment to delivering high quality care within the context of a strong emphasis on recovery and service user involvement certainly provides the scope for full implementation of all the principles outlined in the *Best Practice in Managing Risk* document. Implementation of these principles is also clearly aligned with the implementation of other key national guidance, including the Care Programme Approach and the Recovery Approach, the success of which is also designed to embed the principles of risk management in day-to-day practice.

In my view, the development and implementation of a Trust-wide Clinical Risk Policy has been the most important driver for improving day-to-day practice and implementing the principles outlined in *Best Practice in Managing Risk*, and I would recommend this as a key priority for establishing clear standards against which practice can be audited and improved. Implementing such a policy has, however, highlighted the need for training in both risk assessment and management and in recovery-orientated practice, and this should be considered a second key priority. A third priority is the need to establish clear leadership and lines of accountability, especially in the context of large-scale organizational changes, perhaps establishing a single point of contact, as we did. Our new integrated clinical and managerial leadership and governance structure is proving more successful in the task of reviewing our policy and in meeting the standards set out in both our policy and by external regulatory bodies, including the Care Quality Commission and the NHS Litigation Authority.

Finally, our Risk Management Review Panels and the use of the Root Cause Analysis tool are a very practical way for providing staff support and linking an individual or multidisciplinary team's practice and the organizational strategy, highlighting as it has, gaps in skills and competencies and gaps in service provision.

References

Care Services Improvement Partnership (2007). *Increasing Access to Psychological Therapies, South East Bulletin,* September/October.

Department of Health (2005). *A Short Guide to NHS Foundation Trusts,* available at www.dh.gov.uk/en/Publicationsandstatistics/Publications/PublicationsPolicyAndGuidance/ DH_4126013.

Department of Health (2006). *The National Health Service Litigation Authority framework document,* available at www.nhsla.com/NR/rdonlyres/D872241A-43E3-492B-8F74-32FB0586608F/0/Frameworkdocument.pdf.

Department of Health (2008a). *Best Practice in Managing Risk: Principles and Evidence for Best Practice in the Assessment and Management of Risk to Self and Others in Mental Health Services.* London: Department of Health.

Department of Health (2008b). *Refocusing the Care Programme Approach: Policy and Positive Practice Guidance,* available at www.dh.gov.uk/en/Publicationsandstatistics/Publications/ PublicationsPolicyAndGuidance/DH_083647.

National Patient Safety Agency (2009). *Root Cause Analysis Tool,* available at www.nrls. npsa.nhs.uk/resources/collections/root-cause-analysis.

Norfolk, Suffolk, and Cambridgeshire Strategic Health Authority (2003). *The Independent Inquiry into the Death of David Bennett (The Bennett Report),* available at image.guardian.co.uk/sys-files/Society/documents/2004/02/12/Bennett.pdf.

Social Care Institute for Excellence (2007). *A Common Purpose: Recovery in Future Mental Health Services.* Joint position paper, available at www.scie.org.uk/publications/ positionpapers/pp08.asp.

15

Case Study 3:
Learning from Experience – Using Clinical Risk Data to Influence and Shape Clinical Services

Louise Fountain and Patrick McKee

Introduction

Over the last 20 years, many excellent documents and guidance notes have been produced to support clinicians in the practice of recording and documenting clinical risk assessments and associated care plans. Yet there still seems to be resistance in many mental health trusts across England to implementing a robust set of clinical tools for the measurement and management of risk assessment and care planning. In England, the Care Programme Approach (CPA) was introduced in 1991 in an attempt to standardize care planning, linking CPA to risk assessments. Since that time, the CPA and associated clinical risk management structures have struggled to become established as part of mainstream practice in most mental health services. This has resulted in a number of major revisions to the national CPA policy, most notably in 1994, 1999 and 2007/2008. One of the main reasons cited for practitioner resistance was the correlation between CPA and an ever-increasing bureaucratic burden associated with the paperwork required to document care plans and clinical risk assessments. This, in part, was due to the changing clinical environment associated with the closure of psychiatric institutions and the expansion of community mental health services across England. Many practitioners have reported an increase in defensive practice, which has been directly linked to negative press coverage of high profile mental health service failures, usually linked to homicides and associated with care in the community.

This chapter will explore and attempt to explain some of the essential ingredients required to provide the right conditions to support practitioners to practice with greater freedom. We will attempt to do this by exploring our local practice using internal audit findings and the application of root cause analysis as a problem solving tool. The chapter will conclude by outlining local service changes within the Avon and Wiltshire Mental Health Partnership Trust (AWP) linked to both local and national initiatives that

Self-Harm and Violence: Towards Best Practice in Managing Risk in Mental Health Services, First Edition.
Edited by Richard Whittington and Caroline Logan.
© 2011 John Wiley & Sons, Ltd. Published 2011 by John Wiley & Sons, Ltd.

we believe will help the reader to implement effective care planning and clinical risk assessments while maintaining practitioner support for change.

The Local Context

Avon and Wiltshire Mental Health Partnership Trust is a large, specialist mental health trust. It was formed by the amalgamation, over a number of years, of the mental health services from several general health trusts coming together to create this functionally specialist trust.

The early stages of developing risk assessment

The process of developing clinical risk assessment within the trust took place over a number of years and might reasonably be described as an 'organic' process. This type of development is almost certainly not unusual within large organizations, but brings with it a number of difficulties, which with hindsight – or ideally with pre-planning – could best be avoided.

There were already a number of locality-based risk assessment protocols in use within the Trust, and to try to create a more 'joined up' way of doing things a committee was established to oversee both the development and dissemination of risk assessment and management procedures and the training of staff in their implementation and delivery. The decision was taken to use the same assessment tool throughout the Trust, and the Sainsbury Risk Assessment Tool (Morgan, 2002) was adopted as a template, which was then added to and adapted for local need. It was hoped that this strategy would improve risk assessment both by providing clinicians with a standardized approach to carrying it out and by facilitating better communication about risk between different clinical teams and areas.

While having the appropriate tools is important, the way in which such tools are implemented by practitioners has been found to be closely linked to effectiveness of use. The five-year report of the National Confidential Inquiry, *Avoidable Deaths* (Appleby *et al.*, 2006) identified some key factors in the prevention of homicides and suicide, including ensuring good staff communication, improving training and record-keeping, and aligning CPA and risk management more closely. The recommendations of a homicide inquiry around that time within AWP highlighted similar factors.

Auditing the assessment of risk

Within the Trust, standards for the collection of risk relevant information and the subsequent estimation of level of risk were set out in two key Trust policies/guidelines (*Policy and Tools on Assessment and Management of Risk* (AWP, 2002, and updated in 2005), and *Good Practice Guidelines for the Completion of Health and Social Care Records* (AWP, 2001).) A first step in reaching a better understanding of actual practice was to obtain a clearer picture through audit of the current standards of completion of the Trust risk documentation. The case files of 20% of all service users newly referred or re-referred for a new episode of care to the Adults of Working Age speciality within a calendar year in one locality of the Trust, were examined (Fountain, Shipway and Sidaway, 2007). As the risk assessment tools and procedures were by then standardized throughout the Trust, it was felt that the findings from this one part of the Trust could be generalized to the other areas. At that time, the total risk assessment package in use comprised an initial risk screen (a checklist tool identifying risk factors), a Risk Assessment and Management Plan (consisting of a chronological risk history and a rating of severity of risk), and a Summary and Interim Management Plan in which the risk plan was recorded. According to the policy, risk screening should have been carried out in all cases (100%), but there was no documented evidence in almost one-quarter (23%) of case files that *any* risk screening or assessment had been carried out. This means, of course, that over three-quarters (77%) of case files did have documented evidence of screening for risk, although almost three-quarters of those had been carried out using 'outdated' documentation (i.e., not the then current version). The outcome of those screens indicated that almost all (92%) of them should then have been subject to a full risk assessment, but this was the case for only between one-quarter and one-third (28%). Despite this, it was found that when full risk assessments had been carried out both risk ratings and risk plans had been completed in the majority of cases (94%) and there was evidence that practitioners had good awareness of those factors that predict risk and were able to produce comprehensive written plans to manage it.

The local audit findings and the evidence from the reviews were further supported by findings from the AWP annual Trust-wide CPA audits, which were reporting a similar picture across the majority of our community mental health teams. These findings were also consistent with anecdotal evidence reported from other NHS mental health trusts across England, prompting the most recent review of national CPA policy in 2007/2008.

The way forward

While there were clearly issues of concern arising from these findings, it was nevertheless encouraging that when the risk procedures were carried out fully they were well done. The problem appeared to be in the use of the *process* by which risk was assessed rather than a lack of skill in carrying it out. Having the tools and providing training in their use, which was already well established in the Trust, was simply not enough in itself. Practitioners needed to understand the importance of using all the tools and completing all the procedures – and they needed to be able to get the most up-to-date information about what they should be doing – the process – quickly, reliably, and clearly. It seemed likely, therefore, that the organizations strategic approach to doing this and its ability to take staff along with it needed to be considered further.

As an organization with high aspirations for the delivery of clinical excellence, AWP were keen to understand the reasons for the poor levels of compliance. The Trust therefore signed up to a project being led by one of the authors of the *Best Practice in Managing Risk* guidance (Department of Health, 2009). A small number of mental health trusts were assessed with regard to their strategic approach to managing clinical risk against the standards set out in the *Best Practice* document. This guidance was the first set of standards for the comprehensive assessment and management of clinical risk in mental health services in England, providing a route map to best practice across trusts. The assessment involved completing a self-rated performance review (see *Best Practice in Managing Risk Guidance*, Department of Health, 2009) against the 16 principles described in the guidance and led to the development of an action plan. The performance review demonstrated that AWP could report with confidence that they had a structured framework in place for CPA and Clinical Risk assessment. There were comprehensive policies that had been developed in response to national guidance as well as various local CPA policy amendments based on learning from internal incident reviews of unexpected deaths and the homicide enquiry. The AWP policy framework went into great detail in relation to the level of documentation required for both the completion of the clinical risk assessments, core CPA assessment, and associated care plans. In support of this, AWP were also confident that they had rolled out significant training to all of their staff and, to ensure the new CPA framework was sustainable, the organization made CPA and clinical risk assessment part of their mandatory training programme.

Areas of concern from the self-assessment performance review related to the application of policy and training into practice.

Root causes

Following an initial review of the wider AWP serious untoward incidents recommendations, it was clear that there were some structural blocks that the Trust were going to have to tackle if they were going to move this process forward. The themes identified by the risk committee sub-group thematic review included the following:

- lack of skills or knowledge in clinicians' ability to complete risk assessments;
- over-bureaucratic system resulting in duplication of assessment and care planning information, meaning too much paperwork;
- lack of practitioner time to complete detailed risk assessments;
- disorganized clinical case notes making it very difficult for clinicians to access relevant risk information;
- clinicians assuming that the risk screen was actually the full risk assessment and completing only that part of the process;
- lack of a structured referral process across the Trust resulting in many inappropriate referrals;
- no clear entry and exit criteria for clients coming in or moving through the service;
- poor caseload supervision in some areas;
- lack of an agreed capacity model with appropriate caseload volume controls;
- lack of clear clinical supervision in some teams; and
- poor culture for clinical monitoring of records.

It became apparent that the Trust needed to review their systems and structures regarding capacity management with particular attention to the referral process, case volume, caseload weighting, and administrative systems, including the structure of the health care record. The immediate action required to achieve this would be to develop an appropriate capacity model with an emphasis on volume controls for community teams.

AWP set up a small team of senior clinicians and managers to review team capacity and found that many teams were carrying caseloads in excess of 40 to 50 clients, some as high as 60 to 70. In addition, community mental health teams were being asked to complete the increased CPA documentation, including risk documentation, in order to meet Department of Health (DOH) compliance frameworks. This piece of work also highlighted that a large number of teams were dealing with a high level of inappropriate referrals. Many teams were running with as much as 50% of clinically inappropriate referrals received from a range of colleagues including GPs, local authority partners, and other external referring agencies. (Clinically inappropriate referrals is a term used to indicate referrals that identified a set of needs that did not match the services that AWP were commissioned to provide.)

It was obvious that there was no consistent Trust-wide system for the management of referrals. The impact of this was that there were no agreed acceptance criteria for new referrals, which resulted in staff spending anything up to three hours reviewing clients who were never going to be accepted into secondary mental health services. This activity was not recognized by Primary Care Trust (PCT) commissioners and as such unfunded. This, in turn, impacted on existing caseload activity resulting in a reduction in the number of clinically appropriate clients being seen by the Community Mental Health Team (CMHT). The effect of this was that practitioners were spending less time with their existing clients and completing fewer clinical assessments and supporting documentation. The CMHT response was to be pragmatic and ensure that they maintained direct patient face-to-face contact in response to the increasing demand but at a cost to the completion of risk assessments and CPA core assessment documentation.

The lack of an agreed referral process meant that there was a huge variation in the type and range of conditions being managed from one CMHT to another. We found that some teams were managing serious mental health and long-term conditions, whereas others were dealing with what could best be described as primary care mental health issues, such as mild to moderate anxiety and depression.

Additionally, the local review team observed that many practitioners were reluctant to discharge patients even when teams had clarity regarding discharge criteria. This appeared to relate to the practitioners desire to maintain contact with the patient 'just in case they became unwell in the future'. Many practitioners perceived this as positive practice arguing that ongoing maintenance would reduce future crises even when there were perfectly good primary care mental health services available via the local GP practice. In many areas, this practice remained unchallenged due to a lack of a structured caseload supervision process and an absence of a performance management system.

The Trust quickly realized that if we were going to move forward, we would need to start to develop a centralized approach to both referral systems and the entry and exit criteria underpinned by effective caseload management. This system would need to establish clear processes for volume controls within the structure that would allow for a better balance of direct patient contact to non-direct clinical activities, for example, generic team meetings or telephone activity.

Next Steps

Over the last year, the Trust has been setting up a process to redesign the structure and delivery of community services. As part of this process, AWP are developing a single point of access system with clear referral criteria alongside caseload management systems for all community mental health teams. This system will require a formal threshold for receiving and containing caseload volume within teams and, as a working principle, we are looking towards the Community Mental Health Policy Implementation Guidelines and recommended caseload size of approximately 25 to 35 per whole-time equivalent worker. The over-arching framework for developing this capacity model within AWP will be based on the DOH guidance on currency models, including care clusters, dovetailing with the national work on mental health currencies, particularly the issues relating to payment by results.

Payment by results (PbR) is the term given to a pricing structure based on units of activity within the NHS health care system. To develop this system for mental health, the Department of Health established a mental health PbR development group with the stated aim of further developing work done by the South West Yorkshire Mental Health Trust (2008) on care clusters into a mental health currency. The South West Yorkshire work was developed over a number of years with significant clinical input and advice, with the final product culminating in the development of a Clinical Decision Support Tool (CDST). The current version of the CDST is made up of 21 clinically meaningful care clusters containing groups of service users with similar presentations and care needs. These needs have been assessed and matched with similar sets of resource requirements which could, if required, be matched to a unit cost-based set of clinical interventions and aligned to staff resources. A standardized care package including activities and interventions was then developed to match each of the care clusters incorporating best practice guidance from the National Institute of Clinical Excellence (NICE) emphasizing the need for talking therapies. An additional process using a clinical outcome measure based on the *Health of the Nation Outcome Scale* (HoNOS, now re-titled the *Cluster Allocation Tool*) further reinforced this assessment process.

The national work on care clusters has been embraced by AWP and is central to influencing caseload management and clinical supervision structures. The system offers clear structures to develop acceptance/step up–down criteria, as well as enabling patient flows across the care pathway using pre-agreed assessment criteria. Movement from one cluster to another is supported through what are known as transitional protocols, which are built on a set of assessment rules based on the relevant cluster definitions, including the appropriate clinical outcome measure and associated staff resources. The CDST also offers excellent guidance on the key components of care that a service user can expect in each cluster and is underpinned by a recommended set of clinical interventions based on best practice, primarily NICE guidance.

Avon and Wiltshire Mental Health Partnership NHS Trust have set up three working groups for Adult, Older Adult, and Specialist and Secure Services to test and implement care clusters into operational structures alongside the roll out of a newly commissioned RIO information system. This is all part of a major clinical redesign process and early indications are showing very positive signs with practitioners reporting that care clusters appear to be highly intuitive and easy to understand and apply to practice. It is also becoming apparent that not all of the clusters (or aspects of individual clusters) need to be delivered by secondary care mental health services. Either primary care or third sector providers, such as established voluntary sector organizations, can deliver many interventions and activities within clusters. Critical to this process will be the need to work with both PCT and Local Authority Mental Health Commissioners to ensure that the right systems, funding and services are delivered in a cost effective and efficient manner using the most appropriate providers of mental health care. In effect, this type of agreement, with clear boundaries around referrals into the service, including standards around the quality of referral, should mean that team managers will have greater levels of empowerment to ensure that clinicians deliver the appropriate interventions based on the pre-agreed care packages. With a more efficient application of caseload controls, AWP in partnership with commissioners and managers should also see an increase in patient turnover as inappropriate referrals should be reduced. Interventions should be better targeted and ineffective interventions easily identified and discontinued via more effective measurements of clinical outcomes. With transitional protocols agreed across a plurality of providers, many services users will be discharged from secondary mental health care more quickly due to clarity of acceptance criteria across the care providers. This will reinforce the social inclusion agenda and reduce the stigma associated with secondary mental health care. This combined with the newly commissioned RIO electronic health record, supported by an AWP revised clinical and managerial supervision policy, should ensure that clinical practice and in particular the completion of high quality assessments and care planning processes are effectively addressed in a sustainable operational structure.

Conclusions

This chapter has tried to look at some of the learning that one organization has gone through following concerns about serious clinical incidents and the application of tools and systems to support practitioners in their work. For AWP, the first thing that became clear was the impact that organizational change can have on a service and the time taken to merge and then manage organizational cultures before they start to operate as one system. The second lesson was to acknowledge that change takes time and can best be seen as a journey where things may not always be achieved at the first attempt. For AWP, the application of a root cause analysis approach provided the organization with the opportunity to examine problems from a range of different angles, providing the Trust with a number of themes that needed to be addressed. We discovered that each of the individual themes could not be isolated as the root cause of the problem but collectively the themes converged to adversely influence systems that may have then inhibited rather than supported good practice in clinical risk management.

The learning from this journey has resulted in AWP developing structures and systems to underpin best practice with the desired aim of creating a working environment that is conducive to good clinical practice. This has resulted in the organization aligning clinical service redesign with the development of robust operational structures that support positive risk assessment and care planning. The central theme revolves around effective capacity and caseload management, incorporating clear systems for referral, triage, admission, and discharge criteria to support more effective patient flow through the system. To achieve this, we utilized the most recent national thinking regarding care clusters and clinical outcome measures, underpinned by clear transitional protocols to support patient flows across the care pathway. In addition, we have had to recognize the need for good systems for managing the health and social care records alongside better systems for staff support and supervision. Finally, we are introducing a new electronic records system via the RIO system and reviewed training priorities to ensure staff can take maximum advantage of the new structures and associated clinical recording systems.

We have been fortunate to have been able to align our work to recent Department of Health developments in relation to PbR, clinical outcome measures, and the most recent thinking on care clusters. The learning from our experience is that any organization struggling to deliver a systematic and safe system for the monitoring and management of clinical risk will need to address all of the above points if they are to achieve a robust system that is supported and owned by the staff delivering the service.

References

Appleby, L., Shaw, J., Kapur, N., Windfuhr, K., Ashton, A., Swinson, N., While, D., *et al.* (2006). *Avoidable Deaths: Five-Year Report of the National Confidential Inquiry into*

Suicide and Homicide by People with Mental Illness. Manchester: University of Manchester.

Avon and Wiltshire Mental Health Partnership NHS Trust (2001). *Good Practice Guidelines for the Completion of Health and Social Care Records.* AWP Policy July 2001.

Avon and Wiltshire Mental Health Partnership NHS Trust (2002). *Policy and Tools on Assessment and Management of Risk* (in partnership with the Local authority Social Services Departments within trust Area TW/CPC/012, June 2002 and May 2005 – the 2002 policy was revised in May 2005.

Department of Health (2001). *The Mental Health Policy Implementation Guide.* London: Department of Health.

Department of Health (2002). *Community Mental Health Teams.* Mental Health Policy Implementation Guide. London: Department of Health.

Department of Health (2009). *Best Practice in Managing Risk.* London: Department of Health.

Fountain, L., Shipway, L., and Sidaway, J. (2007). *AWP Clinical Audit Report: Level of Compliance with Trust Risk Documentation Completion in South Wiltshire in 2005.*

Morgan, S. (2002). *Clinical Risk Management: A Clinical Tool and Practitioner Manual.* London: Sainsbury Centre for Mental Health.

South West Yorkshire Mental Health Trust (amended 2008). *Integrated Package Approach to Care (INPAC) – CDST, Clinical Decision Making Tool – Version 2.*

16

Case Study 4:
From Ticking Boxes to Effective
Risk Management

Lorna Jellicoe-Jones, Mark Love, Roy Butterworth and Claire Riding

Service Context

This chapter will discuss the development and revision of risk assessment and management processes within the Guild Lodge medium and low secure mental health service. Guild Lodge is a 122-bedded National Health Service (NHS) unit at the centre of Lancashire, serving a population of approximately 1.9 million people in the north of England. The service incorporates inpatient and community male and female care provision for clients who present with a broad range of mental health needs together with risk and offending behaviours. These needs and behaviours have contributed to their presenting a risk to others which has been assessed as requiring secure service provision. Professional staff within the service includes psychiatry, nursing, pharmacy, occupational therapy, psychology, and social work. These disciplines provide specific and multidisciplinary team (MDT) oriented clinical interventions.

The inpatient client group is drawn from a mixed urban and rural population. It is predominantly male, with over 85% of the current male population being identified as white British. Approximately 17% of the inpatient population are female. The service accepts referrals for adults over the age of 18 with the majority of current inpatients (over 75%) being between the ages of 18 and 48 years. Typically, service developments and policy initiatives require a consideration of clients' clinical and risk presentations and needs, alongside an awareness of the diversity of professional roles, requirements, and standards involved in meeting these.

Within the context of the service in question, this chapter will discuss the development and effective implementation of a revised risk policy and procedure. Our experience in this area suggested that the following issues required attention:

- how far the service or risk assessment and management processes met *Best Practice* guidance;

Self-Harm and Violence: Towards Best Practice in Managing Risk in Mental Health Services, First Edition.
Edited by Richard Whittington and Caroline Logan.
© 2011 John Wiley & Sons, Ltd. Published 2011 by John Wiley & Sons, Ltd.

- the identification of priorities for change and improvement, incorporating clinical, client, staffing and organizational needs; and
- the identification of key motivators and obstacles to improving practice.

While the focus of this chapter is on secure mental health service provision, our contacts and experience of working with community colleagues suggest the issues covered have equal relevance in other service contexts.

Historical Factors and Major Influences for Change

Guild Lodge has a strong tradition for establishing local evidence-based risk assessment and management policy and procedures. The policy development process is multidisciplinary in nature. In 1999, a bespoke comprehensive model for risk assessment and management was devised for the service. Evidence gained from a review of this model in 2003 informed the emergence of 'home grown' comprehensive risk assessment tools (Routine and Elective Risk Assessments: see Box 16.1).

Box 16.1: Initial policy: risk assessment and management tools

Routine review risk assessment is locally developed, evidence-based, structured clinical risk assessment (Webster *et al.*, 1997). It focuses upon historical and collateral data, including details of past risk and offending behaviour, risk vulnerability factors, risk management proposals, risk and clinical formulation points. In conjunction with standardized tools, this assessment supports the process of the situation-specific risk assessment. Responsibility falls on medical staff to complete these, as well as to update at every CPA review, or at any other major changes (in conjunction with the wider multidisciplinary team).

Elective risk assessment supports the day-to-day requirements of managing risks at care transitions and key decision points in care planning. Used to assess dynamic changes in relation to the routine risk assessment and the individual's treatment and progression. Important at various junctures, for example, initial admission, accessing occupational therapy department, transferring from ward to ward, accessing the community. All qualified health care professionals are responsible for completing this tool and it has to be cross-referenced with routine risk assessment.

A subsequent policy and practice review in 2006 noted the existence of elements of good practice which it was felt would benefit from further development. These included the following:

- evidence of multidisciplinary working and perspectives on risk;
- the existence of comprehensive risk assessment and management practices, arising from the above;
- value and ownership of 'home grown' tools for staff (Routine and Elective Risk Assessments, see Box 16.1);

- formal recognition of the benefits of therapeutic risk taking as a core part of the assessment tools;
- provision of structured assessment tools to support clinical reasoning; and
- recognition of the dynamic nature of risk in the assessment tools used in, and for, clinical reviews.

This review, however, also highlighted the need for enhanced multidisciplinary involvement in all aspects of risk assessment and management, and the need for regular clinical evaluation linked to the Care Programme Approach (CPA) process. Concerns had also begun to emerge at this time regarding the quality of staff practice and outcomes in applying the risk management model. Guild Lodge had entered into a frenetic period of unprecedented growth and expansion as a medium secure service. Over a two-year period, the service doubled in size from approximately 60 to 120 beds. This was in the context of increased referrals for long stay and rehabilitation provision. Over time, patient incident reviews contributed to evidence that risk management practice was deviating from the original policy intentions. This appeared to support wider evidence that practice was becoming increasingly fragmented and inconsistent.

The staff recruitment pool that was available to meet the service expansion was predominantly graduates from university with relatively little experience of risk management practice. A lack of formal structured staff training further compounded the problem and contributed to a dependence on uncoordinated experiential learning, an informal cascading of information, and individual uncoordinated disciplinary practices regarding the induction and orientation of newly appointed staff.

Audits highlighted that historical risk assessments were not being routinely completed and that this was impacting on the quality of subsequent risk assessments. Evidence suggested that staff were adopting a number of compensatory practices to address their lack of understanding of risk assessment and management. These included failing to individualize assessments, focusing on historical evidence of risk, and an excessive adoption of information used in previously completed risk documents (a 'cut and paste' approach). These compensatory approaches clearly failed to acknowledge the dynamic relationship between risk history and clients' current situations and needs. The use of electronic record-keeping, which staff had limited skills to implement, further compounded the situation. Additional concerns were raised following routine record-keeping audits where, for example, tools being used to record risk assessments were frequently found to be non-compliant with professional record-keeping standards (e.g., evidence of a lack of, or inaccurate, dating, signing and authorship and multidisciplinary involvement; and a lack of clear client identification).

Research undertaken within the service at this time examined multidisciplinary staff knowledge and awareness of individual clients' index offences (Fallon and West, 2006). This concluded that there were significant gaps in staff awareness of fundamental risk information that should have been recorded on the overarching Routine Risk Assessment. This was sometimes due to staff not being aware of this assessment document, or it not having been completed for individual clients.

The need for a policy review was further reinforced by the Department of Health publication *Best Practice in Managing Risk* guidance (Department of Health, 2009). The need to ensure that the best practice guidance was being adopted within the service became paramount. The following key practice points to address within our local policy were identified: risk management being a required competence for all practitioners;

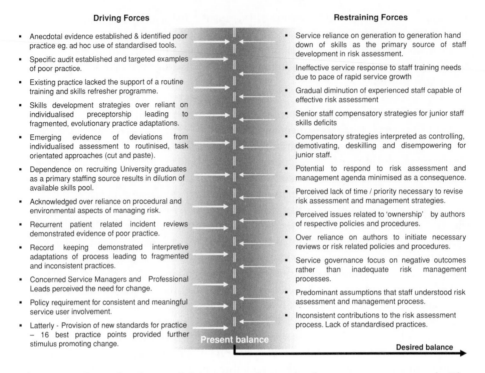

Figure 16.1 Internal and external drivers impacting on the change management agenda. The desired balance would be achievable by overcoming the restraining forces. Adapted from Lewin (1951).

the realization of effective collaboration with clients; the routine inclusion of risk formulation; the need to nurture a consistent approach to risk assessment and management; contemporaneous staff training; and the need for greater consistency in risk communication.

Collectively, these issues can be summarized within a force field analysis framework (Lewin, 1951). Force field analysis facilitates the opportunity to consider forces supporting change and those that might represent obstacles. Within the context of Guild Lodge and the changes required in risk policy and practice at this time, these are provided within the force field analysis outlined in Figure 16.1.

Case Example: Evidence of the Need for Change

The case study outlined below (Box 16.2) demonstrates key clinical and practice concerns experienced at the time (i.e., how *not* to complete a risk assessment). These further contributed to the revision of policy and the review of risk assessment processes. The client in the case study was being considered for greater access to the occupational therapy department in order to facilitate attendance at a broader range of treatment groups. Consistent with policy at the time, the Elective Risk Assessment (see Box 16.1) was presented to the multidisciplinary team, in order to inform their decision on the appropriateness of this change in the client's care arrangements.

Box 16.2: Vignette: Case study – traditional risk assessment

Joe is a 30-year-old male with a diagnosis of schizophrenia. Prior to this admission, he led an itinerant lifestyle travelling around England and being involved in pre-dominantly acquisitive offending behaviours, as well as having several involuntary admissions to local psychiatric hospitals.

His current admission was due to a serious physical assault on a female member of nursing staff, resulting in imprisonment and his eventual transfer to the male acute ward within Guild Lodge. He has a long-standing history of violence and aggression, which appears to be associated with his delusional beliefs, and further exacerbated by excessive alcohol and illicit substance misuse.

Joe has had difficulties sustaining relationships with females in the past and since his admission has had problems working alongside both female staff and peers. Joe has been on the male acute admission ward for nearly nine months and has undergone various neuropsychological assessments that have identified marked cognitive deficits with some mild learning problems. Consequently, Joe has benefited from a structured and consistent approach to his care and engagement (using a combination of visual and verbal prompts and directions to maintain some level of independence).

Most of his therapy sessions have occurred on the ward and within single gender activities in the occupational therapy department. He has now progressed towards, and is requesting to have, greater access to the occupational therapy department to attend various treatment groups (pottery, art, and cooking). The occupational therapy department caters for a mixed gender population, based within the con-fines of the secure perimeter alongside the admission ward. Consequently, an elective risk assessment has been completed in order to support and allow access to the previously outlined activities:

Typical questions outlined in an elective risk assessment:

- What are the main risk behaviours in this case study?
- What factors or variables impact upon the risk behaviours identified?
- From the previous questions, how will the above be managed?
- What benefits will Joe gain by engaging in the above activities?
- What would stop Joe engaging in the above – in other words what are warning signs of risk?
- How can Joe be involved in the risk assessment process?

Abridged and actual content of the elective risk assessment

Joe's main risk behaviours identified by the clinician completing this risk assessment were as follows:

- violence and aggression;
- absconding; and
- illicit substance misuse.

The main factors and variables within the elective assessment undertaken on Joe focused predominantly on his history of risk behaviours. The management plan outlined the need for the nurse in charge to assess Joe's mental state prior to departing from the ward, with all policies and procedures to be adhered to at all times. He was to be escorted by one experienced male at all times – with this member of staff remaining with him for the full duration of his time in the occupational therapy department.

Any deterioration in Joe's mental state would result in him being escorted back to the ward. The perceived benefits of this activity included the following:

- the opportunity to assess Joe away from the ward environment;
- the increased potential for an improvement in the therapeutic relationship with Joe; and
- the potential for an increase in Joe's self esteem.

Factors that would stop Joe from engaging in activities in the occupational therapy department again referred to 'any deterioration' in his mental state or increase in the previously outlined risk behaviours. In addition, non-compliance with his medication and 'breaking rules' either on the ward or within the activities would result in Joe having no access to the occupational therapy department as a risk management response.

Factors Supporting the Need for Change: Further Discussion

The use of the elective risk assessment tool highlighted some important questions and guidance in the overall assessment of risk and how this could potentially be managed in Joe's case. However, as previously outlined in Figure 16.1, there remained a number of key issues to consider in relation to the completed assessment tool and good practice.

Typically, in this and similar cases, there was little focus upon the situation that Joe would be actually engaging in. There was an over-emphasis on procedural and environmental management of generic risk behaviours rather than, for example, relational security. Despite Joe having no history of absconding, this appeared as an identified risk behaviour. Absconding appears to be a popular concern for staff who assess risk behaviours, possibly due to the fact that the client is based within a secure setting and the range of potential negative consequences (clinical, service-wise, and politically) that an absconding involves. Historical factors are clearly important when managing risks. One was left uncertain, however, in Joe's case, about all the other important and relevant current factors that would impact upon Joe's engagement and on his team's understanding and responses.

Within Joe's assessment, there had been no consideration of his cognitive and learning problems, or reference to specific mental state symptoms. There was no mention of potential difficulties working with the opposite gender, or how to manage these. Specific early warning signs relating to deterioration in Joe's behaviour and his mental health were also absent. Joe was not involved at all in the risk assessment process.

Some benefits of the proposed new activity were highlighted, as outlined earlier. There was, however, minimal reference to any strengths or protective factors that could ameliorate against the risk factors and behaviours. Examples might have included the benefit of a highly structured environment and the use of varied prompts by staff to enable positive engagement by Joe. Joe's case study did not explicitly earmark his early warning signs. The elective tool focused upon a 'general deterioration in Joe's mental state or an increase in his risk behaviours'. There was no reference to any specific symptoms or factors that would stop him from accessing, or remaining in, the occupational therapy department.

The assessment failed to consider specific prodromal signs, issues related to cognitive/learning deficits, or potential conflict with females. Finally, Joe's lack of involvement in any part of the risk assessment process resulted in his valued opinions, strengths, and his perceptions of any difficulties not being taken into consideration.

Policy Development and Implementation: Achieving Improved Practice?

In response to evidence regarding both the preceding practice and policy issues, and those highlighted in the case study, a multidisciplinary risk working group was set up in November 2006. This comprised multidisciplinary front line staff and clinical managers. The group's remit was to undertake a systematic review of risk assessment and management processes, culminating in a revised local policy and procedure within the service. The group aimed to facilitate practice development, to address the local concerns previously identified, and to ensure consistency with the *Best Practice* guidance. Key features of the policy and its implementation are outlined in Table 16.1.

Table 16.1 *Best Practice* implementation.

Best Practice *guidance*	Features of policy/implementation
Risk management as a required competence for all mental health practitioners	• Advance policy awareness/training sessions for all senior staff • Training provided to multidisciplinary staff groups • Cascade sessions organized to train staff at all levels • Annual refresher training for all qualified multidisciplinary staff • Electronic induction awareness pack available to all new staff • Three-year refresher training on HCR-20 + START
Risk management to be constructed in a spirit of collaboration (including service with user and carer)	• User and carer involvement as key section in policy • Risk documents record nature and level of service user/carer involvement • Risk assessment reviews as part of CPA process, to which service users are invited • Training to include real-life vignettes to address staff understanding, skills and confidence in this area
Risk assessments to be active 'working' documents	• Changed name from elective to situation-specific • High profile MDT training undertaken on new policy and assessments • Rationale and evidence base for policy and assessments provided to staff • Reality-based training vignettes addressing daily concerns and obstacles of practice

(Continued)

Table 16.1   (*Continued*)

Best Practice *guidance*	*Features of policy/implementation*
Risk management to be based on recognition of service user strength and emphasize recovery	• Service-wide training on recovery models implemented alongside policy (including provision of training by external service user) • Including START in risk assessment policy (focus on service user strengths and needs) • Situation-specific risk assessment includes evidence of progress and benefits of positive risk taking to service user
Risk management as an organizational strategy	• Risk working/policy group as part of service-wide clinical governance processes • Risk policy and implementation group represented on service-wide clinical governance training/research and audit groups • Service multidisciplinary action plan for policy implementation, training, and audit • Regular policy and practice audit; outcomes fed back into service governance forums
Risk management plan to include formulations and actions to be taken including in crisis	• MDT formulation as a key emphasis in policy and procedure • Inclusion of crisis and contingency plans as part of both routine and situation-specific risk assessments
Use of structured clinical judgement approach	• Routine risk assessment and HCR-20 for service user admission and at review
Awareness of capacity for service user change over time	• Required review of routine risk assessment and HCR-20 at each CPA • Use of situation-specific assessments: assessing specific needs at care transition points/changes
Management plans to be developed by multidisciplinary and agency teams	• Advance and annual MDT training sessions on policy and risk assessment • Incorporation of flow chart and procedure outlining specific roles and input by MDT in risk assessment process • Requirement for evidence of MDT input and review in risk assessment documents • Risk assessment review linked to multidisciplinary CPA meetings
To improve consistency in practice	• Advance multidisciplinary training, consultation and feedback opportunities on policy implementation • Attendance monitoring of training to ensure all service and teams had informed staff • MDT training, service-wide, including senior and frontline staff

The 'Elective' risk assessment document was re-named the 'Situation Specific' risk assessment. This was considered to reflect more clearly the aim and purpose of this assessment and to avoid any misinterpretation by staff that they could 'elect' to complete it or not – as had been fed back to the risk working group during the consultation processes!

This review opened up the opportunity for the original authors to broaden the perceived ownership of the risk management policies and procedures, and to share the responsibility for developing systems based upon wider consultation. The previous use of clinical assessment approaches was subsequently bolstered by the inclusion of evidence-based actuarial assessment tools thus adding to the quality of the overall process.

As this local review and change initiative began to gain momentum, key stakeholders from various staff groups within the service were recruited to participate and to provide specific contributions. These included research into alternative evidence-based tools, policy and procedure development, the design of revised documentation, and the design and delivery of robust staff education. Specific standards that were developed included the requirement for all staff involved in risk management to receive a standardized training that would be updated at least every three years. Revised competency frameworks contributing to induction and preceptorship arrangements, and provision of clear expectations for professional practice, were proposed to supplement this.

As part of wider service evaluation aimed at improving MDT working and client involvement in treatment and risk management at this time, an audit project was also undertaken. This examined the processes and practices involved in clinically (i.e., client) oriented multidisciplinary meetings. The audit led to the production of guidelines aimed at clarifying multidisciplinary attendees' roles and responsibilities at such meetings. Consequently, the structure and focus of the meetings and communication and feedback processes all improved (see Figure 16.2). Additional opportunities for client input and involvement were also clarified.

The overall commitment to, and involvement in, implementing the policy was considered extremely positive. Senior staff in nursing, occupational therapy, and psychology jointly coordinated and implemented the training programmes achieving service-wide attendance from all disciplines. Funding was obtained for externally facilitated training sessions on specific risk assessment tools:

- *Historical, Clinical and Risk-20* (HCR-20; Webster *et al.*, 1997) and
- *Short-Term Assessment of Risk and Treatability* (START; Webster *et al.*, 2006).

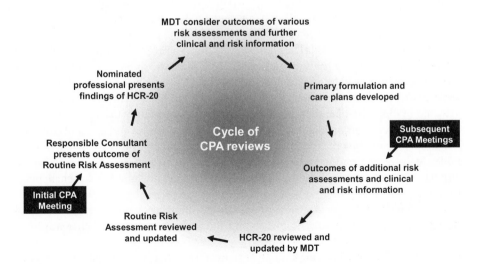

Figure 16.2 Incorporating a multidisciplinary review of risk within the Care Programme Approach (CPA) process.

The HCR-20 is a structured, validated violence risk assessment examining historical and clinical risk factors and risk management variables. The START is also a structured, validated clinical risk assessment for the dynamic assessment of seven often inter-related risks and their treatability.

These workshops were attended by a large number of qualified staff from all relevant disciplines. Consultation processes prior to, and during, training elicited feedback on a number of further key implementation issues. A range of staff perspectives demonstrated positive support and further concerns. (These, and our responses to them, will be discussed shortly.) Further plans and timescales were agreed for implementation and subsequent policy audit and review.

At this point, the reader is invited to consider the following questions in relation to their own service, as questions which were key in informing our policy and practice reviews:

- How far do your service or risk assessment and management processes meet *Best Practice* guidelines?
- What would be your priorities for change or improvement considering clinical, service and staffing issues?
- What key motivators and obstacles to improving practice exist in your service?

What We Have Learnt: Ticking Boxes or Effective Processes?

A planned objective evaluation of the implementation of our policy was undertaken in November 2008 by clinical governance staff and a service-based Modern Matron. The audit was based on a quantitative approach aimed at examining the nature and extent to which key aspects of the policy and procedure had been achieved. Key areas which were examined included the use of the required risk assessments at different stages in the care pathway, evidence of MDT input, and evidence of client and carer input.

Alongside this work, staff across the service were asked to provide feedback on their qualitative experiences of implementing the policy and the new risk assessment measures and documentation that were part of it. The outcomes of the audit suggested that while some positive progress had been achieved a number of the previously identified practice development needs remained. The audit showed, for example, that a number of patients did not have overarching routine risk assessments. There was limited evidence of service user and carer involvement and limited documentation providing a rationale for this. Assessments were frequently difficult to access in service user files and there was inconsistent evidence of multidisciplinary involvement in risk assessment and management.

Feedback from staff highlighted the significant time pressures and demands involved in completing assessments which required a multidisciplinary process, as stated in the policy. Staff also expressed concern about inconsistencies in practice and policy awareness amongst senior clinicians. They highlighted the difficulties often involved in challenging this, due to different power positions and roles in the service.

As previously, the reader is invited to consider the following questions, as key questions which arose for us at this stage, in our attempts to evaluate progress and change:

- If you had been undertaking similar work in your service, what initial outcomes and feedback do you think you would have obtained?
- What factors might have contributed to this?

- Would you say our attempts to improve practice had succeeded? What would you do at this stage?

As part of our commitment to evolving policy and practice, the multidisciplinary risk working group in our service continues to meet. The group is currently undertaking further training and policy review work based on ongoing feedback we have received. External evaluation and perspectives might conclude that our work to date has had limited success in improving practice. Our quantitative audit results, for example, would seem to suggest this and a possible need for actions in the following areas:

- an 'action plan' involving more stringent monitoring activity;
- the design of specific outcomes for 'failing' areas;
- increased training and management input; and
- additional policy and practice development.

The service embraces opportunities for further improvements and learning. Based on feedback from the audit activity, amendments are being made to the policy and training. This will include attempts to ease some of the administration demands, and to increase the 'user friendliness' of the documentation. Other amendments will focus on the inclusion of community service pathways, the need to maintain regular multidisciplinary awareness, and the need to address the real challenges of genuine client and carer collaboration.

Our experience, however, is that successful sustained policy implementation and practice change requires more than a focus on the usual quantitative outcome activities such as action plans, training, consultation, monitoring, and audit. It requires attention to the key issues outlined in Figure 16.3.

These issues require a sustained focus on the process of how outcomes are achieved, as opposed to the outcome alone. In order to remain responsive to client, staff, and service

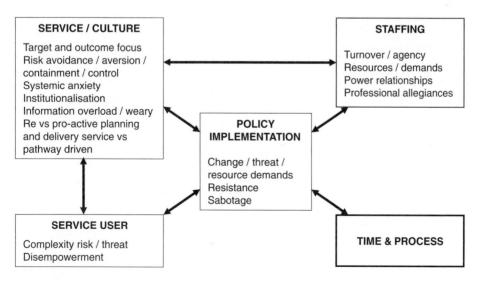

Figure 16.3 The relationships between key organizational dynamics and successful sustained policy implementation and practice change.

needs, change processes must be evolutionary in nature incorporating both planned and emergent processes. Our approaches to change, which have utilized cycles of audit and policy review, have mirrored models advocated by the National Health Service Institute for Innovation and Improvement (NHSI, 2005). The use of the 'plan, do, study, act' cycle will further facilitate opportunities for learning while offering a structured approach to change management.

Future approaches to policy and practice reviews will continue to be supplemented by the development of specific training opportunities, which will be replicated over time as regular refresher programmes for staff. Effective, sustained, and owned change, in our experience, will further involve attention to some of the core aspects of multidisciplinary and secure service working, and the key clinical, cultural, professional, and personal issues previously listed in Figure 16.3.

We continue to maintain and improve our focus on improving practice through training, consultation and review methods, future planned engagement with both staff and clients, and continuous reflective practice and working. These processes will continue to attempt to acknowledge and incorporate the issues listed in Figure 16.3 to enable us to achieve the ideal of both productive and meaningful processes and outcomes. Genuine effective change requires time, leadership and an ongoing commitment to collaborative working. Our final challenge is, perhaps, to maintain this awareness and commitment at all levels of our service provision, whilst managing to achieve the concrete outcomes and goals we aspire to in this fundamental area of secure service practice.

References

Department of Health (2009). *Best Practice in Managing Risk: Principles and Guidance for Best Practice in the Assessment and Management of Risk to Self and Others in Mental Health Services*. London: Department of Health.

Fallon, A. and West, A. (2006). Multidisciplinary Staff's Knowledge of Patients' Index Offences, unpublished study, Guild Lodge Secure Service, Lancashire Care NHS Trust.

NHSI (2005). *Improvement Leader's Guide; Improvement Knowledge and Skills: General Improvement Skills*. Coventry: National Health Service Institute for Innovation and Improvement.

Lewin, K. (1951). *Field Theory in Social Science*. New York: Harper & Row.

Webster, C. D., Douglas, K. S., Eaves, D., and Hart, S.D. (1997). *HCR-20: Assessing Risk for Violence (Version 2)*. Vancouver, BC: Simon Fraser University.

Webster, C. D., Martin, M. L., Brink, J., Nicholls, T. L., and Middleton, C. (2006). *Short-term Assessment of Risk and Treatability (START): A Clinical Guide for Evaluation Risk and Recovery*. Vancouver, BC: Forensic Psychiatric Services Commission, Canada.

17

Conclusions

Caroline Logan and Richard Whittington

In the last two decades, mental health services have found their activities with service users and within their organizational structures increasingly dominated by the belief that risks can be calculated, managed, and ultimately prevented. Service users have increasingly found their distress framed in terms of the risks they may present to themselves or others. Organizations have become increasingly cautious in order to limit the possibility that service users in their care will be harmful, an outcome that could result in very damaging external scrutiny and criticism, even prosecution and litigation. Consequently, practitioners increasingly face the challenge of engaging therapeutically and meaningfully with service users, while at the same time trying to manage any risks they may pose to themselves or others *and* containing the anxieties of their managers and directors fearful of other kinds of risks arising from the care their practitioners provide. In this volume, we have attempted to address the issue of clinical risk assessment and management in mental health services. Specifically, we have attempted to describe this three-way dynamic between service users and carers, practitioners, and service managers and directors in order to acknowledge its existence and offer practical solutions for all tasked with negotiating a way through the complex challenge of risk management. And in this volume, we have one key recommendation: the basis for risk management, whether at an individual or an organizational level, is understanding the risks posed.

This volume has brought together many voices. Kay Sheldon and Sally Luxton have written most powerfully about what it is like to be on the receiving end of risk assessment and risk management, as service user and carer, respectively. Kay describes very distressing experiences of treatment and restriction – her own and others – when it appeared that the risks posed were not well understood, when caution was exercised instead of positive risk management, and collaboration in treatment and care seemed little more than an impossible ideal. Sally's experiences were more positive – because she felt consulted and relevant in the care of her son, because the services with which she was involved tried to understand what it was like both for her son and herself – an example of how liberating

Self-Harm and Violence: Towards Best Practice in Managing Risk in Mental Health Services, First Edition.
Edited by Richard Whittington and Caroline Logan.
© 2011 John Wiley & Sons, Ltd. Published 2011 by John Wiley & Sons, Ltd.

positive risk management can feel, even if the outcomes are not always as hoped. We made the decision to start this volume with their experiences rather than with the evidence or research and clinical practice, because it is the experiences of people like Kay and Sally that are at the centre of all that we do – and could possibly do better. We chose to have their chapters set the tone for the book and we commend both women and the friends, family members, and colleagues they consulted for giving us the means to understand more and to know the value of trying.

The evidence that follows, therefore, needs to be viewed in the content of such personal experience. Maria Leitner and Wally Barr provided a summary of international research on suicide and self-harm risk assessment and management. Informed and accessible, it provides an up-to-date understanding of the strengths of the field and its gaps and weaknesses. Similarly, Richard Whittington, James McGuire, Tilman Steinert, and Beverley Quinn highlighted key findings of recent research into violence and its risk assessment and management. Both these chapters, and the one to follow by Kirsten Windfuhr and Nicola Swinson, in which they highlighted how evidence has come to underpin national policy on homicide and suicide prevention in England and Wales, demonstrate how research has improved understanding and how it can come to inform what we do across complex health systems. In order not to lose sight of what we regard as the necessity of service user and carer involvement, Helen Gilburt finished this first section on evidence with a chapter on empirical research into service user involvement in risk decision-making – making experience real in terms of data and coordinating action on the basis of an understanding of what is really needed.

Continuing in this vein, the following section focused on clinical practice issues. Caroline Logan, Norbert Nedopil, and Thomas Wolf, followed by Ben Thomas, looked into the demanding task of turning vast amounts of research evidence into coherent practice and coordinated national and local policy, while not losing sight of the service user and carer experience. Similarly, Caroline Logan, Rajan Nathan, and Andrew Brown directly tackled the issue of understanding by looking at the practical task of formulation, specifically as it applies to risk – the process of understanding the underlying mechanism of risk in order to prepare hypotheses for change, or risk management. Formulation links risk assessment to risk management – arguably, risk management needs an understanding of the risks posed in order to be relevant and proportionate. This chapter offers a guide to formulation, as do the two chapters that follow – by Paul Clifford and then Richard Whitehead, Ged Carney, and Beth Greenhill. Both offer a guide to positive risk management, another complex and not well understood requirement of modern mental health care made critical by the experiences of service users such as Kay and Sally.

Our volume has concluded with four case studies of ways in which very different services have attempted to put *Best Practice in Managing Risk* into practice. These case studies illustrate the drive to improve care in these representative services and the barriers that can arise in attempting to do so. Because this is the reality of best practice in clinical risk assessment and management – things can get in the way of good intentions to deliver quality mental health care. These case studies offer a guide to how these services tried to avoid and overcome barriers and produce better organized services valued more by their users as a result.

What we do not understand, we cannot risk manage with confidence or with any real expectation of lasting success. This is why improving understanding has been at the heart of all of the chapters and case studies in this volume. Sometimes, an understanding of the risks presented by a service user will not be easy or even possible to achieve. But through the effort of trying in collaboration with the service user will come improved awareness of the problems presented, and out of all this the possibility of a positive risk management plan that is more proportionate in its demands than might otherwise have been the case.

A Route Map

Introduction

We have presented a great deal of experience, evidence, and practice in this volume. Where do we hope you might go from here? In this concluding section, we synthesize the recommendations made by each of our contributors into sections addressing in turn service users and carers, practitioners, and service managers. Recommendations are both for those individual groups to consider, and for the others to examine, in order that they might know what our expectations are for progress in clinical risk assessment and management practice in the next few years.

From service users and carers

In her chapter, Kay Sheldon proposed a manifesto for risk management intended for practitioners and the organizations they work for. Her manifesto consisted of ten rec-ommendations – commandments, if you like:

1. Respect us.
2. Put our experiences at the centre of risk management.
3. Involve us.
4. Base your approach on promoting and protecting our rights.
5. Explain what risk assessment is to us.
6. See us as individuals, and not defined by a particular diagnosis or situation.
7. Give us hope and aspirations.
8. Make your risk assessments accurate, based on facts and kept up-to-date.
9. Involve us in developing your risk management processes, including documenta-tion, training and audit.
10. Independently monitor risk management practice to include service user experi-ences.

Kay's recommendations are both simple and obvious. Yet, they are a lot to ask for in a mental health system that has traditionally viewed service users as patient recipients of care. But now is time for change, in the new century when the voice of service users has never been clearer or louder. Consider Kay's manifesto and improve collaborative working practices with individuals like her who are not made less entitled to these things by virtue of mental disorder.

Sally Luxton proposed a number of top tips for her fellow carers, tips she explicitly wants practitioners to know about and understand as really not negotiable. Sally's top tips for carers are:

- Smile – to encourage you as well as them!
- Have an open attitude.

- Be honest.
- Respect others – and yourself.
- Aim to establish trust in your working relationships with clinical staff.
- Ask to see where your relative will be living.
- Ask anything you need to know.
- Do not feel intimidated.
- Ask for an appointment to meet the psychiatrist.
- Write down questions to ask – and any notes to help you remember what has been discussed.
- Notice even the tiniest signs of recovery in your loved one.
- Tears are okay.
- Explain how you are feeling.
- Write down your feelings.
- Keep lines of communication open.
- Above all, look after yourself.

Sally's top tips for professionals to involve carers in risk management are:

- Remember that welcoming smile.
- And a friendly face and helpful, caring attitude.
- Honesty – tell carers if you are rushed off your feet and if its difficult to talk at that moment, but make an appointment to talk with them later – and keep that appointment.
- Respect your patients and their families, whatever.
- Regard carers as an asset – they know their family members better than anyone, including you, and can give you their history.
- Keep lines of communication open.
- Recognize the strengths of your patients and their carers and families.
- Recognize their stress too.
- Establish trust.
- Tears are okay.
- Listen.
- Look for all windows of opportunity to engage.
- Think of some tips of your own!
- Look after yourself too.

What is striking about the recommendations made by both Kay and Sally is that the cost implications of their implementation are minimal. This is welcome news in these cash-strapped times. Further, their enthusiasm for collaborative working with practitioners is notable – and remarkable given the routine exclusion of both groups from care planning and delivery. There really are no excuses.

For practitioners

Beyond the recommendations given above, for practitioners the message is comparatively simple: keep as up-to-date with the evidence on self-harm and violence as possible. The chapters in this volume, in particular, those by Maria Leitner and Wally Barr and by

Richard Whittington and colleagues, are a very good start. The additional two chapters in the Evidence section of this book are invaluable extra reading. The reference lists for all four chapters contain very recent publications, and all direct the reader to resources from which yet more information can be obtained.

But how can you tell good from not so good evidence in a working week that leaves precious little time if any for continuing professional development? The first chapter of the two chapters by Caroline Logan and colleagues explored evidence-based practice and the purpose of clinical guidelines. While clinical guidelines are far from perfect, they offer a starting point for the busy practitioner seeking a quick way to appraise him- or herself of the latest thinking in the field. Clinical guidelines are derived from the efforts of expert others who have examined the field, extracted its key findings and recommendations, and synthesized them down into a document of concentrated knowledge and guidance, usually available on the Internet. If the busy practitioner has little time to read, he or she could use the precious time available on the websites of the Department of Health, NICE, and NIMHE, as well as those of their professional organizations whose responsibility it also is to highlight key publications and trends in professional practice.

Also, Paul Clifford and, subsequently, Richard Whitehead and colleagues, offer a route map through positive risk management – Paul by defining what it is and is not, and Richard *et al.* describing an example of how it can work. Positive risk management is one of the key themes of this volume. Here we try to provide one of the first descriptions of what it really is and looks like. Both chapters emphasize that positive risk management can happen only when the following conditions are met: (a) there is a good understanding of the risks posed; (b) there is consensus between the service user and carer and the clinical team about the risks posed and how they might be managed; (c) there are the resources available to manage the risks that might ensue; and (d) there is confidence among practitioners that their managers will support them if things do not go according to plan.

For organizations

It is a duty of all mental health services to ensure that their practitioners and service managers have at least some awareness of the importance of clinical skills in risk assessment and management. Risk assessment and management is everyone's business – it is not the prerogative of specialist facilities like forensic services. All services need their leaders – head of service, heads of department – or champions – those practitioners with a special interest in risk – to be a focal point in this work, to drive it in the face of competing demands, as well as to support it in the form of policy as well as learning and development initiatives. The four case studies in the last part of this volume give examples of how leaders may be identified and risk policies prepared and implemented. All the case studies give a view on the following, which other services are encouraged to consider.

1. Determine the *ideal process for risk assessment in your service* – when in a service user's care pathway do you need information about risk and what kinds of information do you need?
2. *Policy review and development* – which risk-relevant policies need review and what new policies need to be developed?

3. Work towards better *collaboration* with service users and carers – how would they like to be more involved?
4. *Risk champions* – if viable, how will they be identified and how will they be made to work in this service, and identify service user/carer representatives as well as practitioners?
5. Decide on *examples of good practice* and effectively managed risk with service users and practitioners, and decide how these examples can be made more widely known (e.g., in ward rounds, case conferences), and copied.
6. *Learning and development* – how can the library, intranet, and other resources be developed to make risk-relevant information noticeable and available for interested staff?
7. *Training* – what is needed and how will a training strategy be developed and implemented and what role there will be for service user/carer involvement in training?
8. *Risk-relevant documentation* – review this to see if it is fit for purpose; consider convening a focus group of practitioners to discuss the documentation and get their opinions about what works and what does not work so well; consider service user/carer involvement in this group.
9. Finally, ask how will your service know if the changes you are making are indeed improvements? *Define three to six standards* that should be met across your organization most of the time – for example, if relevant, 'all care plans will include a risk formulation'; 'all directorates and key services (e.g., early intervention, assertive outreach, older adults, learning disability, crisis resolution home treatment, etc.) will identify a willing risk champion within 12 months and their training will be completed', and so on. Recruit the services of a clinical audit department to monitor improvements, and report progress to the service clinical risk management group.

Consensus is vital in establishing organizational policies and providing formal guidance to staff on what constitutes best practice. However, collaboration between service managers and practitioners is also essential – just as vital as that between practitioners and service users and their carers. The above nine-step plan is a possible way forward in any organization's revision of their strategy on risk assessment and management in which consensus and collaboration are prioritized.

Conclusions

Clinical risk assessment and management in mental health services is a highly demanding undertaking where best practice is not always clear but the stakes are always high. Ideas about the best way to manage this complexity are constantly emerging, as the evidence base increases, as we learn from the past and the good and not so good practice of our colleagues, and as our willingness to collaborate with service users and carers increases. Many of the most current and best ideas are discussed in the chapters of this book and hopefully, overall, the book contributes to the quality and content of the developments underway in the United Kingdom and elsewhere. Recalling the spirit of the *Best Practice in Managing Risk* guidance that started this whole undertaking off – and the reference made to the 16 best practice principles made by Leitner and Barr in this volume – we wish to conclude with our overarching recommendations:

- clinical decisions should be based on established research evidence;
- clinicians should proactively engage with clients as partners in care;
- risk management should be flexible, dynamic, and responsive;
- careful forward planning should be integral to the clinical process;
- care should be multidisciplinary, but well coordinated; and finally
- structural, procedural, and organizational factors should be addressed in addition to individual (client-specific) factors.

Glossary

Actuarial approach: An approach to risk assessment involving the use of statistical models to estimate the likelihood of a harmful outcome such as suicide or harm to others. Actuarial risk assessment tools (e.g., the *Violence Risk Appraisal Guide*, the *Risk Matrix 2000*) depend on the assessed person being exactly comparable with the population from which the tool was derived. Actuarial risk assessments are comprised of static (unchanging) risk factors (e.g., history of mental illness) and, therefore, do not reflect any positive or negative changes in the individual's circumstances that might have had an impact on risk. Actuarial risk assessments can be used only to make a comparison between the client (who is representative of the client group from which the instrument was derived) and this client group, which has a known rate of re-offending; they cannot be used to predict risk in the individual case. In addition, the findings of actuarial risk assessments provide little guidance on risk management (Department of Health, 2008).

Advance directive: A collaborative document in which a person states their future treatment preferences in the event that they become unwell and do not have the capacity to make an informed choice. Advance statements are a means of giving details of the care and treatment a patient would like to receive should they lose capacity at some time in the future, including who they wish to act as a nominated person. Advance directives are intended to promote individual autonomy and empowerment, enhancing communication between patients and those involved in their care.

Assertive outreach team: An intensive and highly integrated approach for community mental health service delivery. Assertive outreach teams serve people whose symptoms of mental illness result in severe functional difficulties that interfere with their ability to achieve personally meaningful recovery goals in several major areas of life, such as work, friendships, independent living, and so on.

***Best Practice in Managing Risk* (Department of Health, 2007, 2009):** A set of clinical guidelines for the management of risk of violence and self-harm published by the

Self-Harm and Violence: Towards Best Practice in Managing Risk in Mental Health Services, First Edition.
Edited by Richard Whittington and Caroline Logan.
© 2011 John Wiley & Sons, Ltd. Published 2011 by John Wiley & Sons, Ltd.

Department of Health in 2007 then updated and re-issued in 2009. Each of the sixteen best practice guidelines is explained and justified by some form of evidence, and it is on that basis that the guidelines should be given consideration by practitioners working with at-risk clients.

Caldicott Guardian: A senior person responsible for protecting the confidentiality of patient and service user information and enabling appropriate information-sharing. The Caldicott Guardian plays a key role in ensuring that the NHS, social services, and partner organizations satisfy the highest practicable standards for handling patient-identifiable information.

Care pathway: Multidisciplinary management tool based on evidence-based practice for a specific group of service users with a predictable clinical course, in which the different tasks (interventions) of the professionals involved in service user care are defined, optimized, and sequenced. Outcomes are tied to specific interventions.

Care Programme Approach (CPA): The Care Programme Approach was introduced in England in the joint Health and Social Services Circular, *The Care Programme Approach for People with a Mental Illness, Referred to Specialist Psychiatric Services*, published by the Department of Health in 1990. CPA was updated in 2008. CPA requires health authorities, in collaboration with social services departments, to put in place specified arrangements for the care and treatment of mentally ill people in the community. CPA has four main elements: assessment; care planning; a chosen care coordinator; and regular review.

Carer's assessment: The Carer's (Recognition and Services) Act 1995 gives people aged 16 and over who provide substantial care on a regular basis the right to request an assessment from Social Services. In addition, standard six of the National Service Framework for Mental Health (Department of Health, 1999) states that all individuals who provide regular and substantial care for a person on CPA should have an assessment of their caring, physical, and mental health needs, repeated on an annual basis, and have their own written care plan, which is given to them and implemented in discussion with them.

Child and Adolescent Mental Health Services (CAMHS): The name for NHS services for children in the mental health arena in the United Kingdom, organized around a four-tier system. Tier 3 services are typically multidisciplinary in nature and staff come from a range of professional backgrounds. Tier 4 services are highly specialist services for young people. These are typically inpatient units for young people who require admission into hospital, but also include a range of other Tier 4 provisions. There are about 90 CAMHS units in England and Wales.

Clinical Decision Support Tool (CDST): Interactive computer programs, which are designed to assist physicians and other health professionals with decision-making tasks.

Clinical guidelines: The synthesis of empirical evidence on a particular subject into an accessible and practical form in order to facilitate improved relevant, effective, efficient, equitable, consistent, and quality health care.

Clinical Negligence Scheme for Trusts (CNST): Provides a means for NHS Trusts to fund the cost of clinical negligence litigation and to encourage and support effective management of claims and risk. The scheme covers claims arising from incidents on or after 1 April 1995. The NHS Litigation Authority (NHSLA), a special health authority, administers the scheme. Membership is voluntary and open to all NHS Trusts, including Primary Care Trusts, in England.

Cognitive Analytic Therapy (CAT): A brief (generally around 16 sessions) therapy developed with the aim of providing effective and affordable psychological treatment. CAT further evolved as an integrated therapy based on ideas from psychoanalytic therapy, cognitive therapy, and Vygotskian ideas. The model of treatment emphasizes collaborative work with the client, and focuses on understanding the patterns and developmental origins of maladaptive behaviours. The aim of the therapy is to enable the client to recognize these patterns and understand their origins, and subsequently to learn alternative strategies in order to cope better.

Cognitive Behavioural Therapy (CBT): A treatment approach that aims to solve psychological problems relating to dysfunctional emotions, behaviours, and cognitions through a goal-oriented, systematic procedure. The title CBT is used in diverse ways to designate behaviour therapy and cognitive therapy.

Community Mental Health Team (CMHT): NHS-funded teams consisting of a group of different mental health professionals who work together to provide specialist mental health services to people living in a particular area. The teams are responsible for the assessment and mental health care of those clients referred to them. They provide one-to-one support, which may take the form of visits in the home or a community setting and referral to other appropriate services, such as a day centre, or home care service, or housing service. Support may be provided on a short- or long-term basis depending on individual need.

Community Treatment Order (CTO): Mental health law derived from the amended Mental Health Act 2007, which allows the compulsory, community-based treatment of individuals with mental illness.

Co-morbidity: The presence of one or more disorders (or diseases) in addition to a primary disease or disorder.

Corporate governance: The system by which organizations direct and control their business. It includes systems, processes, accountabilities, and decision-making.

Crisis Resolution Home Treatment (CRHT) Team: An NHS-commissioned service that provides intensive support for people in mental health crisis in their own home. The teams stay involved until the problem is resolved. CRHT teams are designed to provide prompt and effective home treatment, including medication, in order to prevent hospital admissions and give support to informal carers.

Delphi technique: A systematic, interactive forecasting method that relies on a panel of experts. The experts answer questionnaires in two or more rounds. After each round, a facilitator provides an anonymous summary of the experts' forecasts from the previous round as well as the reasons they provided for their judgements. Thus, experts are encouraged to revise their earlier answers in the light of the replies of other members of their panel. It is believed that during this process, the range of the answers will decrease and the group will converge towards the 'correct' answer. Finally, the process is stopped after a pre-defined stop criterion (e.g., number of rounds, achievement of consensus, stability of results) and the mean or median scores of the final rounds determine the results.

Dialectical Behaviour Therapy (DBT): A therapeutic methodology originally developed to treat persons with borderline personality disorder (BPD). DBT combines standard cognitive-behavioural techniques for emotion regulation and reality testing with concepts of mindful awareness, distress tolerance, and acceptance, largely derived from meditative practice.

Dual diagnosis: The co-morbid condition of a person considered to be suffering from a mental illness and a substance misuse problem. Dual diagnosis is also a term used for people with an intellectual disability and diagnosed with a mental illness. Making a dual diagnosis in substance abusers is difficult as drug abuse itself often induces psychiatric symptoms, thus, making it necessary to try to differentiate between substance-induced and pre-existing mental illness.

Dynamic risk factors: Stable dynamic risk factors refer to those areas of an individual's circumstances that are enduring over a period of time and contribute to the risk of further offending, over months or years, but are amenable to change and, if changed, may be expected to reduce the likelihood or seriousness of further offending. Acute dynamic risk factors are those that change quickly, perhaps over days or hours, and whose emergence indicates a period of critical risk in which serious offending is more likely than not to occur.

Early Intervention Team (EIT):   NHS-funded teams that serve young people with early-onset psychosis – usually between the ages of 14 and 35 years – and their families. EITs bridge youth and adult mental health services and link the community with hospital in each geographical area.

Elective risk assessment: Used to assess dynamic changes in relation to the routine risk assessment and an individual's treatment and progression. Such an assessment supports the day-to-day requirements of managing risk at care transitions and key decision points in care planning. The tool should be cross-referenced with the routine risk assessment.

Equality and human rights impact assessment: The NHS mechanism by which it is ensured that any new or proposed function, policy, or process does not have an adverse impact on any group of individuals with respect to specific equalities strands, namely, disability, race, gender and gender identity, sexual orientation, religion/belief, and age.

Essential Lifestyle Plan (ELP):   A person-centred tool through which the person and the people who are committed to him or her can explore and describe the most important things in a person's life.

Evidence-based Practice (EBP):   Formally referred to as evidenced-based medicine (EBM), EBP is a method of empirically-informed clinical practice grounded on the premise that the carefully scrutinized evidence upon which clinical guidelines are derived maximizes the validity and reliability of decision-making based on those guidelines.

Failure Modes and Effects Analysis (FMEA):   FMEA is widely used in industry and has been adapted as a tool for risk assessment in health care in the United States (Joint Commission on Accreditation of Healthcare Organizations, 2005). It is a proactive tool that helps to evaluate a process or a new product or design of service to identify potential points of failure and the effect these failures could have on individuals and/or the organization. The actions that need to be taken to prevent an incident can then be prioritized.

Force field analysis: A tool used to facilitate the opportunity to consider forces that support change and those that may represent obstacles.

Harmful risk: Relates to behaviours which are illegal or not socially sanctioned, for example, homicidal and suicidal acts, antisocial and criminal behaviour, personal irresponsibility, self-harming patterns of behaviour, and relapse of mental illness. Harmful risk is to be avoided, and treatment goals focus on reducing harmful risk.

Avoidance of harmful risk can also be part of a recovery goal, although this is avoidance for a reason.

Health of the Nation Outcome Scales (HoNOS): The Research Unit of the Royal College of Psychiatrists (CRU) developed scales to measure the health and social functioning of people with severe mental illness. The aim is to provide a means of recording progress towards the Health of the Nation target 'to improve significantly the health and social functioning of mentally-ill people'.

Human Rights Act 1998: An Act of the Parliament of the United Kingdom, which received Royal Assent on 9 November 1998, and mostly came into force on 2 October 2000. Its aim is to 'give further effect' in UK law to the rights contained in the European Convention on Human Rights. The Act makes available in UK courts a remedy for breach of a Convention right, without the need to go to the European Court of Human Rights in Strasbourg. It also totally abolished the death penalty in UK law (although this was not required by the Convention in force for the United Kingdom at that time). The Act makes it unlawful for any public body to act in a way that is incompatible with the Convention, unless the wording of an Act of Parliament means they have no other choice. It also requires UK judges to take account of decisions of the Strasbourg Court, and to interpret legislation, as far as possible, in a way that is compatible with the Convention.

Human Rights-Based Approach (HRBA): In the context of positive risk management, this involves putting human rights and human rights principles at the heart of risk assessment and management planning. The rights implications of the service user's risky behaviours and the ways in which they are managed are made explicit. The HRBA emphasizes organizational leadership and a commitment to empower staff and service users to be aware of and to achieve fulfilment of their human rights in practice. The process should meaningfully involve all key people, including the service user, so that risk management is optimally 'done with' rather than 'done to' service users.

Human Rights Joint Risk Assessment and Management Plan (HR-JRAMP): A document adapted from an original doctoral dissertation, which formulates the risk potential of a person with intellectual disability in order that potential support can be provided from a human rights perspective.

Human rights risk screen: An assessment involving intellectually disabled service users, to the maximum of their insight and ability, to identify their risk areas. The screen asks risk questions in accessible language supplemented by pictures to promote service user inclusion.

Improved Access to Psychological Therapies (IAPT): A UK initiative to improve access to psychological therapies. The aim of the project is to increase the provision of evidence-based treatments for anxiety and depression by primary care organizations. This includes workforce planning to adequately train the mental health professionals required.

International Association of Forensic Mental Health Services (IAFMHS): Established in Vancouver in 2001, where its inaugural meeting was held the same year, the IAFMHS is now established as an Association, paying due attention to establishing a formal structure and a democratic process. The Association focuses on four major areas: clinical forensic psychiatry and psychology including family violence; administrative/legal issues; research in forensic mental health (civil/criminal); violence and abuse and training and education. (For more information, please go to www.iafmhs.org.)

Joint Crisis Plan (JCP):   A record containing a service user's treatment preferences for the management of future crises, created by the service user with the help of their treating mental health team. JCPs have been shown to be an effective way of reducing compulsory treatment in people with psychosis.

Key Performance Indicators (KPIs):   A measure of performance commonly used to help an organization define and evaluate how successful it is, typically in terms of making progress towards its long-term organizational goals.

Mental Capacity Act 2005:   An Act of the Parliament of the United Kingdom, which applies in England and Wales and came into force in April 2007. Its primary purpose is to provide a legal framework for acting and making decisions on behalf of adults who lack the capacity to make particular decisions for themselves. The five principles are outlined in section 1 of the Act. These principles are designed to protect people who lack capacity to make particular decisions, but also to maximize their ability to make decisions, or to participate in decision-making, as far as they are able to do so.

Mental Health Act 1983:   An Act of the Parliament of the United Kingdom which applies to people in England and Wales – the Mental Health Care and Treatment (Scotland) Act 2003 provides for the Scottish jurisdiction. The Mental Health Act covers the reception, care, and treatment of mentally disordered persons, the management of their property, and other related matters. In particular, it provides the legislation by which people diagnosed with a mental disorder can be detained in hospital and have their disorder assessed or treated against their wishes, unofficially known as 'sectioning'. Its use is reviewed and regulated by the Care Quality Commission. The Act was significantly amended in 2007.

Mental Health Act Commission (MHAC):   The Mental Health Act Commission was established in 1983 and consisted of some 100 members (Commissioners), including laypersons, lawyers, doctors, nurses, social workers, psychologists, and other specialists. Its functions were to keep under review the operation of the Mental Health Act 1983 in respect of patients liable to be detained under the Act, to visit and interview, in private, patients detained under the Act in hospitals and mental nursing homes, to investigate complaints which fall within the Commission's remit, to review decisions to withhold the mail of patients detained in the high security hospitals, to appoint medical practitioners and others to give second opinions in cases where this is required by the Act, to publish and lay before Parliament a report every two years, and to monitor the implementation of the Code of Practice and propose amendments to Ministers. The MHAC was replaced by the Care Quality Commission on 1 April 2009.

Mental Health Policy Implementation Guidelines (PIG):   Department of Health document published to support the delivery of adult mental health policy locally. This is a guide and not a prescription. While certain service models are specified there is also emphasis placed on tailoring services to meet local needs.

Multi-Agency Public Protection Arrangements (MAPPA):   The name given to arrangements in England and Wales for responsible authorities tasked with the management of registered sex offenders, violent offenders, and other types of offenders who pose a serious risk of harm to the public. Responsible authorities include probation, prison, and police services. MAPPA is coordinated and supported nationally by the Public Protection Unit within the National Offender Management Service.

Multidisciplinary Team (MDT): A team or group consisting of representatives from several different professional backgrounds all of whom have expertise but in different professional areas. A community mental health team is an example of a multidisciplinary team.

National Confidential Enquiry into Patient Outcome and Death (NCEPOD): The NCEPOD's purpose is to assist in maintaining and improving standards of medical and surgical care for the benefit of the public by reviewing the management of patients, by undertaking confidential surveys and research, and by maintaining and improving the quality of patient care and by publishing and generally making available the results of such activities.

National Health Service Litigation Authority (NHSLA): A branch of the NHS responsible for negligence claims and the improvement of risk management practices in the NHS. The NHS Litigation Authority is also responsible for resolving disputes between practitioners and primary care trusts, giving advice to the NHS on human rights case law, and handling equal pay claims.

National Health Service (NHS) Trust: The basic organizing unit of the UK National Health Service (NHS), which provides general mental health services to a specific catchment area. Some trusts also provide specialist services, such as secure forensic psychiatric care, to an entire region.

National Institute for Clinical Excellence (NICE): An independent organization that produces guidance on public health, health technologies, and clinical practice in England and Wales. NICE has three centres of excellence: the Centre for Public Health Excellence develops public health guidance, with information for patients on diagnosis and treatment of specific illnesses and conditions; the Centre for Health Technology Evaluation recommends medicines and evaluates the safety and efficacy of procedures within the NHS; and the Centre for Clinical Practice develops evidence-based clinical guidelines for clinicians on the appropriate treatment of people with specific diseases. NICE and the National Patient Safety Agency (NPSA) cooperate in the risk assessment of new technology, monitoring safety incidents associated with procedures, and providing solutions if adverse outcomes are reported. In addition, NICE and NPSA share reporting in areas known as confidential inquiries: maternal or infant deaths; childhood deaths to age 16; deaths in persons with mental illness; and perioperative and unexpected medical deaths.

National Patient Safety Agency (NPSA): An NHS special health authority created in July 2001 to improve patient safety within the NHS by encouraging voluntary reporting of medical errors, conducting analysis, and initiating preventative measures. Since 2005, the NPSA has also been responsible for: safety aspects of hospital design, cleanliness and food; safe research practices through the National Research Ethics Service (NRES); and performance of individual doctors and dentists, through the National Clinical Assessment Service (NCAS). The NPSA identifies patient safety deficiencies with the input of clinical experts and patients, develops solutions, and monitors the results of corrections within the NHS. In addition, the National Reporting and Learning System (NRLS) allows NHS employees to provide the NPSA with reports anonymously.

National Service Framework (NSF): Policies set by the NHS in the United Kingdom to define standards of care for major medical issues such as cancer, coronary heart disease, mental health, and diabetes. NSFs are also defined for some key patient groups, including children and older people. The two main roles of NSFs are to set clear quality requirements for care based on the best available evidence of what treatments and services work most effectively for patients, and offer strategies and support to help organizations achieve these.

National Suicide Prevention Strategy (NSPS): A document published by the Department of Health in 2002 outlining a national strategy on suicide prevention. The strategy is designed as an ongoing, coordinated set of activities, which will evolve over several years, and seeks to be comprehensive, evidence-based, specific, and subject to evaluation. It is delivered as one of the core programmes of the National Institute for Mental Health in England (NIMHE).

Order for Lifelong Restriction (OLR): A provision, overseen by the Risk Management Authority (RMA) in Scotland, for the sentencing and treatment of violent and sexual offenders who pose a continuing danger to the public. As a form of life sentence, an Order for Lifelong Restriction can be imposed only by the High Court and differs from a life sentence or a long determinate sentence because of the element of risk assessment that is undertaken prior to sentence being passed. It is an option for dealing with violent, life-endangering, and sexual offenders, and those who in the informed opinion of the court show a propensity to commit such offences.

Patient Environment Action Team (PEAT): An annual assessment of inpatient health care sites in England that have more than ten beds, imposed by the NPSA. It is a benchmarking tool to ensure improvements are made in the non-clinical aspects of patient care, such as cleanliness, food, and infection control. The assessment results help to highlight areas for improvement and share best practice across health care organizations in England.

Positive risk: Relates to behaviours that involve the person taking on challenges leading to personal growth and development.

Primary Care Trust (PCT): A type of NHS trust that provides primary and community services or commissions them from other providers, and is involved in commissioning secondary care.

Probabilistic Risk Assessment (PRA): PRA examines incidents and their contributory factors and determines the likelihood of the event occurring. PRA involves a mixture of quantifying risks and judgement. The PRA approach works out the likelihood of each outcome and what could be done to reduce that likelihood. It attempts to quantify the potential risks by scoring the likelihood of a particular risk or incident actually happening, including a consideration of the frequency with which it may arise. To help with this quantification, incident data can be assessed along with expert estimation of how often a process could fail.

Protective factor: Any circumstance, event, factor, or consideration with the capacity to prevent or reduce the severity or likelihood of harm to self or others (Department of Health, 2008).

Psychodynamic Interpersonal Therapy (PIT): A short-term supportive psychotherapy that focuses on the connection between interactions between people and the development of a person's psychiatric symptoms.

Recovery Model: An approach to mental disorder or substance dependence that emphasizes and supports each individual's potential for recovery. Recovery is seen within the model as a personal journey, which may involve developing hope, a secure base and sense of self, supportive relationships, empowerment, social inclusion, coping skills, and meaning. Originating from the Twelve-Step Programme of Alcoholics Anonymous, the use of the concept in mental health emerged as de-institutionalization resulted in more individuals living in the community. The Recovery Model gained impetus due to a perceived failure by services or wider society to adequately support social inclusion, and by studies demonstrating that many can recover. The Recovery Model has now been explicitly adopted as the guiding principle of the mental health systems of a number of countries.

Risk: The nature, severity, imminence, frequency or duration, and likelihood of harm to self or others. A hazard that is to be identified, measured and ultimately, prevented (Department of Health, 2008)

Risk assessment: The process of gathering information via personal interviews, psychological/medical testing, review of case records, and contact with collateral informants for use in making decisions pertaining to an individual's risk and its most appropriate, effective, and proportionate prevention or minimization.

Risk factor: A condition or characteristic assumed to have a direct relationship to the potential of a person to harm another person or themselves. Examples of risk factors common to risk outcomes of a number of different kinds are major mental illnesses or substance use problems.

Risk formulation: A future-focused explanation of the underlying mechanism of an individual's risk of harmful behaviour, identifying the predisposing risk factors and triggers and the counter-balancing protective factors, and explaining how risk might become unacceptable in the future. A risk formulation should generate hypotheses for change, namely, risk management intended to prevent or minimize harmful outcomes.

Risk management: The actions taken, on the basis of a risk assessment, designed to prevent or limit undesirable outcomes. Key risk management activities are treatment (e.g., psychological care, medication), supervision (e.g., help with planning daily activities, setting restrictions on alcohol use or contact with unhelpful others, and so on), monitoring (i.e., identifying and looking out for early warning signs of an increase in risk, which would trigger treatment or supervision actions), and if relevant, victim safety planning.

Risk Management Authority (RMA): A non-departmental public body established by the then Scottish Executive in 2004 to ensure the effective assessment, management, and minimization of risk of serious violent and sexual offenders. The RMA also acts as a national centre for expert advice on offender risk assessment and management. (For more information, please go to www.RMAscotland.gsi.gov.)

Risk Pooling Scheme for Trusts (RPST): Two separate schemes covering non-clinical risks (the Liabilities to Third Parties Scheme or LTPS and the Property Expenses Scheme or PES) are known collectively as the Risk Pooling Schemes for Trusts (RPST). NHS bodies may join one or both schemes. The RPST dates from 1 April 1999, and cover begins from that date, or from the date when the NHS body joined the scheme if that is later. LTPS covers employers' liability claims, from straightforward slips and trips in the workplace to serious manual handling, bullying, and stress claims. In addition, LTPS covers public and product liability claims, from personal injury sustained by visitors to NHS premises to claims arising from breaches of the Human Rights Act, the Data Protection Act and the Defective Premises Act. There is also cover for defamation, professional negligence by employees, and liabilities of directors.

Root Cause Analysis (RCA): A framework used by the National Patient Safety Agency (NPSA) for reviewing patient safety incidents, as well as claims and complaints. Investigations can identify what, how, and why patient safety incidents have happened. Analysis can then be used to identify areas for change, develop recommendations, and look for new solutions.

Routine risk assessment: Locally developed, evidenced-based, structured clinical risk assessment, focusing on historical and collateral data. Used in conjunction with standardized tools, this assessment supports the process of situation-specific risk assessment.

Service User Reference Panel (SURP): A panel of service users, who act collaboratively with the Care Quality Commission (CQC). SURP is comprised of people who are currently or have recently been detained under the Mental Health Act, and duties include providing a service user perspective on activity around the Mental Health Act, advising on priorities for CQC visits and future plans, contributing to publications, contributing to particular projects through steering groups, and advising on service user involvement within the CQC.

Static risk factor: Static risk factors are factors that reflect elements of an individual's past behaviour thought to have relevance to their potential for future risky behaviour. Static risk factors are generally incapable of change and, thus, are often referred to as 'tombstone' factors.

Staying Well Plan: Completed with the service user, such plans highlight the individual's understanding of their risk triggers and their experience of interventions they know to be helpful in preventing these triggers from occurring.

Stepped-care model: A recovery model which seeks to treat service users at the lowest appropriate service tier in the first instance, only 'stepping up' to intensive/specialist services as clinically required. The level of professional input is augmented gradually, until satisfactory health status is achieved.

Strengths approach: A model of working with service users that focuses on enhancing the strengths of the individual to minimize the negatives and the influence of other life problems. By looking at the person's abilities, interests, and capabilities, and working with these, the service user feels empowered to lead their own programme of growth and change in their recovery.

Structured Professional Judgement Approach (SPJ): A practitioner-based approach moving the emphasis from one of risk prediction to risk prevention through management where the conditions under which the risk will increase and decrease are highlighted. Systematic frameworks have been developed to guide risk assessment that clearly outline the sequence and stages of clinical risk management. An example of an SPJ framework is the HCR-20.

Therapeutic alliance: The relationship between a health care professional and a service user. It is the means by which the professional hopes to engage with, and thereby effect change or recovery, in a service user.

Wellness Recovery Action Plan (WRAP): A tool for use with service users, their carers, and clinical staff, which encourages the service user to think about what they need to do to keep themselves well and to encourage an awareness of their own wellbeing.

Welsh Risk Pool (WRP): A mutual organization funded by all Trusts and Local Health Boards (LHBs) in Wales. It is hosted by Conwy and Denbighshire NHS Trust at St Asaph in Denbighshire. The main functions of the WRP are the reimbursement of losses, the management of claims, encouraging good risk management practice, and assessing of risk management performance. WRP Assessors measure an organization's risk management performance against the WRMS annually. A detailed report is made to each organization, the Welsh Assembly, and the WRP Advisory Board.

Index

Self-Harm and Violence: Towards Best Practice in Managing Risk in Mental Health Services, First Edition.
Edited by Richard Whittington and Caroline Logan.
© 2011 John Wiley & Sons, Ltd. Published 2011 by John Wiley & Sons, Ltd.